THE PROPORTIONALITY TEST IN EUROPEAN PATENT LAW

Does a European patent always entitle its holder to a permanent injunction? This question has sparked vigorous debate in past years but so far remains unresolved. This open access book presents a detailed, practical and comprehensive test to determine when injunctive relief should be limited on proportionality grounds.

The book's three parts guide readers from proportionality's normative foundations to its practical applications. Part I argues that, contrary to conventional wisdom, proportionality is not an open-ended balancing test but rather applies the principle of commensurate scope at the remedies stage. Part II offers an in-depth analysis of situations where a permanent injunction risks upsetting that principle. It draws on a unique qualitative study of all US District Court decisions between 2006 and 2020 granting or denying a permanent injunction in patent cases to stake out circumstances where an injunction might have disproportionate consequences. Part III grounds the inquiry in EU law and proposes a proportionality test along three elements: overreach, abuse, and conflicts with third-party rights.

The book thus provides a distinctly European response to a global problem. It is an invaluable resource for practitioners, clerks and scholars looking not only for the normative, empirical, and legal basis of proportionality in European patent law, but also for guidance on its real-world operation.

The Proportionality Test in European Patent Law

Patent Injunctions before EU Courts and the UPC

Léon Dijkman

•HART•
OXFORD • LONDON • NEW YORK • NEW DELHI • SYDNEY

HART PUBLISHING

Bloomsbury Publishing Plc

Kemp House, Chawley Park, Cumnor Hill, Oxford, OX2 9PH, UK

1385 Broadway, New York, NY 10018, USA

29 Earlsfort Terrace, Dublin 2, Ireland

First published in Great Britain 2023

A catalogue record for this book is available from the British Library.

A catalogue record for this book is available from the Library of Congress.

Library of Congress Control Number: 2023944754

ISBN: HB: 978-1-50997-362-0
ePDF: 978-1-50997-364-4
ePub: 978-1-50997-363-7

Typeset by Compuscript Ltd, Shannon

For Cato

FOREWORD

When I started work as an IP lawyer in 1973, 'proportionality' did not come to mind when discussing injunctions. The view at the time was: a patent is a property right, its essence is a right to exclude, and in case this right is violated the automatic remedy is an injunction. Underlying this view was the assumption that the legislator had carefully weighed the circumstances in which patent exclusivity would be not acceptable by including in the Patent Act exceptions, such as private prior use rights and compulsory license provisions. For decades this was essentially undisputed.

If anything, the tendency was towards strengthening the patentee's rights with auxiliary claims, such as recalls and other measures now routinely granted. Patents were and are considered as an important, maybe even essential tool to stimulate innovation for the benefit of mankind. In my opinion, the recent pandemic has shown that this is true, perhaps all the more so in the present day as we face the challenges of climate change and the provision of food and shelter for a vastly increased world population.

Thus, until around 2000 there was hardly any discussion about proportionality in the field of patent law. In extreme situations the concept of misuse of right was used but such situations were very rare. In my practice it happened only once in 30 years. However, as Dijkman eloquently describes, technology and society changed drastically over the years. Patent law evolved from a specialism for a selected group of people to a domain which holds the attention of society at large. Consequently, it became more and more apparent that the automatic injunction was not a desirable solution in all circumstances and could, in certain circumstances, be an impediment instead of an incentive for further innovation and/or stifle competition in an unacceptable way. In the US, this resulted the decision in *eBay v MercExchange*. In the EU, it resulted in Article 3 of Directive 2004/48/EC (the Enforcement Directive), which states that IP enforcement measures and proceedings, apart from being effective and dissuasive, should also be proportionate. This concept of 'proportionality' was all rather unfamiliar to the classic patent practitioner and the patent judiciary and it took quite a while before it started to have some meaning in practice. In the UPC Agreement, which came into force last June, Article 63 states that the Court in case of infringement 'may' issue an injunction. This wording clearly leaves room for applying the proportionality requirement of Article 3 Enforcement Directive.

The Drafting Committee for the Rules of Procedure for the UPC (consisting of patent judges from the UK, Germany and France, practitioners from these countries, and myself) was heavily lobbied by certain circles to introduce the US *eBay* regime into the Rules, but we considered that went (much) too far in the light of the Enforcement Directive. In our view it was clear that the injunction should be the rule, and refusing an injunction on the basis of proportionality the exception. We nevertheless saw it as our task to provide some guidance for the application of the proportionality test. However, as Dijkman describes, the Public Consultation yielded very different views, and so the Committee eventually threw in the towel and left the formulation of further guidance to the discretion of the Court.

Apart from offering a very rich overview of its history and all the considerations relevant to a proportionality regime in European (and US) patent law, Dijkman tries to proceed where the UPC Rules Drafting Committee and the German legislator during the recent revision of the German Patent Act failed. That is, to give the patent community a concrete test that would allow application of the (vague) concept of proportionality in a more predictable manner. He proposes what he calls the 'commensurability principle', which is both creative and original as it both accepts the exceptional nature of the proportionality defence and, on the other hand, gives the patent practitioner and patent judge concrete tools to make a decision, tools with which the patent specialist feels familiar.

In view of the aforementioned technological and societal developments, in my opinion there is every reason to believe that the UPC will also develop a European proportionality test in the years to come, just as it will decide on a European approach to inventive step and equivalents. Dijkman's work and proposals are a very valuable contribution to that enterprise and the future case law of the UPC. Now that the UPC has opened its doors, Dijkman's book is not only a must read but also a pleasure to read!

Willem Hoyng
Amsterdam, September 2023

ACKNOWLEDGEMENTS

This book is the result of doctoral research at the European University Institute that was concluded on 26 May 2023. It was a privilege to pursue my studies in a place that so stimulates the mind. My supervisor, Peter Drahos, was a constant source of inspiration, both on the substance of this work and for his light-hearted approach to work and life. Willem Hoyng provided advice and feedback from the book's embryonic beginnings to the version now before the reader, and I am much indebted to him for his support and encouragement. I thank my colleagues at HOYNG ROKH MONEGIER for making me the lawyer I am today and welcoming me back, and those at the Erasmus School of Law for giving me a new academic home.

I am grateful to Qualcomm, whose support made possible the research reported in chapter four, and to Intel, whose support helped make this book available open access.

Throughout the writing process, my friends at the EUI offered critical feedback and much-needed distraction, while my friends back home remained sparring partners and party accomplices. I thank them all for the joy and encouragement they brought. To my parents, I owe a debt of gratitude for everything they taught me, for their love and for supporting me every step of the way. To my sister, for her wisdom and camaraderie, and for always having my back. Being a father to Stella is one of the great fortunes of my life and I am grateful for every day she lights up with her smile. Lastly, for everything, I am profoundly thankful to my beloved Cato, to whom this book is dedicated.

TABLE OF CONTENTS

ABBREVIATIONS

AvB	Afdeling van Beroep
BGH	Bundesgerichtshof
BPatG	Bundespatentgericht
CAFC	Courts of Appeals for the Federal Circuit
Cass	Cour de Cassation
CFR	Charter of Fundamental Rights
ECHR	European Convention on Human Rights
ECJ	European Court of Justice
EPC	European Patent Convention
EPD	effective, proportionate, dissuasive
EPO	European Patent Office
EWHC	High Court of Justice
EWCA	Court of Appeal
FRAND	fair, reasonable and non-discriminatory
FTO	freedom to operate
GH	Gerechtshof
GPA	German Patent Act
HR	Hoge Raad
IP	intellectual property
LG	Landgericht
NPE	non-practising entity
OEM	original equipment manufacturer
OLG	Oberlandesgericht
RB	Rechtbank

SDO	standards development organisation
SEP	standard essential patent
SME	small and medium enterprises
TFEU	Treaty on the Functioning of the European Union
TGI	Tribunale de grande instance
TJ	Tribunal Judiciaire
TO	Tribunale Ordinario
TRIPS	Agreement on Trade-Related Aspects of Intellectual Property Rights
UPC	Unified Patent Court
WIPO	World Intellectual Property Organization
WTO	World Trade Organization

LIST OF FIGURES AND TABLES

TABLE OF CASES

European Union

Court of Justice

Court of Justice: AG Opinion

General Court

European Commission

European Court of Human Rights

World Trade Organization Dispute Settlement Bodies

Boards of Appeal of the European Patent Office

England and Wales

Germany

The Netherlands

France

Italy

United States

US Supreme Court

US Court of Appeals for the Federal Circuit

US District Courts

Unified Patent Court

TABLE OF LEGISLATION

Introduction: This is a Rhinoceros

Giovanni de' Medici, son of the legendary Florentine ruler Lorenzo the Magnificent, was born into unimaginable wealth that would nonetheless rise to even greater heights when he was elected pope on 9 March 1513. By the end of 1515, he was promised a gift that was exceptional even by his standards: a living rhinoceros, the first to set foot in Europe since Roman times. Alas, its soul departed Earth before it reached Rome when the ship that carried the rhinoceros was wrecked by Porto Venere, not far from Genova. Short though it may have been, the presence of this noble beast in Europe immediately caused a sensation. Descriptions of its physique were sent to correspondents across Europe for inclusion in bestiaries. The rhinoceros was drawn not just by eyewitnesses, but also on the basis of second-hand or further removed accounts. In fact, the most famous depiction of the animal is a 1515 woodcut by Albrecht Dürer, who never saw it in the flesh (Figure 1). To the modern observer, the woodcut certainly resembles a rhinoceros. But it also contains many a quaint detail, such as the sheets of armour that appear to cover the rhinoceros' body, the second horn on the creature's back and its scaly legs. Many other contemporary depictions exist, each offering their own curious interpretation of what constitutes a rhino.

Figure 1 Albrecht Dürer, *Rhinocerus* (1515)

Fast-forward 500 years and the European Court of Justice (ECJ) finds, for the first time, that a patentee's action for a permanent injunction against an infringer could be considered abusive if the patentee fails to comply with conditions which seek to ensure a fair balance between the interests concerned.[1] The decision marks an important step in a paradigm shift in European patent law, according to which a patentee that prevails on the merits is no longer automatically entitled to a permanent injunction. This doctrinal shift, known colloquially as 'proportionality' in patent law, has in recent years caused a sensation among experts and industry stakeholders not unlike that caused by Dürer's rhinoceros. Just like the rhinoceros five centuries before, the concept of proportionality is exciting but foreign, its main impetus having been a 2006 ruling by the United States Supreme Court that made permanent injunctions in patent cases subject to an equitable test.[2] And just like the rhinoceros, everyone has a general idea what proportionality is, but nobody knows what it looks like exactly. To hear critics say it, proportionality should apply only in the narrowest of cases. Proponents seem to think it a panacea for all of patent law's (presumed) problems, from so-called patent trolls to low patent quality. Many think the proportionality doctrine derives from European law, but others seek it in national concepts such as good faith and abuse of rights. There is a vague sense of agreement that patent exclusivity cannot block patients' access to life-saving medicines where they depend specifically on infringing treatments, but beyond that, we have hardly conceptualised how and when a European proportionality doctrine would work, much less reached any measure of consensus. Because European case law applying proportionality in patent law cases is so scarce, there is virtually no guidance from practice. The result is a muddled debate among polarised stakeholders that may do nothing but discourage courts from applying the proportionality doctrine when they should be leading the way in its development. This book intends to change that.

Definitions and Scope

On the Use of Proportionality and Discretion in this Book

This book contains many references to 'proportionality' and 'discretion' that do not correspond to the generally accepted usage of these words. Proportionality is a mega-concept in law that means many different things in many different contexts. In this book, 'proportionality' refers to a principle according to which immediately effective injunctive relief may not be appropriate in every case where a court finds a valid patent was infringed. Proportionality may require that the injunction's entry into force be delayed or its scope of application limited to exclude specific

[1] Case C-170/13 *Huawei Technologies Co v ZTE Corp* ECLI:EU:C:2015:477, para 55.
[2] *eBay Inc v MercExchange LLC* 547 US 388 (2006).

instances of infringement. The term can be traced back to Article 3(2) of Directive 2004/48 (the Enforcement Directive), which, however, sets other conditions for patent remedies besides proportionality, as chapter five explains in detail.[3] Unless otherwise specified, my use of proportionality refers not to the specific requirement in Article 3(2), but to the more general principle just outlined that encompasses all requirements for intellectual property (IP) remedies set by the Enforcement Directive. Such usage, while not entirely accurate, offers advantages of conciseness and consistency with the European literature, which seems to have uniformly adopted this term for any remedial freedom afforded to patent courts. A proportionality 'test' or 'doctrine' refers to the rules and norms guiding the applicability of this limitation to patent exclusivity, whereas the proportionality 'defence' refers to an infringer's plea to these rules in a given case. A 'disproportionate' injunction would be any injunction issued not in accordance with these rules.

'Discretion' refers to the freedom that proportionality bestows on patent courts to decide whether to limit a patentee's entitlement to injunctive relief, and to what extent. Taken literally, it means a court would be completely free to decide every case as it sees fit, something that in remedies scholarship is often referred to as 'strong' discretion.[4] The framework proposed here bestows on courts 'weak' discretion, to be exercised in accordance with precedent and within boundaries set by applicable legal provisions, in particular the Enforcement Directive and the Charter of Fundamental Rights (CFR).[5] Thus, any reference to discretion over injunctions in this book should be read simply as referring to a court's power to impose temporal or subject matter limitations on injunctive relief in accordance with EU law, not as a suggestion that this power is unlimited and subject only to the court's whim. A related term is 'balancing'. There are European authors who believe that proportionality requires courts to place all interests at stake in a given infringement case on a hypothetical scale to determine whether the aggregated harmful effects of the injunction sufficiently outweigh the patentee's overall interest in immediate injunctive relief. Even though substantive patent law and the Enforcement Directive reflect a balance between the various interests at stake in patent infringement proceedings, these authors support 'ad hoc' balancing by patent courts, ie a case-by-case weighing of interests to determine the appropriate remedy. As explained in section 2.3, this book rejects balancing as the heart of the proportionality test. Instead, it advocates ad hoc a delineated and technically oriented test that comprises minimal, if any, balancing.

Lastly, unless qualified, 'injunctive relief' refers to the issuance, by a court finding a patent valid and infringed, of an order prohibiting all further acts of infringement with immediate effect. It refers to a permanent injunction granted

[3] Directive 2004/48/EC of the European Parliament and of the Council of 29 April 2004 on the enforcement of intellectual property rights [2004] OJ L195/16.

[4] P Birks, 'Three Kinds of Objection to Discretionary Remedialism' (2000) 29 *Western Australian Law Review* 1, 3.

[5] Charter of Fundamental Rights of the European Union [2000] OJ C364/01.

after a decision on the merits, not a preliminary injunction issued in anticipation of the court's final decision. An 'automatic injunction rule' refers to a regime according to which patent courts have no liberty to deviate from this course of action, unless the conditions for a finding of abuse of rights, abuse of a dominant market position (Article 102 of the Treaty on the Functioning of the European Union) or another accepted ground to limit legal entitlements are satisfied. Adoption of a proportionality doctrine would nuance the automatic injunction rule and give courts discretion to 'limit' injunctive relief. By that I mean any exception to the patentee's default entitlement to injunctive relief with immediate effect: staying the injunction or exempting certain acts from its scope would be the most common examples.

The European Literature on Proportionality in Patent Law

Until recently, the European literature primarily addressed whether application of a free-standing proportionality test was mandated by EU law and whether such a test is desirable. The orthodox view has long been that in continental European jurisdictions, courts have no authority to deny successful patentees a permanent injunction and courts thus applied an automatic injunction rule.[6] Under this view, existing provisions safeguarding the interests of infringers and others (eg compulsory licensing provisions, stays of enforcement, abuse of rights provisions, competition law) suffice to prevent disproportionate injunctions from being issued. But a growing number of scholars argue that these limitations do not, or no longer, suffice.[7] Most of them argue that patent courts should apply a free-standing proportionality test to curb disproportionate and/or dysfunctional effects of an automatic injunction rule. Others suggest using abuse or rights provisions more aggressively to achieve the same outcome.[8]

[6] See generally M Husovec and J Contreras, 'Issuing and Tailoring Patent Injunctions: A Cross-Jurisdictional Comparison and Synthesis' in J Contreras and M Husovec (eds), *Injunctions in Patent Law* (Cambridge University Press, 2022).

[7] Important contributions include M Norrgård, 'The Role Conferred on the National Judge by Directive 2004148/EC on the Enforcement of Intellectual Property Rights' (2005) 6 *ERA Forum* 503; A Ohly, 'Three Principles of European IP Enforcement Law: Effectiveness, Proportionality, Dissuasiveness' in J Drexl et al (eds), *Technology and Competition: Contributions in Honour of Hanns Ullrich* (Larcier, 2009); R García Pérez, 'Injunctions in Intellectual Property Cases: What Is the Power of the Courts?' [2016] *Intellectual Property Quarterly* 87; N Siebrasse et al, 'Injunctive Relief' in CB Biddle et al (eds), *Patent Remedies and Complex Products: Toward a Global Consensus* (Cambridge University Press, 2019); M Stierle and F Hofmann, 'The Latest Amendment to the German Law on Patent Injunctions: The New Statutory Disproportionality Exception and Third-Party Interests' (2022) 71 *Gewerblicher Rechtsschutz und Urheberrecht International* 1123; R Sikorski, 'Towards a More Orderly Application of Proportionality to Patent Injunctions in the European Union' (2022) 53 *International Review of Intellectual Property and Competition Law* 31.

[8] A Strowel and A Léonard, 'Cutting Back Patent Over-enforcement' (2020) 11 *Journal of Intellectual Property, Information Technology and Electronic Commerce Law* 3.

The debate over recognition of a proportionality principle in European patent law now seems largely academic. As chapter five explains in detail, all remedies issued in patent cases must satisfy the requirements of Article 3 of the Enforcement Directive, including its proportionality requirement, and strike a fair balance between all fundamental rights at stake. The primacy of Article 3 of the Enforcement Directive when it comes to injunctive relief in patent cases has been acknowledged by several European courts.[9] They have also accepted that an injunction may not be granted where doing so would impermissibly interfere with third parties' rights.[10] According to Article 63 of the Agreement on a Unified Patent Court (UPC Agreement), that court – which became operational on 1 June 2023 – 'may' grant an injunction.[11] As we will see in section 5.4, this wording signifies discretion over permanent injunctions to be exercised in accordance with Article 3 of the Enforcement Directive. Germany, where patent courts were most averse to applying a proportionality test, recently amended its patent law to clarify that courts should apply the directions handed down by the Federal Supreme Court in a case about grace periods. In light of these developments, the automatic injunction regime in European patent law no longer seems tenable and this book takes it as a given that patent courts must respect the requirements of proportionality.

The more difficult question is under what circumstances the grant of a permanent injunction in patent cases can be qualified as disproportionate. This question so far remains unresolved and is at the heart of this book. At the time of writing, there seems to be a cautious consensus on the following points. First, a patentee who succeeds on the merits is presumptively entitled to a permanent injunction with immediate effect, and exceptions to this rule should generally take the form of limited stays.[12] It follows that European patent courts may exercise only weak discretion over injunctive relief, in contrast to the much stronger discretion enjoyed by US patent courts (outlined in chapter four). Second, both the infringer's and third parties' interests can be grounds to limit a patentee's entitlement to injunctive relief.[13] Third, the limitation of injunctive relief does not affect the patentee's entitlement to other remedies and they should be compensated for the duration of the stay.[14]

[9] BGH GRUR 2016, 1031; X ZR 114/13 *Wärmetauscher*, para 49; *HTC Corp v Nokia Corp* [2013] EWHC 3778 (Pat), para 26; Cass civ (1) 12 July 2012, 11-13.666; RB The Hague 18 July 2018, ECLI:NL:RBDHA:2018:8777 (*Nikon v ASML*), para 4.51. In the context of preliminary injunctions: TO Milano 31 July 2017, 27991/2017 (*Radaelli Angelo v Oknoplast*), para 61; and TJ Paris 20 January 2020, 19/60318 (*IPCom v Lenovo*), 14.

[10] *Evalve v Edwards* [2020] EWHC 513 (Pat), para 58; *Edwards Lifesciences v Boston Scientific* [2018] EWHC 1256 (Pat), paras 15, 69. Two European supreme courts have accepted this in the context of copyright disputes: Cass civ (1) 15 May 2015, 13-27.391; HR 3 April 2015, ECLI:NL:HR:2015:841 (*GeenStijl v Sanoma*).

[11] Agreement 2013/C on a Unified Patent Court [2013] OJ L175/01 (UPC Agreement).

[12] *Edwards v Boston* (n 10) para 60; *Wärmetauscher* (n 9) paras 45, 49; Siebrasse et al (n 7) 155.

[13] This is explicitly stated in §139 of the 1980 German Patent Act (*Patentgesetz in der Fassung der Bekanntmachung vom 16. Dezember 1980, BGBl. 1981 I S. 1*) (GPA) after its 2021 revision; for the Netherlands and France, see the decisions cited in n 10 above. For Italy, see TO Torino 16 June 2021, 10009/2020 (*Edwards Lifesciences v Meril Life Sciences*), 3.

[14] This is also explicitly stated in the revised §139 GPA; compare *Virgin Atlantic v Premium Aircraft* [2009] EWCA Civ 1513, para 34 (on the proper compensation).

Beyond these fairly general points, European case law offers hardly any guidance on assessing the (dis)proportionality of patent injunctions. In the USA, there is now a considerable literature analysing patent remedies from a variety of perspectives.[15] But because it is written in so different an institutional context – the *eBay* framework is far removed from the EU concept of proportionality and US substantive- and procedural patent law differs significantly from its European counterparts – the insights this literature yields are often of limited relevance in Europe. Thankfully, an increasing number of authors now study proportionality from a distinctly European perspective, primarily in Germany, but also in France, Italy, the Netherlands and other European countries. This book gratefully builds on their work, with the aim to become a useful stepping-stone for the further development of a European doctrine of proportionality in patent law.

What this Book Does Not Address

While this book aims to provide an exhaustive analysis of proportionality in patent law, three topics that often figure in the proportionality literature are outside its scope. The first is preliminary, interim or provisional injunctions. Patent courts in most European Member States can and regularly do grant such orders, which typically last until the court decides on the merits of the case. Preliminary injunctions raise issues distinct from permanent injunctions because their grant depends primarily on (i) the patentee's likelihood of success in the merits proceedings and (ii) a balance of the parties' interests.[16] It is clear that (i) has no relevance for permanent injunctions and I argue in this book that (ii) should not have, either. Even if proportionality mandates consideration of the parties' interests at the permanent injunction stage, the tests will differ: at the preliminary injunction stage, the question is generally whether the status quo should be preserved pending trial, not the parties' interest in specific relief or its denial more generally. That said, the proportionality framework proposed here may still have some relevance for the grant of preliminary injunctions if the limitations it suggests to the patentee's entitlement to injunctive relief are accepted. After all, there is no principled reason why they should not also apply in preliminary relief proceedings. It is thus possible that, over time, courts deciding on preliminary relief will afford more weight to their estimate of whether the infringer will succeed on their proportionality defence than on a balance of interests.

[15] The literature is vast and cannot be exhaustively cited here. In my view, the best work was done by John Golden. See, eg J Golden, 'Principles for Patent Remedies' (2010) 88 *Texas Law Review* 505; J Golden, 'Complex Economics and Patent Remedies' (2010) 1 *IP Theory* 50. On several occasions, this book draws inspiration from the critique on *eBay* offered in M Gergen, J Golden and H Smith, 'The Supreme Court's Accidental Revolution? The Test for Permanent Injunctions' (2012) 112 *Columbia Law Review* 203.

[16] Contreras and Husovec (n 6) 322.

The second topic not addressed in detail in this book are standard essential patents (SEPs). The ECJ's decision in *Huawei*, referenced in the opening paragraphs, put in place a procedure that EU courts must follow when deciding on a SEP holder's request for a permanent injunction. That procedure applies exclusively to SEPs, and by and large makes clear when an injunction is appropriate, not least because scholars and practitioners have eagerly pored over its intricacies.[17] In addition, at the time of writing, the European Commission has proposed SEP-specific legislation that would further clarify a SEP holder's entitlement to injunctive relief.[18] This is not to say the rules surrounding SEPs are settled, much less in a fully satisfactory manner. It is clear, however, that SEPs are distinct from non-SEPs, and almost no guidance is available for the latter as to what rules should govern the entitlement to injunctive relief, if not an automatic injunction rule. This is therefore where my focus lies. The specific question whether a proportionality test as discussed here can apply in addition to the *Huawei* framework is addressed in section 3.2.5.

The third topic not addressed here are damages, the remedial companion to injunctions. US scholarship has shown an increasing interest in the subject, and massive damages awards sometimes make headlines even in Europe. By contrast, in Europe, damages are awarded in separate quantum proceedings, which are hardly ever pursued; the rare exceptions tend to result in modest awards far removed from the multi-million-dollar verdicts that may spark the imagination. In my view, even if damages and injunctive relief are obviously related subjects from the perspective of the compensation due to a patentee for infringement of their patent, this long-standing practice makes it acceptable not to address damages in detail in this work. Offsetting injunction denials through higher damages, as is sometimes proposed, risks missing the mark in practice simply because damages awards in European patent cases are such a seldom occurrence. This book therefore considers the entitlement to injunctive relief in isolation and proposes a solution that seeks to be balanced without recourse to compensation in the form of damages. The issue of compensation due for the duration of a stay is addressed in section 6.6.

Outline of the Book

Part I: Foundations

Patents exist to promote innovation and the diffusion of the resulting technologies. Aspects of patent law that do not contribute to this goal, let alone hinder it,

[17] An overview is provided by I Nikolic, *Licensing Standard Essential Patents: FRAND and the Internet of Things* (Hart Publishing, 2021).

[18] Commission, 'Proposal for a regulation of the European Parliament and of the Council on standard essential patents and amending Regulation (EU)2017/1001' COM(2023) 232 final.

should be reconsidered because patent protection often imposes high social costs. This truism motivates much of the scholarship on patents, not just by lawyers, but also by economists or political scientists, to name just two other disciplines with an avid interest in patent law. It is also the driving force behind much of the writing on proportionality, the intuition being that injunctions can sometimes have such severe consequences that are not justified by patent law's underlying purpose (or, conversely, that limiting patentees' entitlement to an injunction will have pernicious effects on innovation). I call this the innovation paradigm of proportionality. A second leading vision of proportionality is the diffusion paradigm, which is concerned that patents sometimes result in unjustifiable restrictions on the use of protected technologies. The perennial controversy over patents on pharmaceuticals illustrates these concerns well, though they extend to all fields of technology. The first part of this book is devoted to the idea that a third way may be preferable: the paradigm of commensurate scope.

To understand why, chapter one takes a step back and asks why court discretion over patent injunctions might be desirable. It starts with the observation that patent laws strive for an equilibrium between the interests of patentees (seeking exclusivity to recuperate investments in R&D and effectively commercialise their inventions), their competitors (seeking freedom to pursue their own innovations) and the public (who benefit from innovation, but also seek access to existing technologies on reasonable terms). But the equilibrium is an abstract goal set for patent law in its entirety, whereas patent law's day-to-day effects are highly context-specific. Patents are more important drivers of R&D investments in some industries than in others and their strategic importance varies across business models: for some types of innovators, they are indispensable, whereas they are primarily a nuisance for others. The effects of injunctions, in particular, are highly context-dependent because they are such blunt instruments. If it is accepted that this context dependence has the potential to upset the equilibrium that patent laws strive for, it makes sense to cede at least some authority over patent policy to the institution in the patent ecosystem most sensitive to context: courts. This is commonly accepted for most key doctrines in patent law – in particular, inventive step and scope of protection – and chapter one discusses three examples where legislators accepted this also for patent remedies. However, as we grant courts discretion over patent injunctions, we should be mindful of their institutional constraints. These include, in particular, limited knowledge of industry characteristics and consequently a limited capacity to formulate rules of general applicability with a view to 'improving' the equilibrium that patent law strives for.

The second chapter proceeds to evaluate the innovation and diffusion paradigms in light of these constraints. It suggests that courts are unlikely to oversee properly how the grant or denial of injunctive relief in any given case might affect the innovation or diffusion functions of the patent system. Consequently, 'prevention of harm to innovation' or 'avoidance of excessive costs' are unsuitable principles to guide the application of a proportionality test. Chapter two suggests that, instead, the guiding principle of the proportionality doctrine ought to be commensurate scope. That is, the proportionality test should ensure that the patentee's effective sphere of exclusivity is commensurate with their inventive contribution. This principle has a long history in European patent law and underlies its key doctrines according to European courts and the European Patent Office's Boards of Appeal, so that it would be incongruous to disregard it at the remedies stage. It also aligns well with the boundaries that EU law sets on enforcement in IP cases. It further offers the basis for a test that is more predictable and workable for courts than what follows from the innovation and diffusion paradigms. The leading view in the literature, which generally embraces those two paradigms, is that proportionality is a 'broad scope, high threshold' test: the circumstances potentially relevant to its application are unlimited, but it should apply only in exceptional cases. By contrast, adopting commensurate scope as a guiding principle would narrow down proportionality's scope and possibly lower its threshold for application. Stated differently, not only does the proportionality test become more predictable in its application, but its more frequent application becomes much less objectionable if it is not relied on to remedy any possible undesirable side-effect of injunctions but is focused on specific problems with contemporary patent law.

Part II: A Solution in Search of a Problem?

The second part of the book is devoted to what those specific problems with contemporary patent law might be. The literature is replete with suggestions bearing suggestive epithets: trolls, holdup, patent ambushes or royalty stacking are some of the most common examples. But most of these phenomena are not new. Patent law has been controversial ever since its inception, and complaints – even outrage – about the social costs it imposes have always been around. In my view, such complaints carry normative force primarily where they arise from problems that were not present before or at least are more pronounced today. Otherwise, these complaints serve merely to alter patent law's equilibrium in favour of one group of stakeholders or the other. And if there are no genuine problems proportionality can address, it risks being a solution in search of a problem, as its critics like to quip.

Chapter three observes that one thing has changed for certain: there are many more patents in force today than there were at any time in history. While not a problem in and of itself, this amplifies pre-existing problems to the point where intervention is justified. Put briefly, my main findings are that the great proliferation of patents in recent decades has: (i) subjected to patent protection ever more technologies on which society has an ever greater dependency; (ii) made patentable ever smaller components of that technology; and (iii) made accidental infringement of those patents ever more likely, especially as patent prosecution procedures have become ever more complex and thus offer ever more opportunities for subterfuge. Again, none of these phenomena are new in an absolute sense, but put together, they suggest that cases where injunctive relief is problematic are increasingly more likely to occur.

That suggestion is assayed in chapter four. It surveys developments in the US law of patent injunctions after the seminal decision in *eBay v MercExchange*. That decision bestowed on lower courts remedial discretion in patent cases that is arguably quite strong. Courts' use of that discretion offers something of a natural experiment to test the assumptions in this book. What do we see when we read their decisions? I observe that irreparable harm takes centre stage in the US approach to patent injunctions, that its evaluation according to precedent nevertheless remains murky and that the broad scope of *eBay*'s test contributes to the test's overall unpredictability. But the decisions studied in chapter four serve another purpose within this book: they demonstrate that the concerns discussed in the chapter that precedes it are not theoretical but actually occur in practice. At least in the US, patentees sometimes delay enforcement to lock in infringers, infringing products are sometimes critical to customers and consumers, and patents on small components are sometimes leveraged to extract high royalty payments – and US courts have responded by limiting patentees' entitlement to injunctive relief. While US and European patent law likely differ too much to 'borrow' from one another in terms of outcomes, the problems that inspired them are likely to occur on both sides of the pond.

Part III: Towards a Proportionality Test in European Patent Law

The third and final part investigates what a European proportionality doctrine for patent injunctions might look like. Chapter five analyses in detail the applicable EU law framework, principally the Enforcement Directive and the ECJ's case law applying it. What does it mean that remedies in patent cases, including permanent injunctions, must be 'effective, proportionate, and dissuasive', that they must not create 'barriers to legitimate trade' and that Member States must provide 'safeguards against their abuse'? I argue that the Enforcement Directive strikes an incipient balance between the fundamental rights of the patentee and the infringer, enshrined in the Charter. Thus, whereas Article 17(2) CFR confers on patentees an exclusive right to the invention and a right to oppose infringements and Article 47 CFR guarantees effective remedies to realise these rights, Article 16 CFR protects the infringer's right to engage in legitimate business and Article 47 CFR entitles them to procedural safeguards against the Enforcement Directive's exceptionally strong suite of remedies. The Enforcement Directive reflects a balance between these rights, but because its attainment is so context-dependent, courts must make a case-by-case assessment before imposing remedies, as Recital (17) and the ECJ's guidance make clear. That does not mean courts must balance the patentee's and infringer's rights in every case: that would mean redoing the balance struck by the European legislator. Rather, they must ensure the balance envisioned in the Enforcement Directive is attained by checking that its general conditions, laid down in Article 3, are satisfied. That is different when it comes to third parties because their rights are not specifically foreseen in the Directive's provisions, as opposed to the infringer's rights.

Finally, chapter six ties together the previous chapters and proposes a proportionality test in three categories: overreach, abuse and conflicts with third-party rights. Overreach is present when the effective scope of the injunction exceeds the patentee's inventive contribution to an impermissible degree. To establish overreach, the infringer must demonstrate three things: first, that the patented technology is not indispensable for the core functionality of the products falling within the effective scope of the injunction; second, that the patented technology offers no notable commercial or technical advantages over alternative technologies; and third, a best effort plan to cease infringement on the shortest time reasonably possible. If they succeed, courts should presume that a stay is warranted and grant it for the period requested. The patentee may then rebut the presumption by demonstrating that the requested stay is unreasonable or that the infringer's conduct bars a proportionality plea, for instance because they engage in hold-out tactics or because infringement was wilful. The second category within the proportionality framework proposed here, abuse, exists for rare cases where no overreach is established but the patentee's behaviour was nevertheless so egregiously opportunistic that its entitlement to injunctive relief ought to be limited. The third category deals with cases where the injunction would affect the interests of third parties.

These categories correspond to the conditions for patent remedies set by the Enforcement Directive, but also follow the paradigm of commensurate scope. In overreach cases, the effective scope of the injunction far exceeds the patent's actual scope. The same is true for abuse cases, as the labyrinthine procedures of present-day patent prosecution and the sophistication of large patentees may entice stratagems that put a patentee in a position of power not warranted by their invention or envisioned by the Enforcement Directive. When it comes to third-party rights, the proportionality test proposed here would apply only where the injunction would severely affect the business of third parties engaged in activities unrelated to the infringement, or where it would deprive end users of important technological advances over the patented invention. Also in these cases, the injunction would extend the patentee's effective sphere of exclusivity beyond their inventive contribution, and so intervention at the remedies stage is justified. But it should be noted that the vast majority of cases in which the proportionality test proposed here would apply are those involving component patents. I believe that is justified in light of the findings in Part II: component patents raise problems of unprecedented salience in contemporary patent law. If that finding is accepted, it would be odd to limit the proportionality test's application to outlier cases with exceptional fact patterns. Instead, the limitation should take place at the test's scope: if tailored primarily to the problems raised by component patents, more frequent application becomes unproblematic. In fact, it becomes the rational response to a recognised problem. In sum, I propose that the paradigm of commensurate scope is capable of normatively grounding the proportionality test in a principle familiar to all of patent law; that it brings the proportionality test fully in line with EU law; that it focuses the test on problems of contemporary patent law that are urgent and occur with unprecedented frequency; and most importantly, that it makes the test easier to apply by courts and more predictable for litigants.

Much like Dürer's depiction of Giovanni de' Medici's rhinoceros, my proportionality test is an early sketch of a strange creature about to embark on a journey through Europe. The ambition of this work, which sometimes departs from the apparent consensus in the literature, is to shed light on what proportionality might look like so as to aid European patent courts as they confront this question. To those who are disappointed that my proportionality test is not capable of resolving all problems in patent law (and I do not deny they exist), I point out that I intend to show a rhinoceros, not an elephant: by its nature, a proportionality test cannot trample over established patent law by fundamentally rewriting its boundaries. To those who believe I go too far, I propose that they should not hope that this rhinoceros, like Dürer's, will perish prematurely. Proportionality is here to stay, and the purpose of this book is to help courts, practitioners, scholars and other stakeholders better understand this enigmatic animal.

PART I

Foundations

1

The Role and Limitations of Patent Courts

Our exploration of the proportionality test in patent law must begin with an analysis of the institution tasked with applying it: courts. Should courts be authorised to limit a patentee's injunction entitlement and, if so, what do their institutional strengths and weaknesses suggest about the form and extent of this authority? Like the question it addresses, this chapter consists of two parts.

The first part starts with the observation that in Europe, as elsewhere, courts commonly enjoy considerable leeway in the application and refinement of patent law's key doctrines to protect the equilibrium that the legislator has sought to establish in the patent system. Similar leeway should be accepted when it comes to injunctive relief. In a nutshell, the argument is that the effects of injunctions are so context-specific that it is impossible to reconcile the interests they affect in an abstract, ex ante rule. The clash of interests over injunctive relief in patent cases was on full display during the recent reform of the German Patent Act (GPA), which offers an illustrative case study of why sensitivity to context is critical when deciding on injunctions. We will see that not just the German legislator, but also the European legislator and the states participating in the Unified Patent Court (UPC) accepted the argument and mandated at least some court discretion to limit the patentee's entitlement to injunctive relief in appropriate cases. The book's point of departure, then, is that patent courts in all EU Member States, including the UPC, are authorised to apply a proportionality test.

Before embarking on the analysis of how that authority might best be used, the chapter's second part looks at the institutional constraints faced by patent courts. It is commonly accepted in the US literature that these constraints 'should guide legal design' of remedies.[1] This part notes that courts are resource-constrained, have limited knowledge of their rulings' real-world effects and should be wary of treating individual cases as indicative of structural shortcomings in the patent system. The design of a proportionality test should account for these shortcomings, a thread that is continued in chapter two.

[1] Most notably J Golden, 'Principles for Patent Remedies' (2010) 88 *Texas Law Review* 505, 512.

1.1. Innovation, Property, Diffusion: Patent Law's Search for Equilibrium

1.1.1. Patents as Market-Driven Incentives for Innovation

This book adopts a utilitarian view of patent law, ie that patents exist to promote innovation. That is not a controversial position in Europe. The European Patent Convention does not state its purpose, but a 2007 report commissioned by the European Parliament on ways to improve the patent system found that its fundamental purpose is 'to enhance social and economic welfare by stimulating innovation and diffusion of knowledge'.[2] For its part, the European Patent Office (EPO) considers it its mission to 'deliver high-quality patents … that foster innovation, competitiveness and economic growth'. Recital (4) of Regulation 1257/2012 (the Unitary Patent Regulation) connects patent protection to increased innovation by stating that 'Unitary patent protection will foster scientific and technological advances'.[3] A utilitarian approach is also found in other secondary legislation of the EU that deals with patent protection, as in Recitals (1)–(3) of Directive 2004/48 (the Enforcement Directive), Recital (2) of Directive 1998/44 (the Biotech Directive)[4] and Recital (3) of Regulation 469/2009 (the SPC Regulation).[5] All of these recitals assume a link between legal protection and fostering innovation. A similar view was expressed by the European Commission.[6] All in all, it is clear that in the EU, patents are granted, first and foremost, as an incentive for innovative activity, even if differing views exist on the need for and efficacy of this incentive.

In theory at least, this incentive is provided by (the prospect of) market exclusivity, guaranteed by a property right to the underlying invention. Several consequences attach to fostering innovation through property rights and not, as has been done throughout history, through state-awarded prizes, privileges or other non-proprietary systems. First, the patentee's reward in monetary terms is determined by the market. There are many examples where a patent on sought-after technology made its holder fabulously rich, but many more where, for various reasons, the technology could not be marketed successfully and the patent yielded its holder no benefits. Second, others wishing to use the patented technology may

[2] R Cowan et al, 'Policy Options for the Improvement of the European Patent System' (IP/A/STOA/FWC/2005-28/SC16, European Parliament STOA 2007) 8.

[3] Regulation (EU) 1257/2012 of the European Parliament and of the Council of 17 December 2012 implementing enhanced cooperation in the area of the creation of unitary patent protection [2012] OJ L 361/1.

[4] Directive 98/44/EC of the European Parliament and of the Council of 6 July 1998 on the legal protection of biotechnological inventions [1998] OJ L 213/13.

[5] Regulation (EC) 469/2009 of the European Parliament and of the Council of 6 May 2009 concerning the supplementary protection certificate for medicinal products (codified version) [2009] OJ L 152/1.

[6] Commission, 'Communication from the Commission to the European Parliament, the Council and the European Economic and Social Committee setting out the EU approach to Standard Essential Patents' COM(2017) 712 final, 1 ('Patents provide R&D with incentives and enable innovative companies to receive an adequate return on investment').

do so only with the patentee's consent. Conditions for use of patented technology are thus set by private actors through bargaining processes, and not by courts or government officials. Third, to enable these two mechanisms, patents enjoy protection as property rights under national constitutions as well as Article 17(2) in the EU's Charter of Fundamental Rights (CFR). Patentees are thus protected against unlawful interferences with their rights by their national government, although the latter may regulate property in the public interest. They also enjoy a strong right to enjoin others from using the invention, as opposed to a damages entitlement or other remedy.

An evident drawback of innovation incentives that take the form of property rights is that they afford private sovereignty over technology. This is problematic if we understand the goal of the patent system not just in a narrow sense of fostering innovation by companies for their own benefit, but more broadly as aimed at the diffusion of the innovation that patents generate.[7] These concerns are as old as patent law itself, but gain new urgency as novel technologies become ever increasingly entwined in our daily lives. Stephen Hilgartner has argued that we are witnessing the emergence of a 'new politics' of intellectual property (IP) owing to which 'much of the contemporary debate is not about stimulating innovation, but centres on concerns about who governs technology and in pursuit of what goals'.[8] The participants in this contemporary debate are not just academics and patent professionals, but the public at large. Controversies surrounding access to COVID-19 vaccines, the struggle for global dominance over 5G technologies and the rise of gene patents are but some instances where patent law took centre stage in public discourse. Such discourse takes place outside the traditional confounds of court proceedings or academic journals, as politicians, interest groups, journalists, citizens and others rightly feel entitled to express their views on, and make demands of, the patent system. As Hilgartner points out, these stakeholders are not so much concerned with whether patent law delivers on its utilitarian promise as with democratic values, distributive justice and decision-making power over the processes that shape technological progress. It is fair to say that these 'new politics' of IP translate into increasing pressure on patent institutions to take account of the broader societal context in which patents operate.

Thus, the nature of patents in the EU is aptly summarised as having 'an emphasis on ensuring a high level of protection for inventors, albeit for utilitarian rather than deontological reasons, and still subject to certain Charter-derived third-party rights and societal interests'.[9] Indeed, from this brief (and necessarily incomplete) survey follow two main observations: strong protection for patents, modelled on property rights, is thought necessary to foster innovation; but concerns over the social costs of patents and their potential to impair rights of others have always existed and continue to grow. This field of tension is a red thread running throughout this book.

[7] On the diffusion function of patent law, see esp P Drahos, *A Philosophy of Intellectual Property* (Dartmouth, 1996) ch 8. This function was accepted in the report by Cowan et al (n 2).

[8] S Hilgartner, 'Intellectual Property and the Politics of Emerging Technology: Inventors, Citizens, and Powers to Shape the Future' (2008) 84 *Chicago-Kent Law Review* 197, 207.

[9] J Pila, 'Pluralism, Principles and Proportionality in Intellectual Property' (2014) 34 *OJLS* 181, 194.

1.1.2. Finding Equilibrium in Legislative Design and Ex Post Control Mechanisms

Patent law thus governs a triangular relationship between patentees, competitors and the public. Generally speaking, between patentees and competitors, the goal is to reward patentees sufficiently to ensure patent law achieves its aim of fostering innovation, while ensuring sufficient freedom remains for competitors to develop their own innovations. Between patentees and the public, the latter reap benefits from the innovation and disclosure that patent law induces, but in the short term pay monopoly prices for it. Between competitors and the public, the latter benefit from healthy competition, although patents are generally considered a legitimate and welfare-enhancing exception to free competition. In addition, there may exist dependencies on competitors' specific products or production capacities. Naturally, this is a highly stylised and merely two-dimensional view of the relations that patent law controls. Many nuances and additions would need to be made to capture the real-world dynamics underlying this triangular relationship and their short- and long-term effects on innovation and diffusion. For our purposes, however, the triangle serves as a useful reminder of the three groups of interests that patent law must reconcile as best it can at each stage of its application.

Figure 1.1 The interests that patent law must reconcile

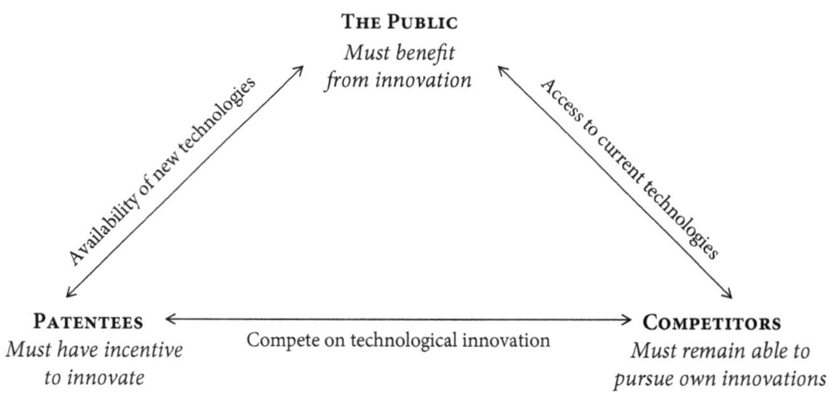

The various doctrines of substantive patent law seek to jointly create an acceptable equilibrium between these three sets of interests, even though many competing views exist on what is 'acceptable'. Thus, to avoid denying competitors the use of technologies they already possessed before the priority date, patented inventions must be novel and exceptions to exclusivity exist for prior users. Sufficiency seeks to ensure that competitors and the public can further develop the patented invention by requiring the patentee to fully disclose it. The inventive step requirement checks that only non-obvious inventions merit burdening competitors and the public with patent exclusivity. In Europe, claim construction explicitly seeks to combine 'a fair protection for the patent proprietor with a reasonable degree of legal certainty for third parties'.[10] As patent courts give substance to these doctrines through their decision-making practice, they strive to reach an acceptable equilibrium between these interests. Indeed, it is fair to say that the equilibrium contemplated by the legislator is effectuated by the choices courts and the EPO's Boards of Appeal make as they fill the inevitable gaps in the applicable legal texts. This, too, is uncontroversial: it is well understood that decisions, even highly consequential ones, on how patent law functions in practice are in the hands of patent courts and the EPO's appeal boards.[11] Taken together, those decisions profoundly influence the contours of patent law's equilibrium.

Even then, because the actual effects of patent exclusivity are so context-specific, there remains a need for corrective mechanisms to limit these effects if they would unacceptably upset the equilibrium in a specific case. The application of such 'ex post' correctives is contingent on circumstances generally unforeseeable at the time of grant. Standards for validity and infringement, even if properly calibrated, therefore do not – and cannot – resolve conflicts of interests falling within the scope of ex post correctives. This also accounts for their rare application: too frequent application of ex post correctives would risk eroding the legislator's intended equilibrium, reflected in substantive patent law. That would not only increase uncertainty about patent law's boundaries, but also make unelected institutions such as courts responsible for drawing them. Specific ex post correctives nevertheless exist for each of the groups of interests outlined above. For instance, if claim construction results in a scope of protection that does not properly reflect the inventive merits of the patented technology, the doctrine of equivalents may be relied upon to extend it. The duration of pharmaceutical patents may be extended if the effective duration of market exclusivity is 'insufficient to cover the investment put into the research' (Recital (4) of the SPC Regulation). On the other hand, if the enjoyment of a patent restricts competition 'unduly in a manner contrary to the Treaty' (Recital (12) of the Enforcement Directive), the rules of competition law may limit the patentee's sphere of exclusivity. And if the public's access to patented technology would be impermissibly limited, their interests may be safeguarded by the grant of a compulsory licence. This book is about a specific ex post corrective that is relatively new in European patent law and has so far been rarely invoked: the proportionality test. The next section considers why patent law may presently have reached a moment where greater reliance on this ex post corrective is necessary.

[10] Article 69 of the Convention on the Grant of European Patents 1973/2000 (European Patent Convention, EPC); see the Protocol on the Interpretation of Article 69 EPC of 5 October 1973 as revised by the Act revising the EPC of 29 November 2000.

[11] A recent example is the Enlarged Board of Appeal's decision on plausibility: G2/21 *Reliance on a purported technical effect for inventive step (plausibility)* [2023] ECLI:EP:BA:2023:G000221.20230323. Many other examples in the field of biotechnology are provided by G Van Overwalle, 'Policy Levers Tailoring Patent Law to Biotechnology: Comparing US and European Approaches' (2011) 1 *UC Irvine Law Review* 433.

1.2. A House Divided, or the Manifold Views on Proportionality

1.2.1. The Context-Specific Effects of Injunctive Relief in Patent Cases

The patent system must cater to many interests. In 2022, for instance, the top 10 technical fields with the most patent filings at the EPO were as diverse as digital communication (first place), medical technology and pharmaceuticals (places 2 and 5), computer technology and electronic machinery (places 3 and 4), transport (place 6) and measurement (place 7).[12] The industries behind these technologies are highly heterogeneous in virtually all aspects, including how and why they innovate. Each industry is characterised by its own, unique innovation incentives, regulatory hurdles to marketing new products and product life-cycles, to name just a few key determinants of the innovation process. Yet patent law applies uniformly across all industries. The relative importance and the practical effects of any given rule, such as the entitlement to injunctive relief, will thus vary greatly from case to case. This diagnosis of the patent system as functioning differently in different industries was popularised by Dan Burk and Mark Lemley in a 2011 book, in which they argue that courts should apply patent law doctrines in industry-specific ways.[13]

However, the notion of distinct 'industries' on which Burk and Lemley rely is becoming harder to sustain as ever more intersections of technologies arise. The recent spate of patent litigation between car makers and telecoms companies illustrates this well, as it pushed an industry that never seemed troubled about patents to the forefront of the debate about proportionality in Europe. If many industries formerly resembled gentleman's clubs where broad cross-licensing agreements warded off litigation, the rise of 'smart' devices exposed club members to patent assertion by industry outsiders. Divestment of patent portfolios to such outsiders creates anxiety among club members as key patents in the industry may suddenly be leveraged by investors seeking to monetise them. At the same time, these industry shifts create opportunities for newcomer firms specialised in R&D or established firms looking to divert their focus further towards 'pure' R&D, such as IBM. These changes inspired much of the contemporary scholarship on patent remedies, but it bears emphasis that they are ongoing: new revolutions in business and technology are surely on the horizon. In sum, the great variation in

[12] The analysis is provided on the website of the European Patent Office: 'Top Technical Fields' (EPO, 30 January 2023) www.epo.org/about-us/annual-reports-statistics/statistics/2022/statistics/patent-applications.html#tab3.

[13] D Burk and M Lemley, *The Patent Crisis and How the Courts Can Solve It* (University of Chicago Press, 2009).

industry characteristics makes the disparate impact – and sometimes awkward fit – of uniform rules of patent law immediately apparent; but at the same time, where the application of those rules presents threats to some, it represents opportunities for others.

The general picture painted by Burk and Lemley should thus be complemented by a closer look at firm structure and strategy. In a recent study, Jonathan Barnett argues that various measures strengthening the patentee's position in the USA since the 1980s led to the rise of small, specialised and highly R&D-intensive firms that were able to successfully challenge larger incumbents.[14] Barnett calls this a 'dynamic analysis' of IP, under which the availability of non-IP alternatives to maintain competitive advantage determines how firms respond to changes in IP regimes. According to Barnett, 'larger, more established, and more integrated entities' have advantages of scale and reputation, as well as accumulated know-how, among other things, so changes in IP strength will have the weakest effects on these entities.[15] Conversely, newcomer firms that specialise only in technology possess none of these advantages and therefore strong IP protection is critical for the viability of this business model. Barnett presents a compelling argument that the prominence of such smaller firms tracks the evolution of US patent law between the mid-nineteenth century and the early twenty-first century. He then offers evidence that at least domestically large, integrated firms prefer (and lobby for) weaker IP rights, whereas R&D-specialist, disintegrated firms prefer (and lobby for) stronger IP rights.[16] Contemporary debates on proportionality in patent law thus represent a clash between business models, some new and some old, and particularly their ways of adapting to industry change spurred by technological developments. Burk, Lemley and Barnett focus exclusively on the USA, and we cannot simply extend their findings to the EU, given the unmistakable differences between both economies, certainly over a 150-year lifespan.[17] Nevertheless, it seems reasonable to infer that both industry characteristics and firms' organisational structures correlate strongly with stakeholder views on injunctive relief and proportionality in Europe. The next section offers support for this inference by analysing German stakeholder positions on proportionality expressed during the recent reform of the GPA in 2019–21.

[14] J Barnett, *Innovators, Firms, and Markets: The Organizational Logic of Intellectual Property* (Oxford University Press, 2021) ch 6.

[15] ibid 3.

[16] ibid 162. Firms' preferences may differ when it comes to setting international standards to govern IP protection abroad. Drahos and Braithwaite show that big US firms were a driving force in the negotiation of the TRIPS Agreement: P Drahos and J Braithwaite, *Information Feudalism: Who Owns the Knowledge Economy?* (Earthscan, 2002) ch 7.

[17] I expect the rise of R&D-intensive innovator forms chronicled by Barnett was less pronounced in Europe and even then was limited geographically to Western European countries, though further research is outside the scope of this book.

1.2.2. Stakeholder Positions During the German Patent Act Reform (2019–21)

1.2.2.1. Background to the Reform

Potential changes to the GPA were first announced in early 2019 by the Federal Ministry of Justice following calls for reform of various aspects of it, particularly the quasi-automatic entitlement to injunctive relief laid down in §139 GPA.[18] In May of that year, the Ministry invited stakeholders for a roundtable discussion on the need for improvement. The roundtable was attended by 35 judges, academics, attorneys and representatives of trade bodies, and a first draft reform bill was published on 14 January 2020.[19] To the surprise of many, the draft bill proposed to add the following caveat to §139 GPA:

> The claim [to injunctive relief] is excluded, insofar as enforcement of the injunction entitlement is disproportionate, because it results in hardship not justified by the exclusive right in light of the special circumstances, having regard to the interests of the patentee vis-à-vis those of the infringer, as well as the requirements of good faith.

The explanatory memorandum accompanying the first draft indicated that German law already provided for the exceptional derogation of a patentee's right to an immediate injunction, referring to a 2016 decision by the Federal Supreme Court (*Wärmetauscher*).[20] In brief, in *Wärmetauscher* the Federal Supreme Court opened the door to derogation from the automatic injunction rule by way of a grace period for selling out infringing stock, but only under very strict conditions. The first draft observed that, due to the strong reluctance on the part of courts to apply the *Wärmetauscher* rule, the societal consequences of an injunction could exceed what would be necessary for the measure to be dissuasive.[21] It concluded that it seemed 'proper' (*sachgerecht*) to 'clarify explicitly' that a patent injunction may – in exceptional circumstances, it emphasised – be disproportionate, in accordance with Article 3(2) of the Enforcement Directive.[22] The Federal Ministry of Justice invited stakeholders to express their views on the draft bill by March 2020.

Thirty-four submissions were received, principally from individual companies or industry bodies.[23] As might have been expected, the proposed revision of

[18] M Stierle and F Hofmann, 'The Latest Amendment to the German Law on Patent Injunctions: The New Statutory Disproportionality Exception and Third-Party Interests' (2022) 71 *Gewerblicher Rechtsschutz und Urheberrecht International* 1123, 1124.

[19] Federal Ministry of Justice, Discussion Bill (*Diskussionsentwurf: Entwurf eines Zweiten Gesetzes zur Vereinfachung und Modernisierung des Patentrechts*) of 14 January 2020 (hereinafter, first draft). See www.bmjv.de/SharedDocs/Gesetzgebungsverfahren/DE/PatMoG_2.html.

[20] BGH GRUR 2016, 1031; X ZR 114/13 *Wärmetauscher*, para 45.

[21] First draft (n 19) 51. The draft indicates that 'parts of the German industry', especially the automobile- and telecom sectors, were particularly concerned about the reluctant application of a proportionality test by lower courts.

[22] First draft (n 19) 32.

[23] Annex I contains an overview of all publicly available stakeholder positions.

§139 GPA stirred great controversy and responses to it were sharply divided. Some stakeholders argued it did not go far enough to protect their interests; others argued it went much too far. A second, revised draft followed on 1 September 2020.[24] Apart from clarifying that the patentee would be entitled to monetary compensation in the event their entitlement to injunctive relief was curtailed, it departed from the previous proposal in two ways. It now applied in case of disproportionate *detriment*, a seemingly lower threshold than *hardship*. And it explicitly required taking into account third-party interests, something lower courts considered to be outside the reach of the *Wärmetauscher* test.[25] The revised explanatory memorandum did not explain the redaction from 'hardship' to 'detriment', but it did address in detail the reason for inclusion of third-party interests. It explained that consideration of these interests is mandatory under the Enforcement Directive, and pointed out important differences between consideration of third-party rights in a proportionality test and a compulsory licence.[26] By early October 2020, another round of stakeholder positions was published, largely the same as those that had commented on the first draft.

1.2.2.2. Overview of Stakeholder Positions on the Revision of §139 GPA

Table 1.1 summarises industry positions on the proposed revision of §139 GPA in response to the first and second draft bills. Coalition groups or companies opposing any codification of proportionality are listed under 'No change'. Those supporting codification but only within the limited contours of the *Wärmetauscher* decision are listed under 'Weak change', supporting what I will call a 'weak', as opposed to a 'strong', proportionality test. Those advocating a further-reaching exception clause that would limit the patentee's entitlement to injunctive relief in a broader set of cases are listed under 'Strong change'.

Table 1.1 Overview of industry positions taken on proposed changes to §139 GPA, 2020

Company/group	Industry	Strong change	Weak change	No change
3M	Industrial technology			X*
AbbVie	Pharmaceuticals			X*
ACT	Tech industry	X		
BASF	Chemicals			X*

(continued)

[24] Federal Ministry of Justice, Draft Bill (*Referentenentwurf: Entwurf eines Zweiten Gesetzes zur Vereinfachung und Modernisierung des Patentrechts*) of 1 September 2020 (hereinafter, second draft). See www.bmjv.de/SharedDocs/Gesetzgebungsverfahren/DE/PatMoG_2.html.

[25] LG Düsseldor BeckRS 2017, 104662; 4a O 28/16 *Herzklappen*.

[26] Second draft (n 24) 63–64.

Table 1.1 ***(Continued)***

Company/group	Industry	Strong change	Weak change	No change
Bayer	Pharmaceuticals		X*	
BDP	Plant breeding		X*	
BIO Deutschland	Biotechnology			X*
Bitkom	IT/telecoms	No position expressed		
BITMi	IT/telecoms	No position expressed		
BVMW	Cross-industry		X	
Canon	Electronics		X	
DABEI	Cross-industry			X**
Deutsche Erfinderverband	Cross-industry		X	
Deutsche Telekom	Telecoms	X		
Ericsson	Telecoms			X
Die Familienunternehmer	Cross-industry	No position expressed		
Fischergroup	Automotive			X*
Fair Standards Alliance	Cross-industry (mostly tech/ automotive)	X		
VFA/VCI	Pharmaceuticals			X
Honda	Automotive	X		
IP Europe	Cross-industry (mostly telecoms)			X
IP2Innovate	Cross-industry (mostly tech/ automotive)	X		
JAMA	Automotive	X*		
JBMIA	Electronics		X	
NVIDIA	Tech	X		
Patentverein	Industrial technology	X		
ProGenerika	Pharmaceuticals		X	
Sanofi	Pharmaceuticals		X	
Siemens	Industrial technology			X
VDA	Automotive	X		
Vodafone	Telecoms	X		

(continued)

Table 1.1 ***(Continued)***

Company/group	Industry	Strong change	Weak change	No change
VPP	Cross-industry	No position expressed		
ZVEI	Industrial technology		X	
Total		10	9	10

Source: German Federal Ministry of Justice; see also Annex I.

* These stakeholders only submitted views in the second round.

** DABEI supported a weak proportionality test in the first round but opposed the amendment altogether in the second round.

The contentiousness of proportionality is immediately apparent from the table, and viewpoints are almost perfectly divided across the two extremes and the more moderate middle ground. For the most part, this division confirms the hypothesis put forward in the previous subsection that preferences for an injunction regime depend on the industry and business model. Tracing exactly the positions outlined by Barnett, 'big tech' came out in favour of strong proportionality whereas Qualcomm, together with other R&D-specialist firms, opposed any codification of proportionality.[27] The automotive industry, which led the reform effort, supported proportionality, whereas an independent and highly specialised supplier of parts (Fischer Group) opposed it. Most pharmaceutical and chemicals companies opposed proportionality, which corresponds to the expectations of Burk and Lemley, as well as Barnett.[28] Lastly, the positions by network operators (Vodafone and Deutsche Telekom) are also wholly in line with Barnett's dynamic theory: third-party IP reduces margins on the sale of phone plans, while the immobility of network infrastructure makes them especially vulnerable to injunctions.

But there are also some seemingly unexpected results. Siemens, a vertically integrated giant with a long-standing reputation and close ties to the government, vehemently opposed the proportionality test. So did 3M, presumably one of the firms that benefited most from the 'semi-bureaucratic innovation architecture' that Barnett attributes to the weak-IP, high-concentration era in the mid-twentieth century.[29] The industry coalitions supporting strong proportionality also represent small and medium enterprises (SMEs, eg Patentverein), particularly tech start-ups (ACT) and a large number of suppliers in the automotive industry (VDA).[30] In the pharmaceutical industry, both generics companies (ProGenerika) and two major innovator companies (Bayer and Sanofi) coalesced around a weak proportionality

[27] Barnett, *Innovators, Firms, and Markets* (n 14) 162 *et seq*. See the positions of IP2Innovate, of which Apple and Google are a part, and IP Europe, of which Qualcomm is a part.

[28] Burk and Lemley (n 13) 4; Barnett, *Innovators, Firms, and Markets* (n 14) 3.

[29] Barnett, *Innovators, Firms, and Markets* (n 14) 100.

[30] Some caution is probably warranted when interpreting these coalitions' positions because they may be influenced by larger members.

test. The latter example in particular suggests that reliance on IP as a means to appropriate returns on investment (as compared to non-IP alternatives) does not fully determine stakeholder positions. Apparently, overly strong patents pose risks even to those firms that otherwise rely heavily on IP, and conversely, firms that enjoy significant non-IP advantages may nonetheless need patents to stay competitive. In sum, while there is indeed a clear correlation between preferences on the injunction regime and industry and firm structure, preferences expressed are ultimately idiosyncratic and driven by strategic goals and obstacles particular to the individual stakeholder.

That conclusion finds particular support in the fact that some stakeholders changed or nuanced previously held views on proportionality.[31] For instance, Qualcomm opposed the introduction of a proportionality test in German patent law and co-signed an open letter together with, amongst others, Nokia, expressing concerns about 'maintaining Germany as a strong research location'.[32] But when Qualcomm was on the receiving end of an injunction in California, it vigorously disputed the patentee's entitlement to injunctive relief, even though the injunction allowed for a 13-month sunset period.[33] And Nokia had filed an amicus brief in *eBay v MercExchange*, arguing that the automatic injunction rule must be abolished because this rule 'could have the unintended consequence of enabling a patent owner whose patent covers a standard to seek exorbitant royalties, stymie competition, and ultimately harm public interests promoted by interoperability standards'.[34] That Qualcomm and Nokia now appreciate an automatic injunction rule differently than they did roughly 15 years ago should hardly surprise us: the industry they operate in underwent tremendous change in this period and their businesses understandably adapted. The observation is not limited to the telecoms industry. For instance, Sanofi, an originator pharmaceutical company, supported the proportionality test, a position that is at odds with the one defended by an industry association to which it belongs.[35] This somewhat surprising position comes at a time when novel therapeutical methods break down the traditional industry divide between originator and generics companies. It is surely no coincidence that just months prior, Sanofi had been denied a compulsory licence for a drug that it claimed had important clinical benefits over the patentee's product.[36]

[31] A similar shift was also observed in the US: M Lemley and AD Melamed, 'Missing the Forest for the Trolls' (2013) 113 *Columbia Law Review* 2117, 2135–36 (citing several examples from the tech and telecoms industries).

[32] M Klos, 'Europe's Industrial Companies Mobilise against Weaker Automatic Injunction' (JUVE Patent, 4 February 2021) www.juve-patent.com/news-and-stories/legal-commentary/europes-industrial-companies-mobilise-against-weaker-automatic-injunction/.

[33] *Broadcomm Corp v Qualcomm Inc* 543 F.3d 683, 701 (Fed Cir 2008).

[34] Brief of Nokia Corporation as Amicus Curiae, 16, *eBay Inc v MercExchange LLC* 547 US 388 (2006). In more recent amicus briefs, Nokia has rather tended to take a position that would preserve the availability of injunctions: J Barnett, 'Has the Academy Led Patent Law Astray?' (2017) 32 *Berkeley Technology Law Journal* 1313, 1374.

[35] Sanofi (Discussion proposal position) 1; the industry association's contrary position is found at VFA and VCI (Discussion proposal position) 7.

[36] BGH GRUR 2019, 1038; X ZB 2/19 *Alirocumab*.

1.2.3. How Should the Legislator Respond?

It follows from the foregoing that the answer that this section started with – is greater reliance on proportionality necessary to maintain patent law's equilibrium? – will differ depending on who you ask. Whether an automatic injunction rule is viewed as the cornerstone of patent law's incentive to innovate or, to the contrary, a grave threat to innovation and diffusion is contingent upon, particularly, industry characteristics and firms' individual strategies. What are we to make of this stark disagreement? It might be tempting to dismiss stakeholder positions as opportunistic, even cynical, lobbying rhetoric, especially where they conflict with positions previously taken in different contexts.[37] To be sure, stakeholder rhetoric should be taken with a grain of salt and serves primarily to change the law to benefit the individual stakeholder's bottom line. Still, these positions help map the disparate effects of, and dependencies on, patent injunctions across industries transformed by technological advancements of the past decades. They suggest that both sides of the argument may be right: a company like BASF may well be in trouble if it cannot reliably obtain injunctions against competitors, whereas the all too reliable availability of injunctions may well force a company like Mercedes to meet licensing demands that are far out of proportion with the technological contribution of the patented technology. It all depends on context. In addition, injunctions may well affect end users of technologies, as especially the network operators and some pharmaceutical companies pointed out. The legislator is then faced with the unenviable task of reconciling these interests in a way that best maintains the equilibrium outlined in section 1.1.2.

The legislator could respond by simply doing nothing, as advocated in Germany by proponents of 'no change' and eminent lawyers like judge Klaus Grabinski.[38] They generally argue that the contemporary patent system requires stronger, not weaker, patent rights and that existing ex post correctives suffice to prevent rare instances of egregious enforcement. In my view, this is not a fair characterisation of patent law today, a point that chapter three develops in more detail. Put briefly, the great proliferation of patents in recent decades (i) subjected to patent protection ever more technologies on which society has an ever greater dependency, (ii) made patentable ever smaller components of that technology and (iii) made accidental infringement of those patents ever more likely. Of course, patents on critical technology, component patents and accidental infringement are not, by themselves, new phenomena, but they have unprecedented salience in the contemporary patent system simply because we have so many more patents. From the immense academic and political debates on both sides of the Atlantic, it seems

[37] G Reilly, 'Patent Litigation Reform in the United States' in T Takenaka, *Research Handbook on Patent Law and Theory* (Edward Elgar, 2019) 387–88 (describing the tech industry's lobby as a 'powerful interest' which clashed in the US Congress with pharmaceutical companies and trial lawyer groups, ultimately stalling attempts at patent litigation reform).

[38] K Grabinski, 'Injunctive Relief and Proportionality in Case of a Public Interest in the Use of a Patent: Different Ways – Same Result' [2021] *Gewerblicher Rechtsschutz und Urheberrecht* 200.

clear that this raises at least some nontrivial issues around injunctive relief, most notably its appropriate limits in component patent cases.

This diversity of views also counsels against paralysis out of fears that uncertainty over injunctive relief will have a destabilising effect on patent markets and innovation, as expressed by Barnett amongst others.[39] Barnett concedes that thickets, holdup and royalty stacking – theories associated with injunctive relief and discussed in chapter three – could potentially 'discourage innovation and inflate intermediate and end-user costs', but finds no evidence that they occur with any regularity.[40] At the same time, policy actions taken to address these theories, in particular denying injunctive relief to non-practising entities, will likely give rise to 'several socially harmful effects'.[41] It is not evident, however, that the assumption supports an automatic injunction regime.[42] Assuming, as Barnett does, that there is a trade-off between preventable social losses owing to court discretion over injunctions and social losses caused by uncertainty stemming from that same court discretion, at least in theory a point exists where overall losses are lowest. Barnett accepts that, as a practical matter, that point cannot be found (as do I). But it does not follow that an automatic injunction regime is the safest bet.[43] To the contrary, if stakeholders across the board take diametrically opposed positions, a prudent middle ground is more likely to resemble the economically optimal regime than the regime favoured by only one side. It is surely no coincidence that all genuinely cross-industry coalitions have either tended towards weak proportionality or expressed no view on the matter. Bitkom, 'Germany's digital association' whose members include 'more than 1,000 SMEs, over 500 startups and virtually all global players' according to its website, in fact explained its unwillingness to comment on the issue of proportionality by citing 'a broad range of viewpoints' among its members.

There are other reasons beyond estimations of economic effects to allow at least some court discretion over patent injunctions. First and foremost, in the EU, patents enjoy constitutional protection under Article 17(2) CFR, albeit subject to other Charter rights. Patent protection cannot be absolute because in each case,

[39] Barnett, 'Has the Academy Led Patent Law Astray?' (n 34) 1379. In Europe, this view was expressed by M Schellhorn, *Der Patentrechtliche Unterlassungsanspruch im Lichte des Verhältnismäßigkeitsgrundsatzes* (Carl Heymanns Verlag, 2020) 352.

[40] Barnett, 'Has the Academy Led Patent Law Astray?' (n 34) 1379, 1361.

[41] ibid 1379.

[42] In fairness, while Barnett plainly rejects the *eBay* framework, it is not clear where he would land on the much more circumscribed proportionality test proposed in this book.

[43] It is worth noting that many scholars taking an economic approach to law and otherwise favouring strong patent rights appear to share the view that some flexibility is better than none at all. See, eg R Epstein, 'The Disintegration of Intellectual Property – A Classical Liberal Response to a Premature Obituary' (2010) 62 *Stanford Law Review* 455, 490; FS Kieff and A Layne-Farrar, 'Incentive Effects from Different Approaches to Holdup Mitigation Surrounding Patent Remedies and Standard-Setting Organizations' (2013) 9 *Journal of Competition Law and Economics* 1091, 1121; B Heiden and N Petit, 'Patent "Trespass" and the Royalty Gap: Exploring the Nature and Impact of Patent Holdout' (2017) 34 *Santa Clara High Technology Law Journal* 179, 204.

EU courts must strike a fair balance between all rights at stake, as chapter five addresses in more detail. An automatic injunction regime is incompatible with this Charter-derived obligation, a conclusion seemingly supported by the European Commission in its 2017 guidelines on intellectual property enforcement.[44] Indeed, the protection of conflicting rights takes precedence over economic considerations. Thus, an injunction cannot be issued where this would impermissibly interfere with another's fundamental right, even if granting it would 'send a message' that would result in overall efficiency gains.[45] Second, if the range of stakeholders' positions summarised in Table 1.1 is representative of German industry as a whole, weak proportionality would seem a compromise position that enjoys most democratic legitimacy. Moreover, a compromise position is most likely to retain longer-term support, as we saw that positions on injunctive relief change even for individual companies.

Accepting that an automatic injunction regime is no longer tenable raises the question who should change it and how it should be changed. Although the legislator could conceivably adopt a tailored injunction regime, the vast majority of authors suggest this should be done by courts on a case-by-case basis. Burk and Lemley, for instance, consider the legislature ill-suited to implement the necessary changes for a number of institutional reasons: they worry that the case-by-case application they advocate cannot easily be captured in a statute; that industry-specific legislation is costly and bound to become obsolete as industries evolve; and that the legislature is prone to capture by interest groups.[46] Indeed, precisely because objections against the automatic injunction regime are so industry- and stakeholder specific, it is unlikely that the legislator will be capable of formulating a better, yet workable alternative. The German legislator was repeatedly requested to clarify the scope of the adopted proportionality test, but it refused to codify even a non-exhaustive list of relevant circumstances, let alone a particular alternative regime. According to the legislator, doing so did not seem 'appropriate' (*angebracht*) in light of the 'multiplicity of possible situations' in which the proportionality test could apply.[47] The better option is thus to move away from a strict rule towards a standard that would leave it for courts to decide whether injunctive relief should be limited; or rather, a 'rule with excuses'.[48] The next section shows that three different European legislators, each operating in a different political

[44] Commission, 'Communication from the Commission to the European Parliament, the Council and the European Economic and Social Committee [providing] guidance on certain aspects of Directive 2004/48/EC of the European Parliament and of the Council on the enforcement of intellectual property rights' COM(2017) 708 final, 9–11.

[45] Barnett, 'Has the Academy Led Patent Law Astray?' (n 34) 1361 (referring to the 1990 shutdown of Kodak's instant camera business as a result of patent infringement proceedings brought by Polaroid).

[46] Burk and Lemley (n 13) 97–99.

[47] Federal Parliament, Proposed Bill (*Gesetzentwurf: Entwurf eines Zweiten Gesetzes zur Vereinfachung und Modernisierung des Patentrechts*) of 31 January 2021, BT-Drucksache 19/25821, 53.

[48] C Sunstein, 'Problems with Rules' (1995) 83 *California Law Review* 953, 963. Burk and Lemley reference the long-standing debate on rules and standards in law: Burk and Lemley (n 13) 103–04 with references.

context but each having an authoritative voice in the European patent landscape, have decided to do just that.

1.3. Ceding Authority Over Patent Injunctions to Courts: Three Examples

1.3.1. The European Parliament Emphasises the Importance of Context (2003)

As is well known, the proposal that would ultimately become the Enforcement Directive was born out of concerns over piracy and counterfeiting.[49] Although the Enforcement Directive ended up as a wholesale harmonisation of enforcement measures for intellectual property rights, the scope of the original proposal was limited to cases where 'infringement is committed for commercial purposes or causes significant harm to the right holder' (Article 2(1)). In line with this scope, the emphasis in the proposal was more on effective enforcement measures for rights holders than on safeguards for infringers. Even so, the European Commission wanted to include a 'general obligation to provide for proportionate remedies'.[50] Concerns about overenforcement grew when it was proposed to extend the directive's scope to all acts of IP infringement. The European Parliament, in particular, foresaw that different types of infringement would raise different issues, making pivotal the discretion afforded to courts to tailor the remedy to the situation at hand.[51] This becomes especially clear from the following explanatory comment from the so-called Fourtou report:[52]

> [Because the Directive should cover any infringement of intellectual property rights] the rapporteur has tabled some amendments to ensure that the penalties and provisional measures will be applied in a graduated and proportionate way, taking into account whether or not the infringement was deliberate, so as to prompt judges to use their power of assessment when facing cases of infringement that are not properly acts of counterfeiting or piracy.

[49] Commission, 'Proposal for a directive of the European Parliament and of the Council on measures and procedures to ensure the enforcement of intellectual property rights' COM(2003) 46 final, 3. The proposal was proceeded by a Green Paper that outlined 'the importance of the fight against counterfeiting and piracy': Commission, 'Combating Counterfeiting and Piracy in the Single Market' COM(98) 569 final. See generally M Leistner and V Pless, 'European Union' in J Contreras and M Husovec (eds), *Injunctions in Patent Law* (Cambridge University Press, 2022) 28.

[50] COM(2003) 46 final (n 49) 19.

[51] EP Committee on Legal Affairs and the Internal Market, 'Report on the Proposal for a Directive on Measures and Procedures to Ensure the Enforcement of Intellectual Property (Janelly Fourtou)' A5-0468/2003. See inter alia comments made under amendments 3 and 16.

[52] ibid 41.

Case-by-case scrutiny of IP remedies was thus considered a necessary check on the strong remedies granted to IP rights holder in the Enforcement Directive after they were expanded to cover all acts of IP infringement, not just acts of counterfeiting or piracy. The need for such scrutiny was emphasised by the Commission in a 2017 guidance paper.[53] The shift resulted in a framework for IP remedies that offered a high, equivalent and homogeneous level of protection throughout the EU for all IP infringement cases, as Recital (10) of the Enforcement Directive makes clear. The European Court of Justice (ECJ) often cites this recital to justify a broad interpretation of the Enforcement Directive's provisions, or when pointing out that Member States remain free to provide stronger measures going beyond the minimum guarantees laid down in the directive. On such occasions, the ECJ often reminds us of the indispensable control mechanism for these strong remedies: the national court's case-by-case assessment.[54] That control mechanism also found its way into the Recital (17) in the final text of the Enforcement Directive.

1.3.2. The German Legislator Adopts a Proportionality Test (2021)

Following the stakeholder consultations discussed in section 1.2.2, the Federal Ministry of Justice prepared a formal draft bill on 28 October 2020 where 'detriment' was changed back to 'hardship'. On 7 December 2020, a legislative committee issued a short advice to the Bundesrat – the chamber of representatives from Germany's provinces (*Länder*) – suggesting the wording of the revised §139 GPA be made to correspond with the *Wärmetauscher* decision.[55] In accordance with the German legislative process, this was followed by a first parliamentary debate (27 January 2021), an expert hearing by a parliamentary committee (24 February 2021) and second and third parliamentary debates (both on 10 June 2021).[56] The amendment of §139 GPA and its precise wording was by far the leading subject throughout these deliberations and it remained fiercely contentious until the end. Despite a refusal of the opposition parties to support the reform bill,

[53] COM(2017) 708 final (n 44) 9–10: 'in order to ensure the balanced use of the civil IPR enforcement system, the competent judicial authorities should generally conduct a case-by-case assessment when considering the grant of measures, procedures *and* remedies'.

[54] Case C-99/15 *Liffers* ECLI:EU:C:2016:173, para 24 ('the objective of that directive is to attain a high level of protection of intellectual property rights that takes into account the specific aspects of each given case'); Case C-531/20 *NovaText* ECLI:EU:C:2022:316, para 49.

[55] Federal Council, Recommendations of the Committee (*Empfehlungen der Ausschüsse*) of 7 December 2020, Drs 683/1/20, 4.

[56] Transcripts of the parliamentary debate can be accessed via https://dip.bundestag.de/vorgang/zweites-gesetz-zur-vereinfachung-und-modernisierung-des-patentrechts/269713. For the expert hearing, see Federal Parliament, Transcript (*Wortprotokoll der 132. Sitzung*) of 24 February 2021, BT-Drucksache 19/2581.

it was ultimately adopted with a single amendment: the inclusion of a reference to principles of reasonableness and fairness (*Treu und Glauben*) that underlie the *Wärmetauscher* ruling. In its final and now current form, Germany's proportionality exception in §139 GPA reads as follows (my translation):

> [The claim for injunctive relief] is excluded insofar as, in light of the special circumstances of the specific case and the principles of good faith, it would cause the infringer or third parties disproportionate hardship, not warranted by the right to exclude. In this case, the aggrieved party shall be granted a reasonable monetary compensation. This does not affect the damages claim laid down in paragraph 2.

The outcome of the legislative process can be fairly characterised as a weak proportionality test in that it sets a high bar for limiting injunctive relief. At the time of writing, it has not yet been successfully invoked in any case.[57] But it also goes beyond the confines of the *Wärmetauscher* case, most notably because it explicitly allows limiting and even denying injunctive relief (rather than just imposition of a sunset period) and allows consideration of third-party interests.[58] For the purposes of this chapter, several aspects of the reform process are worth noting. First, the reform process demonstrates the great importance of the subject. While it is customary for German ministries to open up draft legislation for stakeholder comments (the *Referentenentwurf*, here the second draft), it is quite unusual for them to publish a pre-draft to invite an extra round of comments (the *Diskussionsentwurf*, here the first draft). The fact that the Federal Ministry of Justice did so in this case, after having already organised a roundtable discussion with judges, experts and representatives of affected industries, indicates how consequential the seemingly dry subject of patent injunctions has become to constituencies. Second, the stakeholder positions track the patterns discussed in section 1.2: they point out changing market conditions and technological developments, and how these cause patents to be more of a threat than in previous times. As we saw, depending on the specific facts of the case, all these concerns may be legitimate, and a solution must therefore be context-sensitive. Third, the reform process confirms that only courts can provide that solution. One of the experts at the parliamentary hearing, judge Fabian Hoffmann of the Federal Supreme Court, believed the primary purpose of the amendment of §139 GPA was that it allows 'court practice to clarify the contours of proportionality'.[59] Indeed, despite the exceptionally rich feedback provided to the Federal Ministry of Justice by industry stakeholders, practitioner groups, scholars and judges, it did not include any rule-like constraints on courts in §139 GPA.[60]

[57] The argument was rejected in LG Düsseldorf GRUR 2022, 1665; 4c O 18/21 *Sofosbuvir*, C.II (defendant should have timely requested a compulsory licence); LG Düsseldorf OpenJur 2022, 14333; 4b O 7/22 *Fahrzeugdächer*, III.1.bb.(3) (in light of short remaining lifespan of the patent no severe hardship expected from injunction).

[58] Stierle and Hofmann (n 18) 1126.

[59] Transcript (n 56) 7.

[60] It is worth noting that, on the eve of the second parliamentary debate, several factions had proposed such inclusions, eg specifying the hardships that would justify application of proportionality or duties on the part of the infringer: Federal Parliament, Final Recommendation and Notice

1.3.3. The Unified Patent Court's Discretion Over Injunctive Relief (2023)

Article 63 of the Agreement on a Unified Patent Court provides that this court may, rather than shall, grant an injunction aimed at prohibiting the continuation of the infringement. Such discretion is understandable in light of the fact that the UPC is bound by EU law, including the Enforcement Directive, as per Article 20 of the UPC Agreement. Rule 118(1) of the UPC's rules of procedure,[61] on decisions on the merits, is expressly 'without prejudice' to the UPC's discretion under Article 63. In an earlier version (fifteenth draft), this rule contained an additional section that specified a number of ostensibly cumulative requirements that had to be met before an injunction could be denied. A public consultation of this version was conducted and several stakeholders expressed their opinion on this interpretation of the UPC's remedial discretion, again with some supporting broader and others narrower application.[62] In response, the drafting committee clarified that the subsection sought to extend, not restrain, the discretion of the court and generally stipulated that 'the general rules of Art. 3(1) and (2) of the Enforcement Directive are applicable and allow for alternative relief to injunctions'.[63] A sentence to this effect was added in a next version of the rules of procedure (sixteenth draft), but in the successor version (seventeenth draft) the subsection was deleted altogether, because it was still considered as potentially limiting the Court's discretion. Instead, the drafting committee generally explained that 'Where the Court finds an infringement of a patent it will under Article 63 of the Agreement give order of injunctive relief. Only under very exceptional circumstances it will use its discretion and not give such an order'.[64] This change in the seventeenth draft was maintained in the final version. It was among the more important topics of discussion at an oral hearing on the seventeenth draft in 2014, where the drafting committee apparently 'referred to the experience of the judges in exercising their discretion and that there was no need to develop a detailed scheme limiting [] the discretion of the Court'.[65]

(*Beschlussempfehlung und Bericht*) of 9 June 2021, BT-Drucksache 19/30498. All of these proposals were withdrawn or defeated.

[61] Rules of Procedure of the Unified Patent Court, as adopted by decision of the Administrative Committee on 8 July 2022.

[62] Legal Group of the UPC Preparatory Committee, 'Responses to the Public Consultation of the Rules of Procedure of the UPC' (31 January 2014) www.veron.com/upc/various-documents/?lang=en, 95–98.

[63] ibid 95.

[64] Legal Group of the UPC Preparatory Committee, 'Table with Explanatory Notes to the Changes Made by the Legal Group of the Preparatory Committee in the 17th Draft of the Rules of Procedure' (31 October 2014) www.veron.com/upc/various-documents/?lang=en, 11. It is worth noting that the cautious characterisation of the Court's discretion ('very exceptional circumstances') was the subject of considerable criticism during the oral hearing on this draft: Legal Group of the UPC Preparatory Committee, 'Oral Hearing on the Rules of Procedure' (Trier, 26 November 2014) www.veron.com/upc/various-documents/?lang=en, 464 *et seq*.

[65] S Dorn, 'Those New European Patent Litigation Rules: A Report on the Oral Hearing on the 17th Draft' (*IPKat*, 1 December 2014) https://ipkitten.blogspot.com/2014/12/those-new-european-patent-litigation.html.

In sum, the deliberations on the UPC's discretion over injunctive relief closely track the patterns we saw in the previous subsections. The need for this discretion was clearly acknowledged, with repeated emphasis that outright denial of an injunction would be appropriate only in very exceptional circumstances. What those circumstances might be, and what might lie in between them and the standard case to justify imposition of a grace period, was left to the UPC to determine.

1.4. The Institutional Constraints of Patent Courts

1.4.1. The Limitations of Judicial Lawmaking

So far, the analysis has shown that proportionality is considered a necessary ex post corrective in today's patent laws not just by the European legislator, but also in the European jurisdiction far and away the most experienced in patent law (Germany) and the UPC, which by all expectations will soon be Europe's most authoritative patent court. Because the potential problems that patent injunctions can cause are so context-specific, it makes sense to delegate the task of preventing them to the institution most sensitive to context: courts. But we would do well to delineate that task in a way that fits patent courts' institutional competences and experience, which are surveyed in this final section.

Burk and Lemley valorise courts as the most competent institution to 'solve' their perceived 'patent crisis' because of the flexibility that a 'common-law approach of ongoing judicial oversight' affords.[66] They propose that courts 'profile an industry inductively' by 'hearing cases presenting recurrent themes', suggest that a rule that 'limits injunctions to plaintiffs that really need them might help solve the problems with abuse of the patent system' and even refer to the US four-factor test for injunctive relief as 'our best chance at efficient patent reform'.[67] Burk and Lemley thus eagerly tap into a stereotype of the common law that extols the virtues of incrementally building legal doctrine through court decisions. As a preliminary point, a 'common-law approach of ongoing judicial oversight' may not be feasible in the EU, given the differences between US and European courts. In particular, continental European courts generally do not have the advantage of full discovery or multiday trials where expert witnesses are heard. Judicial tradition also differs as courts are expected to restrict themselves to applying the law without elaborate consideration of its real-world effects. The differences become immediately apparent when comparing English and German or Dutch decisions involving standard essential patents, which often raise complex economic issues. German or Dutch courts are much less likely to engage extensively with those issues, a reluctance

[66] Burk and Lemley (n 13) 104.
[67] ibid 105–06, 139.

doubtlessly caused in part by their much more limited access to evidence on those issues. Thus, even if patent law is primarily developed by courts on both sides of the Atlantic (section 1.1.2), the institutional contexts in which they do so differ vastly. The fact that continental European courts have considerably less access to evidence than their English or American counterparts suggests more caution is necessary when we task these courts with 'profiling an industry inductively', as Burk and Lemley would have it.

Indeed, Burk and Lemley's faith in courts is not even shared universally among Anglo-Saxon authors. Writing before Burk and Lemley, Peter Drahos pointed out that in order to establish efficient regulation of property rights (such as patents), it is crucial for courts to obtain reliable information about the market.[68] Because they are embedded in a narrowly constituted community of specialists, patent courts are relatively unlikely to obtain such information and are therefore relatively prone to err in establishing industry characteristics.[69] Precisely this criticism has been levied against Burk and Lemley's proposal: a court might mistakenly assign certain characteristics to an industry and proceed to decide on this basis in a manner that is in fact harmful to innovation in the given industry, in a decision that sets a precedent that might be hard to ignore in future cases.[70] Notably, two experienced US patent judges have cautioned the UPC against this very temptation.[71] Even if courts could get a full and correct view of the relevant industry characteristics, it is difficult to successfully tailor patent protection to these characteristics, especially since these are subject to constant change. It is not clear, moreover, that individual patent cases have sufficient in common, even within the same industry, for courts to effectively learn from and build on past decisions. This particular criticism – a court's propensity to mistakenly consider a specific case representative of future cases – was expressed against the common law more generally by Frederick Schauer.[72] He writes:

> If judges have a hard time avoiding what they see as the right result for the particular case in all of its contextual richness, and if they are at the same time making law for future cases, then the combination of the salience of the particular case and the pull to decide it correctly may produce a rule that is unrepresentative of the full range of future cases that can be expected to be decided under it.[73]

[68] P Drahos, 'Regulating Property: Problems of Efficiency and Regulatory Capture' in J Braithwaite et al (eds), *Regulating Law* (Oxford University Press, 2004) 186.

[69] ibid 177 (contrasting the Court of Appeals for the Federal Circuit with the English courts in the 17th and 18th centuries, which, unlike the Federal Circuit, had the benefit of juries of merchants that were intimately familiar with custom).

[70] S Baker, 'Can the Courts Rescue Us from the Patent Crisis?' (2010) 88 *Texas Law Review* 593, 595.

[71] K O'Malley and B Lynn, 'Decision-Making in the Unified Patent Court: Ensuring a Balanced Approach' in C Geiger, C Nard and X Seuba (eds), *Intellectual Property and the Judiciary* (Edward Elgar, 2018) 376.

[72] F Schauer, 'Do Cases Make Bad Law?' (2006) 73 *University of Chicago Law Review* 883, 894.

[73] ibid 900.

Courts, of course, are well aware of these limitations. They therefore tend to avoid, when they can, resolving contentious issues with comprehensive precedents, certainly in Europe. In earlier work, Schauer observed that the duty to give reasons constrains courts because a reason given for a decision necessarily derives from a principle of more general applicability.[74] He gives the example of 'I criticized Mary because she did not write a thank-you note'. The reason given ('because she did not write a thank-you note') appeals to the broader principle that people in Mary's situation should write thank-you notes, which, in turn, is derivable from the more general principles 'show appreciation for social kindnesses' and 'do unto others as you would have them do unto you'.[75] It appears to me that the constraining force of the duty to state reasons and the risk of overgeneralisation of the case at hand are communicating vessels. The harder it is to assess whether problems posed by the case at hand are representative of problems existing in the real world, the harder it will be to confidently state reasons for an outcome one way or another. Those reasons, after all, necessarily constrain decision-making space in future cases, ie they operate as rules governing future cases that present at least partially overlapping fact patterns.

1.4.2. How not to Design a Proportionality Test

The observations by Drahos and Schauer suggest that the best way to introduce a proportionality test in European patent law would be to (i) define the values such a test seeks to maximise in a way that facilitates generalisation of specific problems and (ii) provide as much clarity as possible on the test's contours, making it easier for courts to apply it in a reasoned manner.[76] The German legislator, however, has done the exact opposite. As to (i), §139 GPA seeks to prevent 'disproportionate hardship, not warranted by the right to exclude'. But without any guidance on what the right to exclude warrants, courts are essentially instructed to rely on their good judgement to identify cases where patent exclusivity would impose unacceptable social costs. This, as Drahos points out, is very difficult, if not impossible, for them to do without in-depth knowledge of the relevant industry. As to (ii), we saw that the German legislator in fact declined to define the test's contours and instead stated that its application turns on an open-ended range of 'viewpoints' which interact with one another.[77] Legal tests of this kind are often used when courts must engage in interpretive exercises, for example during claim construction,

[74] F Schauer, 'Giving Reasons' (1995) 47 *Stanford Law Review* 633, 653.

[75] ibid 639, 641 ('to provide a reason for a decision is to include that decision within a principle of greater generality than the decision itself').

[76] See also W Tilmann, 'Article 63' in W Tilmann and C Plassmann (eds), *Unified Patent Protection in Europe: A Commentary* (Oxford University Press, 2018) no 33 (arguing remedial discretion needs 'value criteria under which it is to be applied' and 'limits', though opposing it for the UPC because these elements are presumed absent).

[77] Proposed Bill (n 47) 53.

when the claim language's scope must be construed. But they are a poor fit when what must be 'interpreted' is essentially the case at hand against the backdrop of market dynamics in the industry where it arises. As per Schauer, it will be difficult for courts to reason why one or several 'viewpoints' support the outcome at hand when those reasons can be grounded in an infinite number of circumstances. These obstacles are compounded by the fact that German patent infringement courts cannot obtain nearly as much information on industry and social costs as their common law counterparts can and are severely time- and resource constrained as it is. Naturally, this is not to single out the German courts: neither the European Parliament nor the drafting committee for the UPC's rules of procedure provided any guidance at all on how discretion over injunctive relief should be used, leaving it entirely up to the courts to decide this.

The foregoing suggests that we should not be surprised if courts shy away from applying a proportionality test thus formulated.[78] The average European patent judge is along in years and used to the automatic injunction rule that has been the norm in Europe for decades. To derive out of thin air grounds to deviate from this norm, which must justify limiting a property entitlement in the present case and prevent as much as possible legal uncertainty for future cases, is to ask much indeed. What is more, the desire to attract cases is a strong incentive not to deviate from the norm at least for German courts, a dynamic that some fear will also make the UPC decidedly pro-patentee.[79] Far from being puzzling, European patent courts' hesitation so far to apply a proportionality test is thus entirely in line with expectations.[80] After all, granting an injunction requires no reasoning, whereas the road to limiting it is, as we saw, full of hurdles. On the rare occasions that a European court would make an allowance for proportionality, it would likely emphasise the uniqueness of the case.[81] While better than not applying a proportionality test at all, this is still less than ideal if the goal is to come to a European doctrine of proportionality. European patent law is an exemplar of judicial dialogue, a process

[78] Van Dongen rather understates the point by observing 'no strong signals of [proportionality] being picked up by domestic courts' and arguing, rightly in my view, that not applying the proportionality test at all is clearly not in line with EU law: L Van Dongen, 'Proportionality and Flexibilities in Final Injunctive Relief' in L Desaunettes-Barbero et al (eds), *The Unitary Patent Package & Unified Patent Court: Problems, Possible Improvements and Alternatives* (Ledizioni, 2023) 371.

[79] S Bechtold et al, 'Forum Selling Abroad' (2018) 92 *Southern California Law Review* 487, 500.

[80] Those expectations were expressed even by proponents of remedial discretion for patent courts: R Hilty, 'Legal Remedies against Abuse, Misuse and Other Forms of Inappropriate Conducts of IP Right Holders' in R Hilty and K Liu (eds), *Compulsory Licensing: Practical Experiences and Ways Forward* (Springer, 2015) 269 ('it is hardly conceivable that [a European judge] would weigh the legitimate interest of the right holder, on one hand, and those of the (unauthorised) user, on the other hand'); J Sarnoff, 'Lessons from the United States in Regard to the Recent, More Flexible Approach to Injunctive Relief' in C Correa (ed), *Research Handbook on the Interpretation and Enforcement of Intellectual Property under WTO Rules* (Edward Elgar, 2010) 74–75 (arguing that 'policy-based judgments' that require 'nuanced attention by judges to the factual context and the different public interests' are 'often intentionally eschewed by judges').

[81] Schauer (n 72) 900. *cf Wärmetauscher* (n 20) para 45.

whereby courts cite one another's decisions when faced with similar problems to build towards a European *acquis*. This requires explicit reasoning on how such cases should be dealt with, not insistence that they are unrepresentative outliers.

One of this book's main objectives is to overcome this stalemate. Most of the book is devoted to the second task raised at the start of this subsection, ie establishing clear contours for the proportionality test. For the reasons outlined here, I believe the proportionality test will be a dead letter so long as those contours remain undefined. Before embarking on our search for them, the next chapter takes up the first task raised at the start of this subsection: defining the values that a proportionality test should seek to maximise.

2

Justifying Proportionality

We saw in the previous chapter that because patent injunctions are so sensitive to context, it is prudent to allow courts some discretion to tailor them to the circumstances of the case. European patent courts have been granted such discretion and they were instructed to use it when the injunction's effects would be 'disproportionate'. As a first step towards determining what that means, this chapter considers which values should be pursued when courts entertain a proportionality defence. It asks, in other words, what the normative justification is for application of a proportionality test in European patent law.

The chapter's first section introduces two 'paradigms' of proportionality that dominate the European literature. According to the innovation paradigm, injunctions are disproportionate when their effects run counter to patent law's goal of fostering innovation; according to the diffusion paradigm, they are disproportionate if they impermissibly restrict access to critical technology. Building on the analysis of courts' institutional constraints in chapter one, my argument here is that both paradigms suffer from an indeterminacy problem: courts cannot know which outcome would best serve these objectives. In the chapter's second section, I introduce an alternative paradigm that is both workable and grounded in longstanding practice: the paradigm of commensurate scope. The third and final section elaborates on the difference between the different paradigms by comparing what a proportionality test would look like under either. My overall conclusion is that a proportionality test oriented on commensurate scope is superior in terms of workability and predictability, and therefore more likely to find application in practice. With that normative groundwork in place, the next chapter starts the inquiry into which cases risk running afoul of the principle of commensurate scope.

2.1. Three Paradigms of Proportionality

2.1.1. In Search of a Guiding Principle for Proportionality

As we saw in section 1.1, European patent law serves to promote innovation and diffusion, and it sets an equilibrium between three conflicting sets of interests: those of patentees, competitors and the general public. In an ideal world, patent laws would reflect the equilibrium that best achieves their twin goals, ie define patent exclusivity just so that it provides sufficient incentives for innovation without unnecessary constraints on competition and diffusion of technology.[1] Unfortunately, patent laws in the real world may well be far removed from that ideal, because the effects of patents depend on the specific context of enforcement. A static optimum therefore cannot be defined and ex post correctives remain necessary. More fundamentally, the extent to which an equilibrium is considered optimal depends on (i) our knowledge of its effects on innovation and (ii) value judgements on the relative importance of innovation vis-à-vis diffusion. The trouble starts with our limited understanding of how patents affect innovation. Despite a plethora of studies on the subject, whether the benefits of having a patent system outweigh the costs remains a hotly contested question. True, these studies have enhanced our understanding of how patents operate in various contexts, in some cases challenging the notion that they are a necessary incentive to innovate. But the picture that emerges is complicated and generally insufficient to infer that altering some or other aspect of patent law will result in a more optimal equilibrium. Even assuming a demonstrably positive correlation between exclusivity and innovation (which is often lacking), it must still be decided whether the innovation benefits are worth the reduction in diffusion.

This raises the question what overall objective should guide courts' application of the proportionality test. Does the proportionality test seek to promote innovation or diffusion? Perhaps it tries to do both, but if so how do these objectives relate to one another in the context of the test? The answer to these questions informs us of proportionality's scope of application and, particularly, guides its application in cases presenting novel problems. For example, during a future pandemic comparable to the outbreak of COVID-19 in 2019–21, a diffusion-oriented proportionality test would likely limit injunctive relief on vaccines and treatments much sooner than an innovation-oriented test. Despite the question's importance, most European authors are not explicit about the values they believe a proportionality test should promote; most imply it should be a mix of innovation and diffusion, with the latter taking a clear back seat.[2] This chapter introduces the guiding principle of the proportionality test proposed in this book – commensurate scope – and compares it to innovation- and diffusion-oriented paradigms of proportionality. To be sure, these are ideal types, and most authors would be unlikely to commit to a pure version of any one paradigm. But when considering the scope and content of a proportionality test, it is important to first delineate its function because that will give a basic indication of what should – and what should not – fall within the test's ambit.

[1] J Golden, 'Principles for Patent Remedies' (2010) 88 *Texas Law Review* 505, 509.

[2] The ambivalence is particularly palpable in N Siebrasse et al, 'Injunctive Relief' in CB Biddle et al (eds), *Patent Remedies and Complex Products: Toward a Global Consensus* (Cambridge University Press, 2019). This is a statement of consensus among leading patent remedies scholars that clearly accept the innovation rationale (118) but states that they 'failed to reach consensus on the extent to which courts should consider the negative effects of injunctions on third parties or the general public' (150).

2.1.2. The Innovation Paradigm

The innovation paradigm of proportionality is most strongly associated with US authors writing in the law and economics tradition.[3] On this view, injunctive relief should be limited where granting it would risk overcompensating the patentee, particularly by forcing the defendant to agree to payment of royalties in excess of the invention's market value. Such overpayment, it is contended, harms innovation because it causes social losses 'with no clear corresponding benefit'.[4] This view appears to be shared at least implicitly by many European proponents of proportionality.[5] Thus, they advocate limiting injunctive relief when the harms it would cause exceed the 'normal' consequences of patent exclusivity and end up 'unusually' high.[6] Although there have been attempts to identify case groups where this might be the case or formulate principles that courts can apply, a clear definition of situations where injunctive relief should be denied is still missing and courts are generally instructed to find them by taking account of all circumstances of the case.

John Golden has argued persuasively that 'efforts to optimize' patent remedies endorsed by the innovation paradigm face 'fundamental difficulties'.[7] These include the multiplicity of behaviours that injunctions seek to incentivise or steer away from; the aforementioned lack of consensus on the proper equilibrium that patent law should strive for; and the contingency of patents' effects on industry and technology specifics. Chapter one demonstrated that these contingencies were the reason to grant European patent courts a degree of discretion over injunctive relief, but also that their institutional limitations make it difficult to 'improve' patent law's equilibrium by formulating specific rules on injunctive relief. For instance, much ink has been spilled over how (if at all) patent remedies regimes should respond to Non-practising entities (NPEs) and so-called patent holdup. The lack of consensus on these issues despite dozens, if not hundreds, of papers on the subject is a first indication that we should not expect European patent courts to resolve them

[3] See, eg T Cotter, 'Patent Holdup, Patent Remedies, and Antitrust Responses' (2009) 34 *Journal of Corporation Law* 1151, 1177; T Sichelman, 'Purging Patent Law of Private Law Remedies' (2014) 92 *Texas Law Review* 517, 538; M Lemley and C Shapiro, 'Patent Holdup and Royalty Stacking' (2007) 85 *Texas Law Review* 1991, 2009.

[4] Cotter, 'Patent Holdup' (n 3) 1179.

[5] R Sikorski, 'Permanent Injunctions in Patent Law – in Search of Flexibility' in S Frankel (ed), *Is Intellectual Property Pluralism Functional?* (Edward Elgar, 2019) 385. Analyses that also take explicit account of diffusion include M Stierle and F Hofmann, 'The Latest Amendment to the German Law on Patent Injunctions: The New Statutory Disproportionality Exception and Third-Party Interests' (2022) 71 *Gewerblicher Rechtsschutz und Urheberrecht International* 1123, 1125–26; A Strowel and A Léonard, 'Cutting Back Patent Over-enforcement' (2020) 11 *Journal of Intellectual Property, Information Technology and Electronic Commerce Law* 3, para 67; M Norrgård, 'The Role Conferred on the National Judge by Directive 2004148/EC on the Enforcement of Intellectual Property Rights' (2005) 6 *ERA Forum* 503, 511.

[6] A Ohly and M Stierle, 'Unverhältnismäßigkeit, Injunction Gap und Geheimnisschutz im Prozess' [2021] *Gewerblicher Rechtsschutz und Urheberrecht* 1229, 1231 ('*außergewöhnlich hoch*').

[7] Golden, 'Principles for Patent Remedies' (n 1) 511.

in a convincing manner. Even addressing problems on which there is (cautious) consensus is likely to be difficult. This is so because any adaptation of the remedies regime to address such problems is likely to frustrate other, equally legitimate interests served by the current regime.[8] Germany's *Warmetäuscher* case, discussed in more detail in section 3.3, is a good illustration.[9] It involved enforcement of a component patent by an NPE and resulted in a royalty payment far exceeding the (likely) market value of the patented invention, yet it remains impossible to state with confidence that deciding it differently would have resulted in lower overall social costs. After all, a denial of injunctive relief could have incentivised holdout tactics, of which the defendant in that case was also accused, or other undesirable behaviour. Any alteration to the patentee's injunctive relief entitlement is likely to affect behaviour in future cases, but it is impossible to determine whether that will result in a net benefit for innovation, especially given courts' institutional constraints.[10] The US Supreme Court clearly expressed this sentiment in a 2015 decision where it was asked to abolish a rule prohibiting extraction of post-expiration royalties, inter alia on the grounds that this rule hindered innovation. In response, the Court eloquently explained why the goal of 'fostering innovation' cannot guide decision-making by patent courts, which, in my view, illustrates well why an innovation paradigm of proportionality is untenable:

> Kimble also seeks support from the wellspring of all patent policy: the goal of promoting innovation. [Prohibiting post-expiration royalties], he contends, 'discourages technological innovation and does significant damage to the American economy ...' Maybe. Or, then again, maybe not. While we recognize that post-patent royalties are sometimes not anticompetitive, we just cannot say whether barring them imposes any meaningful drag on innovation ... Truth be told, if forced to decide that issue, we would not know where or how to start. Which is one good reason why that is not our job.[11]

2.1.3. The Diffusion Paradigm

The diffusion paradigm can be associated with scholars like Peter Drahos and Alexander Peukert.[12] This view grounds limitations of patent exclusivity in normative entitlements of others to the patent technology, rather than in a strictly economic cost–benefit analysis. These entitlements arise not just on the part of the public, who may have a legitimate claim to things like affordable healthcare, but also on the part of competitors who pursue their own innovations. In the EU

[8] ibid 529. See also Barnett, 'Has the Academy Led Patent Law Astray?' (2017) 32 *Berkeley Technology Law Journal* 1313, 1379.

[9] BGH GRUR 2016, 1031; X ZR 114/13 *Wärmetauscher*.

[10] M Biagioli, 'Weighing Intellectual Property: Can We Balance the Social Costs and Benefits of Patenting?' (2019) 57 *History of Science* 140, 154.

[11] *Kimble v Marvel Entertainment LLC* 576 US 446 (2015).

[12] P Drahos, *A Philosophy of Intellectual Property* (Dartmouth, 1996) 228; A Peukert, 'Intellectual Property as an End in Itself?' (2011) 33 *European Intellectual Property Review* 67, 69–70. See also *Wärmetauscher* (n 9) para 52, which implies that a proportionality defence is more likely to succeed if the patented component is an essential part (*funktionswesentliches Bauteil*) of a complex product.

legal order, such entitlements may enjoy constitutional protection under the EU Charter of Fundamental Rights, and the European Court of Justice (ECJ) has held that intellectual property (IP) rights enforcement must strike a fair balance between all applicable rights.

In my view, the diffusion paradigm is even harder to sustain than the innovation paradigm, not least because it cannot avoid the types of difficult trade-offs the latter gives rise to. Diffusion-oriented limitations of patent exclusivity always face the question whether they do not come at too high a price for innovation.[13] Just as with the innovation paradigm, courts will not be able to oversee this. It is clear that the patent system suffers from many problems and it has been controversial since its inception. Those problems must be taken seriously and we may even conclude one day that society is better off without a patent system and abolish it. Nothing in this book is incompatible with that view, but in light of their institutional constraints, we should resist the temptation to rely on proportionality as a tool to address those problems. In principle, proportionality could be used as a magic wand to address a wide range of perceived dysfunctionalities with the patent system, as denying the patentee an injunction makes many of them disappear. But that would mean courts determine the contours of the patent system from case to case. There are many drawbacks to this, the most glaring of which are a lack of predictability and democratic legitimacy, as well as handing over patent policy to the institution that is arguably most information-constrained in the patent ecosystem. If the proportionality test is to have credibility and integrity, it should be used sparingly and applied in accordance with strict and transparent standards. Only then can we hope to see it applied consistently. Requiring the test to do any more would, in my view, be self-defeating.

2.2. The Paradigm of Commensurate Scope

2.2.1. The Importance and Prevalence of Commensurate Scope in Patent Law

The technical commensurability paradigm can be associated with Robert Merges, who considers the idea that 'The size or scope of an IP right ought to be proportional to the value or significance of the work covered by the right', a 'midlevel principle' in IP law and *the* principle behind the US regime of patent injunctions.[14]

[13] See, among many others, R Merges, *Justifying Intellectual Property* (Harvard University Press, 2011) ch 9.

[14] ibid 150, 160; *cf* also Biagioli (n 10) 160 (arguing that the 'patent bargain' is a better guiding principle than balancing because it 'is not about the social benefits and costs of the patent but about the contractual arrangement between the public and the inventor that defines that a patent is'). In Europe, see M Vivant, 'Intellectual Property Rights and Their Functions: Determining Their Legitimate

On this view, injunctive relief ought to be limited when granting it would effectively extend the patentee's sphere of exclusivity beyond their technical contribution to the art. Because of its emphasis on *technical* commensurability, the inquiry proposed under this paradigm is distinct from proposals that would depart from the patented invention's *economic* value.[15]

In earlier work with Richard Nelson, Merges highlighted the crucial importance of patent scope: 'Property rights that are too narrow will not provide enough incentive to develop the asset, while overly broad rights will pre-empt too many competitive development efforts.'[16] They point out several examples of US patents that slowed the pace of subsequent innovation significantly. Reviewing these examples, they find that in many cases the broad protection granted by the patent was not justified in that it did not correspond to 'what the inventor actually disclosed in his specification as an indicator of what the inventor actually achieved'.[17] A strength of the Merges and Nelson paper is that they shift the intuition driving the innovation paradigm – overcompensation of patentees should generally be avoided – from an economic to a technical inquiry. Their suggestion that courts 'hew more closely to the substance of the inventor's disclosure' when determining claim scope removes the need to consider how their decision might affect future conduct or innovation more generally, which is hard for them to oversee.[18] Conversely, the technical inquiry into the substance of the inventor's disclosure, while not easy, matches well a patent judge's expertise and is part and parcel of virtually any patent suit. At the same time, Merges and Nelson demonstrate it is a good proxy for the innovation and diffusion functions of the patent system. While the breadth of scope that optimally incentivises innovation remains indeterminate, it is very plausible (if not common sense) that exclusivity going beyond the patent's technical contribution risks a skewed equilibrium, as the historical analysis by Merges and Nelson also suggests. Diffusion concerns, too, go to the heart of Merges and Nelson's argument because they demonstrate that an overly broad patent scope inhibits follow-on innovation by competitors and thus deprives the public of the technological progress it would yield. Adopting commensurate scope as a guiding principle for claim scope thus credibly tracks innovation and diffusion while also handing courts a workable, objective and predictable test, at least relative to a test that seeks to maximise either or both values directly.[19]

"Enclosure"' in G Ghidini, H Ullrich and P Drahos (eds), *Kritika: Essays on Intellectual Property*, vol 2 (Edward Elgar, 2017) 51, 62.

[15] See esp C Osterrieth, 'Kriterien der Angemessenheit des Ausgleichs nach § 139 I 4 PatG' [2022] *Gewerblicher Rechtsschutz und Urheberrecht* 299, 301.

[16] R Merges and R Nelson, 'On the Complex Economics of Patent Scope' (1990) 90 *Columbia Law Review* 839, 875.

[17] ibid 909.

[18] ibid.

[19] *cf* M Gergen et al, 'The Supreme Court's Accidental Revolution? The Test for Permanent Injunctions' (2012) 112 *Columbia Law Review* 203, 234 ('Particularly when administrative costs and limitations are considered, overall decisionmaking can be improved through use of presumptions and defenses that mimic the direction expected for fully-informed judgments attentive to accepted goals').

It is therefore no wonder that the principle of commensurate scope permeates all of patent law.[20] In a landmark decision on sufficiency (Article 83 of the European Patent Convention), the European Patent Office's (EPO's) Technical Board of Appeal held that 'the underlying purpose' of this requirement is that 'the patent monopoly should be justified by the actual technical contribution to the art'.[21] The same principle governs inventive step, as claims not inventive in their entirety 'must be amended so as to exclude obvious subject-matter in order to justify the monopoly'.[22] As the UK Supreme Court recently held, all validity doctrines are 'in one way or another directed to satisfying the principle thus expressed'.[23] Technical commensurability also operates during claim construction and when assessing infringement. It is well accepted that patent claims must be given not a literal, but a purposive reading, ie a reading that reflects the inventive concept disclosed in the patent.[24] The inventive concept will thus determine whether a claim element is given a broad or narrow interpretation. Even if a claim cannot be so construed as to encompass a certain product, but that product achieves substantially the same result in substantially the same way as the invention, it may nevertheless fall within the patent's scope of protection by way of equivalence.[25] These examples show that the technical commensurability principle can cut both ways: it can both limit and expand the patent's scope, each time depending on the underlying invention and the protection it is due. Commensurability is applied even to remedies, for instance in cases concerning second medical use claims. When infringed, courts may impose a qualified injunction, such as forbidding sales unless the protected indication is carved out and the infringer informs all buyers that the product is not to be used for that indication, to make the injunction reflect the patent's technical contribution.[26]

2.2.2. Commensurate Scope as a Guiding Principle for Proportionality

My main argument in this chapter is that, like many other doctrines of substantive patent law, the proportionality test should be guided by the principle of

[20] M Lemley and M McKenna, 'Scope' (2016) 57 *William & Mary Law Review* 2197, 2285 ('Scope is *the* critical question that underlies all IP regimes').

[21] T409/91 *EXXON/Fuel Oils* [1994] OJ EPO 653, para 3.4.

[22] T939/92 *AgrEvo* [1995] OJ EPO 309, para 2.4.2.

[23] *Warner-Lamber Co LLC v Generics (UK)* [2018] UKSC 56, para 17.

[24] eg BGH GRUR 2006, 655; Xa ZR 116/07 *Trägerplatte*, para 18; HR 4 April 2014, ECLI:NL:HR:2014:12 (*Abbott v Medinol*), para 3.5.2.

[25] *Icescape v Ice-World Int'l* [2018] EWCA Civ 2219, para 72; but see GH The Hague 25 October 2016, ECLI:N:GHDHA:2016:3368 (*Teva v Synthon*), para 4.15 (limited contribution to the art justifies limitation of claim scope).

[26] TO Milano 24 December 2021, 11933-1/2020 (*Novartis v Medac*).

commensurate scope.[27] That is, the goal of applying the proportionality test should be to ensure that the patentee's effective sphere of exclusivity, as effectuated through the injunction, is commensurate with the patent's contribution to the state of the art. The fact that proportionate and commensurate are synonyms is a good start. Indeed, it would be incongruent for a system that in its design cares so much about commensurate reward to disregard it at the stage of its actual application, and there is some cautious precedent for the position that commensurability of scope is at least a relevant consideration in the proportionality analysis.[28] Notably, checking for technical commensurability at the validity and infringement stages does not guarantee the injunction is also necessarily commensurate with the patentee's inventive contribution. There is not, for instance, a heightened inventive step requirement for component patents to ensure only highly inventive components can be the basis of an injunction, nor stricter claim construction if the invention is embedded in the infringer's own innovations. That is entirely justified because these doctrines care about how the inventive concept relates to the prior art and the public domain. These abstract concepts do not capture the specific circumstances of enforcement and the practical effects of the injunction, nor could they, as they are not foreseeable at the time of grant. But these circumstances and effects can easily result in an effective sphere of exclusivity that goes well beyond the patent's inventive contribution, as chapter three discusses in detail. The consequences to the infringer and public of such 'overreaching' injunctions find no acknowledgement in current patent laws, and the conventional assumption is that the infringer bears the risk of them materialising. But why should this be so? If commensurate scope is a beacon throughout patent law, it should give us pause that injunctions have the potential to upset it.

Consistency with substantive patent law is not the only advantage of adopting a paradigm of commensurate scope for proportionality. Determining how the patented invention contributes to the prior art is a familiar exercise for any patent court. Deciding on that basis the effective scope of exclusivity the patentee is entitled to remains, of course, a subjective exercise. But, as with other ultimately subjective judgements in patent law, specific guidance can be formulated to increase workability and predictability, and chapter six makes a proposal for such guidance. Structuring the proportionality test around a specific legal test would bestow on it a measure of objectivity that allows reasoned discussion over outcomes and judicial dialogue, as we also observe with issues like plausibility or equivalence. Even if not perfect, the resulting test would in any event be more workable and predictable than the judgement calls courts must make under the innovation and diffusion paradigms. What is more, the paradigm of commensurate scope is

[27] *cf* J Golden, 'Complex Economics and Patent Remedies' (2010) 1 *IP Theory* 50 (already pointing out the relation between Merges and Nelson's paper and 'Current debates over the proper remedies for patent infringement').

[28] *Napp Pharmaceutical Holdings v Dr Reddy's Laboratories* [2016] EWHC 1517 (Pat) (granting injunction inappropriate where this 'would effectively extend the scope of the patentee's monopoly'); and, in a copyright case, Cour d'Appel de Paris 22 December 2017, 13/14419 (*USPA/Les editions de minuit*), 26.

more compatible with EU law than either alternative, as is further explained in chapter five.

Adopting the paradigm of commensurate scope is also most consistent with the law of remedies more generally, which principally seeks to 'replicate the content of the defendant's substantive duty'.[29] There are good reasons to treat remedies as analytically distinct from substantive duties even in civil law jurisdictions. But the distinction should serve to check that the remedy does reach beyond the substantive duty enforced, not as a vessel for courts to reconsider the social costs or the distributive justice of that duty. This is sometimes expressed by the phrase 'procedural law follows substantive law', according to which the remedy 'may not contain any more or less' than what is required by the substantive duty underlying it.[30] The proposal for proportionality made in this book embraces that principle and thus rejects strong remedial discretion for patent courts. However, it also asserts that taking 'procedural law follows substantive law' seriously means limiting relief where an immediate injunction would have effects reaching far beyond the substantive duty it enforces.

None of this is to say that it is straightforward to determine the commensurate scope of component patents at the remedies stage. As brilliantly illustrated in William Shakespeare's *The Merchant of Venice*, it is clear that denial of an injunction any time its effect would extend beyond simple removal of the infringing component is untenable. That would render the patent practically worthless in many cases, just as Shylock stood empty-handed before Portia as she upheld Antonio's bond, but warned Shylock not to shed 'one drop of Christian blood' in taking it. The fact that the patented technology drives the functionality of the overall device or is exceptionally inventive may justify a broad sphere of exclusivity. That is a familiar principle in patent law, which affords broad protection to pioneer inventions. Furthermore, if the infringer acted in bad faith, there may also be reason to deny a proportionality defence, for otherwise infringers would have much less of an incentive to seriously engage in licensing negotiations, and over time may not bother to perform clearance searches altogether. Thus, just as construing a claim strictly literally does insufficient justice to the patentee, denying an injunction every time it would affect technology beyond what is claimed would render exclusivity illusory for a large number of patents. At the same time, there should be some sensible limit to the patentee's right to enforcement, as Shakespeare's play – the most vivid illustration of disproportionality I came across – demonstrates.

Chapter six contains a detailed proposal for where that limit should be drawn. The proportionality test proposed here applies in three situations: overreach, abuse and conflicts with third-party rights. Overreach, likely the most important part of

[29] S Smith, *Rights, Wrongs, and Injustices* (Oxford University Press, 2020) 97. See further T Nuninga, 'Recht, Plicht, Bevel, Verbod' (2018) *Nederlands Tijdschrift voor Burgerlijk Recht* 152, 154; F Hofmann, *Der Unterlassungsanspruch als Rechtsbehelf* (Mohr Siebeck, 2017) 60–61.

[30] W Tilmann, 'Article 63' in W Tilmann and C Plassmann (eds), *Unified Patent Protection in Europe: A Commentary* (Oxford University Press, 2018) no 31.

the test in practice, addresses head on the problem of component patents and how courts might ensure that the injunction remains commensurate with the patented invention in these cases. Abuse covers situations where the patentee employs a stratagem to obtain a litigation advantage not contemplated by the Enforcement Directive. And my proposal for addressing conflicts with third-party rights identifies as problematic cases where the injunction would affect bona fide enterprises having nothing to do with the infringement, or deprive end users of significant technological improvements. The principle of commensurate scope is the wellspring for each element of the test, for in each case the injunction would affect interests or activities operating far beyond the scope of the patent claim invoked. In my view, a proportionality test covering these three situation types is capable of addressing well-nigh every legitimate problem with contemporary patent enforcement. It follows that the proportionality test need not be relied on to foster innovation, diffusion or other values beyond commensurate scope. Of course, there are those who consider the open-ended nature of the proportionality test to be its principal strength, and for them commensurate scope might be one among several values that the proportionality test should promote. That is not my preferred interpretation, as a proportionality test that not only checks for commensurate scope but also promotes innovation, diffusion and potentially other values lacks clarity and predictability in its application. Delineation of the test is a feature, not a bug, as it brings focus and legal certainty. Nevertheless, for those who believe the proportionality test must safeguard a broader range of values, my proposals here and in chapter six are perfectly capable of being read as non-exhaustive principles for, and instances of, disproportionate injunctions, alongside others to be identified in the years to come.

2.3. How does the Choice of Paradigm Influence the Proportionality Test?

2.3.1. Innovation and Diffusion: Broad Scope, High Threshold

In the foregoing, I alluded repeatedly to the fundamental indeterminacy problem of the innovation and diffusion paradigms. The problem becomes readily perceptible if we consider what a proportionality test under either paradigm looks like. The leading opinion in the literature seems to be that the proportionality test should seek to prevent harm to the infringer and third parties disproportionate to the harm the patentee would suffer if the injunction does not issue.[31] A wide range of interests, both of a monetary and non-monetary nature, have been suggested as potentially relevant. On the side of the patentee, these may include

[31] Siebrasse et al (n 2) 152.

non-compensable harm; the technical and economic significance of the invention; whether the patent protects the result of high and uncertain R&D investments; or whether the patentee practises the invention. On the side of the infringer, these may include investments made in the infringing technology; the commercial significance of the infringing technology; opportunity costs; or whether the technology was independently developed. On the side of third parties, these may include various interests, including those of suppliers, customers, employees, end users, patients or network subscribers, as well as the general interest more broadly. They could even include the infringer's competitors who invested in avoiding infringement. The general view seems to be that courts should place all relevant interests on a hypothetical scale and determine whether the aggregated harmful effects of the injunction sufficiently outweigh the patentee's overall interest in the injunction.[32] This, it is said, should only be accepted in exceptional cases. The resulting test can be characterised as 'broad scope, high threshold': a virtually unlimited number of case specifics are potentially relevant to the proportionality assessment, but, taken together, they should weigh very heavily against the imposition of injunctive relief.

The characterisation calls to mind good faith or abuse of law doctrines, which, among other behaviours, limit exercises of rights when they would be grossly or manifestly disproportionate in light of all circumstances of the case. Examples are known to every law student, and in property law typically include situations where buildings encroach minimally on adjoining land or owners suffer some modest nuisance, while the consequences of the injunction the aggrieved party is legally entitled to would be extremely severe. Gross proportionality is also an accepted limit to patent enforcement.[33] All such cases involve a balance of interests and set the threshold for court intervention – that is, limitation of an otherwise lawful entitlement – not just at mere or even significant, but at *gross* disproportionality. There are various explanations for this stringent standard, the most relevant of which for our purposes is related to the institutional constraints of courts discussed in section 1.4. Requiring 'gross' disproportionality for intervention avoids difficult estimations of the dispute's real-world context because the implications are that (i) parties' interests should be so skewed that intervention is evidently warranted while (ii) such cases are necessarily rare outliers, which limits the intervention's precedential value. As Golden puts it, 'The intuition seems to be that courts can do significant good by picking out extreme cases of error or dysfunction even when they are incompetent to give precise answers on questions of optimality or value'.[34]

Just like the paradigm of commensurate scope, a gross disproportionality standard thus circumvents the indeterminacy problem, albeit in a different manner: rather than adopting a more workable proxy, it simply sets the threshold

[32] The scale metaphor is suggested by Ohly and Stierle (n 6) 1231.
[33] *Virgin Atlantic v Premium Aircraft* [2009] EWCA Civ 1513, para 37.
[34] Golden, 'Complex Economics' (n 27) 54.

for intervention so high that erroneous application becomes less likely. This may help explain why several European courts have interpreted the proportionality test precisely so.[35] However, requiring gross disproportionality for intervention adds nothing to existing limitations on patent enforcement, since gross disproportionality is already a recognised ground to curtail enforcement in the civil codes of most European jurisdictions. It also sets too high a threshold to tackle the problems that proponents of a proportionality test, but also the German legislator, want it to address (which include, among many others, component patents, patent thickets or conflicts with third-party rights). Even though these proponents say the test will apply only in exceptional cases, they must necessarily intend less exceptional application than would be the case under a gross disproportionality standard, otherwise there would be no need to introduce a proportionality test at all.

But lowering the threshold for intervention brings back the indeterminacy problem. As we saw above, there is simply no way of knowing whether a standard of intervention below gross disproportionality would foster, rather than hinder, innovation writ large.[36] There have been attempts at formulating heuristic principles to identify fact patterns where intervention would be warranted, and if a 'broad scope, high threshold'-type proportionality test has any hopes of widespread adoption, it will be owing to such principles.[37] At the time of writing, however, few such principles enjoy enough (let alone universal) recognition for courts to readily rely on them, and fewer still have been formulated with the specifics of European patent litigation in mind. Those European specifics include, in particular, courts' severely more constrained access to evidence on industry specifics and other aspects of the real-world context. Thus, even assuming an appropriate threshold of intervention could be defined between the 'normal' consequences of enforcement and gross disproportionality, why should we assume courts are able to detect it? Gross proportionality has an 'I know it when I see it' logic to it that (supposedly) suffices to justify intervention. A lower standard for intervention necessitates more rigorous justification of its application lest it seem subjective or even whimsical. For the reasons stated in section 1.4, I fear that European patent courts are not quite able – and are much less willing – to engage in such rigorous justification.

The problems for 'broad scope, high threshold' tests do not stop here. Regardless of the standard for disproportionality one adopts, courts must first determine the interests to be compared. To be sure, none of the authors cited argue for precise calculation of these interests and some concede that this would not be possible or necessary.[38] But in order to apply the proportionality test in a reasoned

[35] *HTC v Nokia* [2013] EWHC 3778 (Pat,) para 32; *Wärmetauscher* (n 9) para 50; RB The Hague 18 July 2018, ECLI:NL:RBDHA:2018:8777 (*Nikon v ASML*), para 4.50.

[36] Golden, 'Principles for Patent Remedies' (n 1) 527. There is even no way of knowing the innovation effects of intervention in grossly disproportionate cases, but, as noted above, we tend to assume they are positive.

[37] T Cotter, 'On the Economics of Injunctions in Patent Cases' (2019) 11 *Zeitschrift für Geistiges Eigentum* 293, 303; W Lee and AD Melamed, 'Breaking the Vicious Cycle of Patent Damages' (2016) 101 *Cornell Law Review* 385, 445.

[38] Cotter, 'On the Economics' (n 37) 300.

manner, as opposed to strictly intuitively, the interests on the scale must at least be estimated. To credibly move beyond the court's own sense about the weight of a given interest, even estimating the size of an interest requires substantive engagement with evidence on, for example, economic performance figures, licensing practices or market structures. Indeed, as chapter four demonstrates, this is what US district courts generally do when deciding on injunctive relief, and perusing these decisions quickly gives an impression of just how complicated it is to come up with reasonable estimates, let alone without the benefit of discovery or expert hearings.[39] If estimating the monetary harm an injunction would cause is hard enough, how should the patentee's claim to exclusivity be valued? The bill proposed by the German legislator contains a reference to the invention's value (*Wert*) and suggests it may be a benchmark for the proportionality assessment.[40] However, we know from cases involving standard essential patents (SEPs) that a hypothetical royalty rate is notoriously difficult and time-consuming to calculate. Supporters of the innovation paradigm argue that the hypothetical royalty is also used in damages proceedings.[41] But in practice, those are virtually never pursued in patent litigation. This should give us pause before adopting the hypothetical royalty rate as a benchmark for the proportionality test, as should the observation that at the time of writing not a single continental European court has ever calculated a fair, reasonable, and non-discriminatory (FRAND) royalty rate in a SEP dispute. Assuming they will readily do so in non-SEP disputes that raise proportionality concerns is fanciful, even leaving aside the question why the hypothetical royalty would be an appropriate benchmark if the patentee made no FRAND commitment.

2.3.2. Commensurate Scope: Narrow Scope, Lower Threshold

If my assumptions about courts in the previous chapter are correct, the difficulties outlined here will all but ensure the proportionality test remains a dead letter in practice. This need not be so. The difficulties can be avoided by adopting a narrower test that focuses primarily on the interaction between the patented technology and the device to be enjoined, as I propose in this book. True, this excludes from the scope of the test various circumstances commonly considered

[39] See, eg *Hynix Semiconductors Inc v Rambus Inc* 609 FSupp2d 951 (ND Cal 2009); *Amgen Inc v F Hoffman-La Roche Ltd* 581 FSupp2d 160 (D Mass 2008). As ch 4 shows in more detail, questions that regularly plague US courts include which sunk costs on the part of the infringer should count? How should non-monetary harms, such as reputational damage, be weighed? How can courts reliably estimate losses to third parties that are not part of the proceedings?

[40] German Federal Parliament, Proposed Bill (*Gesetzentwurf: Entwurf eines Zweiten Gesetzes zur Vereinfachung und Modernisierung des Patentrechts*) of 31 January 2021, BT-Drs 19/25821, 54. I note that 'Wert' could also be read as referring to technical merit. In the same section, the German legislator also considers relevant whether the enjoined technology is functionally essential (*funktionswesentlich*) to the overall device.

[41] Osterrieth (n 15) 301.

relevant to proportionality, especially the balance of interests between the parties. But, as we saw above, safeguards against grossly disproportionate harm to infringers already exist in most European jurisdictions. Why should a lower threshold for intervention specifically for patent law be justified? After all, potentially severe consequences for competitors and the public are not a feature unique to patent enforcement. In my view, because the proportionality test sets new and additional limits on patent enforcement, it is legitimate only insofar as it responds to new problems specific to patent law.[42] Otherwise courts would simply be tinkering with the equilibrium set by the legislator.[43] A proportionality test accommodated to these problems and capable of resolving them effectively would be most compelling to courts and lawmakers, and thereby would have the best chances of making a difference in practice. In my view, that is preferable to a proportionality test broad enough to encompass all conceivable problems with patent enforcement, but for that reason difficult to conceptualise and hardly applied in practice. What is more, a test more narrowly confined to the problems it ought legitimately to solve need not apply only exceptionally. If we believe that an automatic injunction rule regularly expands the patentee's effective sphere of exclusivity beyond their inventive contribution, and if we believe that is undesirable as a matter of patent policy, there is no need to limit the injunction's effects only in rare cases. To the contrary: if such cases regularly occur, more frequent intervention might be necessary. So long as the test seeks to prevent a harm that can reliably be detected by patent courts, and is not an invitation to reimagine the patent equilibrium, such interventions are justified.

This chapter therefore suggests adopting a paradigm of commensurate scope for the proportionality test. By introducing a measure of objectivity into the proportionality test's normative basis, courts do not face a mission impossible every time they are asked to apply it. Decisions applying the test become better capable of scrutiny on appeal, by sister courts and by scholars, for it is easier to debate the merits of a court's technical assessment than its preference for one abstract interest over another. For a doctrine so consequential and yet so underdeveloped, that is a significant advantage. What is more, a technically oriented proportionality test allows for judgement based on subject matter that patent courts are well versed in. They not only have ample experience with various areas of technology, but by the end of a trial any patent court will be highly knowledgeable about the intricacies of the specific technology at hand. This, in turn, may make them more amenable to application of a proportionality test than they would be if it required a value judgement on the social costs of a particular instance of enforcement. It is impossible to say for sure, but I am hopeful that more frequent application of a narrower

[42] *cf eBay Inc v MercExchange LLC* 547 US 388, 396 (2006) (Kennedy J concurring) (justifying the *eBay* decision by 'considerations quite unlike earlier cases' in contemporary patent law); but critically, see J Golden, '"Patent Trolls" and Patent Remedies' (2007) 85 *Texas Law Review* 2111, 2124.

[43] *cf Evalve v Edwards Lifesciences* [2020] EWHC 513 (Pat), para 73(vii).

proportionality test amply compensates for its potential underinclusiveness. I am hopeful in particular because, in my view, problems with the patent system that are unique to our time – and thus justify increased reliance on proportionality as an ex post corrective – can be targeted in a proportionality test without making it turn on an open-ended catalogue of viewpoints. It is to these problems that I turn in the next chapter.

PART II

A Solution in Search of a Problem?

3

A Diagnosis of the European Patent System

The book's first part offered a theoretical justification for the proportionality test. This part asks if proportionality in patent law is nevertheless, as a practical matter, a solution in search of a problem. There have been calls in the literature to curtail the patentee's entitlement to injunctive relief since at least the early 2000s, based on a range of phenomena perceived as problematic. My goal in this chapter is to analyse whether these phenomena are indeed problematic, whether they are likely to occur in Europe and whether they are properly addressed with a proportionality test.

I start with what is arguably the only observation in the proportionality debate that can be stated with certainty: there are more European patents in force today than at any other time in history and the increase occurs in most areas of technology. To be sure, this is not a problem in and of itself.[1] But it provides an objective starting point when investigating how the patent system might operate differently today than it did in previous times. Section 3.1 draws three inferences: first, the average product is covered by more patents than has historically been the case and today a wider range of technology is covered by patents. Second, greater demands on the European Patent Office (EPO) have increased pressure on examiners, which opens up possibilities for strategic prosecution of patents as careful scrutiny of a patentee's application strategy is not feasible. Third, other countries (and particularly the USA) have witnessed similar trends and simultaneously weakened the patentee's entitlement to injunctive relief, which suggests that the EU would be an outlier if it did not adopt a functioning proportionality doctrine. Against this backdrop, section 3.2 reviews the literature calling for reform of the automatic injunction regime and particularly the problems these calls purport to address. In brief, my main finding is that the great proliferation of patents in recent decades has: (i) subjected to patent protection ever more technologies on which society has an ever greater dependency; (ii) made patentable ever smaller components of those technologies; and

[1] A Mossoff, 'The Rise and Fall of the First American Patent Thicket: The Sewing Machine War of the 1850s' (2011) 53 *Arizona Law Review* 165, 204 (arguing that patent thickets are 'contextual, depending on such things as time, available technology, and even commercial or legal norms').

(iii) made accidental infringement of those patents ever more likely, especially as patent prosecution procedures have become ever more complex and thus offer ever more opportunities for subterfuge.

My conclusion is that this is a problem that can and should be addressed through a proportionality test. Section 3.3 discusses and rejects a number of counterarguments, but accepts as legitimate concerns about what is sometimes called patent holdout – essentially wilful infringement and other bad faith behaviour by infringers. The chapter concludes by reviewing a number of European patent decisions in which one could imagine an argument about the disproportionality of the injunction. In so doing, the final section builds up to the next chapter, which demonstrates by reference to US case law that problematic patent injunctions are not imaginary after all.

3.1. Technology, Patents and Politics in the Twenty-First Century

3.1.1. What Else is New?

Chapter one advanced the argument that courts should be granted some degree of remedial discretion because technological developments and concomitant shifts in industry make the practical effects of injunctions highly context-dependent. The underlying assumption is that because these developments are recent, the context dependency must be higher than before. This assumption is often found in the literature and evidently underlay Justice Kennedy's concurrence in the *eBay* case, where he stated that equitable discretion 'is well suited to allow courts to adapt to the rapid technological and legal developments in the patent system'.[2] It is nevertheless imperative to ask what, precisely, are the rapid technological and legal developments to which heightened remedial discretion should respond. Many of the problems associated with these developments, from non-practising entities (NPEs) to component patents, are not new.[3] We should thus be cautious before declaring on the basis of these problems alone that the patent system requires recalibration.[4] If it turns out that the patent system broadly operates as it always

[2] *eBay Inc v MercExchange LLC* 547 US 388, 397 (2006) (Kennedy J concurring).

[3] *cf In the Matter of a Petition of the Robin Electric Lamp Company Ltd* [1915] RPC 202, 215 (NPE refusing to license competitor's improved product); *Applications by Brownie Wireless Co Ltd for the Grant of Compulsory Licences* [1929] RPC 457, 474 (no 'arbitrary exercise' of 'super monopoly' by entity that has acquired all valuable patents on enabling technology); Octrooiraad AvB 20 February 1942, *Bijblad* 1942, 95 (non-use not abusive in and of itself, infringer remains able to produce substitute so no grounds for intervention).

[4] J Golden, '"Patent Trolls" and Patent Remedies' (2007) 85 *Texas Law Review* 2111, 2124 ('Until substantial comparative evidence is assembled … the present situation should not be confidently characterized as 'markedly' different from the past').

has, the case for a proportionality test becomes much weaker. It is understandable that those who are not convinced there exists a problem that proportionality should solve tend to view pleas for its adoption as cynical attempts to change the system for the financial benefits of large companies.[5] Of course, questioning the functioning of the patent system is legitimate even without changed circumstances, but the patent system has always imposed static social costs and legislators so far have resisted the temptation to intervene, for better or for worse. Conversely, if there is reason to believe, again citing Justice Kennedy, that patent cases today present 'considerations quite unlike earlier cases', then the case for intervention to correct dysfunctional effects becomes much more compelling.[6]

There is by now a very considerable literature debating whether phenomena often associated with proportionality, such as holdup, royalty stacking or NPEs, occur with any regularity and, if so, whether this merits reform. These debates are not and likely cannot be resolved because measuring the impact of something as diffuse as any of these phenomena on something as complex as innovation is exceedingly difficult. Even the seemingly easier task of just measuring their occurrence can be daunting, given, inter alia, definitional issues, informational constraints and substantial disagreement about what the appropriate compensation of patent holders should be.[7] Then again, specific problems may be worth addressing even if they are not (yet) proven to be widespread.[8] If there is reason to believe these problems may plausibly occur, it may be preferable to equip courts with the means to address them over doing nothing at all. Thus, while this chapter cannot begin to definitively resolve the question of whether the phenomena associated with proportionality are empirically salient in Europe and undesirable as a matter of patent policy, it need not do so to contribute to the task of developing a proportionality test for European patent law. Its more modest task is to inquire which issues may *plausibly* arise from the quasi-automatic grant of patent injunctions.

In a way, the question of empirics has become obsolete since it is clear that European courts have the authority to limit the patentee's entitlement to injunctive relief (section 1.3). During the reform of the German Patent Act (GPA), the German legislator explicitly stated its assumption that the 'increasing complexity of many products' means that an immediate injunction may have disproportionate effects.[9] In its wake, the Dutch Minister of Economic Affairs responded to

[5] eg J Barnett, 'Has the Academy Led Patent Law Astray?' (2017) 32 *Berkeley Technology Law Journal* 1313, 1373.

[6] *eBay v MercExchange* (n 2) 396 (Kennedy J concurring).

[7] J Golden, 'Principles for Patent Remedies' (2010) 88 *Texas Law Review* 505, 527 (outlining 'five basic problems' that 'haunt efforts to optimize patent remedies').

[8] J Contreras, 'Much Ado about Hold-Up' (2019) *University of Illinois Law Review* 875, 896 (referring to insistence on empirical evidence of systemic holdup as the 'Ebola fallacy').

[9] German Federal Parliament, Proposed Bill (*Gesetzentwurf: Entwurf eines Zweiten Gesetzes zur Vereinfachung und Modernisierung des Patentrechts*) of 31 January 2021, BT-Drs 19/25821, 54.

questions from parliament that Dutch patent law offers courts the 'necessary flexibility' to ensure injunctions are proportionate, citing the increasing 'complexity and digital functionality' of many products. Similar questions were raised in the French parliament, and there, too, the government answered that French patent law respects the requirements of the Enforcement Directive and offers a 'margin of appreciation' to courts to ensure remedies are proportionate.[10] These are prominent patent jurisdictions in Europe and the ministries tasked with overseeing patent law have accepted that, indeed, the patent system today does not operate quite like it did historically, and that remedial discretion is needed to respond to the changes. But asking what changed and why that should cause problems remains worthwhile because it can, and should, inform our views on when intervention is necessary.

3.1.2. The Rise in Patenting and Patent Creep

Contemporary society, it is often said, is characterised by technological development proceeding at an unprecedented pace. This trite observation may not survive close scrutiny as there are serious indications that the rate of research and innovation productivity is declining.[11] Without engaging in that more normative debate, it seems reasonable to accept that technology has at least achieved an unprecedented penetration into our daily lives. That is, we are more reliant than ever on technology simply because it permeates many, if not all, aspects of our lives. The observation logically extends to the businesses that provide us with these technologies: their products must provide increasing technological sophistication to remain competitive. For our purposes, the most important consequence is that the range of businesses potentially affected by patents is ever increasing. We can see this in the steady increase in classes and groups of patented subject matter, suggesting that new or at least more fine-grained areas of technology must be added every year to catalogue the full range of technologies across which patents apply.[12] Indeed, the EPO has seen a rise in patent applications across almost all categories of technology. Figures 3.1 and 3.2 show the total number of patent applications and grants at the EPO between 1980 and 2021.

[10] For the Netherlands: Dutch Minister of Economic Affairs and Climate, Letter of 20 June 2022, DGBI-I&K/22257631; for France: Assemblée Nationale, Rep min no 4621 JOAN 16 May 2023, p 4467 (Christophe Blanchet).

[11] R Gold, 'The Fall of the Innovation Empire and Its Possible Rise through Open Science' (2021) 50 *Research Policy* 104226, 3.

[12] The main system for classification of patents per technology is the WIPO-administered International Patent Classification (IPC) system. The IPC divides technology in classes, subclasses, groups and subgroups, and every patent is assigned one or more IPC classifications. In 2006, the IPC included a total of 129 classes and 68,718 groups. In 2022, it included 131 classes and 77,736 groups.

Figure 3.1 Total patent applications (direct and Patent Cooperation Treaty (PCT) national phase entries), 1980–2021

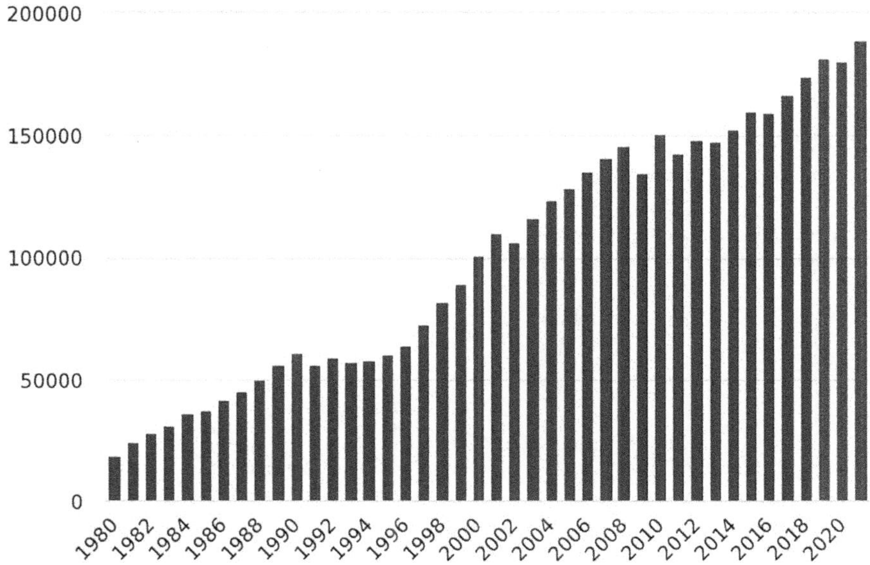

Source: WIPO IP Statistics Data Center.

Figure 3.2 Total patent grants (direct and PCT national phase entries), 1980–2021

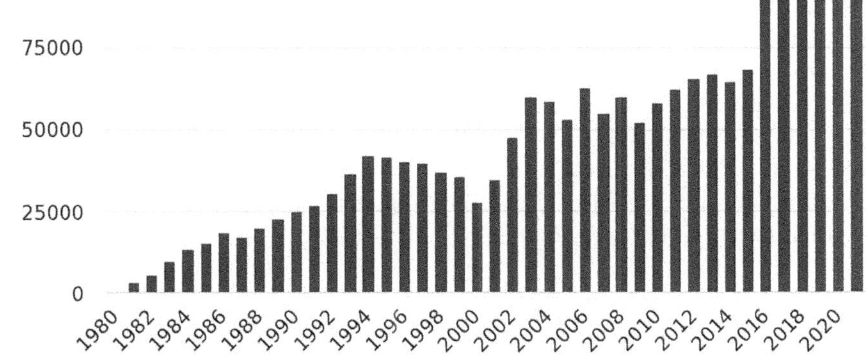

Source: WIPO IP Statistics Data Center.

The increase in numbers is spectacular: from 18,596 applications in 1980 to 188,778 in 2021 and from 484 patent grants in 1980 to 108,799 in 2021, down from a record high of 137,782 in 2019. European patents, of course, are not necessarily validated in all European Patent Convention (EPC) contracting states, so it is also important to look at the numbers of patents in force per individual country. The World Intellectual Property Organization (WIPO) has full data on these numbers since 2010, and in five of the EU's six biggest economies, the number of patents in force shows a year-by-year increase (Figure 3.3).

Figure 3.3 Total patents in force (Germany, France, the UK, Italy, the Netherlands and Spain), 2010–21

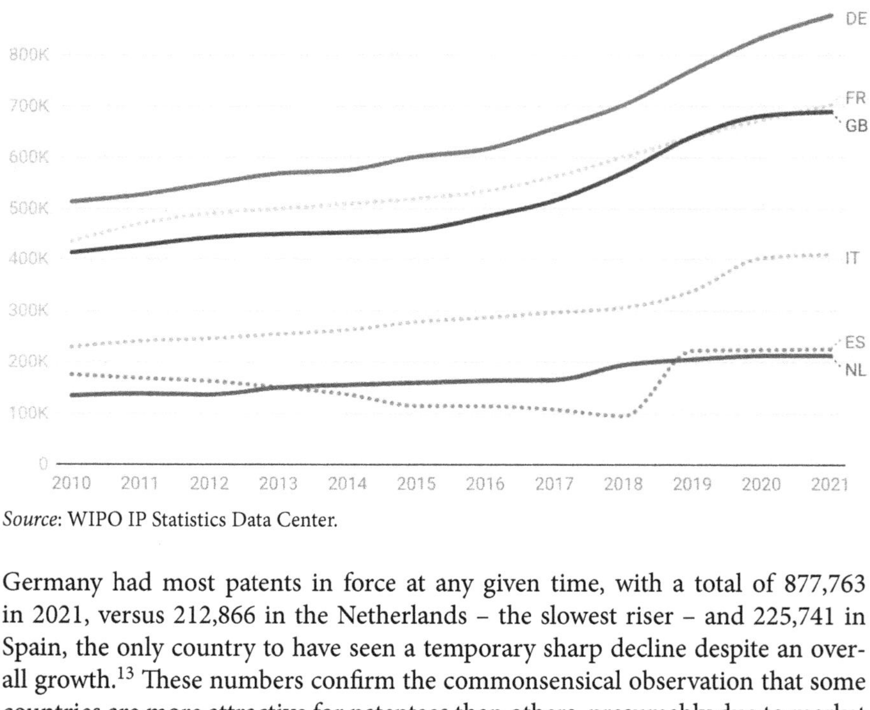

Source: WIPO IP Statistics Data Center.

Germany had most patents in force at any given time, with a total of 877,763 in 2021, versus 212,866 in the Netherlands – the slowest riser – and 225,741 in Spain, the only country to have seen a temporary sharp decline despite an overall growth.[13] These numbers confirm the commonsensical observation that some countries are more attractive for patentees than others, presumably due to market size and possibilities for enforcement. Germany, a patentee-friendly jurisdiction to the point of notoriety, did not just have most patents in force at any given time, but was also the fastest riser, displaying an increase in validated patents of approximately 113 per cent since 2004.[14] That seems a rather steep increase over

[13] It should be noted that these numbers are dwarfed by US numbers, where 3,063,494 patents were in force in 2018. The problems outlined in this chapter are therefore likely to be much more severe in the USA, which cautions against overreliance on US advocacy and scholarship.

[14] In 2004, the first year for which WIPO has data for Germany, 411,671 patents were in force in Germany.

a 17-year period. As Figure 3.3 demonstrates, all major European patent jurisdictions witnessed a rise in patenting in the past decade, even accelerating in pace in recent years.

Furthermore, the rise in patent applications can be observed in almost all areas of technology. The EPO offers a tool to track patent applications across 35 categories of technology in the period between 2012 and 2021. In 28 of these categories, the number of applications was higher in 2021 than it was in 2012 (Table 3.1).

Table 3.1 Patent applications at the EPO per category, 2012–21

Areas with an increase in applications			Areas with a decrease in applications		
Category	**2012**	**2021**	**Category**	**2012**	**2021**
Electrical machinery, apparatus, energy	9744	12,054	Telecommunications	4116	4092
Audio-visual technology	4129	5440	Basic communication processes	1040	988
Digital communication	9753	15,400	Analysis of biological materials	1335	1260
Computer technology	8537	14,671	Organic fine chemistry	6587	5923
Civil engineering	4306	4598	Microstructural technology and nanotechnology	238	146
IT methods for management	1491	2438	Environmental technology	2068	1823
Semiconductors	3241	3748	Engines, pumps, turbines	5877	4318
Optics	3381	4242			
Measurement	6631	9167			
Control	2092	3360			
Medical technology	10,497	15,321			
Biotechnology	5539	7611			
Pharmaceuticals	6301	9026			
Other consumer goods	3072	5130			
Furniture, games	2778	3348			
Macromolecular chemistry, polymers	3493	4033			

(continued)

Table 3.1 ***(Continued)***

Areas with an increase in applications			Areas with a decrease in applications		
Category	2012	2021	Category	2012	2021
Surface technology, coating	2290	2686			
Handling	3956	4719			
Food chemistry	1587	2010			
Basic materials chemistry	4246	4432			
Materials, metallurgy	2959	3890			
Chemical engineering	3602	4026			
Transport	7000	9399			
Machine tools	3461	3549			
Textile and paper machines	2235	2359			
Other special machines	4352	6450			
Thermal processes and apparatus	2465	2641			
Mechanical elements	3765	3925			

Source: EPO Statistics & Trends Centre.

The ascent of networked technologies and 'smart' devices anticipate the considerable rise observed in 'digital communication' and 'computer technology' patent applications. But the data show that the rise in patent applications is not limited to just these two categories. Even intuitively low-tech categories such as 'furniture and games', 'textile and paper machines' or 'food chemistry' witnessed rises in applications, albeit only small ones. Patent applications for 'other consumer goods' rose by almost 67 per cent in this short time span. True, a decline in applications is witnessed in 7 out of 35 categories, but most of these declines are modest. For three categories they are below 10 per cent, and for two more they are barely over 10 per cent. A significant drop (38.6 per cent) occurred for 'microstructural technology and nanotechnology', but that category had far and away the fewest applications to begin with. That leaves 'engines, pumps, turbines', showing a 26.5 per cent decline between 2012 and 2021, as the only real outlier. In all other areas of technology, the number of patent applications has either declined minimally or (much more likely) increased, sometimes significantly so. I take this as an indication of what I call 'patent creep': the expanding reach of patent law across industries and technologies.

3.1.3. Incremental Innovation and Patent Density

Part of the explanation for the increase in patent applications is the gradual lowering of patentability standards in roughly the three decades preceding 2015. Software patents are perhaps the most infamous example and there is certainly tension between the case law of the EPO's Boards of Appeal and Article 52(2) EPC, which provides that programs for computers 'in particular' shall not be regarded as patentable inventions. Of particular interest is the inventive step requirement, which in many ways acts as a gatekeeper of the patent system by setting the qualitative bar for inventions. There are indications that the inventive step standard has been applied loosely in the early 1990s and early 2000s, precisely the periods in which the patent grant rate rose quickly (see Figure 3.2).[15] In recent years, the pendulum seems to be swinging in the opposite direction, and many European courts today apply validity standards quite strictly. Even so, the numbers decidedly show a strong increase in patent grants, which suggests either lower validity standards or a less than thorough examination process.

Lower standards of inventiveness imply minor innovations already suffice to obtain a patent. That is surely most controversial in the pharmaceutical industry, where 'evergreening' strategies are well documented.[16] More generally, it has been argued that awarding patents for relatively minor improvements incentivises devoting research efforts to such improvements as opposed to more audacious, breakthrough innovations.[17] Again, this has important normative implications that cannot be considered here. But it also has implications that are directly relevant for a proportionality doctrine, because granting patents for granular innovation means more patents can read on products and technologies that operate in the market as individual commodities. Admittedly, innovation always occurs incrementally. However, an increment's threshold to warrant patent protection is a policy choice, and in recent decades, the policy adopted and technological developments have converged to stimulate the patenting of many increments, particularly small ones. Smartphones are an oft-cited example: in 2011, a US patent aggregation company estimated that there are 'more than 250,000 active patents relevant to today's smartphones'.[18] The estimate should

[15] G Van Overwalle, 'Policy Levers Tailoring Patent Law to Biotechnology: Comparing US and European Approaches' (2011) 1 *UC Irvine Law Review* 433, 461 (suggesting the EPO's Boards of Appeal applied a lower standard of inventive step in the biotech industries 'to compensate for the risk of failure' in this young industry).

[16] Evergreening refers to the prolongation of exclusivity by patenting ostensibly minor improvements such as dosage regimes. See O Granstrand, 'Evergreening and Patent Cliff Hangers' (2019) 2 *Stockholm Intellectual Property Law Review* 4, 7. Due to their interaction with regulatory requirements, such patents can have extremely high commercial value.

[17] Gold (n 11) 5.

[18] RPX Corp, 'Form S-1 Registration Statement under the Securities Act of 1933' (filed 2 September 2011) 59, www.sec.gov/Archives/edgar/data/1509432/000119312511240287/ds1.htm. Although the number appears in a financial statement and no details on the cited 'research' were disclosed by RPX, the number is frequently cited by advocates of patent reform.

certainly be lower in Europe because in all European jurisdictions the number of patents in force is significantly lower than in the USA. But even if the number were closer to 10,000, that is still a considerable number of patents covering a single device. Despite the dearth of objective data on this issue, it seems reasonable to assume that smartphones are not unique in this respect. The steep increase in patenting since the 1980s, coupled with increasing technological complexity and particularly an inventiveness standard that allows and even encourages patenting incremental improvements, cannot but mean that in many cases the number of patents covering the same product or device is higher than ever. I refer to this phenomenon as 'patent density'.

3.1.4. The Consequences of the Ever-Growing Pressure on the EPO

Patent applications are evaluated by the EPO's examiners, which are known for their rigour as compared to their colleagues at the US and Japanese patent offices.[19] But as the number of applications increases, so does the pressure on the examiners conducting the evaluation. Between 1996 and 2021, the increase in patent examiners at the EPO (118 per cent) fell far behind the increase in patent applications (195 per cent).[20] In recent years, the number of EPO examiners has fluctuated but with an overall decline, from a record number of 4378 examiners in 2017, down to 3945 in 2020 and back up to 4026 in 2021. The EPO's resources to examine each application are thus decreasing as the number of applications to examine keeps growing. In addition, applications tend to increase in length: one study reports that between 1988 and 2005, the average number of pages per patent application more than doubled, whereas the average number of claims increased by 85 per cent.[21] These developments are generally understood as creating a pressure to grant patents, a perception strengthened by the fact that the EPO is primarily funded through user fees.[22] In 2018, an open letter signed by 924 examiners expressly lamented this state of affairs, complaining that they are 'far too often put in front of the dilemma of either working according to the European Patent Convention (EPC) and respecting the Examiner's Guidelines, or issuing

[19] P Drahos, *The Global Governance of Knowledge: Patent Offices and Their Clients* (Cambridge University Press, 2010) 77.

[20] The WIPO IP Statistics Data Center shows that over this period, the number of applications rose from 64,035 to 188,778, while the number of examiners rose from 1851 to 4026.

[21] N Van Zeebroeck et al, 'Patent Inflation in Europe' (2008) 30 *World Patent Information* 43, 44. The average number of claims may since have decreased because in 2008, the EPO introduced a new fee rule whereby applicants pay per claim.

[22] Drahos (n 19) 75 (finding that even though examiners requested more time to properly examine applications, managers focused on 'the overriding importance of meeting production targets').

'products' as our hierarchy demands'.[23] And in 2019 and 2020, the EPO itself estimated that it had properly granted only three out of four patents.[24] It thus seems plausible that the high application numbers contribute to lower patent quality, an important subject with a long history of debate but preciously little consensus. I nevertheless do not address it in detail here because, at least in non-bifurcated systems, it relates to proportionality only indirectly.

Another consequence of the burgeoning workload at the EPO is that it further upsets the playing field between examiners and applicants. In particular, examiners have limited time to assess individual applications and are certainly too resource-constrained to make inquiries beyond that assessment into the strategic value of the patent and its relation to the social value of the invention.[25] By contrast, there is no limit to the amount of resources applicants can spend on their applications and the tactical development of their portfolio – and spend on this they do. The literature on proportionality tends to overlook the fact patentees draft their own property entitlements and the enormous strategic advantages this confers on them.[26] If we are genuinely concerned about the inability of market participants to perform patent clearance (as I argue below we should be), it is of course critically important that the patentee can make it even harder.[27] Applicants might do this by obscuring the ultimate owner of the patent, which has raised concerns in the literature and in US practice.[28] But the application process itself also provides means for subterfuge.

In particular, patentees can keep applications pending indefinitely and amend their description and claims at any time, provided any amendments are derivable from the application as filed (Article 123 EPC). In the USA, it used to be the case that pending applications were not published and the patent's term started running at the date of grant, which resulted in egregious submarine patent tactics. It took legislative changes in 1995 and 2005 to make the term run from the date of application and to make publication of the application mandatory after 18 months, measures that were part of the EPC from the start. However, it can be seriously

[23] Chairman of the EPO Central Staff Committee, 'Petition from EPO Examiners' (9 March 2018) https://regmedia.co.uk/2018/03/15/epo-examiners-letters.pdf.

[24] EPO, 'Quality Report 2020', 34, www.epo.org/about-us/annual-reports-statistics/annual-report/2020.html. The quarterly numbers range between 75% and 76.8%, and are based on internal audits.

[25] Drahos (n 19) 294.

[26] ibid 80 ('It is in the drafting of the claims that so much of the relentless gaming of the patent system is to be found').

[27] D Harhoff and S Wagner, 'The Duration of Patent Examination at the European Patent Office' (2009) 55 *Management Science* 1969, 1973 ('Patent law leaves sufficient leeway for applicants to modify their applications in ways that can impose costs and uncertainty on rivals, even if the initial application has been published').

[28] A Gorbatyuk and A Kovács, 'Patent Notice (Failure) in the Era of Patent Monetization' (2022) 53 *International Review of Intellectual Property and Competition Law* 506, 529. For a case where confidentiality arguments were cited (and rejected) to keep ultimate ownership of enforced patents confidential, see *Uniloc 2017 LLC v Apple Inc* 2019 WL 2009318, *1 (ND Cal 7 May 2019) ('generalized assertions of potential competitive harm fail to outweigh the public's right to learn of the ownership of the patents-in-suit, which patents grant said owner the right to *publicly* exclude others').

questioned whether publication of the application after 18 months provides sufficient notice of pending applications in all cases. First, it means that, at any given time, pending applications filed up to 18 months prior are unfindable. In many industries, 18 months is a long time to be in the dark about potential patent claims. Second, and more fundamentally, there is nothing to stop patentees from filing broadly worded applications and to slim them down only after competitors have launched their own products. In fact, this is customary practice, at least for patentees that can afford it (because fees remain due during pendency). The search for patents potentially relevant to a projected product is clearly complicated if the validity and scope of protection of the patents found cannot be properly evaluated because the contents of the application are deliberately overly broad. Third, through the use of divisional applications – essentially exact copies of the original application 'reset' to the first stages of the application – patentees can 'perpetuate commercial uncertainty' even after a patent is revoked.[29] Because there is no time limit to file divisional applications (contrary to what is the case in, for example, China), patentees can always keep at least one divisional application pending even for patents granted years ago.[30] Thus, if a court should revoke such a patent, it is possible to start over from the original application and tackle any validity concerns raised, all the while maintaining at least some commercial uncertainty about whether the patent will issue or not.[31]

3.1.5. Comparative Notes Amidst a Global Struggle for Dominance

As we will see below, these developments create problems for an automatic injunction regime. It is therefore unsurprising that other jurisdictions, faced with similar developments, are moving away from it. The USA did so famously in 2006, as the next chapter discusses at length. Many of the problems discussed in this chapter had already been mentioned in a 2003 report from the Federal Trade Commission,

[29] *Fujifilm Kyowa Kirin Biologics Co, Ltd v AbbVie Biotechnology Ltd* [2017] EWHC 395 (Pat), para 396. See generally K Foss-Solbrekk, 'The Divisional Game: Using Procedural Rights to Impede Generic/Biosimilar Market Entry' (2022) 53 *International Review of Intellectual Property and Competition Law* 1007. At the time of writing, the European Commission is investigating the use of 'divisional shields' as potentially anti-competitive behaviour: Commission, 'Antitrust: Commission Sends Statement of Objections to Teva over Misuse of the Patent System and Disparagement of Rival Multiple Sclerosis Medicine' IP/22/6062.

[30] A time limit was introduced in 2009, but after fierce resistance from users it was removed again in 2013: Decision of the Administrative Council of 16 October 2013 amending Rules 36, 38, and 135 of the Implementing Regulations of the European Patent Office [2013] OJ EPO 501.

[31] In *Neurim Pharmaceuticals v Generics (UK)* [2022] EWHC 109 (Pat), para 160, the English court refused to find an abuse on the facts of that case, but expressly considered that strategic use of divisional applications as 'backups' 'can raise serious problems' and that the argument it amounts to abuse 'would be an important and complex one'.

which Justice Kennedy cites in his aforementioned concurrence.[32] In China, injunctions were granted to prevailing patentees in over 90 per cent of cases in 2014, but in 2016 the Supreme People's Court issued guidelines on the adjudication of patent infringement suits, which state that the People's Court may refuse an injunction 'in light of national interests and public interests'. Then, in 2020, an amendment to the Patent Act was passed that states that patent enforcement 'shall follow the principle of good faith' and that 'The patent right shall not be abused to damage the public interest or the legitimate rights and interests of others'.[33] This change seems to have been inspired specifically by the US Supreme Court's *eBay* decision.[34] Especially when it comes to standard essential patents (SEPs), China appears to consciously pursue a weak injunction regime to achieve an 'across-the-board discount on the price of technology inputs in wireless-enabled markets'.[35] For its part, Japan considered limiting a patentee's entitlement to injunctive relief as early as 2010 and the issue was put on the agenda again in 2019, once more following developments in the USA and Germany.[36]

It should give the EU pause that all these jurisdictions are limiting access to injunctive relief. Maintaining an automatic injunction regime would place European companies at a competitive disadvantage: they are threatened by an immediate injunction in case of enforcement in the EU by overseas competitors, but if they countersue in the competitor's home jurisdiction the measure may be unavailable. That risk is far from illusory because over half of patent applications before the EPO come from non-European applicants (see Figure 3.4). In 2021, application numbers from the USA and Korea increased by 5.2 per cent and 3.4 per cent, respectively, as compared to 2020. In that same year, applications from China rose by a staggering 24 per cent.[37] Most applications by far came from the USA, and only two EU countries made it into the top six. For the next-generation telecommunications technology, 5G, only the non-European countries in the top

[32] Federal Trade Commission, 'To Promote Innovation: The Proper Balance of Competition and Patent Law Policy' (October 2003) www.ftc.gov/sites/default/files/documents/reports/promote-innovation-proper-balance-competition-and-patent-law-and-policy/innovationrpt.pdf. It is worth noting that even the strategic reliance on divisional applications, discussed in the previous section, is already flagged in the report: see, eg recommendations 7–8 on pp 15–16.

[33] X Jinping, 'Order of the President of the People's Republic of China No 55' of 17 October 2020, http://www.npc.gov.cn/englishnpc/c23934/202109/63b3c7cb2db342fdadacdc4a09ac8364.shtml.

[34] P Wu and C Xiao-chuan Weng, 'Old Wine in a New Bottle? Assessing the Injunction Remedy for Intellectual Property Disputes in China' (2021) 11 *Queen Mary Intellectual Property Law Journal* 295, 300 ('The equitable standards in the US *eBay* case noticeably influenced legal practices and research of intellectual property injunctions in China'); L Yu, 'Permanent Injunction on Intellectual Property Rights: Judicial Experiences in China' (2023) 45 *European Intellectual Property Review* 154, 160 (concluding that, since 2009, Chinese courts regularly deny injunctions on public interest grounds).

[35] J Barnett, 'Antitrust Mercantilism: The Strategic Devaluation of Intellectual Property Rights in Wireless Markets' (2023) 37 *Berkeley Technology Law Journal* 259, 266.

[36] T Hatori, 'Restriction to an Injunctive Relief in Patent Infringement Proceedings under the Japanese Patent Act' (Master's Thesis, Max Planck Institute for Innovation and Competition, 2020) 17 *et seq*, https://papers.ssrn.com/sol3/papers.cfm?abstract_id=3904030.

[37] If the rise in patent grants is steep at the EPO, it is positively breathtaking in China: it went from 3393 in 1995 to 695,946 in 2021, according to the WIPO IP Statistics Data Center.

six (USA, China, Japan and South Korea) are true leaders holding the most critical patents.[38] If the same is true in other fields of technology, that does not bode well for the patent leadership of EU countries.

Figure 3.4 European patent applications per country by origin (2021)

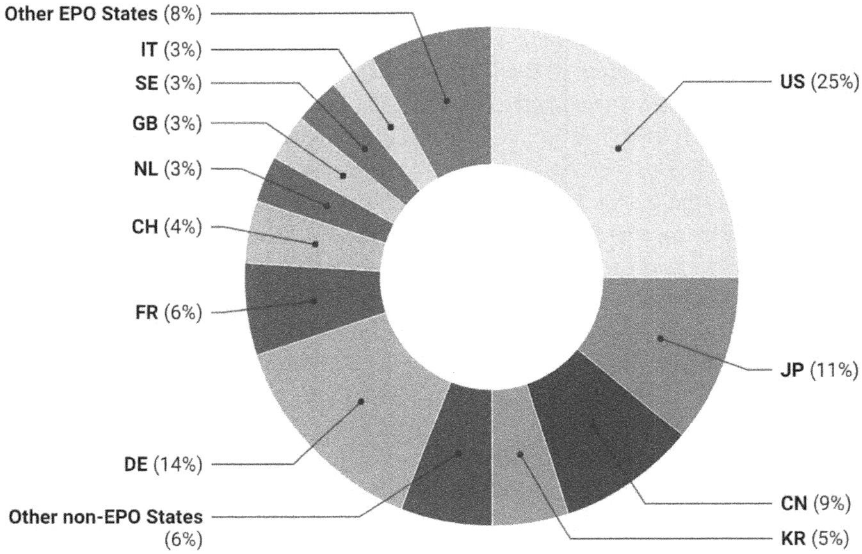

Source: EPO Patent Index 2021.

These developments should be understood as part of a worldwide race for technological and economic dominance. Recent skirmishes over 5G offer a fine illustration. China announced its 'Made in China 2025' plan in 2015, according to which it strives to upgrade its industries to become global leaders in technological innovation. A Chinese telecoms firm, Huawei, has since made waves as it became not only the world's leading smartphone manufacturer by global sales, but also the single biggest holder of 5G patent applications.[39] Its success did not go unnoticed in Washington, and in 2018, the Office of the US Trade Representative issued a report accusing China of a wide range of unfair trade practices, including the theft of intellectual property.[40] President Trump issued trade sanctions

[38] P-L Parcu, N Innocenti and C Carrozza, 'Ubiquitous Technologies and 5G Development: Who Is Leading the Race?' (2022) 46 *Telecommunications Policy* 102277, 9.

[39] IPLytics, '5G Patent Study 2020' (24 February 2020) 11, www.iplytics.com/report/5g-patent-study-2020/ (measured by number of declarations of essentiality). In 2021, Huawei was the leading applicant at the EPO, having filed 3544 patent applications in that year alone.

[40] Office of the US Trade Representative, 'Findings of the Investigation into China's Acts, Policies and Practices Related to Technology Transfer, Intellectual Property, and Innovation under Section 301 of the Trade Act of 1974' (22 March 2018) 17–18, https://ustr.gov/sites/default/files/Section%20301%20FINAL.PDF?mod=article_inline.

against China shortly thereafter, many of them ostensibly intended to specifically hurt Huawei. In addition, the USA put pressure on EU states to ban Huawei from supplying 5G infrastructure in Europe. The trade war continues under President Trump's successor, President Biden, and it is clear that the USA fears not just the rise of Huawei, but China's technological dominance more generally. It is also clear that patents play a key role in this struggle, and the year-on-year increase in patenting by Chinese firms is no coincidence but part of a long-term geopolitical strategy. Against this background, having an automatic injunction regime is a liability because it creates threats for strategically or economically significant industries. The concessions that the US demands from China are emblematic of the advantages that such a regime creates for foreign companies: part of the very first step towards resolution of the trade war were commitments to 'strengthen protection and enforcement of IP in China', including the grant of preliminary injunctions in the pharmaceutical sector.[41] This geopolitical dimension is only tangential to the actual application of a proportionality test, but nevertheless provides important context to understand its broader function.

I now turn to the various symptoms associated with the increase in patenting outlined here that have received attention in the literature. Where possible, I build on stakeholder positions expressed during the reform of the GPA (section 1.2.2).

3.2. Patent Law under Pressure: Problems with Patent Injunctions

3.2.1. Patent Thickets and Accidental Infringement

The term 'patent thicket' was first coined by Carl Shapiro, who defined it as 'a dense web of overlapping intellectual property rights that a company must hack its way through in order to actually commercialize new technology'.[42] Patent thickets are thus high concentrations of patents, hemming in specific technologies, that contribute to what I called patent density in section 3.1.3. The ever-increasing number of patent grants make their occurrence quite plausible and there are anecdotal reports confirming this. The aforementioned example of the smartphone gained particular traction; German car manufacturers have cited the example of complex semiconductors, which, according to their estimates, may be covered by more than 10,000 patents. New cars can contain dozens of such semiconductors,

[41] Executive Office of the President of the US, 'Economic and Trade Agreement between the United States and The People's Republic of China Fact Sheet: Intellectual Property' (January 2020) https://ustr.gov/sites/default/files/files/agreements/phase%20one%20agreement/Phase_One_Agreement-IP_Fact_Sheet.pdf.

[42] C Shapiro, 'Navigating the Patent Thicket: Cross Licenses, Patent Pools, and Standard-Setting' in A Jaffe, J Lerner and S Stern (eds), *Innovation Policy and the Economy*, vol 1 (MIT Press, 2001) 120.

so the number of potentially relevant patents multiplies – and those are just the semiconductor patents. These kinds of estimates are hard to verify, but there is some empirical support for the occurrence of patent thickets,[43] and in a 2012 report, the EPO's Economic and Scientific Advisory Board concludes that 'patent thickets are a natural outcome (or symptom) of the other aspects of the current system'.[44] All in all, there seems to be some agreement that patent thickets occur. The controversy is whether they make freedom-to-operate searches unreasonably difficult and, if so, what the consequences thereof should be.

High patent density, potentially running into the tens of thousands of patents per device, may cause two problems: it may be difficult to identify all relevant patents (search problems) and, once identified, it may be difficult to obtain permission from all patentees (clearance problems). Clearance problems are addressed in section 3.2.2; here, I address only search problems. On the one hand, stakeholders from different industries (VDA – automotive, Sanofi – pharmaceutical, BVMW – cross-industry small and medium enterprises (SMEs)) have argued that it is simply not possible to identify all relevant patents if patent density is high. Judge Fabian Hoffmann of Germany's Federal Court of Justice, who was heard as an expert during the parliamentary hearing on the reform bill, accepted without reservation that in such cases a patent might easily be overlooked.[45] SMEs, in particular, also feared the prohibitive costs these searches would entail if made mandatory for an appeal to proportionality. Note that these are not just patent attorney fees: in some cases, experiments need to be performed to see if a product falls within the claim's scope (eg functional claims in the pharmaceutical industry, section 3.2.7), and those may impose significant additional costs. On the other hand, conducting freedom-to-operate analyses is routine work for patent attorneys and there is a suite of databases available to facilitate the search.[46] Automated searches and outsourcing to specialised search firms can help keep costs manageable for smaller players. Most importantly, the fact that conducting a proper clearance search is sometimes costly does not mean companies cannot be expected to perform them.

Still, the question remains: with so many patents, can one ever be sure that a search will yield all patents relevant to a projected product? Recall that patent applications are kept secret for 18 months and can be amended at any time, including after grant of the patent, through use of divisional applications. Of course, patent attorneys can anticipate possible amendments, but this further raises costs and uncertainty, especially if patent applications run to hundreds of pages. All in all, it strikes me as undeniable that an individual patent or a specific claim might

[43] B Hall et al, *A Study of Patent Thickets* (Intellectual Property Office, 2013) 2013/26.

[44] EPO, 'Report: Workshop on Patent Thickets' (2013) 17, www.epo.org/mobile/news-events/news/2013/20130313.html.

[45] German Federal Parliament, Transcript (*Wortprotokoll der 132. Sitzung*) of 24 February 2021, BT-Drs 19/2581, 25.

[46] Mossoff (n 1) 204.

be overlooked despite a diligent search. Even the two experts appearing before the German parliament who were most adamantly opposed to the reform, Renate Weisse and Alissa Zeller, had to admit that searches could never be 100 per cent accurate.[47] Additionally, once found, there will always be at least some uncertainty over the validity and scope of patent claims. As we saw, the EPO itself concluded in recent years that it was wrong to grant one in four patents, and invalidation rates before national courts approach (and sometimes exceed) 50 per cent in many European jurisdictions. This is one place where patent quality and proportionality intersect: lower patent quality means more uncertainty for competitors who have identified relevant patents in the course of bringing to market a new product. With such high rates of invalidation, it would be unreasonable – and undesirable as a matter of innovation policy – to require companies to abandon new products just because some patent may potentially read on it.[48] Therefore, awareness of an application alone should be insufficient to deny infringers a proportionality defence, an issue I return to in section 6.2.2.

In sum, I consider it plausible that (i) more and more areas of technology are characterised by high patent density and that (ii) this creates search problems, in terms of both finding relevant patents and ascertaining their relevance to a projected product. The more fundamental question is whether these observations should have legal consequences. In a recent, thought-provoking book, Patrick Goold argues that a negligence standard should apply in cases of 'accidental' infringement, ie where the infringer at the time of acting 'could reasonably foresee only a risk that their conduct would result in an IP infringement'.[49] Goold draws an analogy to the introduction of the tort of negligence in response to 'the increase in accident cases that accompanied the Industrial Revolution', when economic and social changes made accidents of various kinds much more likely.[50] So, too, the risk of 'IP accidents' is greatly augmented by the increase in number of IP rights, and Goold argues this is a reason to exonerate from liability infringers who took reasonable care to avoid infringement. As I have written elsewhere, I believe Goold takes the argument too far.[51] Still, he captures exactly the dilemma that so vexed stakeholders and experts in the German reform process. Deviation from a strict liability standard is certain to invite opportunistic behaviour by infringers and makes patent protection even more probabilistic than it already is. Nevertheless, it is unfair and inefficient to penalise persons who could reasonably assume their actions were legal, and a patent regime that allows this risks

[47] Transcript (n 45) 13, 18.

[48] Drahos (n 19) 299 reports an Australian case where a product was dropped after 'arse-covering' advice from counsel on the basis of a US patent, whereas seemingly no protection was applied for in Australia.

[49] P Goold, *IP Accidents: Negligence Liability in Intellectual Property* (Cambridge University Press, 2022) 9.

[50] ibid 48.

[51] L Dijkman, 'Guest Book Review: IP Accidents' (*IPKat*, 14 September 2022) https://ipkitten.blogspot.com/2022/09/guest-book-review-ip-accidents.html.

stifling innovation. To illustrate, think of the massive investments pharmaceutical companies must make (eg initiating clinical trials) to bring a new product to market. Naturally, such a company's board will want to know of any legal risks, including the risk of patent infringement, before proceeding with such investments. If my intuition is correct that on many occasions that risk is difficult to assess, whether the innovation proceeds will depend primarily on a board's risk appetite. If we can mitigate the worst of the risks faced by companies in these positions through a proportionality test, that would seem like a clear improvement of the status quo.

Indeed, the right to exclude that attaches to property entitlements (including patents) is premised at least in part on the idea that exclusion rights facilitate private ordering, and if a patent cannot be located despite reasonable efforts, the justification for the right to exclude is weakened.[52] In addition, dismissing as irrelevant an infringer's reasonable precautions creates undesirable incentives not just on the part of infringers (abandoning innovation, as we have seen, or investing excessively in patent searches), but also on the part of patentees, who might be tempted to obscure their patent position to maximise leverage. We saw that the increasing pressure on the EPO makes it harder for examiners to detect such strategies, and their effects may only become known during the infringement proceedings. In my view, then, the increased risk of accidental patent infringement today is an important consideration for the proportionality test in European patent law. Section 6.2.2 addresses in more detail how the test's structure might incorporate this consideration.

3.2.2. Anticommons and Royalty Stacking

The anticommons and royalty stacking theories are essentially variations of the patent thicket hypothesis based on perceived clearance problems. In 1998, it was feared that the sharp rise in biotechnology patents would seriously stifle innovation in this field because the sheer number of patents and patentees would make it difficult to obtain all necessary licences.[53] Relatedly, royalty stacking theory posits that large numbers of patents held by different patentees will cause implementers to overpay for licences, particularly where individual patentees are capable of charging a holdup value (see section 3.2.4 below).[54] The commonality to both

[52] O-A Rognstad, *Property Aspects of Intellectual Property* (Cambridge University Press, 2018) 99.

[53] M Heller and R Eisenberg, 'Can Patents Deter Innovation? The Anticommons in Biomedical Research' (1998) 280 *Science* 698.

[54] M Lemley and C Shapiro, 'Patent Holdup and Royalty Stacking' (2007) 85 *Texas Law Review* 1991, 2013.

theories is the inference that patent thickets make cost-efficient clearance of all relevant patents impossible.

So far, however, the inference seems to be faulty. There is no evidence that a patent anticommons materialised in the biotech industry.[55] In fact, this industry has arguably been characterised by unusually high rates of innovation in past decades.[56] Likewise, despite fierce enforcement campaigns against them, smartphone producers seem to pay moderate aggregate royalty rates.[57] The telecoms industry certainly displays a very high patent density, but historical experience suggests that systemic clearance problems will be avoided through the formation of patent pools.[58] That is precisely what happened as most patentees came together in pools like ETSI or 3GPP, which offer relatively easy access to most, if not all, relevant patents (see further section 3.2.5 below). Indeed, generally speaking, patentees have an incentive to set low royalty rates to encourage broad adoption of their technology, which, in turn, increases the royalty base and provides an entryway to pitch future technologies.[59]

Furthermore, if and when anticommons or royalty stacking problems do materialise, it is not clear how a proportionality test can solve them. It is conceivable, for instance, that a car manufacturer ends up with an aggregate royalty rate that is in excess of what is necessary to compensate individual patentees, if it is the subject of consecutive patent assertions that can leverage holdup value. During the German reform process, the automotive industry in fact expressed fear of this happening. But patent enforcement is not rendered disproportionate just because the infringer must also pay other patentees. The mere fact that there are several other patentees to whom royalty payments are due should be irrelevant for the propriety of any individual instance of enforcement. Royalty stacking is problematic primarily when structural features of the patent system allow each individual patentee to extract royalties (far) in excess of a reasonable market price. If those structural features are curbed through a proportionality test, the 'royalty stack' at most comprises a series of royalty payments approaching market value. To the extent that this is considered problematic, the solution most likely lies with patentability standards (making it too easy to obtain commercially valuable patents) or industry practices (making it too easy to assert outsider patents), but not with injunctive relief.

[55] J Contreras, 'The Anticommons at 20: Concerns for Research Continue' (2018) 361 *Science* 335, 337.

[56] J Barnett, *Innovators, Firms, and Markets: The Organizational Logic of Intellectual Property* (Oxford University Press, 2021) 117.

[57] A Galetovic et al, 'An Estimate of the Average Cumulative Royalty Yield in the World Mobile Phone Industry: Theory, Measurement and Results' (2018) 42 *Telecommunications Policy* 263, 271 (estimating an aggregate rate of 3.4% in 2016).

[58] R Merges, 'Contracting into Liability Rules: Intellectual Property Rights and Collective Rights Organizations' (1996) 84 *California Law Review* 1293, 1328.

[59] Barnett, *Innovators, Firms, and Markets* (n 56) 132–33.

3.2.3. Component Patents

If a product is covered by several patents, each individual patent will relate only to one part or feature of the product. In this book, patents that do not relate to a device as a whole but only to a part thereof are referred to as 'component patents'. Component patents may cover relatively 'large' parts of a product (eg a patent on the grip of a knife), but most problematic cases will arise where the patent covers only a 'small' part of a device, as can happen when many patents read on the device (eg a patent covering one of several semiconductors used in a car).[60] Of course, if a component patent is infringed, the court will enjoin only the use of the specific component: the rest of the device is unaffected and, so long as the infringing component is omitted or replaced, its sale or production may continue. As a practical matter, however, it may not be possible to omit or replace the infringing component, or doing so may take time. In these cases, the practical effect of the injunction will be to prohibit not just the infringing component, but the entire device. In other words, the practical effects of the injunction expand the patentee's exclusivity beyond the claims to the device as a whole. This results in a problem that is as old as patent law itself but defies resolution in the abstract: is it fair in such cases to grant the injunction?[61]

In the USA, courts apply a causal nexus test to determine whether injunctive relief should issue on a component patent and inquire whether the patented technology was a 'significant reason' for consumers to purchase the infringing product.[62] As explained in section 4.2, the causal nexus test stems from the irreparable harm requirement and seeks to establish whether competitive harm suffered by the patentee is caused by the infringement (in which case an injunction will issue) or by legitimate competition, ie the non-infringing features of the device (in which case an injunction will be denied). Because a showing of irreparable harm is not required for a permanent injunction in any European jurisdiction, the causal nexus test is extraneous to a European proportionality doctrine. Indeed, the problem posed by component patents was for a long time completely ignored in European patent practice. This attitude doubtlessly stems from a strong conviction that the infringer bears the full risk of all consequences of patent infringement. But why should this always be so? One could imagine the rule being overly harsh where infringement was accidental, let alone where the

[60] N Siebrasse, et al 'Injunctive Relief' in CB Biddle et al (eds), *Patent Remedies and Complex Products: Toward a Global Consensus* (Cambridge University Press, 2019) treat the problem discussed here as one of complex products, which incorporate 'inventions claimed in not just thousands, but tens or even hundreds of thousands of individual patents' (1). These products will present the hardest cases, but strictly speaking the problem is not confined to such products.

[61] See *Hoe v Boston Daily Advertiser Corp* 14 F 914 (CCD Mass 8 February 1883) (injunction denied where the 'improvement in question is but part of a large machine').

[62] *TEK Global Srl v Sealant Systems Int'l* 920 F3d 777, 792 (Fed Cir 2019).

patentee deliberately obscured their patent position. A hard and fast rule according to which component status is irrelevant for injunctive relief would also elevate the value of component patents in industries where the instant removal of a device component is very difficult. For instance, in industries where strict regulatory requirements apply for marketing products or where long supply chains are the industry norm, the proprietor of a component patent can usually expect to obtain an effective sphere of exclusivity beyond the patented component simply because ceasing infringement instantly is more difficult than it is for other products. As these considerations illustrate, component patents by definition raise problems of commensurate scope. Far from arguing that injunctive relief should never be issued on the basis of such patents, I believe it is necessary for European patent law to offer a reasonable approach to these problems, certainly if it is correct that these days there are more component patents, covering smaller components, than has historically been the case.

Fortunately, the tide seems to be turning in the European case law.[63] Issues with component patents were flagged in several position papers during the GPA reform and are now acknowledged even by those who generally oppose a proportionality test.[64] However, during the debates, the component patent problem was often conflated with (and thus implicitly limited to) cases of accidental infringement, cases where no alternative exists for the patent technology or other fact patterns. In my view, this is incorrect: at its heart, the component patent problem is one of overreach, and that threat exists regardless of other circumstances. To be sure, accidental infringement is more likely where a device is covered by a large number of component patents. Conversely, there are certainly cases where an injunction is justified even for a small component patent that is hard to remove from the device as a whole. But it is important to keep in mind that component patents raise issues distinct from accidental infringement: in the first case, the problem is one of commensurate scope, whereas in the second case, it is one of protecting good-faith actors. Both problems have a role to play in the proportionality test, but their respective roles are best determined if considered separately, as opposed to being conflated.

3.2.4. Patent Holdup and Patent Holdout

Patent holdup is a variant of the component patent problem. I discuss it separately because it rejoices in copious scholarly attention, though, much like anticommons

[63] *HTC Corp v Nokia Corp* [2013] EWHC 3778 (Pat) (finding that 'the mere fact that the injunction only relates to a small component of a larger whole' (61) is insignificant, but that 'the availability and cost of non-infringing alternatives' (62) may render injunction disproportionate); RB The Hague 9 May 2022, ECLI:NL:RBDHA:2022:6079 (*Ericsson v Apple*), para 4.30 (relevant to grant of preliminary injunction that patented technology was 'only an especially small part' of Apple's products).

[64] M Schellhorn, *Der Patentrechtliche Unterlassungsanspruch im Lichte des Verhältnismäßigkeitsgrundsatzes* (Carl Heymanns Verlag, 2020) 379.

theory and royalty stacking, the concept does not play a significant role in this work. The definition of patent holdup is passionately contested, but it is generally understood to comprise: (i) an ex ante moment when an infringer, had they been aware of a patent, could either have licensed it on reasonable terms or implemented alternative technology; and (2) an ex post moment when an injunction has inflated threat value because of the infringer's sunk costs or high switching costs, or both.[65] As Thomas Cotter and co-authors explain:

> The intuition is that if the patent holder can credibly demand to enjoin the use of the infringing technology *ex post*, the manufacturer often would be better off agreeing to pay a royalty that exceeds the technology's *ex ante* value, rather than to write off those asset-specific sunk costs as a loss.[66]

The difference between the ex ante and ex post valuations of the technology, it is said, is the 'holdup' value of the injunction.

There is considerable debate in the literature about the theoretical and empirical merits of patent holdup theory. However, that debate need not be resolved here because, in any event, patent holdup theory has several limitations in the context of this book. First, almost all work on patent holdup concerns SEPs, ie patents that their holders committed to license on fair, reasonable and non-discriminatory (FRAND) terms, covering technology that cannot be replaced because it is essential to a technical standard. But as I explain below, under EU law, the risk of patent holdup is substantially mitigated for SEPs following a key European Court of Justice (ECJ) ruling. Second, patent holdup theory presumes that 'the correct or baseline royalty for a patented technology is its "ex ante" value over the next-best available nonpatented alternative'.[67] But here, too, EU law differs critically from US law by generally allowing recovery of damages beyond the hypothetical ex ante value of the technology.[68] Rightly so, in my view, because there is generally no legal basis for capping royalties at the patented technology's ex ante value, certainly not for non-SEPs. In addition, the 'ex ante value' of a technology is very difficult to calculate.[69] Most importantly, any rule that would result in an adjudicated infringer being no worse off than a voluntary licensee, in that they would be shielded against remedies that could induce them to accept a royalty beyond the ex ante value, would seriously undermine incentives to take out a licence. Because detecting and following up on infringement is costly for patentees and because there is always a chance the patent's validity

[65] T Cotter, E Hovenkamp and N Siebrasse, 'Demystifying Patent Holdup' (2019) *Washington & Lee Law Review* 1501, 1518–28. The authors offer some nuances that I omitted here, but the basic idea is the same.

[66] ibid 1521.

[67] ibid 1519.

[68] *cf* Case C-367/15 *Stowarzyszenie Oławska Telewizja Kablowa (OTK)* ECLI:EU:C:2017:36, para 30–31. In addition, the ex ante value appears to be impossible to calculate in practice.

[69] I Nikolic, *Licensing Standard Essential Patents: FRAND and the Internet of Things* (Hart Publishing, 2021) 96–99.

can be successfully challenged, a company might as well take its chances infringing. This type of opportunistic behaviour is known in the literature as 'reverse holdup' or patent holdout, though it simply boils down to wilful infringement.[70] Holdout is a serious problem even under the automatic injunction rule, and all stakeholders opposing a proportionality test expressed fears that adopting it would make it worse.

Still, there is one basic insight from the patent holdup literature that is relevant to this book: in cases where the patentee is willing to license the patent or even initiated enforcement proceedings for that specific purpose, the harm threatened by the injunction (and only secondarily the value of the underlying technology) will determine the patentee's leverage. I refer to this phenomenon as the injunction's threat value. Any patent case can involve threat value, for instance where the infringer faces liability from being unable to fulfil supply contracts if the injunction takes immediate effect.[71] But it is most likely to arise in component patent cases because of the potential that the injunction effectively extends (far) beyond the patented technology, as we just saw. This is another place where patent quality and proportionality intersect: lower standards of inventiveness make it easier to patent one among several solutions to a technical problem. If more or less equivalent alternatives to a component patent exist, the value of that patent is likely to consist entirely of threat value.

During the GPA reform, the automotive industry in particular emphasised that extremely high costs of production stops lead to extraordinary threat value, while straightforward alternatives often exist but are costly to implement due to production chain complexity and regulatory requirements. Of course, for opponents of proportionality, threat value is precisely the point of injunctions.[72] If proportionality is to have any meaning in practice, it should be capable of limiting threat value in appropriate cases but leaving it intact in other cases to maintain the integrity of the patent system. In my view, this can be done without recourse to economic theories of holdup or scrutiny of the patentee's ultimate interest in enforcement, as is sometimes suggested in the literature. Instead, the principle of commensurate scope should serve as guidance to distinguish between cases, as further elaborated in section 6.3.

3.2.5. Standard Essential Patents and Patent Ambush

As noted above, the telecoms industry is notable for the prevalence of standards development organisations (SDOs), which formulate technical standards that allow interoperability between devices, even if from different manufacturers.

[70] Cotter et al (n 65) 1551.

[71] For an example, see *Virgin Atlantic v Premium Aircraft* [2009] EWCA Civ 1513, para 30.

[72] Mary-Rose McGuire, an academic expert heard by the German parliament, likened it to a price increase in case of fare evasion: Transcript (n 45) 8.

SDOs have proven effective fora for the joint development processes typically required to establish technical standards while also avoiding anticommons problems. They do so by requiring, from each participating organisation, disclosure of patents relevant to the standard, and a commitment to license them on FRAND terms. Patents that read to a technical standard are known as SEPs. In a landmark case, the ECJ held that the holder of a SEP may only obtain an injunction if they 'comply with conditions which seek to ensure a fair balance between the interests concerned'.[73] In brief, those conditions include making the infringer a licence offer on FRAND terms, provided the infringer has expressed their willingness to conclude a licence on such terms. As a practical matter, this substantially mitigates the risk of patent holdup because so long as an infringer conducts itself as a willing licensee, it is shielded from an injunction. Conversely, at least in theory, no proportionality concerns should arise if an infringer is not a willing licensee, as that implies opportunistic behaviour, which may bar a proportionality plea (with the possible exception of third-party rights concerns: section 6.5.3.1). This is not to suggest that the European approach to SEP enforcement operates flawlessly: continental European courts have been criticised for applying the *Huawei* framework so strictly that its safeguards for the infringer are practically meaningless and in any event many open questions remain.[74] For the purposes of this book, however, such issues should be addressed through clarifying and improving the existing *Huawei* framework and not through the additional application of a proportionality doctrine.[75]

The proportionality test will nevertheless have a role to play in cases involving SEPs that fall outside the scope of the *Huawei* framework. This might occur, for instance, if the SEP holder does not hold a dominant market position within the meaning of Article 102 of the Treaty on the Functioning of the European Union (TFEU)[76] or when targeting suppliers. Some authors have argued that a FRAND commitment may not extend to every party interested in the technology and that excluded parties 'cannot nurture any legitimate expectations' obtaining a FRAND licence.[77] This is certainly true, but contrary to what these authors assert, it is not apparent that excluded parties 'will benefit from the *Huawei v ZTE* negotiation

[73] Case C-170/13 *Huawei Technologies* ECLI:EU:C:2015:477, para 55.

[74] At the time of writing, the European Commission is considering the implementation of SEP-specific legislation which would address many of these issues: Commission, 'Proposal for a regulation of the European Parliament and of the Council on standard essential patents and amending Regulation (EU)2017/1001' COM(2023) 232 final.

[75] For a different view, see P Picht and J Contreras, 'Proportionality Defenses in FRAND Cases – A Comparative Assessment of the Revised German Patent Injunction Rules and US Case Law' (2023) 72 *Gewerblicher Rechtsschutz und Urheberrecht International* 435, 447 (arguing that there should be room for an additional proportionality assessment at least in those cases where the infringer's FRAND defence is rejected without considering whether the patentee's licensing offer is in fact FRAND).

[76] This condition had 'not been contested' in the case that came before the ECJ, so that it is unclear whether a SEP automatically confers dominance on the holder: *Huawei* (n 73) para 43.

[77] J-S Borghetti, I Nikolic and N Petit, 'FRAND Licensing Levels under EU Law' (2021) *European Competition Journal* 1, 216.

framework' 'in the context of injunction proceedings', since the applicability of that framework depends on the same legitimate expectations these authors claim excluded parties cannot nurture.[78] Furthermore, some SDOs are witnessing a trend of 'negative letters of assurance', a rather unfortunate misnomer for a declaration of SEPs without committing to the SDO's FRAND policy.[79] Whether the *Huawei* framework will apply to such SEPs remains to be seen. SEP holders might also attempt to circumvent the *Huawei* framework and their obligations under it in various ways. A practice that has received some attention in the literature (but was allowed by a German court) is to divest part of a SEP portfolio to outside entities under royalty-sharing agreements to increase the aggregate royalty yield, possibly beyond FRAND levels.[80] SEP holders could sue customers to put pressure on manufacturers 'at terms they might not otherwise accept'.[81] They could seek a preliminary injunction under a complementary non-SEP to force the infringer to accept a licence agreement, again possibly on non-FRAND terms.[82] In sum, it is not evident that the *Huawei* framework will apply in all cases where SEPs are enforced and, if it does not, those cases should fall within the ambit of a proportionality test.

A final intersection between SEPs and proportionality is where an SDO member strategically conceals its patent position so that, after adoption of the standard, they may assert non-FRAND-encumbered patents to extract higher royalties. This practice is known as patent ambush.[83] Rambus, a semiconductor NPE, gained worldwide notoriety for its attempted patent ambushes. In the early 1990s, it took part in SDO meetings, then left the SDO and filed divisional applications to cover specifically the technology that was to be incorporated in the standard.[84] When it asserted those patents in the USA, Rambus's reliance on this tactic, while not amounting to unclean hands, was an important reason to deny it injunctive relief.[85] In Europe, Rambus's conduct was investigated by the European Commission as a violation of Article 102 TFEU, which ended with Rambus committing to put a cap on the royalties it would seek.[86] Even if patent ambush is a rare occurrence, the Rambus saga illustrates two points made in this

[78] ibid 216–17. See expressly *Huawei* (n 73) paras 53, 59.

[79] K Gupta and G Effraimidis, 'An Empirical Examination of Impact' (2019) 64 *The Antitrust Bulletin* 151, 163–64.

[80] D Geradin, 'European Union Competition Law, Intellectual Property Law and Standardization' in J Contreras (ed), *The Cambridge Handbook of Technical Standardization Law Competition, Antitrust, and Patents* (Cambridge University Press, 2018) 90–91.

[81] ibid.

[82] *Ericsson v Apple* (n 63) para 4.30.

[83] Cotter et al (n 65) 1541.

[84] *Rambus Inc v Infineon Technologies AG* 318 F3d 1081, 1107 (Fed Cir 2003). While the district court had held that this conduct amounted to fraud, the majority on appeal did not, though it did find that 'such actions impeach Rambus' business ethics' (1104).

[85] *Hynix Semiconductors Inc v Rambus Inc* 609 FSupp2d 951, 985 (ND Cal 2009).

[86] *RAMBUS* (Case COMP/38.636) Commission Decision C(2009) 7610 [2010] OJ C30/17.

chapter well. First, if patent law does not take account of the realities in which the patent system operates, dysfunctional incentives may be created for patentees. Second, precisely because the strategic behaviour of players like Rambus does not necessarily amount to sanctionable abuse under Article 102 TFEU, a proportionality test is a necessary check on such behaviour. How it may do so is addressed in detail in section 6.4.

3.2.6. Non-practising Entities

Surely no perceived problem of contemporary patent law has so captivated scholars and the public at large as NPEs, or 'patent trolls', which have generated not only stacks of scholarship, but also newspaper attention, podcasts and documentaries, and even their own emoji.[87] Although the definition is disputed, the epithet NPE generally refers to entities that enforce patents without themselves practising them, ie without bringing to market products that incorporate the patented technology. Such entities include firms buying up patents with the purpose of monetising them through enforcement, but also small inventors, universities and IP divisions of multinational companies. In light of their notoriety in the public imagination, it is unsurprising that NPEs featured prominently throughout the German patent reform process, particularly in the position papers of the Big Tech–automotive alliance and the parliamentary debates. One could say that NPEs have become a rallying cry for critics of the patent system and eponymous for the various problems they perceive with it.

Whether NPEs as such are worrisome depends on one's view of the patent system. If one understands its utilitarian premise as being strictly oriented towards the domestic production of useful technologies, as exemplified by historical working requirements, then the case can be made that patentees who themselves contribute nothing towards this production ought not, through patent assertions, tax others that do. But this understanding has a high argumentative burden to meet because it is undeniable that non-manufacturing, R&D-focused entities of various kinds can and do make important contributions to innovation.[88] And the dominant view today seems to be that it is not possible to reliably distinguish between 'good' and 'bad' NPEs.[89] The aforementioned example of Rambus illustrates this

[87] The most thorough study on the subject to date is M Stierle, *Das nicht-praktizierte Patent* (Mohr Siebeck, 2018), who provides an extensive overview of the literature. See further I Glass, 'When Patents Attack!' (*This American Life*, 22 July 2011) www.thisamericanlife.org/441/when-patents-attack; A Meyer (dir), *The Patent Scam* (Genesis Studios, 2017); B Knott, 'A New Emoji for the IP World – the Emoji Troll Is Born' (*IPKat*, 20 May 2022) https://ipkitten.blogspot.com/2022/05/a-new-emoji-for-ip-worldthe-emoji-troll.html.

[88] Barnett, *Innovators, Firms, and Markets* (n 56) 129.

[89] D Geradin, A Layne-Farrar and J Padilla, 'Elves or Trolls? The Role of Nonpracticing Patent Owners in the Innovation Economy' (2012) 21 *Industrial and Corporate Change* 73, 90; M Lemley and DA Melamed, 'Missing the Forest for the Trolls' (2013) 113 *Columbia Law Review* 2117, 2125–26; Stierle, *Das nicht-praktizierte Patent* (n 87) 23–34.

well: it is an NPE with a track record of strategic litigation, but it is also a leading innovator in the semiconductor industry that annually invests very large sums in R&D. It is thus more accurate and productive to focus on the flaws in the patent system that opportunistic actors – whether NPEs or not – seek to exploit. In the USA, these include high litigation costs, the absence of fee shifting outside exceptional cases, potentially high damages awards and swathes of broad patents of doubtful validity.[90] These features of the US patent system make it attractive for 'bottom feeding trolls', entities hoping to 'induce parties to settle for small amounts of money rather than pay millions to their lawyers' and which have attracted the most attention in policy debates.[91] But European systems differ significantly on each of these points.[92] Fighting dubious patent claims is a feasible strategy in jurisdictions where it will be a rare case where 'millions' are spent on lawyers. At the same time, Germany's patent system has its own weakness – bifurcation – that is also prone to exploitation. Bifurcation no doubt contributes significantly to the finding that while NPE suits in Europe seem to be rising, the majority of these suits are filed in Germany.[93] Again, this proves the point that the practising/non-practising status of a patentee is far less relevant than the systemic weaknesses they seek to exploit.

In my view, therefore, the practising/non-practising status of the patentee should receive limited, if any, weight in a proportionality analysis.[94] That also seems to be the dominant opinion among European patent courts.[95] The main exception are requests for preliminary injunctions, which in most European jurisdictions (and contrary to permanent injunctions) are granted on a balance of convenience. It seems reasonable to assume, as several courts have, that NPEs generally do not have an urgent interest in injunctive relief because the infringement harms them so irreparably that they cannot await the outcome of merits proceedings.[96]

[90] Lemley and Melamed (n 89) 2173–77.

[91] ibid 2126.

[92] I Nikolic, 'Are Patent Assertion Entities a Threat to Europe?' (2019) 14 *Journal of Intellectual Property Law & Practice* 477, 481; B Love et al, 'Patent Assertion Entities in Europe' in DD Sokol (ed), *Patent Assertion Entities and Competition Policy* (Cambridge University Press, 2017) 115; S Fusco, 'Markets and Patent Enforcement: A Comparative Investigation of Non-practicing Entities in the United States and Europe' (2014) 20 *Michigan Telecommunications and Technology Law Review* 439, 454.

[93] Darts-IP, 'NPE Litigation in the European Union: Facts and Figures' (February 2018) https://clarivate.com/lp/npe-litigation-in-the-european-union-facts-and-figures/ (finding an increase in 'NPE-related actions' from 56 in 2007 to 173 in 2017; most of these suits were filed in Germany); N Thumm, 'The Good, the Bad and the Ugly – the Future of Patent Assertion Entities in Europe' (2018) 30 *Technology Analysis & Strategic Management* 1046, 1051 ('Whilst the large size of the German market is probably a contributing factor, this choice also reflects a deliberate attempt to exploit Germany's bifurcated patent system').

[94] The same is true for the practised/not-practised status of individual patents, which Stierle, *Das nicht-praktizierte Patent* (n 87) has argued extensively is a better measure of potential abuse. However, shifting the focus from entities to patents creates problems of its own: Lemley and Melamed (n 89) 2171.

[95] OLG Düsseldorf 13 January 2016, I-15 U 65/15 (*Zwangsvollstreckung*), para 17; GH The Hague 2 July 2019, ECLI:NL:GHDHA:2019:3613 (*Philips v Wiko*), para 4.61; Cour d'Appel de Paris 15 December 2004, 03/12780 *GIE Marechal v STE Proconect*, 15; *HTC* (n 63) para 54–56.

[96] GH The Hague 17 March 2020, ECLI:NL:GHDHA:2020:711 (*Sisvel v Xiaomi*), para 4.15; Tribunal Judiciaire de Paris 20 January 2020, 19/60318 *IPCom v Lenovo*, 16.

3.2.7. Broad Claims and De Facto Essentiality

A wholly different problem that is rarely addressed in the proportionality literature are so-called broad claims, which rose to prominence as a result of breakthrough developments in biotechnology and other fields. Broad claims define an invention in functional as opposed to structural terms. Thus, they delineate inventions by what they *do* instead of what they *are*, so they have a potentially very wide scope because they cover any embodiment of the invention that possesses the claimed functionality, including embodiments undiscovered at the priority date. Such claims raise potential sufficiency issues (Article 83 EPC) if the patent application does not enable the skilled person to make substantially all embodiments falling within the claim.[97] It is commonly assumed that sufficiency requirements were long applied loosely to stimulate the growth of the underlying technologies, but are now being applied more strictly, which follows precisely the pattern discussed in section 3.1.3. More fundamentally, broad claims capture perfectly the old dilemma of optimal claim scope: breakthrough inventions warrant patents with a broad scope, but a broad scope inhibits follow-up innovation.[98]

From the perspective of proportionality, broad claims raise two issues that relate to the accidental infringement problem discussed in section 3.2.1. First, they create a novel type of search problem because, as a technical matter, it may be very difficult to establish whether a proposed product falls within the claim scope. This problem has been signalled in relation to antibody claims: often the only way to determine whether a substance or antibody performs a function within the claimed range requires conducting experiments, and these can be very costly. Here, search problems are caused not so much by patent thickets – though those certainly do not help – as by the technical difficulty of ascertaining claim scope. The problem is not unique to biotechnology and antibodies patents, but they have been the site of most conflicts so far. Another area of technology affected by this problem is polymers (which, as Table 3.1 shows, have also seen increased patenting). Plastics producers compete primarily on improving the strength of their materials, but the strength is determined by the structure of the polymers, ie the precise way in which the molecules are chained together. As a technical matter, however, it is impossible to observe the polymer structure of a material beyond identification of the molecules used. Patent claims seeking protection for plastics with improved strength are often difficult to write and even harder to interpret for outsiders not privy to the patentee's know-how. Thus, practically speaking, when faced with broad claims, it may be very difficult to take the reasonable precautions Goold advocates, raising in particular the question of what can still be considered 'reasonable' in this context.

[97] *Regeneron Pharmaceutical v Kymab Ltd* [2020] UKSC 27, para 56.

[98] R Merges and R Nelson, 'On the Complex Economics of Patent Scope' (1990) 90 *Columbia Law Review* 839, 908–09.

Second, broad claims raise the distinct possibility of infringement that is not just accidental but also superfluous to the infringing product. Although this may be a rare occurrence in practice, at least in theory it is possible that an antibody or compound is developed for a different purpose but coincidentally also performs the claimed function. In a clear-cut case, the correct approach would likely be to deny infringement, in line with an old decision of the Dutch Supreme Court that there can be no infringement where the invention's purpose is not achieved.[99] But I suspect it is quite possible that functional claiming will yield cases that are less clear-cut. Such cases are all the more plausible because sufficiency remains a poorly understood ground of invalidity and applicants evidently seek to make their claims as broad as possible. It is much easier to isolate antibodies today than it was when the field was younger so that broad claims no longer seem warranted, and those granted can have a palpable blocking effect.[100]

More plausibly, because broad patents cover an entire area of technology once discovered, competitors may be precluded from developing follow-up innovations. Another instance of this problem is 'de facto essential' technology, ie technology not subject to a formal standard but nevertheless indispensable to operate in a market due to its widespread adoption.[101] Of course, some view the ability to control downstream innovation as the very purpose of the patent system. And both patent law (dependency licences) and competition law (essential facilities doctrine) make provision for this problem, albeit on very strict conditions. But if a competitor independently develops a superior technology and infringement of a broad patent is either accidental or based on a reasonable assumption of non-infringement, a case could be made for lower standards to ensure continued access for the public to the infringer's superior technology.

3.2.8. Conflicts with Third Party Rights

The field of tension between the interests of patentees and those of third parties dependent on the infringing technology goes back to patent law's beginnings. Patent law itself contains various provisions to safeguard the interests of third parties, most notably compulsory licensing provisions. Despite insistence by opponents that these provisions suffice, the outcome of the GPA reform is that third-party interests must (also) be taken into account in the proportionality test. One of the arguments advanced in favour of this solution is that the ECJ's

[99] HR NJ 1942/519; ECLI:NL:HR:1942:170 (*Handley Page v KLM*).

[100] Compare L Druedahl et al, 'A Qualitative Study of Biosimilar Manufacturer and Regulator Perceptions on Intellectual Property and Abbreviated Approval Pathways' (2020) 38 *Nature Biotechnology* 1253, 254 (finding, based on 25 interviews with industry stakeholders and regulators, that 'the patent landscape for originator biologics led to considerable uncertainty and risk for biosimilar companies').

[101] Nikolic, *Licensing Standard Essential Patents* (n 69) 14 cites as examples Microsoft's '.doc' format for text files and the QWERTY layout of keyboards.

proportionality case law requires it. Section 5.3.3 shows that this is correct and it was also accepted by courts in France, the Netherlands and Italy.[102] At least in continental European jurisdictions, the duty to take account of third-party rights when issuing relief is new, as patent courts have traditionally assumed otherwise.[103] It is a development that aligns well with diffusion concerns and the 'new politics' lens on patent law discussed in section 1.1.1. However, the question arises how the consideration of third-party rights at the remedies stage relates to the ex post corrective traditionally relied on to balance patent exclusivity against the public interest: compulsory licences.

It is sometimes argued that exempting acts of patent infringement from the injunction in the interest of third parties is equivalent to the grant of a compulsory licence and should thus be allowed only when the (strict) conditions for such a grant are met.[104] I believe this is incorrect. There are several doctrinal distinctions between the compulsory licences and a proportionality test, as also acknowledged by the German legislator.[105] Thus, whereas a compulsory licence exonerates its recipient from any liability for infringement, the proportionality test cannot negate the act of infringement so that liability for damages and even compensation for the specific duration the injunction is denied remain. Those damages, moreover, are not capped at a reasonable remuneration, as is the case with compulsory licences, but can also take the form of a disgorgement of profits. The scope of a proportionality test is narrow and limited to specific infringing devices, while a compulsory licence constitutes a broad permission to use patented technology, including, for example, improvements of an initial product. Because of these differences, grants of compulsory licences must satisfy the requirements of Article 31 of the Agreement on Trade-Related Aspects of Intellectual Property Rights (TRIPS)[106], whereas applying a proportionality test arguably does not. Article 44(1) TRIPS, which governs injunctive relief, states only that courts shall have the authority to issue an injunction, not that they are obligated to do so in every case.[107] Lastly, the proportionality test derives from EU law and is partially harmonised through the Enforcement Directive, whereas the grounds for the grant of a compulsory licence differ between Member States, with the Unified Patent Court (UPC) lacking any authority to grant them.

[102] Cass civ (1) 15 May 2015, 13–27.391; HR 3 April 2015, ECLI:NL:HR:2015:841 (*GeenStijl v Sanoma*); TO Torino 16 June 2021, 10009/2020 (*Edwards Lifesciences v Meril Life Sciences*), 3.

[103] HR NJ 1996/462; ECLI:NL:HR:1995:ZC1705 (*Boehringer Mannheim v Kirin Amgen*), para 3.7; LG Düsseldorf BeckRS 2017, 104662; 4a O 28/16 *Herzklappen*, para IV.2.b.

[104] *Evalve v Edwards Lifesciences* [2020] EWHC 513 (Pat), para 51; LG München BeckRS 2019, 11305; 7 O 10261/18 *Steuerventil*, para 61.

[105] Proposed Bill (n 9) 55. See M Stierle, 'Patent Injunctions – Identifying Common Elements' (2019) 11 *Zeitschrift für geistiges Eigentum* 334, 355–56.

[106] Agreement Establishing the World Trade Organization (Marrakesh, 15 April 1994) 33 ILM 619, Annex 1C.

[107] G Dinwoodie and R Dreyfuss, 'Injunctive Relief under Patent Law and TRIPS' in J Contreras and M Husovec (eds), *Injunctions in Patent Law* (Cambridge University Press, 2022) 15 (though expressing some reservation about the applicability of Art 31 TRIPS to denials of injunctive relief).

The difference between the proportionality test and compulsory licences can also be appreciated by looking at their function and scope. As argued in the previous chapter, the proportionality test embodies the principle of commensurate scope at the remedies stage. By contrast, compulsory licences serve to (exceptionally) boost diffusion of patented technologies. Consequently, the two instruments operate differently. While the proportionality test checks whether the effective sphere of exclusivity is commensurate with the inventive contribution, the compulsory licence operates within a variation of the diffusion paradigm. Ostensibly a balancing tool, compulsory licences in fact focus only on one specific interest: the public interest. So long as the public interest in diffusion of technology weighs sufficiently heavy, a compulsory licence will be granted, in principle regardless of the patentee's interest. For instance, it is entirely imaginable that a country would grant a compulsory licence to treatments of COVID-19 (and many considered doing so between 2019 and 2021), even if it knew that the patentee made substantial investments in the technology that it needs to recoup. This makes the grant of compulsory licences arguably even more constrained than tests for gross disproportionality: the granting authority must be satisfied that the public interest at stake is so urgent that it outweighs any imaginable interest on the side of the patentee. By contrast, a proportionality test as proposed here is principally concerned with the relationship between the patented and infringing technology, and thus comprises an entirely different inquiry.

These differences notwithstanding, it is clear that a long-term denial of injunctive relief is, in practical terms, equivalent to the grant of a compulsory licence. I therefore suggest, in section 6.5.3.2, that in the specific case of longer stays to protect third-party interests, the weight of those interests should be such that they would justify the grant of a compulsory licence. But consideration as part of the proportionality test does not require these interests to have a particular social significance, as is often required for compulsory licence grants.[108] To the contrary: the ECJ's fair balance jurisprudence, which is the basis for consideration of third-party interests as part of the proportionality test, sets a specific and apparently lower standard for the limitation of injunctive relief. Because the proportionality test gives courts considerable freedom to tailor the injunction to the specific circumstances of the case, it can yield outcomes that traverse the infringer's proportionality claim as well as the rights of third parties in a manner compulsory licences could not. That includes, in particular, short-term stays to avoid harms that may not be very significant on the individual level, but that are large in the aggregate. In addition, section 6.5.2 argues that there are different classes of third-party interests raising different concerns under the proportionality test, and what is referred to there as 'non-party interests' would hardly be cognisable under most

[108] eg in the Netherlands: Minister of Economic Affairs BIE 1981, 185 (*Weidepomp*) (compulsory licence grants limited to cases where their grant would promote policy goals pursued by the government, which must not lightly be given preference over patent exclusivity).

compulsory licensing regimes. Conversely, many such regimes expressly provide for political decisions on the national or regional importance of an infringing technology, ie consideration of a more abstract public interest. For instance, in 2010, MSD planned to lay off 2175 people in Oss, a Dutch city in a rural region where its subsidiary Organon was based, by closing and relocating the company's R&D division. This would have been a tremendous blow to the region's employment and innovative capacities, and in response, the government contemplated granting a compulsory licence under MSD's patents so that Organon's activities could continue.[109] Ultimately, the licence was not granted because the reorganisation was prevented, but it illustrates well the use that can be made of a compulsory licence outside the realm of health crises to pursue strategic or economic goals of political importance. In fact, part of the reason European states agreed to the EPC in the first place was that they would retain a measure of autonomy through compulsory licensing regimes.[110] These regimes are thus an important backstop on matters of strategic importance for countries, which are not for courts to consider in the context of a proportionality test.

A final difference between the proportionality test and compulsory licences is that a court applying a proportionality test will have heard and considered all the parties' infringement and, in non-bifurcated proceedings, validity arguments. This gives courts an understanding of the specifics of the case that is hard for any parallel institution to obtain. Nevertheless, tasking an outside agency or different court with the decision to limit injunctive relief through the grant of a compulsory licence would result in duplicative litigation and associated complications. To point out some of the more arresting ones: should infringement proceedings be stayed pending consideration of the compulsory licensing request?[111] Would positions taken by either party prejudice their position in the parallel proceedings? In particular, should the request for a compulsory licence by the infringer be construed as an admission of infringement? In a recent case, Germany's Federal Patent Court granted a provisional compulsory licence to Shionogi's raltegravir patent, but in parallel proceedings, the High Court in England invalidated the English part of Merck's patent for lack of inventive step and insufficiency.[112] Yet the Federal Patent Court ruled that a remuneration under the compulsory licence was due even if the patent was later revoked – in other words, even if it turned out the applicant never needed it in the first place.[113] That outcome seems undesirable from a policy perspective, as it rewards holders that use invalid patents to block the production of goods that are so essential that they warrant the grant of a compulsory licence. Then again, does failure to

[109] Minister of Economic Affairs, Letter of 14 September 2010, Kamerstukken II 29 544, Nr 261, 3.

[110] J Pila, 'The European Patent: An Old and Vexing Problem' (2013) 62 *International & Comparative Law Quarterly* 917, 927.

[111] A stay request was denied in LG Düsseldorf GRUR 2022, 1665; 4c O 18/21 *Sofosbuvir*, C.II.

[112] *Merck, Sharp and Dohme Ltd v Shionogi & Co Ltd* [2016] EWHC 2989 (Pat).

[113] BPatG GRUR 2018, 803; 3 Li 1/16 (EP) *Zwangslizenz für AIDS-Medikament*, para 1(c).

request a compulsory licence preclude consideration of proportionality arguments or third-party interests? This seems to be the view in Germany.[114] In my opinion, this is incorrect, inter alia because it puts the infringer at an important disadvantage and may even require them to pay royalties despite invalidation of the patent. Perhaps it would be possible to construe a system of shared competence between courts and an administrative agency that solves these and the various other issues it gives rise to in a satisfactory manner, but I am doubtful. Whether any of these arrangements would stand up to scrutiny from the ECJ, which requires that courts remain fully competent to review all circumstances of the dispute, is (yet) another matter.

3.3. Is Proportionality the Answer?

3.3.1. Arguments against Proportionality

My attempt has been to start from objective, or at least more or less universally recognised, statements about the patent system (section 3.1) and to connect these to the problems they might cause in contemporary practice (section 3.2). As was also observed by one of the experts that appeared before the German parliament, there seems to be consensus on surprisingly many counts.[115] It is undeniable that patent density and patent creep keep increasing, and most stakeholders acknowledge that, as a result, patent clearance searches are becoming more difficult to perform. I suspect most commentators would recognise that it is unacceptable for patent exclusivity to put patients' lives at risk. And everyone agrees that patent injunctions can have enormous threat value – though they may disagree whether that is good or bad. I conclude this chapter by examining some of the objections against a proportionality test frequently expressed by its opponents.

During the GPA reform, the near-universal position among those opposing the introduction of a proportionality test was that it was an opportunistic attempt by large players from two big and politically well-connected industries to weaken patent protection and lower their costs. There is certainly truth to this allegation. After all, the automotive industry was the main driver of the reform process, and efforts of the tech industry to weaken patent protection have been extensively documented.[116] These observations are consistent with the preference of large, vertically integrated businesses addressed in section 1.2. But we also saw that some small companies supported a proportionality exception. Patentverein and

[114] *Sofosbuvir* (n 111) C.II; K Grabinski, 'Injunctive Relief and Proportionality in Case of a Public Interest in the Use of a Patent: Different Ways – Same Result' [2021] *Gewerblicher Rechtsschutz und Urheberrecht* 200, 202.

[115] Transcript (n 45) 9 (Ansgar Ohly).

[116] Barnett, *Innovators, Firms, and Markets* (n 56) ch 7.

the coalition of German inventors, for instance, feared 'layoffs and bankruptcies' for smaller companies, and the risk that deep-pocketed industry giants could 'ruin' these businesses. During the parliamentary hearing, the automotive industry's representative stated that his coalition represented 'over 600' smaller suppliers.[117] The picture is thus a bit more nuanced than opponents might suggest. More fundamentally, adopting a proportionality test does not become a bad idea just because it is favoured by some big companies. The whole purpose of the consultation was to get their and others' views, and it is understandable that they argue for a solution that best serves their business needs, just as opponents do. If the analysis presented in section 1.2 is correct, injunctions may threaten disproportionate outcomes across industries and business models, and companies' individual preferences will shift over time. It is therefore not surprising that, looking at the stakeholder positions in their entirety, there seemed to be broad support for a cautious middle ground.

The search should therefore be for proper calibration of the proportionality test. But opponents fear that its mere codification will open the proverbial floodgates to proportionality arguments in every case, raising costs of litigation and ultimately weakening patent protection.[118] This argument does not strike me as very compelling. First, cases where a plausible proportionality argument arises have been rare, even since the reform, and that is not expected to change. The law provides for many other exemptions from infringement liability besides proportionality, but none of them is argued very often, let alone in every case. It is hard to see why this would be different for proportionality, especially because the onus is on the infringer to substantiate its proportionality argument. If the infringer cannot do so, as is expected in the majority of cases, courts can and will give the argument short shrift.[119] Second, judicious application of a proportionality test ought not weaken patent rights. SMEs and bigger innovators expressed concerns about counterfeits, but it is hard to imagine a proportionality argument succeeding in cases of wilful infringement. Pharmaceutical companies expressed concerns about policy-oriented proportionality pleas, but those fall outside any proposed scope of the test. Instead, a successful proportionality argument will require a demonstrated set of circumstances that suggest an immediate injunction cannot be issued in all fairness. As we have seen, disregarding such circumstances risks creating perverse incentives. Conversely, it should not impair the incentive function of patents because the grant of an injunction will remain the norm and it seems implausible that a company would forego applying for a patent (let alone

[117] Transcript (n 45) 19 (Kurt-Christian Scheel).

[118] See, eg the testimony by Renate Weisse: ibid 19, 30–31. More generally, see J Contreras and M Husovec, 'Issuing and Tailoring Patent Injunctions: A Cross-Jurisdictional Comparison and Synthesis' in Contreras and Husovec (n 107) 339 ('The predominant concern of patent judges in EU countries seems to be opening the floodgates to a new avenue of pleading at the remedial stage').

[119] The point was also made by Fabian Hoffmann: Transcript (n 45) 24. This is consistent with the first German decisions on proportionality after adoption of §139 GPA, which do not dwell terribly long on the issue: *Sofosbuvir* (n 111) C.II; LG Düsseldorf OpenJur 2022, 14333; 4b O 7/22 *Fahrzeugdächer*, III.1.

pursuing some innovation) because it might face a successful proportionality argument in the future. Even if these intuitions are wrong, there is no indication that any benefits 'stronger' patent protection might yield will outweigh the avoidance of costs associated with disproportionate enforcement.

Incentives for holdout are a different matter. As stated in section 3.2.4, patentees frequently encounter difficulties when offering licensing agreements to implementers of their technology. Readers with experience representing licensor companies and particularly smaller NPEs will know that it is often extremely difficult to get prospective licensees to engage. It is a matter of common sense that, where costs of detection and enforcement are high, chances of success uncertain and penalties for infringement modest, infringers will have an incentive to take their chances. But sticking to an automatic injunction regime will not solve these problems. A better way to address them is through a dissuasive damages regime, which was initially discussed during the reform but later dropped, or through establishment of a court with Europe-wide jurisdiction, as has happened with the UPC. True, the threat of an injunction provides an important incentive for implementers to engage. But if the analysis in this chapter – and in the sizeable literature on which it builds – is correct, there are cases where that incentive is rather too strong, inducing implementers to overpay. That does not seem economically efficient and, more to the point of this book, clearly suggests a reward for the patentee that is not commensurate with its inventive contribution. With respect, just as we should not take claims about harmful effects of NPE enforcement and patent holdup at face value, we should be critical of claims that the European innovation ecosystem will break down the moment patent courts are afforded some degree of remedial discretion. After all, opponents of the proportionality test also ultimately act out of self-interest. The best way forward, then, seems to be the development of a proportionality test that takes account of the concerns on both sides of the debate, as is proposed in chapter six.

3.3.2. Disproportionate Injunctions

The general expectation is that cases where an injunction would be disproportionate will be rare. During the German parliamentary hearing, one expert estimated that in the past 15 years, there had been 'barely a handful' of instances of abusive enforcement, while German courts hear approximately 800 cases a year.[120] Stakeholders supporting a proportionality test did not refer to instances where they were subjected to an injunction they felt was disproportionate (at least not publicly) and their advocacy was driven by fears of abusive patent assertions in the future. That was also the impression I got from one industry group that lobbied for

[120] Transcript (n 45) 52, 9 (Mary-Rose McGuire). Another expert, Fabian Hoffmann, considered these numbers 'plausible' (24).

a strong proportionality exception, which I asked for instances where its members had suffered disproportionate consequences from an injunction. They could not cite any credible examples.[121] At first glance, then, it may seem that proportionality is a solution in search of a problem after all.

In my view, that conclusion would be premature for several reasons. First, fears of abusive litigation may just as well have consequences. For instance, in 2012, Microsoft decided to move its distribution centre from Germany to the Netherlands because it feared getting enjoined in patent proceedings initiated by Motorola.[122] Second, court decisions are a poor indicator of proportionality problems. If a company is faced with a high likelihood that an injunction will be granted, the most rational course of action is to settle proceedings before a decision is issued. Many stakeholders indicated that this is the reason we see so few decisions on proportionality, particularly by higher courts, as infringers will normally not be able to pursue appeals if faced with severe hardship. And settlement agreements will almost invariably be confidential. Thus, disproportionate outcomes may be hidden from sight if the most common outcome is a pre-decision settlement, which seems to be a plausible assumption.[123] Third, the fact that manifestly disproportionate injunctions are not a systemic problem does not mean that they can never occur.[124] It goes to the heart of proportionality that it applies only in small numbers of cases, and if my conclusions in this chapter are correct, it is at least conceivable that such cases may arise, perhaps even with increasing frequency. I end this chapter with some historical examples.

The 1985 injunction issued in the USA against Kodak for infringement of Polaroid's instant photography patent is perhaps the most chronicled patent injunction of all time. The injunction forced Kodak out of the instant photography business, resulted in a massive recall campaign, and led to the reassignment of 800 full-time workers from its US manufacturing site.[125] Twenty years later,

[121] The group referred to LG München OpenJur 2019, 41364; 7 O 16945/15 *Software zur Verwaltung digitaler Bilder*, where an NPE had obtained an injunction against Yahoo, as a result of which the picture service Flickr was unavailable on mobile devices for a period of about two months (it remained available on desktop computers). The Flickr help forum contains a post dated 31 May 2016 announcing: 'We're sorry to share that as a result of a patent infringement injunction issued by a German Court, you will no longer be able to upload photos to your Flickr app via iOS & Android or through the Flickr mobile web page. You can still upload photos to your Flickr account from your desktop computer, and we encourage you to do so.' See www.flickr.com/help/forum/en-us/72157668329100100/. This hardly strikes me as disproportionate hardship on the users' part.

[122] M Palmer, 'Microsoft to Move Out of Germany' *Financial Times* (2 April 2012) www.ft.com/content/08b5913c-7ce2-11e1-a676-00144feab49a. Microsoft stated that 'We would have preferred to keep our European distribution centre … in Germany, as it has been for many years, but unfortunately the risk of disruption from Motorola's patent litigation is simply too high.'

[123] Compare M Lemley, K Richardson and E Oliver, 'The Patent Enforcement Iceberg' (2019) 97 *Texas Law Review* 801, 807 (finding that, in a US sample, 70% of assertions were settled without a lawsuit being filed).

[124] Cotter et al (n 65) 1547.

[125] D Gellene, 'Ruling Forces Kodak to Quit Instant Camera Field' *LA Times* (9 January 1986) www.latimes.com/archives/la-xpm-1986-01-09-fi-14373-story.html.

the District Court of the Hague issued a comparably impactful injunction against Cordis, a medical device manufacturer with a production plant in a rural part of the Netherlands.[126] A local court halted the enforcement of the injunction because it would result in termination of four production lines and hundreds of layoffs, but the stay was reversed on appeal.[127] Shortly after the appeal judgment, Cordis announced it would lay off 462 people as a direct result.[128] These are undeniably hard cases because, as severe as the consequences may appear, the very essence of a patent is to offer a right to exclude in precisely these types of cases. Some celebrate the Polaroid decision for its 'demonstration effect on the market', which 'undoubtedly strengthened patent owners' hand in negotiating licensing terms with potential partners in the commercialization process'.[129] Maybe so. But Kodak reportedly could not have been more diligent while attempting to design around Polaroid's patents.[130] And in the Dutch case, the District Court's decision was reversed on appeal as Cordis was held not to infringe the patent.[131] This is not to suggest that these cases were wrongly decided, and there is an argument to be made that the hardship attributable to the injunction was not as severe as it might seem.[132] Still, they show that injunctions can have consequences that are difficult to reverse and that may not always be justified in light of the particulars of the case.

The best-known example from Germany is the aforementioned decision in *Wärmetauscher*. There, an inventor named Ludwig Schatzinger enforced a patent against Daimler, the producer of Mercedes-Benz cars. The patent related to a hot air blower in a car seat headrest, which Mercedes incorporates in its convertible cars as the AIRSCARF® feature. In first and second instance, Daimler successfully fended off Schatzinger's infringement claim. But the Federal Supreme Court reached a different conclusion and, as a result, Daimler was forced to instantly cease all sales of cars incorporating the AIRSCARF® feature.[133] The parties quickly settled and the case offers unique insight into the amount paid by Daimler because it was so high that it had to be listed in its 2016 annual report: €64 million.[134] At the time of writing, the AIRSCARF® feature is offered as an

[126] RB The Hague BIE 2007/13, ECLI:NL:RBSGR:2005:BA0329 (*Schneider v Cordis*).

[127] RB Assen NJF 2005, 291;ECLI:NL:RBASS:2005:AT8164 (*Cordis v Schneider*); GH Leeuwarden 12 NJF 2005, 446; ECLI:NL:GHLEE:2005:AU4338 (*Schneider v Cordis*).

[128] Editorial, 'Meer ontslagen bij Cordis in Roden' *NRC Handelsblad* (21 October 2005) www.nrc.nl/nieuws/2005/10/21/meer-ontslagen-bij-cordis-in-roden-11032009-a768204.

[129] Barnett, *Innovators, Firms, and Markets* (n 56) 75.

[130] *Polaroid Corp v Eastman Kodak Co* 1990 WL 324105, *79 (D Mass 11 January 1991) (finding that the record 'shows a patent clearance process that could serve as a model for what the law requires').

[131] GH The Hague 15 March 2007, ECLI:NL:GHSGR:2007:BA1903 (*Cordis v Schneider*).

[132] The *LA Times* reported that 'Investment analysts said Kodak wouldn't suffer much as a result of its decision to withdraw' (n 125). Cordis relocated all of its production facilities from the Netherlands to Mexico shortly after its success on appeal, citing competitive pressure and rising prices: Editorial, 'Doek valt voor Cordis Roden' *Groninger Internet Courant* (17 October 2007) www.gic.nl/nieuws/doek-valt-voor-cordis-roden-700-medewerkers-staan-op-straat.

[133] BGH GRUR 2016, 1031; X ZR 114/13 *Wärmetauscher*, paras 52–53.

[134] Daimler, 'Annual Report 2016', 104, https://group.mercedes-benz.com/documents/investors/reports/annual-report/daimler/daimler-ir-annualreport-2016.pdf.

add-on for convertible cars at a price of €533. There is thus no question that the settlement was driven by the injunction's threat value. During the parliamentary hearing, Judge Hoffmann cited this case as an example of overpayment: he stated that a patentee may well rely on an injunction to receive 'multiple times' what a 'normal license' would be, though not 'a thousand times'.[135] On the other hand, by repeatedly refusing to take out a licence, Daimler took a calculated risk that its non-infringement argument would be upheld by the Federal Supreme Court, and this is the archetypical case where a much smaller party is facing an industrial giant and may need injunctive relief to get them to engage. Thus, here, too, the point is not so much to argue that *Wärmetauscher* was wrongly decided as to show that, in practice, injunctions can have enormous threat value. If that is reason for concern (as I argue it is), courts should pay close attention to the circumstances surrounding the injunction's grant.[136]

Lastly, when it comes to third-party rights, the most infamous example is no doubt the *Hertzklappen* decision by the Düsseldorf regional court.[137] That case concerned transcatheter heart valves for patients suffering from serious heart defects, and the infringer argued that some patients could only be treated with their product. Parallel litigation in England (where the patent was held valid and infringed) resulted in a carved-out injunction to ensure patient safety.[138] Although the German court acknowledged that there existed differences between the patented and infringing heart valves and refused a recall on those grounds, it did not allow a future carve-out as the English court did simply because it held that consideration of third-party interests at the injunction stage was outside its scope of competence.[139] This decision was certainly the *bête noire* of the GPA reform process and Judge Hoffmann implicitly referenced it when pleading for extension of the proportionality proviso to third parties, saying it would prevent courts from having to sign orders that they knew would make real people 'suffer'.[140] With §139 GPA thus amended, there no longer seems to be any question that proportionality allows exceptions to patent exclusivity where patients' lives depend on the infringing technology. A more interesting case, also heard by the Düsseldorf court, concerned Sanofi's antibody drug Praeluent®. It was enjoined following an infringement suit brought by Amgen.[141] Insofar as I could establish, the decision in fact resulted in Sanofi stopping all supplies to the German market. Sanofi, however, had argued that its drug possessed superior properties to Amgen's, which

[135] Transcript (n 45) 28.

[136] Another example of a settlement driven by significant threat disparity is the 2013 settlement between IPCom and Deutsche Telekom, which allegedly ran into the 'low-to-medium triple-digit million euro' range: Editorial, 'IPCom Lands Cash Bonanza from D.Telekom Settlement-Sources' (Reuters, 3 July 2013) www.reuters.com/article/deutschetelekom-patent-idUSL5N0F72GN20130703.

[137] *Herzklappen* (n 103).

[138] *Edwards Lifesciences v Boston Scientific* [2018] EWHC 1256 (Pat), para 67.

[139] *Herzklappen* (n 103) para IV.2.b.

[140] Transcript (n 45) 25.

[141] LG Düsseldorf BeckRS 2019, 18224; 4c O 39/16 (*Monoklonaler Antikörper*).

resulted in a lower mortality rate. The Federal Supreme Court had declined to issue a compulsory licence on this ground and, consequently, the Düsseldorf court declined to take it into account during the hearing.[142] But, as argued above, compulsory licences and the proportionality defence are distinct, and there is no reason why clinical superiority should not be considered as part of the proportionality test, because depriving patients of a clinically superior treatment obviously directly impacts their access to healthcare rights. Once again, it is not clear that this case should have been decided differently: when asked about it during the hearing, Sanofi's counsel was apparently unable to name a single case where a switch to Amgen's product caused problems for patients.[143] As with the other examples, the point is merely to indicate that cases raising serious third-party interest concerns do arise and different circumstances may justify a different outcome.

In sum, there are certainly cases where one could have imagined a proportionality defence going either way. Following the observations in the preceding sections, this should not surprise us: *Wärmetauscher*, in particular, reflects many of the developments that the literature argues should give us pause in granting injunctive relief without more in every patent case. There is, however, another rich source of data on the real-world effects that patent injunctions might have and how courts, having the discretion to deny or limit or deny such injunctions, have responded. That source is the case law of US courts since 2006, to which I turn in the next chapter.

[142] BGH GRUR 2019, 1038; X ZB 2/19 *Alirocumab*, para 33.

[143] *Monoklonaler Antikörper* (n 141) para 97. Following the issuance of the injunction, a patient representation group (DACH) also mentioned in a press release that there should be no significant therapeutical differences between Sanofi's product and Amgen's.

4

Lessons from America: *eBay* and its Applications

We observed in the previous chapter that there are more patents in force today than at any other time in history and that this has the potential to cause problems. But are they likely to arise in practice? To complement my findings in chapter three, this chapter turns to what might be considered a natural experiment in remedial discretion for patent courts: decisions by lower US courts after the Supreme Court's 2006 decision in *eBay v MercExchange*.[1]

eBay heralded a seminal change in US patent law by abandoning what was close to an automatic injunction regime in favour of equitable discretion for district courts, to be exercised in accordance with a four-pronged test. After a discussion of the decision's context and outcome, its subsequent interpretation by the Court of Appeals for the Federal Circuit (CAFC) is analysed. The CAFC's case law is important because it outlines the US law of patent injunctions as it currently stands. But the heart of this chapter is a detailed analysis of 419 US district court decisions handed down between 2006 and 2020. Because the district courts are the only fact-finding instance in the US system, we need to look at their decisions to get a view of the circumstances under which US patentees sought injunctions in this period. The goal is not legal comparison: the vast differences in substantive patent law, procedural rules and institutional characteristics of courts between the USA and Europe would make it difficult to draw meaningful conclusions. Instead, I treat the decisions primarily as an empirical source, for they inform us of the fact patterns that arose before US courts and gave them pause about the grant of injunctive relief. Indeed, this collection of court cases may be the most objective source of information available to scholars on how patent injunctions affect parties, having been authored by a neutral but sophisticated party (a judge) after hearing extensive evidence on the issue. Even if there is probably some variance between the types of cases that make it to court between the USA and Europe, I consider it at least plausible that similar fact patterns could arise in Europe as well. The purpose of this chapter, then, is to offer support for the conclusions drawn in the previous chapter by looking at the considerations of US courts that led to the grant or not of injunctive relief in real-world patent cases.

[1] *eBay Inc v MercExchange LLC* 547 US 388 (2006).

Section 4.3 offers general statistics on the district court decisions studied, whereas section 4.4 analyses them in detail. The chapter's final section considers the lessons they contain for the European proportionality test. Bearing those lessons in mind, the book moves on to its third and final part, where it ties them together into a proportionality test firmly grounded in EU law.

4.1. A Shift in the Law of Patent Remedies: *eBay v MercExchange*

Before 2006, infringement of a valid patent more or less automatically resulted in an injunction under US patent law, much like the system in place in Europe today.[2] This had long been established practice, but around the turn of the century it had become the subject of criticism, and in 2005 a proposal for patent law reform that would have given district courts the discretion to deny injunctive relief was put before Congress.[3] Much like the case of German patent law reform, discussed in chapter one, these reform efforts were driven by industry stakeholders who saw their business models threatened by the strong rights of exclusion afforded to patentees.[4] These worries are reflected in the amicus briefs filed before the US Supreme Court in the case that led to the landmark decision in *eBay v MercExchange* and, as we will see, also motivated the justices in coming to their decision.

The *eBay* case concerned a patent on the creation of a secure online marketplace for used goods. MercExchange had itself tried to monetise it by launching a virtual marketplace, but failed. eBay, one of its competitors, launched a 'Buy it now' feature that infringed the patent. MercExchange filed suit and requested a permanent injunction. The district court held that the entitlement to an injunction is governed by traditional equitable principles and proceeded to apply them.[5] It concluded that although MercExchange's patent was valid and infringed, it had to be denied an injunction, and emphasised the fact that MercExchange did not practice the patent itself, its willingness to license it and growing concern over business method patents such as the one held by MercExchange.[6] On appeal, the Court of Appeals reversed, stating that 'the general rule is that a permanent

[2] *Richardson v Suzuki Motor Co, Ltd*, 868 F2d 1226, 1247 (Fed Cir 1989) ('It is the general rule that an injunction will issue when infringement has been adjudged, absent a sound reason for denying it').

[3] D Burk and M Lemley, *The Patent Crisis and How the Courts Can Solve It* (University of Chicago Press, 2009) 101. The earliest harbinger of change was probably a report by the Federal Trade Commission. 'To Promote Innovation: The Proper Balance of Competition and Patent Law Policy' (October 2003) www.ftc.gov/sites/default/files/documents/reports/promote-innovation-proper-balance-competition-and-patent-law-and-policy/innovationrpt.pdf.

[4] G Reilly, 'Patent Litigation Reform in the United States' in T Takenaka, *Research Handbook on Patent Law and Theory* (Edward Elgar, 2019) 378–79.

[5] *MercExchange LLC v eBay Inc* 275 FSupp26 695, 711 (ED Va 2003).

[6] ibid 712–14.

injunction will issue once infringement and validity have been adjudged'.[7] The US Supreme Court disagreed, and in a remarkably short opinion it laid down a four-factor test that it billed as 'the' traditional test for equitable relief, but in fact introduced a quite radical new regime.[8] This test is as follows:

> A plaintiff must demonstrate: (1) that it has suffered an irreparable injury; (2) that remedies available at law, such as monetary damages, are inadequate to compensate for that injury; (3) that, considering the balance of hardships between the plaintiff and defendant, a remedy in equity is warranted; and (4) that the public interest would not be disserved by a permanent injunction.[9]

According to the Supreme Court, 'Neither the District Court nor the Court of Appeals below fairly applied these traditional equitable principles in deciding respondent's motion for a permanent injunction'.[10] It held that, while the district court ostensibly applied the four-factor test for injunctive relief, it appeared to adopt a categorical rule according to which a certain class of patentees – those who do not practice the invention – would not suffer irreparable harm. This was impermissible, according to the Supreme Court, because 'traditional equitable principles do not permit such broad classifications'. The Court of Appeals, on the other hand, had 'departed in the opposite direction from the four-factor test' by articulating a general rule, unique to patent disputes. The Supreme Court concluded that 'Just as the District Court erred in its categorical denial of injunctive relief, the Court of Appeals erred in its categorical grant of such relief'.[11] Instead, 'the decision whether to grant or deny injunctive relief rests within the equitable discretion of the district courts, and … such discretion must be exercised consistent with traditional principles of equity'.

Two concurring opinions were issued: one by Justice Roberts, who was joined by Justices Scalia and Ginsburg, the other by Justice Kennedy, who was joined by Justices Stevens, Souter and Breyer. Both concurring opinions accept that the decision to grant or deny injunctive relief depends on the district court's equitable discretion, but interestingly both suggest a different manner in which that discretion should be exercised. The Roberts concurrence recalled that, from at least the early nineteenth century, 'courts have granted injunctive relief upon a finding of infringement in the vast majority of patent cases'.[12] Although that historical practice does not justify a general rule in favour of injunctive relief, the opinion urges courts to exercise their equitable discretion in line with it. Thus, under the Roberts concurrence, the decision in *eBay* would have little impact on existing practice.

[7] *MercExchange LLC v eBay Inc* 401 F3d 1323, 1338 (Fed Cir 2005).

[8] Gergen et al, 'The Supreme Court's Accidental Revolution? The Test for Permanent Injunctions' (2012) 112 *Columbia Law Review* 203, 207. For broader context on the US regime of patent injunctions as it came to a head in *eBay*, see J Golden, 'United States' in J Contreras and M Husovec (eds), *Injunctions in Patent Law* (Cambridge University Press, 2022) 293–95.

[9] *eBay v MercExchange* (n 1) 391.

[10] ibid 393.

[11] ibid 394.

[12] ibid 395 (Roberts CJ concurring).

By contrast, the Kennedy concurrence seems to view the affirmation of equitable principles as a chance to deviate from historical practice to bring patent law more in line with current-day circumstances. According to Justice Kennedy, 'To the extent earlier cases establish a pattern of granting an injunction against patent infringers almost as a matter of course, this pattern simply illustrates the result of the four-factor test in the contexts then prevalent'.[13] Nowadays, however, 'in many instances the nature of the patent being enforced and the economic function of the patent holder present considerations quite unlike earlier cases'. Justice Kennedy goes on to cite the examples of non-practising entities (NPEs), which monetise their inventions through licensing income, and the case where the patent covers 'but a small component of the product the companies seek to produce', which may give patentees 'undue leverage in negotiations'. Lastly, Justice Kennedy also refers to a 'burgeoning number of patents over business methods', which he believes suffer from 'potential vagueness and suspect validity'.[14] In sum, quite contrary to the Roberts concurrence, Justice Kennedy urges district courts 'to adapt to the rapid technological and legal developments in the patent system'.

4.2. The Court of Appeals for the Federal Circuit's Post-*eBay* Case Law

4.2.1. Irreparable Harm and Causal Nexus

The CAFC hears all appeals in patent cases which, in contrast with many European jurisdictions, are not heard by specialised courts in first instance. Consequently, the CAFC formulates standards and guidelines to be applied by fact-finding courts in all areas of patent law, often as the court of last resort. Entitlement to permanent injunctions is no exception, and by my count the CAFC issued 37 reasoned decisions on a district court's grant or denial of a permanent injunction between 2006 and 2020.[15] *eBay*'s first prong – whether a patentee has suffered irreparable harm as a result of the infringement – has received the most attention by far in these decisions. The CAFC established that *eBay* 'jettisoned' a presumption of irreparable harm on the part of the patentee, so that it must be proven on a case-by-case basis.[16] Two key considerations emerge from the CAFC's case law: the nature of the competition between the parties and the causal connection between the infringement and harm suffered by the patentee.

[13] ibid 396 (Kennedy J concurring).

[14] ibid 397.

[15] This excludes so-called 'Rule 36 affirmances', whereby the CAFC affirms a case without providing reasoning, and other opinions in which the majority does not discuss the merits of the district court's decision to grant or deny the permanent injunction in any way.

[16] *Robert Bosch LLC v Pylon Mfg Corp* 659 F3d 1142, 1149 (Fed Cir 2011).

While direct competition with infringers is not a prerequisite for injunctive relief, it will make irreparable harm easier to establish.[17] The presence of additional competitors in the market does not alter this, as long as some competitive harm can be attributed to the infringement.[18] This harm will typically consist of lost sales or market share, but may also consist of harm to the patentee's reputation as an innovator, loss of distinctiveness and market lure of the patentee's product, or even lessened attractiveness to potential new hires.[19] The harm need not concern the patentee's core business; injuries to non-core aspects of a business may be irreparable regardless.[20] Some markets will have special characteristics that must be taken into account. For instance, in *Broadcom*, the parties were chipmakers that would each pitch their respective technologies to equipment manufacturers, which would then incorporate the 'winning' technology in their products for the entire life cycle of the product.[21] Thus, even if they did not compete on a product market, they were still considered direct competitors, and the incumbency effect enjoyed by the winning party reinforced the finding of irreparable harm.[22] Conversely, where the infringer competes with the patentee's licensee, so that the patentee is not itself active on the relevant product market but earns licensing income from this market, its harm may not be irreparable.[23] That may be particularly true if the patentee actively solicited the infringer to join the licensing programme as well.[24] On the other hand, the CAFC has repeatedly held that a willingness to license the patent, even to the infringer, does not rule out a finding of irreparable harm.[25] All past licences must be examined on their own merits to see if unlicensed use of the particular patent invoked irreparably harms the patentee in the particular circumstances of the case. Failure to seek a preliminary injunction does not establish an absence of irreparable harm, though a patentee's willingness to extend a 'sunset period' until the injunction takes effect beyond what the infringer considers necessary may.[26]

[17] ibid 1151; *Mytee Products Inc v Harris Research Inc* 439 FedAppx 882, 887 (Fed Cir 2011).

[18] *Bio-Rad Laboratories Inc v 10X Genomics* 967 F3d 1353, 1378 (Fed Cir 2020); *Merial Ltd v Cipla Ltd* 681 F3d 1283, 1306 (Fed Cir 2012).

[19] *Douglas Dynamics LLC v Buyers Products Co* 717 F3d 1336, 1344–45 (Fed Cir 2013); *i4i Ltd Partnership v Microsoft Corp* 598 F3d 831, 861–62 (Fed Cir 2010); *O2 Micro Intern Ltd v Beyond Innovation Technology Co Ltd* 449 FedAppx 923, 932 (Fed Cir 2011); *Endo Pharmaceuticals Inc v Teva Pharmaceuticals USA Inc* 731 FedAppx 962, 975 (Fed Cir 2018).

[20] *Bosch v Pylon* (n 16) 1152.

[21] *Broadcom Corp v Emulex Corp* 732 F3d 1325, 1337 (Fed Cir 2013).

[22] See also *Broadcom Corp v Qualcomm Inc* 543 F3d 683, 703 (Fed Cir 2008); *Mytee v Harris* (n 17) 888 (indirect competition sufficient to establish irreparable harm because patentee showed that franchisees rely on patented features in the marketplace).

[23] *ActiveVideo Networks Inc v Verizon Communications Inc* 694 F3d 1312, 1338 (Fed Cir 2012); *Voda v Cordis Corp* 536 F3d 1311, 1329 (Fed Cir 2008).

[24] *ActiveVideo v Verizon* (n 23) 1339.

[25] *Acumed LLC v Stryker Corp* 551 F3d 1323, 1328–29 (Fed Cir 2008); *Presidio Components v American Technical Ceramics* 875 F3d 1369, 1383 (Fed Cir 2017).

[26] *Mytee v Harris* (n 17) 888; *Genband US LLC v Metaswitch Networks Corp* 861 F3d 1378, 1385 (Fed Cir 2017); but, as regards the sunset period, see *ActiveVideo v Verizon* (n 23) 1339.

As regards the causal connection between infringement and harm, the CAFC has developed the so-called 'causal nexus' requirement in four opinions in the *Apple v Samsung* litigation.[27] Establishing irreparable harm requires showing a causal nexus between the infringement and the harm suffered by the patentee as a result of the infringer's sales. In *Apple II*, the CAFC stated that the patentee must show 'that the infringing feature drives consumer demand for the accused product'.[28] That rule was somewhat nuanced in *Apple III*, where the CAFC required 'some connection between the patented feature and demand for [the infringer's] products'.[29] Subsequent decisions further specified that infringing features need not be the sole reason customers bought it, but that there must be more than an insubstantial connection between the infringing features and the purchase decision.[30] In a more recent decision, the CAFC settled on the presence of patented features in the infringer's device having been a 'significant reason' consumers bought it.[31]

The purpose of the causal nexus requirement is to exclude a finding of irreparable harm – and therefore deny a patentee injunctive relief – where demand for the competitor's product is not driven by the infringing feature.[32] The CAFC has stated that in such cases, 'even if the competitive injury that results from selling the accused device is substantial, the harm that flows from the alleged infringement (the only harm that should count) is not'.[33] A causal nexus between infringement and lost sales may be absent, in particular, in component patent cases. Still, it applies equally to 'simple' products, ie where the patented technology is one of only few features or perhaps even the product itself.[34] Essentially, the CAFC's application of the irreparable harm prong in general and the causal nexus requirement in particular have restricted injunctive relief to cases where the patentee suffered some unquantifiable harm in its market position that can be directly attributed to the infringer's usurpation of the patented technology. That is a considerable change from the virtually automatic entitlement to an injunction before *eBay*.

[27] *Apple Inc v Samsung Electronics Co Ltd* 678 F3d 1314 (Fed Cir 2012) (*Apple I*); *Apple Inc v Samsung Electronics Co Ltd* 695 F3d 1370 (Fed Cir 2012) (*Apple II*); *Apple Inc v Samsung Electronics Co Ltd* 735 F3d 1352 (Fed Cir 2013) (*Apple III*); *Apple Inc v Samsung Electronics Co Ltd* 809 F3d 633 (Fed Cir 2015) (*Apple IV*). Although *Apple I* and *Apple II* concerned preliminary injunctions, the CAFC has held that its observations on irreparable harm apply equally in the permanent injunction context: *Apple III*, 1361.

[28] *Apple II* (n 27) 1375.

[29] *Apple III* (n 27) 1364.

[30] *Genband v Metaswitch* (n 26) 1384.

[31] *TEK Global Srl v Sealant Systems Int'l* 920 F3d 777, 792 (Fed Cir 2019). But see *Apple IV* (n 27) 644: 'it is enough that Apple has shown that these features were related to infringement and were important to customers when they were examining their phone choices'.

[32] *Apple I* (n 27) 1324.

[33] *Apple II* (n 27) 1374–75.

[34] *Apple III* (n 27) 1362.

4.2.2. Other Prongs: Adequacy of Damages, Balance of Hardships and Public Interest

eBay's second prong – whether monetary damages are adequate to compensate the patentee for harm suffered – is closely related to the irreparable harm inquiry and courts often discuss these two prongs together. After all, 'irreparable' means that the harm is not capable of being adequately compensated with a money payment so that a finding of irreparable harm more or less implies that monetary damages are not adequate to make the patentee whole, and vice versa.[35] Generally speaking, the CAFC considers incapable of monetary compensation harms in the patentee's market position such as loss of market share, brand recognition or reputation.[36] This is particularly the case where the infringing acts have significantly changed the relevant market, for instance where the infringer gained substantive market share or a first mover advantage.[37] In addition, an infringer's inability to pay a damages award may demonstrate inadequacy of remedies at law.[38] Much of the CAFC's discussion of this *eBay* prong focuses on whether a patentee's willingness to license the patent means they can be adequately compensated for infringement with money. The answer is generally no. Commercial considerations surrounding past licensing deals, the identity of past licensees, developments in the market since then and the circumstances under which the infringement took place must all be taken into account – and will generally provide no ground for a finding that the patentee can be compensated just as well with an ongoing royalty.[39] On the other hand, if the licensing pattern suggests the infringement causes only straightforward monetary harm, a damages payment may be adequate. This could be the case where a patentee monetises the invention exclusively through licensing and the identity of the licensee has no bearing on its income or business.[40]

The third *eBay* prong – balance of hardships – 'assesses the relative effect of granting or denying an injunction on the parties'.[41] Only consequences for the parties themselves may be taken into account in this part of the test: adverse consequences for consumers or other third parties are considered under the fourth prong.[42] The CAFC's reasoning on this prong is often sparse and sometimes contradictory. In particular, it is not clear what harms on the infringer's side

[35] *ActiveVideo v Verizon* (n 23) 1338.
[36] *Douglas v Buyers* (n 19) 1345.
[37] *i4i v Microsoft* (n 19) 862; *Bio-Rad v 10X* (n 18) 1378; *Broadcomm v Qualcomm* (n 22) 703.
[38] *Bosch v Pylon* (n 16) 1156; *ActiveVideo v Verizon* (n 23) 1340. The reverse is not true: 'a defendant's ability to pay a judgment does not defeat a claim that an award of damages would be an inadequate remedy', *Apple III* (n 27) 1369.
[39] *Nichia Corp v Everlight Americas, Inc* 855 F3d 1328, 1343 (Fed Cir 2017); see also *Acumed v Stryker* (n 25) 1328; *Apple III* (n 27) 1370; *O2 v Beyond* (n 19) 933.
[40] *ActiveVideo v Verizon* (n 23) 1338; *Voda v Cordis* (n 23) 1329.
[41] *Apple IV* (n 27) 645.
[42] *Acumed v Stryker* (n 25) 1330.

count for the balance. The CAFC has repeatedly held that sunk costs in development of the infringing product, redesign costs and the centrality of the infringing product to the infringer's business may not be taken into account.[43] This restriction rests on the theory that 'one who elects to build a business on a product found to infringe cannot be heard to complain if an injunction against continuing infringement destroys the business so elected'.[44] At the same time, an infringer's successful plea under the balance of hardships prong will often involve just these same considerations. In a later case, for instance, the CAFC ruled that the balance of hardships tipped in favour of the infringer where 'a much smaller company' depended 'entirely on the sales of the enjoined products for its revenue'.[45] Section 5.4.4 shows that district courts also have difficulty applying the balance of hardships prong consistently. What is clear is that the availability of non-infringing alternatives will mitigate the hardship suffered by the infringer.[46] If the infringer delays in developing such alternatives, it may be held against them when they argue injunctive relief should be denied.[47] Hardship will also be mitigated by sunset provisions which allow the infringer time to switch to non-infringing alternatives or sell out remaining stock.[48] All in all, the CAFC seems to set a high threshold for the balance of hardship prong. In addition, in the rare case where the infringer would suffer substantial hardship, this can be remedied by appropriately tailoring the injunction. As a result, this factor has not played an important role in the CAFC's practice to date.

Lastly, *eBay*'s fourth prong – the public interest – provides a similarly exceptional ground to deny injunctive relief. This factor takes stock of harm to customers, downstream suppliers and other third parties. Notably, the CAFC has held that the public interest would be disserved by being deprived of 'access to a large number of non-infringing features', as can happen when component patents are enforced.[49] Infringers have often argued that competition or cheaper alternatives to the patentee's products are in the public interest, particularly where it concerns medicines.[50] As a general matter, the CAFC has rejected such attempts, finding that 'the public has a greater interest in acquiring new technology through the protections provided by the Patent Act than it has in buying "cheaper knockoffs"'.[51] Later, the CAFC added that 'Injunctions are vital to this system'.[52] Thus, under this *eBay* prong, there seems to be a baseline assumption that

[43] ibid. Notably, on the side of the patentee, the same considerations frequently *do* carry substantive weight: eg *i4i v Microsoft* (n 19) 863.

[44] *Windsurfing Int'l Inc v AMF Inc* 782 F2d 995, 1003, n 12 (Fed Cir 1986).

[45] *Bio-Rad v 10X* (n 18) 1379.

[46] *Douglas v Buyers* (n 19) 1345.

[47] *Broadcomm v Qualcomm* (n 22) 704.

[48] ibid.

[49] *Apple III* (n 27) 1372–73.

[50] *Douglas v Buyers* (n 19) 1346; *Apple IV* (n 27) 647; *WBIP LLC v Kohler Co* 829 F3d 1317, 1343 (Fed Cir 2016).

[51] *Douglas v Buyers* (n 19) 1346.

[52] *Apple IV* (n 27) 647.

upholding patent exclusivity is in the public good, which effectively comes down to a baseline assumption in favour of granting a patentee injunctive relief. To be sure, a sufficiently significant and specific public harm can, and sometimes does, result in denial of the injunction.[53] But here, too, the injunction's potential disservice to the public interest can be mitigated by tailoring the injunction, or by appropriately narrowing its scope.[54]

4.3. District Court Cases: General Statistics

Using the LexMachina legal search engine, I found 419 US district court cases handed down between May 2006 and March 2020 in which permanent injunctions were either granted or denied to patentees who had prevailed on the merits (ie had proven infringement of a valid patent). Previous studies covering the period up to December 2013 found that injunctions were granted in 72.5 per cent of cases while granted injunctions were stayed in 24 per cent of cases.[55] I found 97 denials (~23 per cent) and 52 stays (~12.4 per cent), though the percentage of stays is likely to be under-representative because I did not consider stays ordered by the CAFC pending appeal.[56] The 97 denials include 11 pharmaceutical cases where an injunction was not necessary because the court ordered the effective date of the marketing authorisation for the generic drug to be no sooner than the patent's date of expiration.[57] In the remaining 86 cases, or 20.5 per cent, an injunction was denied because the court considered the patentee was not entitled to it. That is better for patentees than what previous studies found, which may be due to a pushback against *eBay* in the literature, but could also reflect selection effects as some plaintiffs may no longer request injunctive relief in the first place. Either way, in one out of three cases (approximately 33 per cent), an injunction with immediate effect did not issue. From a European perspective, that number is considerable.

It is striking that in 171 cases (approximately 40.8 per cent) the decision contains no reasoning on injunctive relief at all, given that the CAFC held that failure to consider any of the *eBay* factors is an abuse of discretion.[58] An injunction

[53] The CAFC has not yet explicitly sanctioned specific public interest considerations, but it has upheld injunction denials by district courts on the basis of this factor as not abusive of discretion. See *Bard Peripheral Vascular v WL Gore & Associates* 670 F3d 1171, 1192 (Fed Cir 2012). The district court practice, which is discussed below, is more instructive in this respect.

[54] *Broadcomm v Qualcomm* (n 22) 704; *TEK v Sealant* (n 31) 793; *i4i v Microsoft* (n 19) 863.

[55] C Seaman, 'Permanent Injunctions in Patent Litigation after eBay: An Empirical Study' (2016) 101 *Iowa Law Review* 1949, 1983; R Holte and C Seaman, 'Patent Injunctions on Appeal: An Empirical Study of the Federal Circuit's Application of eBay' (2017) 92 *Washington Law Review* 145, 182.

[56] Holte and Seaman (n 55) 182 (reporting a stay rate of 24%, with roughly one-fifth of stays having been ordered by the CAFC).

[57] 35 USC § 271(e)(4)(a). This is a peculiar feature of US patent law that generally obviates the need for injunctive relief: *Alcon Manufacturing Ltd v Teva Pharmaceuticals USA Inc* 2010 WL 3081327 (D Del 5 August 2010).

[58] *Ecolab Inc v FMC Corp* 569 F3d 1335, 1352 (Fed Cir 2009).

was granted in almost all of these cases, apparently without challenge by the defendant.[59] These numbers should assuage fears in Europe that a proportionality defence will be raised in every case, raising the cost and duration of infringement proceedings (section 3.3.1). That certainly has not been the case in the USA, where it might have been expected since *eBay* placed the onus on the patentee to prove their entitlement to an injunction. If US courts grant injunctions without further discussion in four out of 10 cases, that number is likely to be far higher in Europe, where the onus lies with the infringer. Moving on to the remaining 248 cases where court reasoning is available, a picture emerges of the circumstances most commonly considered by courts in their decision to grant or deny the injunction, which is show in Table 4.1.

Table 4.1 Circumstances most commonly considered by US courts when deciding on permanent injunctions (n = 248)

Circumstance	Favours patentee	Favours infringer	Neutral	Not discussed
Public interest	163	36	9	40
Harm to the patentee's competitive position	152	48	1	47
Balance of hardships	102	37	9	100
Prior licens-ing activity by patentee	71	27	1	149
Availability of non-infringing alternatives	60	12	0	176
Invention's centrality to patentee's business	55	9	2	182
Non-infringing features in infringer's product	39	19	0	190

(continued)

[59] An injunction was denied in 16 out of these 171 cases. Of these, 10 concerned the aforementioned 35 USC § 271(e)(4)(a)-pharmaceutical cases (n 57), whereas in the remaining six, the opinion granting the injunction was confidential, referred to arguments made at oral argument or was a party settlement.

Table 4.1 ***(Continued)***

Circumstance	Favours patentee	Favours infringer	Neutral	Not discussed
Likelihood of repeat infringement	41	16	0	191
Infringer's capacity to pay damages	16	4	2	226

When it comes to sheer frequency of mention, *eBay* factors three and four (balance of hardships and public interest) finish in third and first place, respectively. This is somewhat misleading because courts often pay mere lip service to these factors, stating without further analysis that the public interest favours protecting patents or deciding on the balance of convenience in the slipstream of the first two factors. I return to these observations below. Otherwise, the list is dominated by 'patentee-side' considerations: harm to their competitive position, prior licensing activity and the invention's centrality to their business. This suggests that *eBay* factor one, irreparable harm, is the most important consideration in practice, a picture that is confirmed by a closer look at the injunction denials. Readers are referred to Annex II for a complete overview of these decisions; here, I focus on the 86 decisions that remain if the eleven 35 USC § 271(e)(4)(a) pharmaceutical cases (see above) are left out. Out of these decisions, eight contain no reasoning on irreparable harm, while 75 contain an express finding that the patentee was not irreparably harmed by the infringement. These 75 decisions are broken down in Table 4.2.[60]

Table 4.2 Breakdown of US decisions finding no irreparable harm ($n = 75$)

		Patentee status (if known)	
	# of decisions	**Competitor**	**NPE**
Infringement does not affect patentee's market position	25	16	5
Patentee willing to accept licence	17	4	13
Infringer unlikely to enter or remain on market	14	7	–

(continued)

[60] I note that slightly different distributions across categories (especially 1 and 2) would be possible because every decision was assigned to only one category, even though some decisions display multiple factors. Assignment was done on the basis of which factor seemed to weigh heaviest in the court's mind.

Table 4.2 ***(Continued)***

	# of decisions	Patentee status (if known)	
		Competitor	**NPE**
Absence of causal nexus	11	7	3
'The horse has left the barn'	6	5	1
Miscellaneous	2	1	–
Total	**75**	**40**	**22**

Categories 3 and 7 stand on their own: in 14 cases, the court found no irreparable harm because infringing activities had ceased or were unlikely to commence due to regulatory obstacles.[61] It seems reasonable to assume that in these cases no future harm is threatened to the patentee (though the argument can also be reversed to say that imposing an injunction here is harmless, as US courts have done on other occasions). The other categories are all variations on a lack of irreparable harm. Three things are worth noting in this respect.

First, the goal of enforcement (licence or exclusivity) is not the primary determinant of irreparable harm, as some European authors seem to suggest.[62] True, the patentee's willingness to license the patent either to the infringer or to other competitors drove the decision to deny irreparable harm in a good number (17) of cases. But it was more common for patentees – often direct competitors of the infringer – to fail to prove that the infringement would materially affect their market position (25). This included cases where the patentee operated in a different segment of the market (wholesale versus retail, luxury versus low-cost products, etc), where the market counted many competitors, or simply where the patentee's evidence was deemed insufficient to make the required showing. Another fairly common (11) scenario was that the patentee failed the causal nexus test, ie failed to establish that the patented features drove demand for the infringing product. Second, and relatedly, my findings suggest that the truism that it is especially difficult for NPEs to obtain injunctive relief before US courts may need to be nuanced. Annex II shows, for each decision where this could be derived, whether the patentee was a competitor of the infringer or an NPE.[63] Table 4.2 summarises the results per category. In the majority of cases (40), the patentee

[61] In the Miscellaneous category, no injunction was awarded in one case because of the patentee's unclean hands, while the damages awarded in the other case adequately compensated the patentee also for future infringement.

[62] eg M Stierle and F Hofmann, 'The Latest Amendment to the German Law on Patent Injunctions: The New Statutory Disproportionality Exception and Third-Party Interests' (2022) 71 *Gewerblicher Rechtsschutz und Urheberrecht International* 1123, 1128.

[63] I marked as 'competitor' those patentees who made a substantiated pleading that they competed with the infringer. I marked as 'NPE' patentees who the court found not to market any product and/or who were repeatedly willing to license the infringer and its competitors.

in fact competed with the infringer for sales, yet nevertheless could not establish irreparable harm. Only in category 2, where this finding was based on the patentee's willingness to license, did the majority of cases involve NPE enforcement. Even then, not every patentee displayed characteristics frequently associated with abusive NPE enforcement, which is in line with the argument, in section 3.2.6, that it is difficult to distinguish between 'good' and 'bad' NPEs. As shown in the full overview in Annex II, out of 22 NPE suits, one involved a university, four involved patentees that until recently were active on the market (formerly practising entities) and six involved enforcement for the benefit of established licensees whose prices were undercut by the infringer. In other words, half of the NPE suits appear to have involved what many would consider 'benign' NPEs as opposed to 'bottom-feeder trolls' that are 'interested in quick, low-value settlements for a variety of patents'.[64]

Third, the overview shows that narrowing down the irreparable harm inquiry to demonstrable harm to the patentee's market position leads to outcomes that, it is submitted, would be untenable from a European perspective. This means that even direct competitors of the infringer may be denied exclusivity for evidentiary reasons. It also means they may be denied exclusivity because they happen to operate in a multi-player market, or at a different level of the distribution chain. It even means they may be denied injunctive relief where a wilful infringer so successfully cornered the market that even an injunction can no longer turn the tide for the patentee. These cases (6) are labelled 'The horse has left the barn' in Table 4.2, and *Bard v Gore* offers a particularly instructive illustration. There, the court found that the infringer had engaged in 'objectively reckless and wilful conduct' over a 30-year period towards the patentee, and consequently obtained a 62 per cent market share on the market for vascular grafts. Yet the court ruled that the patentee could be 'adequately made whole through legal remedies', citing public health concerns, and denied an injunction.[65] It may be tempting to consider this an outlier decision, but it was affirmed on appeal, and, as the table shows, there are others like it. Section 4.5 contains further reflections on how US courts have applied the irreparable harm standard and what Europe can learn from this, but I note here that in many cases, the outcomes would likely be unpalatable to the vast majority of the European patent judiciary.

It was noted above that *eBay*'s first factor is far and away the most important consideration for US courts. Indeed, among all 322 cases in which an injunction was granted (and for which reasoning is available), there is not a single one where the court found against the patentee on irreparable harm. Table 4.3 considers the 86 denials in three categories: those where the court found no irreparable harm (75); those where it made no finding on irreparable harm (8); and those where it found for the patentee on irreparable harm (3).

[64] M Lemley and AD Melamed, 'Missing the Forest for the Trolls' (2013) 113 *Columbia Law Review* 2117, 2126.

[65] *Bard Peripheral Vascular Inc v WL Gore & Associates Inc* 2009 WL 920300, *5 (D Ariz 31 March 2009).

Table 4.3 Breakdown of US decisions denying an injunction ($n = 86$)

		Balance of hardships			Public interest		
	Total	**Not mentioned or neutral**	**Favours infringer**	**Favours patentee**	**Not mentioned or neutral**	**Favours infringer**	**Favours patentee**
No irreparable harm	75	42	26	7	39	25	11
No finding	8	8	–	–	6	2	–
Irreparable harm	3	1	2	–	–	2	1

35 USC § 271(e)(4)(a) pharmaceutical cases are omitted.

As the table shows, in the majority of cases where courts found against the patentee on irreparable harm, they did not even consider the balance of hardships or the public interest. Where they did, they usually found for the infringer on these factors, with reasoning that often built on their findings on irreparable harm.[66] On occasion, courts found for the patentee on balance of hardships and/or public interest, but this was never enough to outweigh the absence of irreparable harm and justify the grant of an injunction. The reverse scenario, where courts found for the patentee on irreparable harm but for the infringer on the other prongs and denied the injunction, occurred only three times.[67] Table 4.4 shows how the *eBay* factors were weighed by the court in these three cases.

Table 4.4 Breakdown of three US decisions denying an injunction

	Irreparable harm	**Adequacy of damages**	**Balance of hardships**	**Public interest**
Conceptus v Hologic (2012)	+	–	– –	– –
Server v American (2015)	+	– –	n	–
EMC v Zerto (2016)	+	–	– –	+

+ = favours injunction; – = favours denial; – – = heavily favours denial; n = neutral.

[66] There are two cases where the public interest weighed against the injunction so heavily that the court did not rule on irreparable harm: *Medtronic Sofamor Danek USA Inc v Nuvasive Inc* No 8 Cv 1512-MMA transcript, 7 (SD Cal 26 January 2012) (but stating, at 6, that 'the court is not convinced that [patentee] will suffer irreparable injury if [infringer] is not enjoined'); *WBIP LLC v Kohler Co* No 11-10374-NMG, *2 (D Mass 12 August 2013) (but overturned on appeal for failing to discuss other prongs: see above (n 50) 1343).

[67] *Conceptus Inc v Hologic Inc* 2012 WL 44064 (ND Cal 9 January 2012); *Server Technology Inc v American Power Conversion Corp* 2015 WL 1505654, *4 (D Nev 31 March 2015); *EMC Corp v Zerto Inc* 2016 WL 1291757, *13 (D Del 31 March 2016).

In *Server v American*, the patentee may have been irreparably harmed but nevertheless sought a licence, so the injunction was denied. *Conceptus* and *EMC* are notable because they appear to have been the only two cases where the balance of hardships drove a denial of the injunction despite a finding of irreparable harm. In *Conceptus*, the hardship was having to lay off 300 employees and losing an investment of US$ 215 million in a product with important advantages over the patented technology (which is why denial was also in the public interest). In *EMC*, arguably the only 'pure' infringer hardship case out of all 419 decisions studied, the patentee's lost sales represented about 0.001 per cent of its annual revenues, whereas the products targeted by the injunction would comprise the entirety of the infringer's business. These decisions are real outliers and, in my view, are a call for caution to those who advocate a balancing-type proportionality test in Europe and look to the USA for inspiration. I return to this point in section 4.5.

A final aspect of the US case law worth considering are appeals. As noted above, over the period studied, there have been 37 reasoned CAFC decisions specifically addressing the district court's grant or denial of injunctive relief, as indicated in Annex II. Table 4.5 shows the overall statistics:

Table 4.5 Outcomes of injunction-specific appeals ($n = 419$)

	Total	Upheld on appeal	Reversed on appeal
Injunction grants	322	11	7
Injunction denials	97	8	11

Three things stand out. First, there were almost as many CAFC decisions addressing injunction grants as there were injunction denials, whereas the latter category comprises significantly fewer cases. Injunction denials were thus much more likely to be the subject of appeal and were also more likely to be reversed, which is in line with previous findings.[68] Second, nearly half of all appeals ended in a reversal (18 out of 37, 48.6 per cent). This number strikes me as rather high and suggests that there is considerable uncertainty among district courts on *eBay*'s proper application. Third, when compared to the total number of district court decisions (419), the number of CAFC decisions (37) is very low. This is perhaps understandable as district court decisions on injunctive relief are reviewed for abuse of discretion, which sets a high bar for reversal.[69] But that standard itself is instructive, because it implies that it is hard to meaningfully criticise the application of broad-scope tests, such as the one laid down in *eBay* – a point I also made in section 2.3. In other words, if it is entirely up to the court's discretion to weigh all the circumstances of the case, it is difficult to argue about whether it did so correctly, even on appeal. That is not a good basis for the development of a

[68] Holte and Seaman (n 55) 189.
[69] *Bio-Rad v 10X* (n 18) 1377.

European proportionality test, as explained in section 1.4.2. Either way, the small number of appeals decisions further confirms that to really understand how the *eBay* framework is applied in practice, we must study district court decisions. It is to them I turn now, analysing them across six categories: parties, markets, products, hardships, public interests and order modalities.

4.4. District Court Cases: Analysis of Case Specifics

4.4.1. Parties

4.4.1.1. Patentee Characteristics – Enforcement for Exclusivity

Although Table 4.2 shows this is not decisive, the fact that the patentee and the infringer are direct competitors is often considered a strong indication that the grant of an injunction is warranted.[70] The harm felt from infringement should be to an actual, rather than hypothetical, market position.[71] The pursuit of exclusivity partially, or even primarily, for the benefit of licensees was likewise often considered deserving of injunctive relief, because infringement of the patent would decrease the value of a licence.[72] If infringers are not stopped, others may be less willing to take a licence, and existing licensees may be underbid by cheaper, infringing products.[73] As the next subsection will show, the irreparable harm inquiry is complicated to the point of sheer unpredictability where patentees have established licensing programmes, so how the court perceives the patentee's goals can be important: are they interested primarily in maximising licensing income or are they pursuing exclusivity, if not for themselves, then for their licensees, or even to maintain the asset value of the patent?[74] Generally speaking, where a patentee can plead the latter, US courts will grant an injunction.

[70] eg *Brocade Communications Systems Inc v A10 Networks Inc* 2013 WL 140039, *4 (ND Cal 10 January 2013) (direct competition means 'loss of exclusivity is particularly injurious').

[71] Market exclusivity can be 'hypothetical', eg where the patentee is itself prevented from entering the market by other patents: *Tyco Healthcare Group LP v Applied Medical Resources Corp* 2010 WL 11469881, *3 (ED Tex 17 May 2010) or where it operates in a regulated market and requires a licence: *IGT v Bally Gaming International Inc* 675 FSupp2d 487, 491 (D Del 2009).

[72] *Bendix Commercial Vehicle Systems LLC v Haldex Brake Products Corp* 2011 WL 14372, *6 (ND Ohio 3 January 2011). See also *Waterton Polymer Products USA v Edizone, LLC* 2015 WL 1186258, *7 (D Utah 16 March 2015), where denial of an injunction would force the patentee to change its exclusivity-based business model.

[73] *Insituform Technologies Inc v Cosmic-Sondermaschinenbau GmbH* No 1:08-cv-333-TCB, *9 (ND Ga 4 January 2011).

[74] For an injunction granted specifically with an eye to preserving the patent's value on the market, see *Joyal Products Inc v Johnson Electric North America Inc* 2009 WL 512156, *11 (D NJ February 26 2009). But see *MercExchange LLC v eBay Inc* 500 FSupp2d 556, 588 (ED Va 2007), where the patentee's publicly stated intention to sell its patent portfolio was held to weigh against the grant of injunctive relief (though combined with many other factors indicative of rent-seeking behaviour).

A circumstance commonly cited in support of an injunction is that the patentee is a small company facing a much bigger infringer.[75] These situations not only present an appealing David-versus-Goliath narrative, but also correspond with findings in the literature that smaller firms must usually rely on strong intellectual property rights protection to get a foothold in markets dominated by incumbents.[76] If market leaders can infringe newcomers' patents with impunity, the capacity of those newcomers to build a leadership position in the relevant market will be seriously undermined.[77] Incumbents usually possess strong advantages that can effectively foreclose competition. Two examples taken from US practice are allowing customers to consolidate their supply lines if they stay with the incumbent,[78] or being able to pressure retailers into stocking the incumbent's product and not the patentee's.[79] Patent exclusivity can thus be a critical means for smaller patentees to establish long-term business relationships that offer the basis to grow the patentee's business.[80] Needless to say, that will particularly be the case where the patented technology is at the core of the patentee's business.[81]

Relatedly, US courts have tended to favour patentees who themselves developed the patented technology over those who purchased it from others. To be sure, lack of self-development is not dispositive, and there are certainly cases where injunctive relief was granted for infringement of an acquired patent,[82] but a patentee's significant investments in the technology that resulted in the patents has almost always weighed heavily in favour of an injunction.[83]

A special case of exclusivity-oriented enforcement occurs where the patent covers a technology not practised by the patentee, but which it would nonetheless

[75] *SiOnyx LLC v Hamamatsu Photonics KK* 2019 WL 3358599, *3 (D Mass 25 July 2019); *Halo Electronics Inc v Pulse Electronics Inc* 2013 WL 3043668, *8 (D Nev 17 June 2013); *Retractable Technologies Inc v Becton Dickinson and Co* 2010 WL 9034911, *2 (ED Tex 19 May 2010); *800 Adept Inc v Murex Securities Ltd* 505 FSupp2d 1327, 1338 (MD Fla 2007). The reverse is not true: a smaller defendant is not shielded from an injunction just for that reason, *Broadcom Corp v Emulex Corp* 2012 WL 13036855, *6 (CD Cal 16 March 2012).

[76] J Barnett, *Innovators, Firms, and Markets: The Organizational Logic of Intellectual Property* (Oxford University Press, 2021) 140.

[77] *i4i Ltd Partnership v Microsoft Corp* 670 FSupp2d 568, 600 (ED Tex 2009).

[78] *Presidio Components Inc v American Technical Ceramics Corp* 2013 WL 4068833, *6 (CD Cal 12 August 2013).

[79] *Innovention Toys LLC v MGA Entertainment Inc* No 07-6510, *5 (ED La 13 January 2010).

[80] *Sealant Systems International Inc v TEK Global Srl* 2014 WL 1008183, *25 (ND Cal 7 March 2014); *Bendix v Haldex* (n 72) *6.

[81] *Asetek Danmark A/S v CMI USA Inc* 2015 WL 5568360, *14 (ND Cal 22 September 2015); *Vertical Doors Inc v JT Bonn Inc* 2008 WL 11343051, *4 (CD Cal 15 December 2008); *TIVO Inc v Echostar Communications Corp* 446 FSupp2d 664, 670 (ED Tex 2006).

[82] eg *Callaway Golf Co v Acushnet Co* 585 FSupp2d 600, 618 (D Del 2008), where the patent was acquired from a bankruptcy.

[83] *Bio-Rad Laboratories Inc v 10X Genomics Inc* 2019 WL 3322322, *4 (D Del 24 July 2019); *Harris Corp v Federal Express Corp* No 6:07-cv-1819-Orl-28KRS, *24 (MD Fla 16 August 2011); *Smith & Nephew Inc v Arthrex Inc* 629 FSupp2d 1176, 1180 (D Or 2008); *Fresenius USA Inc v Baxter International Inc* No C 03-1431, *4 (ND Cal 21 March 2008); *Sanofi-Aventis Deutschland GmbH v Glenmark Pharmaceuticals Inc* 821 FSupp2d 681, 696 (D NJ 2011).

like to suppress to promote its other, competing technologies. In one case, the court noted under reference to an older US Supreme Court case that such a strategy is 'entirely equitable', yet proceeded to deny an injunction.[84] A later decision confirmed that even if the patentee's product does not incorporate the patented technology, it may still compete with the infringing product, and consequently an injunction may be appropriate.[85]

4.4.1.2. Patentee Characteristics – Enforcement to Obtain Licensing Revenue

It is commonly assumed that, since *eBay*, it has become much more difficult for NPEs to obtain injunctive relief. It is certainly true that the first two prongs of the *eBay* test, as they have been interpreted by the Federal Circuit, are more difficult to satisfy for NPEs. And there are decisions where the court's misgivings about the plaintiff's NPE status are clearly palpable as they refuse an injunction.[86] But, as Table 4.2 shows, the picture that emerges from the lower courts' case law is much too complex to support anything beyond a crude assumption that NPEs bear a special burden when it comes to irreparable harm. In many instances, entities that do not practise the patent themselves were able to obtain injunctive relief; conversely, there are also numerous cases where practising entities were unable to show irreparable harm and therefore denied an injunction. For instance, most commentators agree that universities and research institutions are unlike 'harmful' NPEs, which would suggest they are usually deserving of patent exclusivity.[87] Indeed, in an early and oft-cited case, one such institute – the Commonwealth Scientific and Industrial Research Organization (CSIRO) – sought to enforce a patent related to wireless local-area network (WLAN) technology and was granted injunctive relief. The court reasoned that CSIRO 'relies heavily on the ability to license its intellectual property to finance its research and development'; that it competes with others 'for resources, ideas, and the best scientific minds to transform those ideas into realities'; and that the loss of these opportunities and the reputational harm suffered by infringement is likely to be undercompensated with an ongoing royalty.[88] Surely these are compelling reasons to justify the need for patent exclusivity. But 12 years later, CSIRO was denied an injunction in a case against plant science company BASF Plant Science, concerning algae-based substitutes for fish oil supplements. Here, the court essentially reasoned

[84] *Hynix Semiconductors Inc v Rambus Inc* 609 FSupp2d 951, 968 (ND Cal 2009).
[85] *Sealant v TEK* (n 80) *24.
[86] *Amado v Microsoft Corp* No 03-242, *19 (CD Cal 13 March 2007) ('Amado does not compete with Microsoft, does not sell a product covered by the patent and is no longer even attempting to commercialize or license the patent').
[87] eg Lemley and Melamed (n 64) 2125–26.
[88] *Commonwealth Scientific and Industrial Research Organisation v Buffalo Technology Inc* 492 FSupp2d 600, 604–05 (ED Tex 2007).

that CSIRO and its commercialisation partner had been insufficiently diligent in bringing the invention to market, whereas BASF Plant Science was ready to launch.[89] It also held that in a market saturated with fish oil products, it would be unlikely to enjoy a first mover advantage.[90] This shift in the position of the same research institute is exemplary of the many contingencies on which the grant or denial of an injunction depends beyond the mere question of whether the patentee is an NPE.

How the patentee's licensing behaviour affects the entitlement to injunctive relief is a complicated question. On the one hand, there are cases where a patentee primarily interested in monetising the patent through licensing was denied an injunction because the harm from infringement was essentially limited to the loss of the infringer as customer, which could be compensated with an ongoing royalty.[91] The validity of this argument was seemingly confirmed by the Federal Circuit.[92] Even practising entities can be denied injunctive relief if they have a history of licensing the patent, particularly to (major) competitors.[93] Courts often attempt to establish whether the willingness to license means the patentee is in fact not interested in market exclusivity: in one case, a court accepted that the patentee had 'gambled away' its exclusive rights by granting a single party a licence to its portfolio with the right to grant any third party a royalty-free, worldwide sublicence.[94] Patentees merely seeking payment might be denied an injunction as some courts have held that 'bargaining leverage is neither an appropriate reason to seek an injunction, nor an appropriate reason to grant an injunction'.[95] In this respect, a pattern of seeking licences through litigation could be considered indicative of rent-seeking behaviour, though the cases are remarkably divided in this respect. The point was often argued and some courts accepted it, while others did not.[96]

But not all prior licensing activity precludes injunctive relief and in a large number of highly fact-specific decisions, US courts have justified a finding of irreparable harm and inadequacy of monetary damages despite an earlier willingness to license. The most straightforward justification is that, when granting a

[89] *BASF Plant Science LP v Commonwealth Scientific and Industrial Research Organization*, 2019 WL 8108116, *18–19 (ED Va 20 December 2019).

[90] ibid *17.

[91] *z4 Technologies Inc v Microsoft Corp* 434 FSupp2d 437, 440 (ED Tex 2006); *Paice LLP v Toyota Motors Corp* 2006 WL 2385139, *5 (ED Tex 16 August 2006).

[92] *ActiveVideo v Verizon* (n 23) 1338.

[93] *Johnson & Johnson Vision Care Inc v CIBA Vision Corp* 712 FSupp2d 1285, 1289 (MD Fla 2010).

[94] *Cordance Corporation v Amazon.com Inc* 730 FSupp2d 333, 341 (D Del 2010). See also *Harris v Federal Express* (n 83) *22 (distinguishing the patentee's licensing practices from entering into 'boilerplate license agreements with any interested party').

[95] *BASF v Commonwealth* (n 89) *19; *Ricoh Co Ltd v Quanta Computer Inc* 2010 WL 1607908, *4 (WD Wis 19 April 2010); *MercExchange v eBay* (n 74) 582.

[96] Denying injunctive relief: *Server v American* (n 67) *4; *Advanced Cardiovascular Systems Inc v Medtronic Vascular Inc* 579 FSupp2d 554, 560 (D Del 2008); *MercExchange v eBay* (n 74) 576. Granting injunctive relief: *Broadcom v Emulex* (n 75) *4; *Bendix v Haldex* (n 72) *6.

prior licence, the patentee may have been in a different competitive position than it was at the time of enforcement.[97] In particular, investing in partnerships with key licensees to increase adoption of the patented technology is far removed from a general willingness to grant licences.[98] An earlier licence may also have been granted in a different context, for instance as part of a joint venture,[99] or with a narrow scope, for instance to develop a spin-off product.[100] Lastly, if an infringer refuses to accept a patentee's licence offer, that may limit the credibility of their argument that damages in lieu should be awarded instead of an injunction.[101] Here, too, the inquiry is highly context-sensitive: an established industry player will be irreparably harmed by a competitor's infringement even if they offered them a broad portfolio licence prior to litigation.[102] However, where a licence to the patent-in-suit was offered not just to the infringer but also to numerous other competitors, particularly as part of a litigation strategy, damages in lieu might sufficiently compensate the patentee even if they are a practising entity.[103]

4.4.1.3. *Infringer Characteristics*

The large variety of patentee characteristics just discussed all affect their entitlement to injunctive relief under the first two prongs of the *eBay* test. Infringer characteristics are almost never relevant under these prongs but primarily under the third prong: the balance of hardships. Thus, while US courts often discuss in detail whether the patentee's business model and licensing history entitle it to injunctive relief, there seem to be no structural traits on the side of infringers to help decide whether it would be appropriate to issue injunctive relief against them. Once irreparable harm and inadequacy of monetary damages are established, only a public interest in the availability of the infringing products (rare) or considerable hardship on the part of the infringer (even more rare) can defeat the injunction claim.

A last aspect to consider in this section are prior relationships between the parties. We have already seen that prior licence offers may, but certainly do not always, preclude a finding of irreparable harm. In rare cases, a licence to the patent-in-suit may be implied in a licence to different patents, or prior contacts

[97] *Asetek v CMI* (n 81) *15; *Smith & Nephew v Arthrex* (n 83) 1182; *Acumed LLC v Stryker Corp* 2007 WL 4180682, *6 (D Or 20 November 2007).

[98] *Peach State Labs Inc v Environmental Manufacturing Solutions LLC* 2011 WL 13140668, *4 (MD Fla 12 August 2011) (adoption of technology); *Veracode Inc v Appthority Inc* 137 FSupp3d 17, 89 (D Mass 2015) (key licensing partner). The argument may not be available to companies that already have an established market position: *Belden Technologies Inc v Superior Essex Inc* 802 FSupp2d 555, 578 (D Del 2011).

[99] *ION Inc v Sercel Inc* 2010 WL 3911378, *5 (ED Tex 16 September 2010).

[100] *Innovention v MGA* (n 79) *4.

[101] *Omega Patents LLC v Fortin Auto Radio Inc* 2007 WL 9719177, *6 (MD Fla 4 April 2007).

[102] *General Electric Co v Mitsubishi Heavy Industries Ltd* No 3:10-CV-276-F, *55 (ND Tex 9 July 2012).

[103] *Server v American* (n 67) *4.

may give rise to a legitimate expectation that a licence would be granted.[104] More plausibly, a pre-existing relationship will give rise to suspicions of wilfulness, as when the infringer is a former customer of the patentee.[105] Parties may also have a litigation history: injunctions will almost certainly be issued against repeat infringers who disobeyed or circumvented prior injunctions.[106] By the same token, continued sales after it became clear that those sales infringe the patent (eg following a jury verdict) stress the need to impose injunctive relief.[107] But the most common 'antecedent' argument is that a patentee's delay in bringing the infringement suit, or their failure to request a preliminary injunction, indicates an absence of irreparable harm. Such arguments are usually rejected, but exceptions occur, particularly when other indications exist against irreparable harm.[108] The argument may become more compelling when the infringer succeeded in defeating a motion for a preliminary injunction on substantive grounds,[109] or where substantial investments were made by the infringer during the delay.[110]

4.4.2. Markets

4.4.2.1. Easily Contestable Markets

In many cases, the patentee and infringer compete in a market that is contestable and characterised by a relatively high degree of demand elasticity. As a rule of thumb, markets are easily contestable if customers will quickly switch to products incorporating the patented technology following the grant of an injunction.[111] This is often the case with inexpensive consumer goods, but may also occur

[104] *cf TruePosition Inc v Andrew Corp* 568 FSupp2d 500, 533 (D Del 2008) (finding that an injunction was appropriate precisely because of 'the lack of evidence of an intentional false promise by plaintiffs to license the [patent] followed by a demand for royalties'); *Omega v Fortin* (n 101) *6.

[105] *LC Eldridge Sales Co Ltd v Azen Manufacturing Pte Ltd* No 6:11cv599, *3–4 (ED Tex 22 September 2014); *Peach v Environmental* (n 98) *3.

[106] *Vertical v JT Bonn* (n 81) *5; *MGM Well Services Inc v Mega Lift Systems LLC* 505 FSupp2d 359, 379 (SD Tex 2007) (where, following a preliminary injunction, the infringer filed for bankruptcy and chanced its corporate name while retaining the same employees, office and practice of infringement); *Muniauction Inc v ThomsonCorp* 502 FSupp2d 477, 483 (WD Pa 2007) (where the court noted that 'defendants apparently have every intention of continuing to offer their infringing system in the absence of an injunction').

[107] *Asetek v CMI* (n 81) *15.

[108] Delay in bringing suit: *Halo v Pulse* (n 75) *6; *i4i v Microsoft* (n 77) 599; *800 Adept v Murex* (n 75) 1335; but see *MercExchange v eBay* (n 74) 573. Failure to request preliminary injunction: *WCM Industries Inc v IPS Corp* 2016 WL 7448709, *3 (WD Tenn 16 May 2016); but see *Ameritox Ltd v Millennium Health LLC* 2015 WL 3825499, *2 (WD Wis 19 June 2015) ('If ongoing infringement had been such a concern for plaintiffs, one might reasonably ask why plaintiffs failed to seek a preliminary injunction earlier in the litigation').

[109] *Sanofi v Glenmark* (n 83) 695.

[110] *Cave Consulting Group LLC v OptumInsight Inc* 2016 WL 4658979, *23 (ND Cal 7 September 2016).

[111] *Johnstech International Corp v JF Microtechnology SDN BHD* 2018 WL 3036759, *2 (ND Cal 19 June 2018).

with B2B technology, especially where product life cycles are relatively short. Such markets often have low barriers to entry, so that tolerating infringement may attract further infringers, quickly lead to price erosion or cause a shrinkage in sales outlets willing to stock the patentee's product.[112] Not infrequently, the infringing product will be of lower quality than the original, which may harm the reputation of the patentee's product.[113] In these types of markets, injunctive relief is usually warranted because the window in which to reap benefits from patented exclusivity is limited.[114] At the same time, there will rarely be circumstances weighing against the grant of an injunction as these markets are often for simple technology that does not implicate public interests, and the infringer should be able to recover market share if they succeed in developing a non-infringing alternative or lifting the injunction. At least in the US context, most patent litigation appears to occur within these types of markets.[115]

4.4.2.2. Markets with Incumbency Effects

A recurring example in US practice of a market that is not easily contestable is a so-called 'design wins' market. The term was used in three cases concerning the design of microchips. Competitors in these markets often do not manufacture goods themselves, but pitch their technology to companies that do. These companies incorporate the winning design into their product lines and so are bound to the chosen technology for that product cycle. Thus, winning a design competition shields the technology provider from competitive products for some time and enhances their ability to compete in subsequent design competitions. Because of the critical importance of design 'wins', patentees have an evident interest in injunctive relief to ensure that they do not compete against infringing technology for wins.[116] At the same time, an injunction was denied where a patentee's chances in the design competition were lowered by its own licensees and third-party competitors, while an injunction would 'decimate' the infringer's business after the patentee had strategically 'locked-in' the relevant standard.[117] The decision reveals other key characteristics of design win markets. First, because market players compete on innovation, each of them tends to

[112] *Hydrodynamic Industrial Co Ltd v Green Max Distributors Inc* 2014 WL 2740368, *3 (CD Cal 10 June 2014).

[113] *Whirlpool Corp v Global Purification* LLC 2017 WL 2099771, *3 (ED Tex 15 May 2017) (concerning replacement parts for a branded product); *ALPS South LLC v The Ohio Willow Wood Company* 2013 WL 12164676, *2 (MD Fla 9 May 2013) (where inferior infringing products created a perception in the market that a competing technology was superior).

[114] *Atlanta Attachment Co v Leggett & Platt Inc* 2007 WL 5011980, *8 (ND Ga 23 February 2007).

[115] J Golden, 'Litigation in the Middle: The Context of Patent-Infringement Injunctions' (2014) 92 *Texas Law Review* 2075, 2097 (finding that, in 2010, the typical US patent case involved 'patents on relative mundanities or curiosities that appear to have less than stratospheric economic value').

[116] *Broadcom v Emulex* (n 75) *4; *Hynix v Rambus* (n 84) 981; *Broadcom Corp v Qualcomm Inc* No SACV 05-467 JVS, *9 (CD Cal 31 December 2007).

[117] *Hynix v Rambus* (n 84) 984–85.

perform their own substantial R&D. Second, these markets tend to be dominated by standards, access to which can be indispensable to compete. To the extent the standards are set by standards development organisations and subject to fair, reasonable and non-discriminatory declarations, this is not normally problematic, but they can also be de facto standards that block a competitor's own innovations.[118]

The market for microchip designs is unique, but the characteristics it exemplifies – long-term effects of initial commercial successes – also appear in other markets. Incumbency effects make winning new or regaining lost market share difficult. These effects may be caused by 'sticky' customers that do not easily switch due to product lifetime or the need to procure servicing contracts from the seller,[119] or where sales occur through intermediaries (such as large retailers or healthcare organisations) that cannot easily switch between providers.[120] Building up long-term relations with these customers is critical, especially where they provide feedback for further improvements of the product.[121] Some products display 'ecosystem' effects whereby interproduct compatibility is a key consideration in purchasing decisions, so that a lost initial sale often results in losing potential subsequent sales.[122] The 'win' may be a procurement contract or a sponsorship deal that lasts a fixed period and serves important advertising purposes.[123] These are but some examples of market features that create incumbency effects, and it should be noted that they can also occur in markets that are otherwise easily contestable. In fact, most cases will have elements of incumbency effects, at least to some degree.

What are the implications for injunctive relief? Where infringement threatens to create incumbency advantages for the infringer, eg where it results in a 'design win' or a procurement contract, the patentee will have a strong interest in (urgent) injunctive relief.[124] Especially where infringers obtained incumbency advantages through wilful infringement at a critical phase of the market's growth, courts have been willing to grant injunctive relief.[125] We see a variety

[118] *Broadcom v Emulex* (n 75) *4.

[119] *The Western Union Co v Moneygram International Inc* 2009 WL 8660103, *31 (WD Tex November 17 2009) (money transfer services); *TIVO v Echostar* (n 81) 670 (digital video recorders).

[120] *Hydrodynamic v Green* (n 112) *3 (sea scooters); *Sanofi v Glenmark* (n 83) 695 (pharmaceuticals); *Innovention v MGA* (n 79) *3 (laser board games); *Atlanta v Leggett & Platt* (n 114) *7 (rufflers).

[121] *Smith & Nephew Inc v Synthes-Stratec Inc* 466 FSupp2d 978, 983 (WD Tenn 2006).

[122] *SIMO Holdings Inc v uCloudlink Network Technology Ltd* 396 FSupp3d 323, 345 (SDNY 2019); *The Chamberlain Group v Techtronic Industries Co Ltd* 315 FSupp3d 977, 1010 (ND Ill 2018); *Black & Decker Inc v Robert Bosch Tool Corp* 2006 WL 3446144, *4 (ND Ill 29 November 2006) (concerning a loss of sales of cordless power tools as a result of sales of infringing radio chargers).

[123] *Tarkett Inc & Fieldturf USA Inc v Astroturf LLC* No 10-cv-12492, *14 (ED Mich 11 May 2016); *Callaway v Acushnet* (n 82) 619.

[124] *Broadcom v Emulex* (n 75) *5. See also *Amgen Inc v F Hoffman-La Roche Ltd* 581 FSupp2d 160, 212 (D Mass 2008), where an injunction was granted to prevent the infringer from developing 'infrastructure that would make [them] a viable competitor not only in the [original] market, but also in markets for future drugs'; *Bendix v Haldex* (n 72) *6, finding that patent exclusivity was 'especially important in a market that both parties agreed is heading into a period of tremendous growth'.

[125] *Bio-Rad v 10X* (n 83) *3; *Callaway v Acushnet* (n 82) 621.

of wilfulness scenarios here, for instance where an infringer was only able to obtain market share as quickly as it did by infringing the patent or where it employed a variety of tactics to usurp the patentee's market share and reputation as an innovator.[126] At the same time, incumbency effects create several complicating factors. First, the infringer's market position may have been obtained through non-infringing sales and without even offering the infringing item to customers.[127] In these cases, an injunction that would have the effect of substantially harming the infringer's market position may not be appropriate. Second, a sunset period may be necessary to accommodate the interests of clients and the public where design cycles are long: for instance, in both design wins cases where an injunction was awarded, it was stayed for at least a year.[128] In the case of capacitors with uses in 'government, military, space, and infrastructure projects', a sunset period was ordered to allow shipping orders placed prior to oral argument.[129] Long design cycles may also necessitate carve-outs from the injunction, as occurred in cases involving wind turbines and oil rigs, where maintenance of existing projects was allowed.[130] Third, as the 'Horse has left the barn' cases in Table 4.2 show, the incumbency effects now enjoyed by the infringer may be so strong that they would be hard to undo even with an injunction.

4.4.3. Products

4.4.3.1. General Aspects of the Infringing Product

The nature of the infringing product matters to how infringement impacts the patentee, so courts have considered it relevant to the irreparable harm inquiry. For instance, they differentiated between knock-off products developed specifically to compete with the patented invention on the one hand[131] and independently developed technology on the other.[132] One court found a 'notable difference' between infringement through a business practice and situations where the infringer 'saturates the market with a tangible product whereby the purchase of one company's product *eliminates the demand* for the other'.[133]

[126] *RMH Tech LLC v PMC Industries Inc* 352 FSupp3d 164, 202 (D Conn 2018); *Polara Engineering Inc v Campbell Co* 237 FSupp3d 956, 988 (CD Cal 2017); *Global Ground Automation Inc v Groundrez LLC* 2011 WL 13098293, *6 (ED Tex 29 June 2011); *Smith & Nephew v Arthrex* (n 83) 1181; *800 Adept v Murex* (n 75) 1338.

[127] *Inventio AG v Otis Elevator Co* 2011 WL 3480946, *1 (SD NY 4 August 2011); *MercExchange v eBay* (n 74) 580.

[128] But see *SynQor Inc v Artesyn Technologies Inc* 2011 WL 238645, *8 (ED Tex 24 January 2011), where the infringer's customers were not 'innocent bystanders'. Thus, the clients' absence of goods faith may mitigate against a stay.

[129] *Presidio v American* (n 78) *8.

[130] *LC Eldridge v Azen* (n 105) *6; *General Electric v Mitsubishi* (n 102) *58.

[131] *Polara v Campbell* (n 126) 988.

[132] *Amgen Inc v Sanofi 2017* WL 61725, *3 (D Del January 5 2017); *Cordance v Amazon* (n 94) 339.

[133] *MercExchange v eBay* (n 74) 580.

Here, as elsewhere, what matters ultimately is whether the patentee is irreparably harmed by the infringement so none of these considerations is by itself dispositive.[134]

US courts have also dealt repeatedly with supposed *de minimis* infringements or allegations that the infringement was discontinued. In the European context, these types of problems are usually resolved at the level of (exceptions to) infringement, rather than proportionality.[135] In the USA, however, they are generally considered under *eBay*'s first and third prongs. For example, an injunction was not considered necessary in a case where the only instance of infringement had been the demonstration at a trade show of a prototype device years before.[136] Arguments that an injunction should not issue because infringement was discontinued were more common and sometimes accepted, though more often the court turned them against the infringer by finding that, if the arguments were true, the infringer would suffer no hardship from an injunction. Sometimes, sales of the infringing product have ceased but products already sold require aftersales services. Such services would be enjoined where they constituted a novel act of infringement,[137] though the damages award could also be construed as an implied licence to allow continued performance of those services.[138] In one interesting case, a database was built with infringing technology but, once completed, itself no longer infringed the patent. Should such 'fruits from the poisonous tree' be enjoined? The court ruled no, deciding that the damages payment would sufficiently compensate the patentee.[139]

4.4.3.2. Component Patent Cases

As explained above, US courts developed a causal nexus standard according to which the presence of patented features in the infringing device must impact customers' buying decisions. Its most significant use to date has been in components cases, though it applies generally to all infringement cases.[140] The causal nexus test seeks to establish whether competitive harm suffered by the patentee is essentially due to legitimate competition (through non-infringing components) or at least in part through the advantages provided by the patented technology. That is a sensible approach on paper, but it places on the patentee a burden of proof that can be hard to satisfy, particularly in

[134] *Broadcom v Emulex* (n 75) *4.

[135] For a recent English case on *de minimis* infringement, see *IPCom v Vodafone* [2021] EWCA Civ 205, paras 182–85.

[136] *Respironics Inc v Invacare Corp* 2008 WL 111983, *5 (WD Pa January 8 2008).

[137] *Transamerica Life Insurance Co v Lincoln National Life Insurance Co* 625 FSupp2d 702, 718 (ND Iowa 2009).

[138] *Polara v Campbell* (n 126) 991.

[139] *Veracode v Appthority* (n 98) 96.

[140] See, eg *EL DuPont de Nemours and Co v Unifrax LLC* 2017 WL 4004419, *5 (D Del 12 September 2017) (concerning laminates with flame barrier properties).

high-tech products.[141] It is therefore unsurprising that courts have accepted a wide range of circumstances as indicators that a causal nexus between the infringement and the patented technology was present. These include the fact that the patent 'is the core technology' embodied in a technical standard;[142] that it constitutes 'the central function' that the overall product performs;[143] that this product 'could not function' without the patented technology;[144] that the patented technology 'is highly desired by consumers and of benefit to them';[145] that the patented technology was 'the decisive factor for the commercial success' of the infringing products;[146] that there is a stand-alone market for the small components;[147] that the patented technology solved a key problem occurring in the prior art;[148] that the infringer 'markets some of the patented features as advantages of its products';[149] or even that product sales are 'also driven' by properties resulting from the claimed composition.[150] In each case, the causal nexus must be proven in relation to the infringer's product, not the patentee's product incorporating the technology: customers may have different reasons for buying the infringing product, even if both products incorporate the patented technology.[151]

4.4.3.3. The Patent and its Claims

Lastly, US courts have also considered the merits, inventive or otherwise, of the patent in suit. In *eBay*, the fact that the patent-in-suit was a business method patent weighed against the grant of an injunction.[152] In a high-stakes standard essential patent dispute, the court apparently considered relevant to the denial of an injunction that 'patents in the field of information technology often have little if any value except defensively'.[153] And in a controversial decision concerning snowploughs, the district court refused to grant an injunction in part because the patents in suit were 'minor improvements to

[141] As one court cautioned, an infringing component might be so substantially integrated with the product's other features 'that its isolation and specific attribution of consumer demand to it [may be] exceedingly difficult': *Veracode v Appthority* (n 98) 90.

[142] *Commonwealth v Buffalo* (n 88) 606; *Transocean Offshore v Globalsantafe Corp 2006* WL 3813778, *5 (SD Tex December 27 2006).

[143] *SIMO v uCloudlink* (n 122) 345.

[144] *ActiveVideo Networks Inc v Verizon Communications Inc* 827 FSupp2d 641, 653 (ED Va 2011). See also *Sealant v TEK* (n 80) *23.

[145] *Broadcom v Qualcomm* (n 116) *8.

[146] *MeadWestvaco Corp v Rexam PLC* No 1:10-cv-511, *77 (ED Va 12 April 2012).

[147] *i4i v Microsoft* (n 77) 591.

[148] *Halo v Pulse* (n 75) *5.

[149] *EMC v Zerto* (n 67) *13.

[150] *Invista North America SÀRL v M&G USA Corp* 35 FSupp3d 583, 609 (D Del 31 March 2014).

[151] *Power Integrations Inc v Fairchild Semiconductor International Inc* 2015 WL 604582, *3 (ND Cal 12 February 2015).

[152] *MercExchange v eBay* (n 74) 574.

[153] *Apple Inc v Motorola Inc* 869 FSupp2d 901, 917 (ED Ill 2012).

existing … technology'.[154] Even the type of claim invoked could be relevant to the decision to grant injunctive relief. In the aforementioned *Conceptus* decision, the denial of injunctive relief was supported by the fact that only the procedure used for inserting the infringing intrafallopian conceptive device infringed the patent; the device itself did not.[155]

A short remaining lifespan of the patent usually weighs against an injunction. US courts generally find that the burden of having to comply with a short-lived injunction is excessive for the infringer and potential third parties, depending on the infringing technology.[156] Here, as elsewhere, the argument has also been reversed: one court held that the infringer would suffer only limited hardship if they would soon be able to revert back to the enjoined product.[157]

4.4.4. Hardships

4.4.4.1. eBay's Enigma: The Inscrutable Nature of the Balance of Hardships Test

Sitting as a district court judge, Richard Posner observed that the 'insight' behind the balance of hardship prong in patent cases is that 'An injunction that imposes greater costs on the defendant than it confers benefits on the plaintiff reduces net social welfare'.[158] Application of the balance of hardship test along these lines may be expedient as a matter of abstract economic analysis, but it is far removed from how the test applies in practice. In fact, in most cases, the costs that the injunction imposes on the infringer are disregarded altogether under reference to a 1986 CAFC decision, where it held that 'one who elects to build a business on a product found to infringe cannot be heard to complain if an injunction against continuing infringement destroys the business so elected'.[159] The CAFC reaffirmed that decision post-*eBay* by holding unequivocally that sunk costs on the part of the infringer and 'the consequences [of] infringement, such as the cost of redesigning the infringing products' should be 'ignored' under the balance of hardships test.[160] Consequently, pleas that an injunction would

[154] *Douglas Dynamics LLC v Buyers Products Co* No 09-cv-261-wmc, *6 (WD Wis 25 February 2011). On appeal, the CAFC held that the district court erred in characterizing the patents-in-suit as minor: *Douglas v Buyers* (n 19) 1345.

[155] *Conceptus v Hologic* (n 67) *4.

[156] *The Dow Chemical Co v Nova Chemicals Corp* 2010 WL 3083023, *1 (D Del 30 July 2010) (remaining lifespan of slightly over a year, given substantial issues for appeal, counsels against injunction); *Humanscale Corp v CompX International Inc* 2010 WL 1779963, *4 (ED Va April 29 2010); *Insituform v Cosmic* (n 73) *13–14.

[157] *RMH v PMC* (n 126) 203.

[158] *Apple v Motorola* (n 153) 922.

[159] *Windsurfing v AMF* (n 44) n 12.

[160] *i4i v Microsoft* (n 19) 863.

harm the infringer are often dismissed out of hand, even if the harm would be severe.[161] That is true not just where the infringer argues for denial of an injunction, but also for application of a sunset period.[162]

Of course, it is understandable that courts are unwilling to reward companies for successfully infringing others' patents through generous application of the balance of hardships prong.[163] But ignoring most or all of the infringer's harm regardless of the circumstances makes the balance of hardships test devoid of purpose. On two occasions, this was recognised by the District Court for the District of Massachusetts, which held that 'hardships that may appropriately be considered' on the part of the infringer are limited only where infringement was wilful.[164] And in a recent decision, the CAFC reversed, for abuse of discretion, a decision where the district court enjoined 'a much smaller company' that depended 'entirely on the sales of the enjoined products for its revenue', even though its infringement was wilful.[165] This decision seems hard to reconcile with the CAFC's earlier insistence that courts should ignore the consequences that having to cease infringement would have for the infringer. It exemplifies the general confusion that seems to exist about the proper application of the balance of hardship test: no other part of the *eBay* test is so erratically applied.

4.4.4.2. The Parties' Relative Blameworthiness

One element that is surely relevant to any balancing exercise is the parties' conduct. As the previous chapter showed, the patent prosecution process offers various opportunities for strategic behaviour and subterfuge. In US law, such behaviour can render the patent unenforceable if it rises to the level of misconduct under the specific doctrines of inequitable conduct or unclean hands.[166] As a result, opportunism on the part of the patentee is generally not considered as part of the *eBay* test. At the same time, opportunism that does not rise to the level of misconduct can still be relevant under the balance of hardships test. For instance, where an infringer had incurred large sunk costs and was

[161] *Presidio Components Inc v American Technical Ceramics Corp* 2016 WL 4377096, *17 (SD Cal 17 August 2016); *Retractable v Becton* (n 75) *3; *Momentus Golf Inc v SwingRite Corp* No 4:02-cv-40252, *4 (D Iowa 16 February 2007).

[162] *Callaway v Acushnet* (n 82) 622 ('The court is not in the business of making defendant's infringements easier to unravel'). For examples where hardship stemming from the difficulty of obtaining a timely design-around were dismissed, see *Haemonetics Corp v Baxter Healthcare Corp* 2009 WL 10692802, *3 (D Mass 1 June 2009); *Acumed v Stryker* (n 97) *6.

[163] *Broadcom v Qualcomm* (n 116) *16 ('The argument as made here borders on a contention that successful exploitation of infringing technology shields a party from injunctive relief, and the more successful it is, the more it should be shielded').

[164] *Veracode v Appthority* (n 98) 94; *Smith & Nephew Inc v Interlace Medical Inc* 955 FSupp2d 69, 79 (D Mass 2013). *cf* Gergen et al (n 8) 227–28 (suggesting that an undue hardship defence might be made 'unavailable' in cases of wilful infringement).

[165] *Bio-Rad v 10X* (n 18) 1379.

[166] *Therasense Inc v Becton, Dickson & Co* 649 F3d 1276, 1288 (Fed Cir 2011); *Gilead Sciences, Inc v Merck & Co Inc* 888 F3d 1231, 1240 (Fed Cir 2018).

locked in to the technology in large part because the patentee did not disclose its patents until the relevant technology had enjoyed nearly five years of success, the balance of hardships weighed against the grant of an injunction.[167] Likewise, a patentee's 'specialization in obtaining fees through threatened litigation' may also affect negatively its position under this prong.[168]

Naturally, the infringer's conduct is equally relevant to the balance of hardships test. In one case, the employment of a 'scorched-earth litigation strategy' by an infringer in a superior financial position was considered to weigh strongly in favour of an injunction.[169] Infringers might also be faulted for not having taken reasonable care to avoid patent infringement, for instance by obtaining outside counsel[170] or by vetting their competitors' products to ensure they do not embody patented technology.[171] These examples show that even short of wilful infringement, the infringer might be sufficiently to blame for the infringement to reject a hardship argument. An infringer's efforts in developing a non-infringing alternative are particularly noteworthy in this respect. Where such an alternative was readily available or would have been available had the infringer shown proper diligence in developing it, courts often found the balance of hardships favoured the patentee.[172] The time that should be allowed to developed a work-around and when 'the clock starts running' are further discussed below in the modalities section.

4.4.4.3. Cases in which the Balance of Hardship Favoured the Infringer

It follows from the previous subsections that cases where the balance of hardships weighed against the grant of an injunction are rare, certainly where other factors did not also favour denial. Where courts took harms for the infringer into consideration they mostly found that they did not outweigh the hardship the patentee would suffer if no injunction would issue.[173] A mitigating factor often cited against infringers was that they also sold other, non-infringing products,[174]

[167] *Hynix v Rambus* (n 84) 985.
[168] *MercExchange v eBay* (n 74) 584.
[169] *Eko Brands v Adrian Rivera Maynez Enterprises Inc* 325 FSupp3d 1116, 1129 (WD Wash 2018).
[170] *Smith & Nephew v Arthrex* (n 83) 1183.
[171] *FenF LLC v SmartThingz Inc* 2014 WL 1431692, *4 (ED Mich 14 April 2014).
[172] *Bio-Rad v 10X* (n 83) *4; *WCM v IPS* (n 108) *4; *Broadcom v Emulex* (n 75) *9; *ActiveVideo v Verizon* (n 144) 654; *Vertical v JT Bonn* (n 81) *5; *Fresenius v Baxter* (n 83) *5; *Transocean v Globalsantafe* (n 142) *6.
[173] *Becton Dickinson Co v Tyco Healthcare Group LP* 2008 WL 4745882, *4 (D Del 29 October 2008) (balance of hardships a 'close question' where harm is great and business relationships would suffer, but ultimately not enough because 'that is the risk that [infringer] took when it placed a potentially infringing product on the market'); *Smith & Nephew v Arthrex* (n 83) 1183 (loss of 8.7% of sales not unreasonable); *Atlanta v Leggett & Platt* (n 114) *8 (injunction would 'have little effect on [infringer's] total sales').
[174] *Apple Inc v Samsung Electronics Ltd* 2014 WL 7496140, *21 (ND Cal August 27 2014); *Transamerica v Lincoln* (n 137) 718; *MGM v Mega Lift* (n 106) 379; *Muniauction v ThomsonCorp* (n 106) 483.

an argument that held particular weight in David-versus-Goliath scenarios, which, as we saw above, invariably favour patentees.[175] Commercial success with the infringement has also been cited against the infringer under this prong because it may offset any costs caused by the injunction.[176]

A denial or limitation of injunctive relief on balance-of-interests grounds usually required gross disproportionality between the parties' interests. For instance, forcing an infringer to shut down oil rigs to replace an infringing element 'at a cost of $500,000 per day, per rig [was] disproportionate to the harm [the patentee would] suffer'.[177] Losing an investment of $40.2 million on R&D over a three-year time span supported denial of an injunction.[178] True to the nature of the balance prong, it was found to weigh against an injunction where it would target 'the entirety of [the infringer's] business', whereas the lost sales identified by the patentee represented 'about 0.001 per cent of its annual revenues'.[179] There is no absolute threshold of harm that will tip the balance in favour of the infringer. That point is nicely illustrated by a decision where the court observed that 'Bankruptcy is perhaps the ultimate hardship' (and would likely follow from an injunction), but nevertheless considered the hardship factor neutral.[180] Although potential bankruptcy or decimation of a business sometimes carried weight, most of the time this 'ultimate hardship' was insufficient to defeat an injunction as courts considered the infringer brought these consequences on itself.[181] Rather, the hardship should be substantial in relation to the harm the infringement causes to the patentee.[182]

Hardship need not be understood in strictly financial terms: other considerations, discussed elsewhere in this overview, could also result in the balance of hardship tipping the infringer's way. Significant investments in an independently developed, alternative product with important advantages over the patented

[175] *Inventio v Otis* (n 127) *2 (where infringer had itself represented that 'the infringing system is, if not inconsequential, then of limited relevance to its market success'); *Arlington Industries v Bridgeport Fittings* 2010 WL 817519, *4 (MD Pa 9 March 2010) (no hardship because the infringing products constitute 'but thirty of [infringer's] 2,000 different products').

[176] *Bendix v Haldex* (n 72) *7.

[177] *LC Eldridge v Azen* (n 105) *6.

[178] *Verinata Health Inc v Ariosa Diagnostics Inc* 329 FSupp3d 1070, 1122 (ND Cal 2018).

[179] *EMC v Zerto* (n 67) *14.

[180] *Fitness Anywhere LLC v Woss Enterprises LLC* 2018 WL 6069511, *12 (ND Cal 20 November 2018).

[181] *Global Traffic Technologies LLC v Emtrac Systems Inc* 2013 WL 5964454, *2 (D Minn 8 November 2013); *Retractable v Becton* (n 75) *5.

[182] As with every part of the *eBay* test, outliers exist where seemingly trivial hardship sufficed. See, eg *Tyco v Applied Medical* (n 71) *4 (balance neutral because infringer would have to explain effects of injunction to customers, 'which may engender confusion'); *KFX Medical Corp v Arthrex Inc* 2014 WL 11961953, *4 (SD Cal 18 February 2014) (hardship consisting in costs of reprinting marketing materials and coming up with a new branding strategy). See also *LaserDynamics Inc v Quanta Computer Inc* No 2:06-CV-438-TJW, *5 (ED Tex 22 June 2010); *Metso Minerals Inc v Powerscreen International Distribution Ltd* 788 FSupp2d 71, 76 (ED NY 2011); *Cave v OptumInsight* (n 110) *23 ('Optum's reputation with customers will likely be diminished if those customers are forced to expend the time, effort, and costs necessary to acquire and implement a replacement product'). But see, for a case where this type of hardship was dismissed, *Halo v Pulse* (n 75) *10.

product are one example.[183] An injunction that, due to the nature of the market or arrangements with distributors, would also affect the infringer's capacity to sell other, non-infringing goods is another.[184] Similarly, in many instances, the balance of hardships inquiry intersects with the other *eBay* prongs. For example, the balance could favour the infringer because only one component of its products was found to be infringing.[185] Overlaps with third-party interests (usually addressed under the fourth prong) also occurred frequently, as where the infringer's customers would suffer hardship from the injunction due to the long sales cycle of the infringing products.[186] Another frequent argument is that the injunction will force the infringer to lay off employees. In a case where there was also substantial uncertainty about the validity of the claims pending Patent and Trademark Office re-examination, the potential laying off of 159 employees was held to weigh against the grant of an immediate injunction.[187] In a case concerning an independently developed alternative, having to lay off nearly 300 employees also weighed against an injunction.[188] Conversely, the balance of hardships tipped against the infringer where it had only two employees, also because they knew about the patented product and nonetheless decided to proceed with infringement.[189]

4.4.5. The Public Interest

4.4.5.1. The Nature and Application of the Public Interest Prong

US courts' treatment of *eBay*'s public interest prong stands out for two reasons. First, it is the only prong under which effectively a presumption in favour of injunctive relief operates. While it is nominally for the patentee to prove that the grant of an injunction would not disserve the public, in practice, courts assume that public interest favours protecting patent exclusivity. It is then for the infringer to show that an injunction should nevertheless be stayed, limited or denied, and this should only be accepted in 'rare and limited circumstances'.[190] Second, this prong operates largely independently of the other prongs. Irreparable harm, adequacy of monetary damages and the balance of hardship are often weighed together to determine whether an injunction should be issued, such that findings under

[183] *Conceptus v Hologic* (n 67) *3.
[184] *Commonwealth v Buffalo* (n 88) fn 1.
[185] *Douglas v Buyers* (n 154) *9 ('Entering the injunction ... would in essence require [the infringer] to junk some or most of its snowplow business ... simply because they infringe minor improvements taught in [the patents in suit]'); *Humanscale v CompX* (n 157) *4.
[186] *Carnegie Mellon University v Marvell Technology Group Ltd* 2014 WL 1320154, *35 (WD Pa 31 March 2014).
[187] *Smith & Nephew v Interlace* (n 164) 80.
[188] *Conceptus v Hologic* (n 67) *3.
[189] *FenF v SmartThingz* (n 171) *5.
[190] *Commonwealth v Buffalo* (n 88) 607.

one prong can compensate for findings under another. But every time a court found that an injunction would materially affect the public interest, it required a carve-out or stay to ameliorate public interest concerns (or outright denied the injunction). *eBay*'s fourth prong thus operates more as an external limitation on patent exclusivity than as an integral element of a proportionality test.

To outweigh the public interest in protecting patent exclusivity, 'the harm should be of a unique or socially valuable type'.[191] Potential harm to patients is the archetypal example on both sides of the Atlantic, but other harms have been considered sufficient as well; both categories (healthcare/other) are discussed separately in the following subsections. It should be noted that infringers bear a special evidentiary burden under this prong because, in addition to persuading the court that an interest is sufficiently 'socially valuable', they must also prove that the injunction will in fact harm that interest. Any argument to that effect is inherently speculative, and in many cases, courts have dismissed the infringer's objections for that reason. Parties might try substantiating potential harms through affidavits by affected parties (eg doctors), but those will often be self-serving and of low probative value.[192] If a court considers limiting the injunction on public interest grounds but is unsure of the size or plausibility of the effects, the best way to proceed might be to request supplemental briefing or hear expert testimony.[193] In many cases, however, the point will simply be decided on the basis of what strikes the court as plausible.[194]

Whether the injunction would actually result in demand for the relevant technology going unmet is often a decisive factor in the public interest inquiry. If the patentee or other competitors can easily meet demand, no public interest will be implicated.[195] The infringer's admission that it will have a non-infringing alternative ready soon may thus work against them under the public interest prong.[196] Conversely, if the patentee has insufficient production capacity,[197] or if their product is not yet ready to go to market[198] or the patentee's product was previously discontinued,[199] potential shortages in the technology may necessitate a stay or denial of the injunction. In case of doubt, at least one court has expressed a

[191] *ActiveVideo v Verizon* (n 144) 652.

[192] *Joyal v Johnson* (n 74) *12; *Acumed v Stryker* (n 97) *8. For a unique counterexample where a competitor was able to testify on the effects of an injunction because they had themselves been enjoined under the patent, see *Johnson & Johnson v CIBA* (n 93) 1291.

[193] *Innogenetics NV v Abbott Laboratories* 578 FSupp2d 1079, 1105 (WD Wis 2007); *IMX Inc v Lendingtree LLC* 469 FSupp2d 203, 226 (D Del 2007).

[194] *Advanced Cardiovascular v Medtronic* (n 96) 561; *z4 v Microsoft* (n 91) 443–44.

[195] *SynQor v Artesyn* (n 128) *5; *ION v Sercel* (n 99) *7; *Smith & Nephew v Arthrex* (n 83) 1184. Note that there exists a squeeze on this point in US law because the availability of non-infringing alternatives may be relevant for obviousness, damages, etc and parties are held to their statements on those points, eg *Muniauction v ThomsonCorp* (n 106) 484.

[196] *Bio-Rad v 10X* (n 83) *4. The patentee might also point out that major customers have already started switching to them: *Innogenetics v Abbott* (n 193) *1.

[197] *WBIP v Kohler* (n 66) *2.

[198] *BASF v Commonwealth* (n 89) *20.

[199] *Verinata v Ariosa* (n 178) 1122.

preference for guaranteed continued availability over modification of the injunction 'if an emergency arose'.[200] It is therefore unsurprising that patentees have sought to pre-empt public interest concerns by suggesting limited sunset periods and smoothing transition to the patentee's products, for instance by offering to train customer staff.[201] Another strategy might be to exempt from an injunction support for products already sold, subject to a royalty payment.[202] Even without such concessions on the part of the patentee, in the majority of cases public interest concerns could be resolved through narrowly tailoring the injunction or imposition of a sunset period.[203] It should be noted that these periods have sometimes been quite long (at least for a European observer): for instance, in one of the microchip design cases, an 18-month sunset period was imposed in light of the complexity of the products.[204]

4.4.5.2. Public Interest Considerations – Healthcare

In an early decision upheld by the CAFC, the infringer was allowed to continue supplies of a product for which 'there is no appropriate alternative' so that an injunction 'would increase patient risk and may lead to preventable deaths'.[205] It no longer seems controversial to exempt specific groups of patients from an injunction on these grounds, even in Europe. But competing pharmaceuticals or medical devices are often not identical, which raises the question whether clinical superiority of the infringing product is also grounds for limiting injunctive relief and, if so, how superior the product should be. Additional choice of treatments, while beneficial for patients, was held not to be enough to justify denial of injunctive relief if the infringer's product did not offer appreciable advantages over the patentee's product.[206] Moreover, these advantages must be more than just appreciable, at least on paper.[207] But in practice, US courts have tended to be relatively lenient, apparently wishing to avoid any risk of jeopardising patients' health.[208] For instance, it was considered enough that healthcare professionals 'express concern for the success of their surgeries' in the absence of

[200] *Retractable v Becton* (n 75) *4.
[201] *Haemonetics v Baxter* (n 162) *4; *Bendix v Haldex* (n 72) *7 (patentee would 'work with [infringer] to ensure that [its] existing customers could obtain replacements for previously purchased [infringing] products').
[202] *Bio-Rad v 10X* (n 83) *4. For an unsuccessful attempt, see *Cave v OptumInsight* (n 110) *23.
[203] *Sealant v TEK* (n 80) *28.
[204] *Broadcom v Emulex* (n 75) *8.
[205] *Bard v Gore* (n 65) *8.
[206] *Amgen v Hoffman-La Roche* (n 124) 213. In *Amgen v Sanofi* 872 F3d 1367, 1381 (Fed Cir 2017), the CAFC clarified the issue by holding that 'eliminating a choice of drugs is not, by itself, sufficient to disserve the public interest'.
[207] *Innogenetics v Abbott* (n 193) *1.
[208] *Bard v Gore* (n 65) *9. See also *Conceptus v Hologic* (n 67) *4 ('the public benefit of having two products with different qualities in the transcervical hysteroscopic sterilization market militates strongly against an injunction').

the infringing product,[209] that they had been specifically trained to use it[210] or even that they preferred it over the alternatives.[211]

Pharmaceutical- and medical device cases have also posed more general challenges over what best serves the public interest in these industries. In one particularly well-reasoned decision, the court addressed the oft-heard suggestion that patent exclusivity in these areas may harm the public interest by structurally increasing prices.[212] Perhaps unsurprisingly, after a very lengthy analysis, the court concluded it was impossible to say whether allowing the infringing product to stay on the market would in fact lower prices given uncertainties surrounding pricing by both parties and the system's incentive structures.[213] It added that 'separation of powers considerations' dictated caution 'before attempting to intervene on Medicare's behalf' and that, in any event, the relative savings (if any) on Medicare's budget would be minimal.[214] Also relevant in the context of pharmaceuticals is public funding of the invention, which (perhaps counter-intuitively) was held to weigh in favour of exclusivity.[215] But in another case, the court accepted that the public interest would be served by fostering competition and diversity in specific healthcare markets and denied an injunction.[216]

4.4.5.3. Public Interest Considerations – Other Technologies

Outside of the healthcare industry, there have frequently been calls on courts to deny injunctive relief on the basis of abstract propositions of policy, as opposed to threatened harm to specifically identified third parties. Most of these attempts have been unsuccessful.[217] But outlier decisions exist on this point, too, and one court found that an injunction would not be in the public interest because there was no evidence 'to suggest that [the patentee] was particularly innovative'.[218] In another case, the availability of 'a significantly cheaper alternative for customers' was considered a sufficiently important public interest to counsel against an injunction.[219] The argument was reversed in one of the *Apple v Samsung* cases, where the court held that patent exclusivity promotes product diversity by

[209] *Advanced Cardiovascular v Medtronic* (n 96) 561.

[210] *Braun Melsungen AG v Terumo Medical Corp* 778 FSupp2d 506, 525 (D Del 2011).

[211] *Smith & Nephew v Interlace* (n 164) 80 (but inquiry 'substantially affected' by ongoing reexamination proceedings).

[212] For a more succinct dismissal of this argument, see *Sanofi v Glenmark* (n 83) 696.

[213] *Amgen v Hoffman-La Roche* (n 124) 225.

[214] ibid 225–26.

[215] *Carnegie Mellon v Marvell* (n 186) *36.

[216] *Advanced Cardiovascular v Medtronic* (n 94) 562.

[217] *Haemonetics v Baxter* (n 162) *4 (undesirability of a monopoly in a critical market); *ION v Sercel* (n 99) *7 (thwarting the development of a particular technology); *Douglas v Buyers* (n 154) *10 (fostering competition and servicing an 'untapped market segment', initially accepted but overturned on appeal: n 19 1346.

[218] *XpertUniverse Inc v Cisco Systems Inc*, 2013 WL 6118447, *13 (D Del November 20 2013).

[219] *Server v American* (n 67) *5.

forcing the infringer to design around it.[220] Because injunctions go to the heart of patent exclusivity, the line between law and policy will sometimes be thin.[221]

Outside of the medical field, harms that would have so disserved the public interest that they warranted a denial of injunctive relief included services performed for the federal government, for instance where an injunction would halt repairs to municipal sewer systems.[222] In this context, courts seem to be a bit stricter than in healthcare: a mere preference by 'government and infrastructure clients' to keep using the infringing products was not enough to deny an injunction.[223] Hardship for third parties can also count under this prong. In one of the design–win chip cases, one of the infringer's customers had invested over US$ 2 billion in upgrading its network to accommodate the infringing technology, which offered great benefits to the network users.[224] Even though the infringing technology could easily be switched off, the court considered the consequences of forgoing it too severe and ordered a sunset period for modification of the technology. Hardship suffered by dealers and suppliers may also weigh against the grant of an injunction.[225]

Lastly, a large number of minor harms will suffice to find disservice to the public interest, as demonstrated in a case involving the best-selling contact lens in the USA. If enjoined, 5.5 million users would have to be refitted with alternative lenses when their supply ran out and bear the costs for this and potential follow-up visits (about US$ 100). The court found these 'deleterious effects of the injunction on the general public … simply too great to permit' and refused the injunction.[226] Likewise, in a case where the injunction would target the functionality of Microsoft Windows and Office, the court found disservice to the public even in the case of minor disruptions, given 'the public's undisputed and enormous reliance on these products'.[227]

[220] *Apple v Samsung* (n 174) *23. See also *Hydrodynamic v Green* (n 112) *3 (public interest supports removing from market product copies of inferior quality).

[221] Compare *Carnegie Mellon v Marvell* (n 186) *36 (public interest disserved by forcing innovative businesses offshore); *MercExchange v eBay* (n 74) 586–87 (public interest disserved by strategic enforcement of patents whose validity is in doubt).

[222] *Insituform v Cosmic* (n 73) *14; see also *SynQor v Artesyn* (n 128) *6 (sales to the US government not enjoined).

[223] *Presidio v American* (n 161) *18 (but 90-day sunset period granted).

[224] *Broadcom v Qualcomm* (n 116) *8–9.

[225] *Fractus SA v Samsung Electronics Co Ltd* 876 FSupp2d 802, 854 (ED Tex 2012); *LaserDynamics v Quanta* (n 182) *5; *Paice v Toyota* (n 91) *6. But see *Apple Inc v Samsung Electronics Co Ltd* 909 FSupp2d 1147, 1162 (ND Cal 2012) ('third party retailers should not be protected from the disruption when they have been benefiting from Samsung's infringement').

[226] *Johnson & Johnson v CIBA* (n 93) 1292. But see *ALPS v Ohio Willow Wood* (n 113) *3 ('While an amputee may have to return prosthetic devices to be refitted with another liner from a different manufacturer, there is no evidence that the amputee would experience any substantial inconvenience, additional costs or adverse consequences').

[227] *z4 v Microsoft* (n 91) 442. In a later case concerning Microsoft Word, the patentee had learned from this case and did not request disabling customers' products if sold prior to the injunction's effective date: *i4i v Microsoft* (n 77) 601. See also *Brocade v A10* (n 70) *5 (customers who had already purchased the infringing device exempted from injunction).

4.4.6. Order Modalities

4.4.6.1. Sunset Periods and Stays

Even though this chapter tends to overrepresent cases where an immediately effective injunction was not granted because it omits the large number of routine injunction grants, US courts certainly grant sunset periods and stays more liberally than their European counterparts. Some courts operate under the assumption that a gradual imposition of injunctive relief is, by definition, preferable to an injunction with immediate effect.[228] Still, sunset periods are not costless for patentees. In many cases, the threat value of an injunction is justified and needed for dissuasive effect. This is nicely illustrated in a case where the infringer stated it was pursuing a non-infringing substitute product that 'may make [the patentee's] products obsolete', which the court took as an indication that injunctive relief should be issued immediately because of the apparently short time left to the patentee in which to enjoy 'the benefits of its exclusivity'.[229] That logic applies even more strongly to indeterminate stays (eg pending appeal), and US courts rarely grant them.[230] If the duration of a stay is hard to oversee, courts generally believe that the infringement verdict should be given the force of law.[231] Meanwhile, infringing stock can usually simply be preserved during the pendency of the appeal, mitigating harm to some extent.[232] Cases where a stay was granted usually involved post-trial developments that cast new light on the court's findings, for instance developments in parallel litigation, coupled with high costs caused by the injunction.[233] In one case, the court granted a short stay precisely to offer the defendant the chance to file an (expedited) appeal.[234]

Key considerations in the context of sunset periods are how long they should be and when they start running. The infringer's estimates for how long they need are often accepted, especially when the infringing product has implications for health.[235] That is perhaps surprising, given the 'inherent self interest' in making the estimate, and sometimes the court considers in detail specific evidence on how long the infringer really needs, arriving at some middle ground.[236] The time required may not only depend on the infringer's own capacities, for instance if

[228] *Metso v Powerscreen* (n 182) 76.

[229] *SynQor v Artesyn* (n 128) *4.

[230] *Braun v Terumo* (n 210) 525 (imposing a sunset period but rejecting a stay pending appeal as the latter would be 'too generous' to the infringer).

[231] *e2Interactive Inc et al v Blackhawk Network Inc* 2012 WL 13000524, *2 (WD Wis 6 December 2012); *General Electric v Mitsubishi* (n 102) *60; *Inventio v Otis* (n 127) *3; *TIVO v Echostar* (n 81) 671.

[232] *Eko v Maynez* (n 169) 1128.

[233] *Smith & Nephew v Interlace* (n 164) 79; *Belden v Superior* (n 98) 579; *Arlington v Bridgeport* (n 175) *6.

[234] *Amgen v Sanofi* (n 132) *3.

[235] *Metso v Powerscreen* (n 182) 77; *Fresenius v Baxter* (n 83) *8 (granting a requested nine-month period despite finding infringer's long period of inactivity 'somewhat bewildering').

[236] *Broadcom v Emulex* (n 75) *9, 7.

they are dependent on third-party suppliers to (help) redesign the product.[237] As for the starting point, US courts normally set it at the date of the (jury) verdict that confirmed infringement of a valid patent.[238] However, case specifics (such as parallel litigation) may indicate that diligence would have required starting even before the jury verdict.[239]

Courts often specify what conduct remains allowable during the sunset period. If it was granted to prevent supply disruptions, allowed sales were usually limited to existing customers or even to completing pending orders.[240] Sales could also be limited to specific variations of the infringing technology, eg because substitutes exist for other variations or because the court will not allow use of the sunset period to pitch improved (but still infringing) versions of the product.[241] If the sunset period was granted to allow the development of a non-infringing product, accommodations may be necessary for infringing R&D activity not covered by statutory exceptions to infringement.[242] Delays for purposes of a design-around also raise the question of allowable conduct in the interim: it is possible that the infringer could revert back to prior art alternatives while developing the alternative product, alleviating hardship and obviating the need for a sunset period.[243] Another issue with design-around delays is what to do when the non-infringing alternative is not done in time. Some courts have extended the period or denied the injunction altogether to avoid this and other problems.[244] But such cases are rare and, as one court put it, if the patented technology proved 'more essential to the product than [the infringer] predicted', it had 'no entitlement to continue infringement'.[245]

4.4.6.2. *Formulation of the Injunction and Carve-Outs*

While in the USA, contrary to Europe, an injunction is 'a drastic and extraordinary remedy, which should not be granted as a matter of course', courts have recognised that it may serve important goals apart from preventing irreparable harm.[246] In particular, courts often observed that refusing an injunction might create incentives for others to start infringing the patent.[247] Difficulty of

[237] *Ricoh v Quanta* (n 95) *3.
[238] *Broadcom v Qualcomm* (n 116) *12; *Broadcom v Emulex* (n 70) *8.
[239] *Presidio v American* (n 161) *20. See also *SynQor v Artesyn* (n 128) *8 (customers should have made preparations to switch products from the moment they were subpoenaed).
[240] *Broadcom v Emulex* (n 75) *9.
[241] *Broadcom v Qualcomm* (n 116) *19, 13.
[242] *Broadcom v Qualcomm* (n 116) *22. Compare *Sealant v TEK* (n 80) *28 (allowing 'incidental infringement' to develop design-around).
[243] *Muniauction v ThomsonCorp* (n 106) 483.
[244] *Solutran Inc v US Bancorp and Elavon Inc* 2018 WL 6681748, *3 (D Minn 19 December 2018); *Apple v Motorola* (n 153) 921.
[245] *Brocade v A10* (n 70) *7.
[246] *Apple III* (n 27) 1359.
[247] *Whirlpool v Global* (n 113) *4; *Global v Groundrez* (n 126) *7; *Smith & Nephew v Arthrex* (n 83) 1183; *Amgen v Hoffman-La Roche* (n 124) 212.

recovering ongoing royalties, for instance due to an infringer's lack of solvency or because they were domiciled abroad, were also accessory reasons to issue an injunction.[248] At the same time, the corrective, forward-looking – as opposed to punitive – nature of an injunction was repeatedly considered as limiting its propriety in cases where it would have unduly burdensome effects.[249]

As noted above, use by customers that have already purchased their infringing device is often exempted from the scope of the injunction.[250] In Europe, courts may order a recall of infringing products subject to an express proportionality requirement and so regularly reach the same result. Relatedly, US courts tend to exclude from the scope of an injunction services for such products, for instance if that is necessary to guarantee their safety or proper operation.[251] Products with substantial non-infringing uses generated a mixed picture: sometimes they were excluded from the scope of the injunction because monitoring them would present 'evidentiary difficulties',[252] at other times it was considered the infringer's responsibility not to risk contempt.[253]

Sometimes the claim language created difficulties for the precise form of the injunction. One case concerned a patent on synthetic turf fields having an infill depth of 61–72 per cent, which in practice was not uniform over the entirety of the field and could change over time due to natural settlement factors. The court ordered that depth measurements should be averaged across the field and be taken 'immediately upon completion of a field's construction' to avoid a finding of contempt due to natural processes beyond the control of the infringer.[254] In another case where crafting an appropriate injunction proved difficult, instead of forbidding further infringement, the court ordered the infringer to perform modifications that would place the infringing products outside the claim's scope.[255] What went too far, however, was inclusion of a 'court-approval condition' in the injunction, which would prevent the infringer from introducing any redesigned product without prior permission from the court.[256]

4.4.6.3. *Calculation of Ongoing Royalties*

Courts staying or denying the injunction commonly (though not necessarily) award an ongoing royalty to compensate the patentee for the continued

[248] *Carnegie Mellon v Marvell* (n 186) *29; *Global v Groundrez* (n 126) *7.

[249] *Brocade v A10* (n 70) *5; *Sanofi v Glenmark* (n 83) 697.

[250] *ION v Sercel* (n 99) *8.

[251] *Kolcraft Enterprises Inc v Chicco USA Inc* 2019 WL 4242482, *18 (ND Ill 6 September 2019). A peculiar exception is a case concerning elevator systems that, once built, could not be deconstructed. The court granted an injunction to improve the patentee's bargaining position for royalty payments on existing systems: *Inventio v Otis* (n 127) *2.

[252] *800 Adept v Murex* (n 75) 1339. See also *XpertUniverse v Cisco* (n 218) *13.

[253] *Bestop Inc v Tuffy Security Products Inc* 2016 WL 8232230 fn3 (SD Mich 29 April 2016); *e2Interactive v Blackhawk* (n 231) *4; *Atlanta v Leggett & Platt* (n 114) *8.

[254] *Tarkett v Astroturf* (n 123) *20, *22.

[255] *Transocean v Globalsantafe* (n 142) *10.

[256] *Chamberlain v Techtronic* (n 122) 1011.

infringement. Table 4.6 breaks down the approach taken in the 86 reasoned cases where an injunction was denied (see section 4.3 above).

Table 4.6 Decisions on ongoing royalties after denial of the injunction (*n* = 86)

Decision	Number of decisions
Court orders party negotiations	11
Court orders supplemental briefing	7
Court sets amount without upward adjustment	6
Court sets amount with upward adjustment	5
Ongoing royalty claim denied	5
Determination stayed pending appeal	4
Determination deferred to subsequent proceedings	4
Infringer ordered to file quarterly reports	2
Future infringement covered by damages award	2
Total	**46**
Order contains no reference to ongoing royalty	40

The table paints a mixed picture. In almost half of the cases, there was no mention of the ongoing royalty. This need not mean it was not awarded, just that it was not awarded in the order denying the injunction. When the issue was addressed, the most common outcome (11) was for the court to order parties to negotiate a royalty rate for the period the injunction is denied before setting it itself. That is in line with guidance from the Federal Circuit.[257] Such orders have been issued even where previous negotiations were unsuccessful.[258] Having parties set the terms of compensation for future infringement is certainly attractive, not just because it absolves the court of the task of setting the appropriate royalty rate but also because the agreement would likely cover non-monetary terms.[259] At the same time, where the litigation has caused bad blood between the parties, it may not be feasible to expect them to come to an agreement.[260] For one court, that was reason not to award damages in lieu in the first place, at least not for a prolonged period of time.[261]

[257] *Prism Technologies LLC v Sprint Spectrum LP* 849 F3d 1360, 1377 (Fed Cir 2017).
[258] *Hynix v Rambus* (n 84) 987.
[259] *Transocean v Globalsantafe* (n 142) *5.
[260] *Eko v Maynez* (n 169) 1128; *Bendix v Haldex* (n 72) *6. See also *Haemonetics v Baxter* (n 162) *4 (accounting cannot easily be performed if there is no minimum level of trust between the parties).
[261] *Omega v Fortin* (n 101) *6 ('It would be unjust to force [the patentee] to enter an agreement with an entity that he did not trust').

In an equal number of cases, however, the court set the ongoing royalty itself. Here, it is important to keep in mind that at this stage of the proceedings the jury will normally have awarded damages for past infringement, which serve as a starting point for the calculation of the future compensation.[262] One of the key issues that has attracted attention also among European scholars (see section 6.6) – whether an upwards adjustment of the reasonable royalty is justified – has divided US courts, as Table 4.6 shows.[263] Some courts have reasoned that any ongoing infringement is wilful by definition,[264] while others held that court-sanctioned infringement (during a sunset period) can never be wilful.[265] There may, however, be other justifications beside wilfulness for an upward adjustment of the hypothetical royalty, for instance to take account of monitoring and enforcement costs.[266] In addition, care must be taken that the value of a technology to the infringer may change over time, which would justifying higher, or lower, royalty rates.[267] Similarly, the parties' changed bargaining position has been used as a basis to modify past royalty rates.[268]

Apart from these two typical scenario's, Table 4.6 shows a variety of other approaches, such as requesting supplemental briefing on party preferences and/or the appropriate rate (seven cases), staying the determination pending appeal (four) or deferring it to subsequent proceedings (four), ordering an infringer to file quarterly reports of profits for the benefit of party negotiations or future damages proceedings (two), or even denying the ongoing royalty claim altogether (five). The latter outcome strikes me as rather extreme, but was reached in an elaborately reasoned opinion in *Apple v Motorola*, a precedent occasionally followed by other courts. Judge Posner found that Apple had insufficiently substantiated its ongoing royalty claim, and considered it 'ridiculous' to allow it 'a second chance to prove damages'.[269] It would appear that in these types of case the patentee was faulted for not having sufficiently substantiated their claim; they do not alter the conclusion that, in principle, a patentee whose injunction is denied is entitled to an ongoing royalty award.

4.5. Insights for a European Proportionality Test

4.5.1. The Empirics of US Patent Injunction Decisions

Chapter three presented a 'diagnosis' of Europe's patent system today, but, as stated, it is difficult there to present irrefutable evidence of the various

[262] *z4 v Microsoft* (n 91) 442.
[263] See also Golden (n 8) 307.
[264] *Broadcom v Qualcomm* (n 116) *20; *Broadcom v Emulex* (n 75) *9.
[265] *ActiveVideo v Verizon* (n 144) 656.
[266] *Monsanto Co v Gastel* 2009 WL 10672488, *3 (WD Mo 22 March 2009).
[267] *Commonwealth v Buffalo* (n 88) 606; *Hynix v Rambus* (n 84) 987.
[268] *ActiveVideo v Verizon* (n 144) 658.
[269] *Apple v Motorola* (n 153) 924.

phenomena that the chapter discusses, let alone the best way to address them. The primary purpose of the fine-grained overview of US case law presented here is to overcome, at least in part, this dearth of evidence. To be sure, court decisions do not come close to capturing the functioning of the patent system comprehensively, as most cases are settled before court proceedings terminate or even begin. In addition, there are structural differences between the US and EU economies and their patent systems; the most notable in this respect is the far greater number of US patents in force and the availability of nationwide injunctions. And by looking just at decisions from 2006 onwards, it is impossible to say whether any of the fact patterns observed occur more frequently today than historically. These are all important limitations on what the decisions studied here can tell us about European patent law. Nevertheless, I consider it at least plausible that any given fact pattern that has arisen before a US court might just as well arise before a European patent court. The major US litigants are also involved in European patent cases, not infrequently in parallel proceedings involving the same product and invention. It seems reasonable to assume that, by and large and in most industry sectors, patents function similarly in Europe and the USA, certainly now that the Unified Patent Court has the authority to enforce patents for a large number of EU Member States. I therefore assume that fact patterns from US patent cases are capable of supplementing the empirical basis of the proportionality test proposed in this book.

My main finding in chapter three was that the rise in patent creep and density made patentable ever smaller components of technologies, resulting in a greater risk of accidental infringement, further augmented by the strategic opportunities that patent prosecution procedures afford patentees. That finding is borne out in the US case law. The prevalence of component patent cases sparked the adoption of the causal nexus test as part of the irreparable harm test, and section 4.4.3.2 cites numerous examples where courts applied it. Even outside the application of the causal nexus test, we saw various cases where the injunction would somehow affect non-infringing technology or activities: the non-infringing device that would be forced off the market with an injunction on the procedure to implement it in *Conceptus*; the database, obtained with infringing technology, that at the time of trial no longer infringed in *Veracode*; the provision of aftersales services for infringing devices in *Polara* …[270] These and other decisions show how infringing technology is often deeply entwined with non-infringing technology and activities. While it is, again, impossible to state this with certainty, I expect that patent density and patent creep have made such cases more common than ever, a trend likely to continue in the years to come. If so, it is vital that European patent law develops a way to ensure that in these cases, the patentee's effective sphere of exclusivity does not exceed what is justified by their invention's contribution to the art.

[270] See, respectively, *Conceptus v Hologic* (n 67) *4; *Veracode v Appthority* (n 98) 96; *Polara v Campbell* (n 126) 991.

We have also seen the substantial impact of the parties' relative blameworthiness on the determination surrounding injunctive relief. On the patentee side, cases involving more egregious misconduct are unlikely to make it to the remedies stage as the patent-in-suit may be declared unenforceable on the basis of the unclean hands or inequitable conduct doctrines. But opportunism not quite rising to this level may still affect the patentee's entitlement to an injunction, for instance in cases involving patent ambush or litigation money-making schemes.[271] On the side of the infringer, findings of wilfulness are a regular occurrence and severely limit the infringer's chances of success under *eBay*'s third prong (in addition to opening the door to treble damages). Notably, however, US courts rarely require infringers to demonstrate best efforts at performing patent clearance or other indications of good faith before considering their position under the balance of hardships.[272] Such a requirement would be at odds with the *eBay* test, under which the patentee bears the burden of the evidence. But the observation also hints at a more fundamental insight: it is very difficult for infringers to offer credible evidence of innocence after the fact. One might think that, in a jurisdiction with such elaborate disclosure requirements as the USA, courts could get a reasonable view of the infringer's innocence; yet they rarely address this, and 35 USC §298 even states that 'failure of an infringer to obtain the advice of counsel … may not be used to prove that the accused infringer wilfully infringed'.[273] I return to this point in section 6.2.2.

Most importantly, the analysis in section 4.4 confirms that the effects of patent injunctions are highly context-sensitive, as set out in section 1.2. They may drive an infringer into bankruptcy, or they may hardly have any effect on them; they may be critical to restoring a patentee's capacity to compete, or they may be incapable of undoing the infringement's effects on the market; they may put patients in danger and threaten important public services, or they may simply require users to switch to a readily available alternative. On the one hand, that supports my argument in chapter one that at least some court discretion over patent injunctions is to be preferred over none at all. On the other hand, it can seriously be questioned whether courts are the right forum to consider all potentially relevant circumstances and grant or deny the injunction based on how they view them. Recall the observations in section 1.4: do courts have a sufficient understanding of industry dynamics and decision consequences to find the 'optimal' outcome in every case? I doubt it. In the next subsection, I address the most obvious downside of this approach: an insurmountable lack of legal certainty. But simply telling courts to do what they think is best in each specific case also blurs the line between substantive and procedural law, and consequently between law and policy. There are several examples of this in the US case law: consideration of

[271] See, respectively, *Hynix v Rambus* (n 84) 985; *MercExchange v eBay* (n 74) 584.

[272] Two exceptions are *Smith & Nephew v Arthrex* (n 83) 1183 and *FenF v SmartThingz* (n 171) *4.

[273] *cf Halo Electronics v Pulse* 136 SCt 1923 (2016), 1936–37 (Breyer J concurring) (explaining the rationale behind this statute).

the patent's inventive merits or the nature of infringement (*de minimis*, equivalence) are among the more salient ones. And broadly defined, the public interest prong essentially invites courts to (re)define the purpose and corresponding limitations of patent exclusivity on a case-by-case basis, as shown in section 4.4.5.3. In Europe, these issues would be addressed through substantive law, and I expect there are few patent judges willing to override it at the remedy phase.

4.5.2. *eBay*'s Fuzzy Boundaries

The post-*eBay* development with the most significant policy implications is no doubt the calibration of the irreparable harm prong around demonstrable harm to the patentee's business. That shift rather fundamentally alters the nature of patents, at least relative to how they are viewed in Europe: as constitutionally protected property rights which guarantee the exclusive right to an invention.[274] By contrast, contemporary US patent law appears to protect with exclusivity a fairly narrow class of deserving interests, even if they still represent about two-thirds of all cases. Reasonable disagreement is possible on whether this is a sensible approach to injunctive relief. However, it is clear that in redefining the patentee's entitlement to injunctive relief as it did, the CAFC decisively changed US patent law. It may be the case that this seems inappropriate from a continental European perspective, but an open-ended legal test under which all circumstances of a case are relevant hardly leaves patent courts with a different option. Such a test requires courts to reach, from these circumstances, a reasoned outcome in the given case, but, as we saw in section 1.4, such reasons necessarily constrain decision-making space in future cases and in fact courts value these constraints because they facilitate predictable and efficient decision-making. In other words, it is a mistake to think that any doctrine limiting injunctive relief could only apply in exceptional, isolated cases with limited precedential value, at least if the test is to make some difference to the status quo. Instead, a broad-scope test will require the formulation by courts of more detailed rules of application, as the CAFC has done.[275]

Putting to one side the separation-of-powers implications of this task, it might be acceptable if the outcome would be a clear and predictable legal test. But that is fundamentally at odds with a broad scope test, as the American experience demonstrates. True, the CAFC has formulated guidance on various aspects of the *eBay* test, particularly its first prong. As others have noted, the general effects of these standards have been that patentees are more likely to be

[274] Case C-15/74 *Centrafarm BV v Sterling Drug* ECLI:EU:C:1974:114, [1974] ECR I-1147, para 9.

[275] Indeed, this is what some proponents of the proportionality test argue for: Stierle and Hofmann (n 62) 1128 ('German courts will need to build a mid-level framework by establishing factors refining the application of the new exception').

awarded an injunction if they directly compete with the infringer.[276] But we also saw that there are so many exceptions to this rule that it is hardly more than a working assumption. As a general rule to govern injunctive relief, such substantial uncertainties seem undesirable because a large class of patentees – essentially anyone in the grey area between 'hard-core trolls' and direct competitors with a rock-solid case on irreparable harm – will have little guidance to go by when seeking to enforce their patents. Take, for example, the decisions in *ActiveVideo v Verizon* and *Douglas v Buyers*.[277] Both decisions were handed down in 2011 and contain elaborate reasoning on the irreparable harm prong. Reading them, one gets the impression that they apply wholly different patent laws; and on appeal, both decisions resulted in scathing reversals on multiple grounds.[278] The statistics may suggest a fairly straightforward picture on irreparable harm, but they can easily deceive as it seems far less straightforward to apply the precedents to an actual case. One is genuinely left wondering what the law is on issues like willingness to license and the degree of competition that must exist between parties, even though these would appear to be routine questions in patent cases. And this part of the *eBay* test is still relatively clear.

I called the balance of hardships prong '*eBay*'s enigma' above, and I believe it is hardly an exaggeration, as its correct application is shrouded in mystery. First, what counts as hardship on the side of the patentee? Is it 'harm in the market place, including constrained growth and reputational damage', as the court assumed in *Riverbed*, or does the mere loss of patent exclusivity also count as hardship, which the court in *Commonwealth* held can have 'far reaching effects'?[279] Or perhaps it should be assumed that 'without establishing irreparable harm, the [patentee] cannot demonstrate that it will be faced with a hardship if an injunction does not issue'?[280] Second, what counts as hardship on the side of the infringer? As we saw in section 4.4.4.1, it is not clear which hardships on the infringer's side are properly considered in the balance and which should be 'ignored', and there appears to be conflicting CAFC precedents on this point. Moreover, it is not clear how wilful infringement affects the balance of hardships, if at all. Third, when does the hardship to the infringer sufficiently outweigh the patentee's hardship to refuse the injunction? Is it enough, as Judge Posner suggested, that the injunction 'imposes greater costs on the defendant than it confers benefits on the plaintiff'?[281] Or does it require a grave imbalance between how parties are affected, as in *EMC* (see Table 4.4 and accompanying

[276] Seaman (n 55) 1988–90.
[277] See, respectively, nn 144 and 154.
[278] See, respectively, nn 23 and 19.
[279] See, respectively, *Riverbed Technology Inc v Silver Peak Systems* 2014 WL 4695765, *13 (D Del September 12 2014) and *Commonwealth* (n 88) 606.
[280] *Texas Advanced Optoelectronic Solutions Inc v Intersil Corp* 2016 WL 1615741, *5 (ED Tex 22 April 2016); reversed on appeal, but only because of the 'deficient irreparable-harm analysis': 895 F3d 1304, 1332 (Fed Cir 2018).
[281] *Apple v Motorola* (n 153) 922.

text)? In sum, substantial uncertainty and conflicting precedents exist on each element of the balance of hardships prong. This is a sobering outcome, to say the least, after 419 district court decisions and 37 CAFC decisions over the course of 14 years.

4.5.3. Lessons Learned Across the Atlantic

These criticisms notwithstanding, *eBay* is an obvious source of inspiration for those who advocate a European proportionality test. For deciding *eBay* the way it did, European authors invariably tip their hat at the United States Supreme Court and proceed to propose a range of potentially problematic aspects of patent injunctions, typically to be included as factors in an open-ended balancing test.[282] For them, the overview in section 4.4 offers a catalogue of such factors. In my view, however, it should give them pause, for the catalogue is expansive indeed. It shows that making a realistic assessment of how grant or denial of the injunction affects parties requires consideration, in any event, of both parties' business models and the centrality of the patented technology to their business; the market(s) in which they operate and their particular features; and the type of infringing product at stake. It is worth noting that in the US, the patentee's claim to injunctive relief is typically considered as a post-trial motion: parties file a supplemental briefing after the court and jury decide on the validity of the claim and the infringement, occasionally resulting in a hearing dedicated to this subject alone. By contrast, proportionality is a remedial-stage defence that I expect very few European courts are able (or willing) to consider separately from the substance of the case. If we further take account of their much more limited access to evidence as compared to US courts, it is clear that properly assessing the real-world effects of an injunction grant or denial is a fraught and time-consuming task. Even if European patent courts were to engage in it, it would be very difficult for them to overcome the fundamental problem of legal uncertainty that their US colleagues are still faced with almost two decades after *eBay*.

Of course, the proportionality test need not be modelled after *eBay*'s four prongs. But a rebuttable presumption that the patentee has an interest in injunctive relief, as the aforementioned authors effectively suggest, seems incapable of overcoming the problems just signalled. It would shift the onus on infringers to rebut the presumption, but would do little to clarify what considerations are relevant in this respect, or when they weigh sufficiently heavily for the infringer to succeed. European courts would thus still face the onerous task of evaluating the relevance of, for instance, the patentee's previous licensing practices or a

[282] eg Stierle and Hofmann (n 62)1128; R Sikorski, 'Towards a More Orderly Application of Proportionality to Patent Injunctions in the European Union' (2022) 53 *International Review of Intellectual Property and Competition Law* 31, 53.

temporary inability to come to market. In my view, the better approach is to take the patentee's interest in an injunction as a given, which is also most compatible with the EU's legal framework for patent remedies (see further section 6.1). Once this is accepted, it is questionable whether conceiving of proportionality as a balancing test continues to make sense. As we saw in section 4.3, there were only two cases out of 419 where harm to the infringer weighed sufficiently to deny the injunction despite a finding that the patentee was irreparably harmed. If proportionality is to apply only so rarely, it is not clear that the game is worth the candle.

This is not to say the US approach to patent injunctions has nothing to teach us. In my view, three elements stand out as sources of inspiration: the causal nexus test; the application of the public interest prong; and the principal approach to ongoing royalties. The causal nexus test is part of the irreparable harm inquiry, but notably reduces that inquiry to a single, well-delineated question: are the patented features a significant reason end users buy the infringing product? This is not to say the question is devoid of subjective elements or that its answer is easy to substantiate. Also, the question is too heavily influenced by the CAFC's approach to irreparable harm to be transposed to European patent law. It does, however, show that it is possible to address a specific issue – component patents – in a test that is generally applicable yet does not turn on a balancing exercise. As the cases discussed in section 4.4.3.2 show, US courts have accepted different circumstances as evidence of causal nexus, but the test's contours, its application and its outcomes remain straightforward and predictable, at least relative to the outcomes on irreparable harm in cases where the causal nexus test is not explicitly applied.

A second source of inspiration is how US courts approach the public interest prong. Identifying third parties that would in fact be materially affected by the injunction by asking what alternatives they have available strikes me as a commendable approach. Furthermore, it is interesting to observe that, in practice, the public interest prong usually stands on its own, even though formally it is one of four factors to be considered together. That is, if sufficiently deleterious consequences for third parties are made out, the injunction is denied, stayed or carved out on that ground alone, regardless of the outcome on the other prongs. This, too, seems sensible: why should the relative weight of third-party interests increase if the injunction also affects the infringer's business? Yet the scale metaphor suggests that infringer interests and third-party interests that, taken alone, do not quite suffice to limit the injunction may suffice when taken together, or may suffice when the patentee's interest in an injunction is weaker. Perhaps this approach can be justified if what matters for proportionality are the overall social costs imposed by the injunction. But, for reasons set out in chapter two, I do not find that view convincing. And the analysis in this chapter shows that even courts that are formally required to weigh the interests of third parties together with the patentee's and the infringer's tend to approach third-party interests in isolation. I take this to confirm my intuition that it is difficult to meaningfully 'mix and match' entirely different types of interests as part of an overall balancing exercise.

Lastly, when it comes to the ongoing royalty for the duration of the stay, it is instructive that US courts are most likely to leave its determination to party negotiations. That approach was expressly endorsed by the CAFC.[283] In my view, it would be most practical for European courts to take a similar approach, especially because they will almost never have performed a calculation of past damages when deciding on the proportionality defence. Unlike their US counterparts, they therefore have no starting point for the future royalty. Section 6.6 explores this idea further, building on the approach in two early US cases where the infringer was ordered to submit quarterly reports of profits.[284] But first, the insights of this part and the previous are combined to formulate a European proportionality test in the next, starting with its basis in EU law.

[283] *Prism v Sprint* (n 257).
[284] *z4 v Microsoft* (n 91) 444; *Voda v Cordis Corp* 2006 WL 2570614, *6 (WD Okla 5 September 2006).

PART III

Towards a Proportionality Test in European Patent Law

5

Conditions and Requirements for Patent Injunctions under EU Law

Having set out, in parts I and II respectively, the normative and empirical bases of the proportionality test in European patent law, it is now time to formulate its contents. Like virtually all commentators, this book takes the position that the proportionality test in patent law derives from European Union (EU) law, particularly Directive 2004/48 (the Enforcement Directive) and the EU Charter of Fundamental Rights (CFR). The present chapter analyses these instruments, their provisions relevant to patent law and the interpretation of these provisions by the European Court of Justice (ECJ).

Proportionality has many meanings in EU law. The first section of the chapter therefore sets out how the use of proportionality in the context of patent injunctions relates to the broader use of this term in EU law, and why in this specific context it imposes limits on patent enforcement separately and independently from existing limitations. The second section addresses the complex issue of how the Enforcement Directive, and particularly the general conditions for enforcement laid down in Article 3, relate to the respective parties' Charter rights. I argue that enforcement proceedings are an instance of the clash of Charter rights between right holders and infringers. The Enforcement Directive's conditions reflect the balance between these rights that the EU legislator envisioned in this instance. It is thus neither necessary nor allowable for patent courts to balance the Charter rights of the patentee and the infringer 'ad hoc' when deciding on remedies. Ad hoc balancing nevertheless remains necessary where remedies would affect the Charter rights of third parties, because those were not (and could not be) exhaustively considered in the Enforcement Directive's provisions. The third section analyses, by reference to the ECJ's decisions, what the various safeguards contained in Article 3 of the Enforcement Directive mean for patent enforcement proceedings. The fourth and final section shows that, like Member State courts, the Unified Patent Court (UPC) will need to apply these safeguards. A schematic overview of the chapter's argument is provided in Figure 5.1.

Figure 5.1 Overview of primary and secondary EU law applicable to patent enforcement

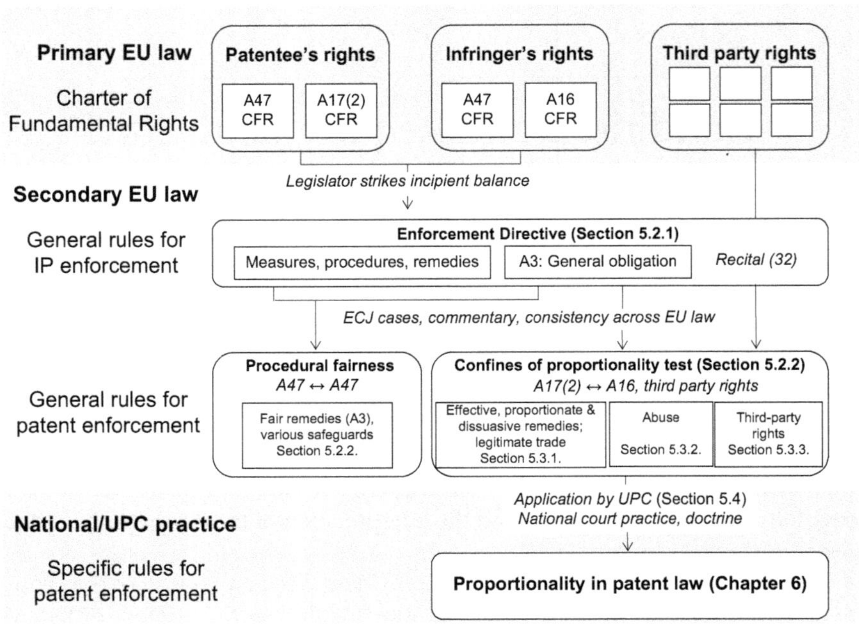

A caveat is in order before the analysis begins. Article 3 of the Enforcement Directive is the bedrock of the proportionality test in European patent law, but this provision is phrased in very general terms. This is understandable, given that it applies to all intellectual property (IP) rights enforcement measures and seeks to leave Member States with sufficient leeway as to its implementation. It could thus be said that Article 3 in fact contains not one but many proportionality tests. Not only will its effects differ depending on the IP right enforced, the specific relief sought and the context of enforcement; but even when it comes to permanent injunctions in patent cases, Member States may implement it differently in light of the specific features of their patent and civil procedure codes. This chapter therefore does not offer a definitive interpretation of Article 3 of the Enforcement Directive, but rather traces the confines of the policy space the provision sets in light of (i) the underlying Charter rights at stake in patent litigation and (ii) the specific features of patents, as per Recital (17). The next and final chapter fills the contours with a concrete proposal for a European proportionality test that matches not only the legal basis set out here, but also the principle of commensurate scope (chapter two) and the problems an automatic injunction rule causes in the contemporary patent system (chapter three).

5.1. Proportionality in EU Law: Remedial Discretion under the Enforcement Directive

5.1.1. The Many Meanings of Proportionality in EU Law

Proportionality has been a cornerstone principle in European constitutional law for decades. The ECJ employs proportionality to assess the compatibility of national or EU measures with primary Union law, just like several national constitutional courts do when ruling on the constitutionality of their domestic legislation. This classic instantiation of proportionality has limited relevance for patent remedies, and in any event it is hard to pin down the contours of the ECJ's constitutional proportionality test as its application varies widely between cases.[1] Proportionality also exists as a general principle within the EU legal order and requires that measures adopted by Union institutions do not go beyond what is necessary to attain the objectives pursued (Article 5(4) of the Treaty on European Union). The proportionality requirement in Article 3(2) of the Enforcement Directive operates in a similar fashion. Lastly, proportionality is an important element of the methodology for resolving conflicts between EU fundamental rights as laid down in Article 52 CFR.

As was addressed in the Introduction, in the context of European patent law, 'proportionality' is commonly understood as a ground that courts may employ to limit the patentee's entitlement to immediate injunctive relief. The terminology no doubt derives from Article 3(2) of the Enforcement Directive, which stipulates that remedies in IP rights enforcement cases must (among other things) be effective, proportionate and dissuasive. This threefold norm, which will be referred to as the EPD (effective, proportionate, dissuasive) standard in the remainder of this chapter for the sake of brevity, lies at the heart of Article 3(2) of the Enforcement Directive according to most commentators.[2] While the ECJ regularly refers to Article 3 when interpreting the Enforcement Directive, at times it also – or instead – applies a seemingly different standard: that a fair balance be struck between the various fundamental rights at stake in the proceedings. Roughly speaking, then, two lines of cases have developed in the ECJ's IP remedies jurisprudence. A first line of cases started with the interpretation of Article 8(1) of the Enforcement Directive, which lays down a right of information for holders of IP rights. The ECJ held that when implementing and applying this provision, Member States and their authorities must in all

[1] T-I Harbo, 'The Function of the Proportionality Principle in EU Law' (2010) 16 *European Law Journal* 158, 180.

[2] Two often-cited examples include A Ohly, 'Three Principles of European IP Enforcement Law: Effectiveness, Proportionality, Dissuasiveness' in J Drexl et al (eds), *Technology and Competition: Contributions in Honour of Hanns Ullrich* (Larcier, 2009); M Norrgård, 'The Role Conferred on the National Judge by Directive 2004148/EC on the Enforcement of Intellectual Property Rights' (2005) 6 *ERA Forum* 503, 512.

cases strike a fair balance between the various applicable fundamental rights.[3] An offshoot of these cases declared the same principle applicable to injunctions against intermediaries, while also setting parameters for such injunctions derived from Article 3 of the Enforcement Directive.[4] Yet another subgroup of cases evaluated specific instances of such injunctions, sometimes only on the basis of the fair balance standard,[5] sometimes mixing fair balance arguments with scrutiny under Article 3 of the Enforcement Directive.[6] Lastly, in the ECJ's only case on standard essential patents (SEPs) to date, it evaluated a SEP holder's request for an injunction according to Article 102 of the Treaty on the Functioning of the European Union (TFEU), but held that in this context a fair balance between the interests concerned was also to be struck.[7] In parallel, a second line of cases developed concerning, inter alia, Articles 9 (provisional measures), 13 (damages) and 14 (attorney's fees) of the Enforcement Directive. The ECJ established that all national measures implementing these provisions, as well as any other provision in Chapter II of the Enforcement Directive, must comply with the general obligations in Article 3 thereof.[8] This second line of cases contains no references to the fair balance test that was applied in the first line of cases.

As a consequence, it is not always clear how pleas for adoption of proportionality in European patent law relate to the Enforcement Directive and the ECJ's case law it sparked. In one view, the criteria for deciding on the entitlement to injunctive relief are supplied by Article 3. A competing view instead embraces the ECJ's fair balance cases as the main limiting factor for IP remedies.[9] In this view, the decision to grant an injunction, and under which conditions, requires 'careful balancing in light of the principle of proportionality'.[10] The difference is consequential, first and foremost because it determines the nature of the proportionality test: is it a matter of checking that an injunction satisfies all elements of Article 3, or is it a more open-ended balancing test? Secondly, both views are

[3] The main cases are Case C-275/06 *Promusicae* ECLI:EU:C:2008:54, [2008] ECR I-271; Case C-461/10 *Bonnier Audio* ECLI:EU:C:2012:219; Case C-580/13 *Coty Germany* ECLI:EU:C:2015:485; Case C-149/17 *Bastei Lübbe* ECLI:EU:C:2018:841; Case C-264/19 *Constantin Film Verleih* ECLI:EU:C:2020:542.

[4] The main cases are Case C-324/09 *L'Oréal and others* ECLI:EU:C:2011:474, [2011] ECR I-6011; Case C-494/15 *Tommy Hilfiger* ECLI:EU:C:2016:528.

[5] The main cases are Case C-314/12 *UPC Telekabel Wien* ECLI:EU:C:2014:192; Case C-484/14 *McFadden* ECLI:EU:C:2016:689; Joined Cases C-682/18 and C-683/18 *YouTube and Cyando* ECLI:EU:C:2021:503.

[6] The main case is C-70/10 *Scarlet Extended* ECLI:EU:C:2011:771, [2011] ECR I-11959. For the purposes of this overview, it is comparable to Case C-597/19 *MICM* ECLI:EU:C:2021:492, where an information request based on Art 8(1) of the Enforcement Directive was evaluated according to both the fair balance test and Art 3 of the Enforcement Directive.

[7] Case C-170/13 *Huawei Technologies* ECLI:EU:C:2015:477, para 55.

[8] The main cases are Case C-235/09 *DHL Express France* ECLI:EU:C:2011:238, [2011] ECR I-2801; Case C-57/15 *United Video Properties* ECLI:EU:C:2016:611; Case C-367/15 *Stowarzyszenie Oławska Telewizja Kablowa (OTK)* ECLI:EU:C:2017:36; Case C-688/17 *Bayer Pharma* ECLI:EU:C:2019:722; Case C-666/18 *IT Development* ECLI:EU:C:2019:1099; Case C-531/20 *NovaText* ECLI:EU:C:2022:316; Case C-44/21 *Phoenix Contact* ECLI:EU:C:2022:309; Case C-355/221 *Perfumesco.pl* ECLI:EU:C:2022:791.

[9] This view is seemingly embraced by the Dutch and French supreme courts: HR 3 April 2015, ECLI:NL:HR:2015:841 (*GeenStijl/Sanoma*), para 5.2.5; Cass civ (1) 15 May 2015, 13-27.391, 5.

[10] R Sikorski, 'Towards a More Orderly Application of Proportionality to Patent Injunctions in the European Union' (2022) 53 *International Review of Intellectual Property and Competition Law* 31, 46.

animated by different iterations of the proportionality principle. The first view would appear to draw primarily on proportionality as a formal principle that penalties must not exceed what is necessary to pursue the stated goal, whereas proportionality in the second view appeals more to the balancing methodology laid down in Article 52 CFR. This, in turn, has implications for the guidance that can be drawn from the ECJ's broader case law for the development of a proportionality test in patent law.

This chapter demonstrates that both views can be reconciled. Most, if not all, patent disputes represent a conflict between, on the one hand, the patentee's fundamental rights to intellectual property and an effective remedy (Articles 17(2) and 47 CFR); and, on the other hand, the infringer's right to conduct a business (Article 16 CFR). In addition, a patent dispute may implicate a variety of third-party rights. The Enforcement Directive, and in particular Article 3 thereof, is best understood as a framework for reconciling these rights clashes and must be interpreted in light of the applicable underlying rights. At the same time, the specific conditions these provisions set for patent remedies subsumes the balance that must be struck between the rights of the infringer and those of the patentee. The Enforcement Directive thus obviates ad hoc balancing of fundamental rights in most cases. By contrast, ad hoc balancing remains necessary where third-party rights are involved because those are not specifically accounted for in the Enforcement Directive's provisions.[11] Thus, Article 3 of the Enforcement Directive sets general requirements for enforcement that must be satisfied in every case, whereas the Charter sets additional limitations that become relevant where enforcement would affect third parties. Importantly, Article 3 sets conditions for each individual instance of enforcement, not for a Member State's system of remedies in their entirety, as I explain in the next subsection.

5.1.2. Is Proportionality a Free-Standing Test?

Writing before the amendment of § 139 of the German Patent Act, Klaus Grabinski argued that all requirements of Article 3 of the Enforcement Directive are subsumed in a number of existing limitations on the patentee's exclusive right, including Article 102 TFEU, the abuse of rights doctrine and the availability of a compulsory licence.[12] This view has long been dominant in Germany, where Grabinski is not alone among the judiciary to hold it.[13] Similarly, in the

[11] *HTC Corp v Nokia Corp* [2013] EWHC 3778 (Pat), paras 26–27.

[12] K Grabinski, 'Injunctive Relief and Proportionality in Case of a Public Interest in the Use of a Patent: Different Ways – Same Result' [2021] *Gewerblicher Rechtsschutz und Urheberrecht* 200, 203. For a similar view, see M Schellhorn, *Der Patentrechtliche Unterlassungsanspruch im Lichte des Verhältnismäßigkeitsgrundsatzes* (Carl Heymanns Verlag, 2020).

[13] U Scharen, 'The Practice of Claiming Injunctive Relief for Patent Infringement in Germany' (2019) 14 *Journal of Intellectual Property Law & Practice* 112, 118; K-J Mellulis, 'Zur Notwendigkeit und Sinnhaftigkeit von Beschränkungen des Patentrechts' [2016] *Mitteilungen der deutschen Patentanwälte* 433, 439–40.

Netherlands, the Hague District Court suggested that the proportionality test of Article 3(2) of the Enforcement Directive has no independent effect but is subsumed in the abuse-of-law provision in Article 3:13 of the Dutch Civil Code.[14] In other words, if an infringer cannot successfully invoke external limitations to an injunction, it must be considered a proportionate measure that is compliant with the limitations set by EU law, and no separate proportionality inquiry is required. With respect, this view should be rejected and proportionality should be understood as a free-standing test that sets separate and independent limits on patent enforcement.

Whether proportionality should be a free-standing test evidently depends on how the limits this requirement sets for patent enforcement are interpreted: under a very narrow interpretation, it would add nothing to existing exceptions. How broadly one interprets proportionality will, in turn, depend on beliefs on the appropriate degree of interference by courts with patent enforcement. The long-standing caution against such interference can presumably be explained by the complexity of innovation dynamics and the fear of distorting them by unwarranted intervention, coupled with a perception of patents as constitutionally protected property. But the ECJ held early on that the right to intellectual property is not absolute and must be viewed in relation to its social function.[15] This suggests that judicial scrutiny of enforcement is appropriate and may need to become more intensive if the right's social function threatens to be impaired as a result of current practices. A national penalty provision may well be legitimate in the abstract but will result in disproportionate outcomes in the specific context of its application – a risk that we saw in part II is plausible in the contemporary patent system. In such cases, national courts must disregard 'that part of the national legislation from which the disproportionate nature of the penalties stems' and so ensure proportionate remedies in fact.[16] What is more, the plain text of Article 3 of the Enforcement Directive and the ECJ's case law mandate case-by-case scrutiny of injunctions in terms that a senior European patent judge recently described as 'crystal clear'.[17] I would add that the language also suggests a degree of judicial scrutiny going beyond traditional limits on enforcement. Generally speaking, those require 'gross disproportionality' to apply, but the inference that patent injunctions are allowed to be disproportionate, just not grossly so, is hard to reconcile with the text of Article 3 of the Enforcement Directive. Indeed, this chapter shows that this article sets clear limits on enforcement, which, in my view, require more intensive scrutiny of patent enforcement than existing limitations allow.

[14] RB The Hague 18 July 2018, ECLI:NL:RBDHA:2018:8777 (*Nikon v ASML*), para 4.45.

[15] Case C-200/96 *Metronome Musik v Music Point Hokamp* ECLI:EU:C:1998:172, [1998] ECR I-1953, para 21.

[16] Case C-205/20 *Bezirkshauptmannschaft Hartberg-Fürstenfeld* ECLI:EU:C:2022:168, para 42.

[17] R Arnold, 'Injunctions in European Law: Judicial Reflections' in J Contreras and M Husovec (eds), *Injunctions in Patent Law* (Cambridge University Press, 2022) 68.

There are other reasons why proportionality should not be considered subsumed in existing limitations. First, insofar as these limitations set specific conditions to apply, they are incapable of ensuring proportionate outcomes in every case. This is most obvious for the requirement of dominance under Article 102 TFEU: there seems to be no cogent reason why non-dominant undertakings should be allowed to disregard proportionality and countervailing rights when enforcing their patents. Second, if proportionality is to be ensured by a variety of national provisions, the limits it poses on patent enforcement would differ across Member States. That creates legal uncertainty and is at odds with the goal of providing an 'equivalent and homogeneous level of protection', as stated in Recital (10), particularly because the differences can be substantial. For instance, the scope and applicability of general principles of fairness as well as abuse of rights doctrines inevitably differs between jurisdictions; the availability of safeguards like stays of enforcement, bond posting requirements or specific carve-outs from an injunction depends on the intricacies of national civil procedure; and the grounds for the grant of compulsory licences differ so substantially across Member States that in the wake of the COVID-19 pandemic, the European Commission is seeking to harmonise the issue to overcome such 'fragmentation'.[18] Lastly, it is not clear how reliance on external limitations to ensure proportionate remedies would work before the UPC, which issues remedies separately from the national law context that lays down these limitations, but will issue injunctions in accordance with Article 3 of the Enforcement Directive, as is addressed in section 5.4.

It has been argued that even if Article 3 of the Enforcement Directive sets conditions for patent enforcement, observation of these conditions is not mandatory to the extent they protect the infringer's interests, because the Directive constitutes minimum harmonisation and leaves Member States free to adopt rules 'more favourable for rightsholders' (Article 2(1)).[19] This argument is unconvincing. First and foremost, the ECJ has held that where a directive requires national remedies to be effective, proportionate and dissuasive, the proportionality requirement has direct effect.[20] The directive at stake in that case was comparable to the Enforcement Directive in that it laid down enforcement measures for the benefit of a class of plaintiffs (there, posted workers) and the proportionality requirement was invoked by their counterparty (there, the representative of a company posting workers). The ECJ held that if the proportionality safeguard only became effective when expressly transposed by Member States, that

[18] In 2022, the European Commission started exploring possibilities for a harmonised EU framework for compulsory licences, describing the different national regimes as fragmented and lacking coordination: Commission, 'Proposal for a regulation of the European Parliament and of the Council on compulsory licensing for crisis management and amending Regulation (EC) 816/2006' COM(2023) 224 final.

[19] M Stierle, 'Zum Verhältnismäßigkeitsvorbehalt im patentrechtlichen Unterlassungsrecht' (2020) 111 *Mitteilungen der deutschen Patentanwälte* 486, 492–93.

[20] *Bezirkshauptmannschaft Hartberg-Fürstenfeld* (n 16) para 30.

'would amount to preventing the individuals concerned from invoking, where appropriate, the prohibition on adopting disproportionate penalties imposed by that requirement'.[21] This, the Court continued, would run counter to Article 288 TFEU, which states that directives shall be binding on Member States. Similarly, if Member States were free to disregard safeguards for the infringers laid down in the Enforcement Directive, those safeguards would be deprived of their binding nature.[22] Second, as is further explained below, the Enforcement Directive represents a balance struck between the Charter rights of holders of IP rights and infringers. The safeguards for the infringer that the EU legislator laid down as part of that balance include not only the proportionality requirement, but also safeguards against abuse and barriers to legitimate trade (also in Article 3(2)), as well as a variety of specific procedural safeguards (eg Articles 7(2)–(5), 9(3)–(7) and 10(2)). Some of these safeguards are expressly formulated as optional (*cf* 'may', eg in Article 9(6)), but most are not (*cf* 'shall', eg in Article 9(7)). It would be anomalous if Member States could simply override these non-optional safeguards and allow, for example, abusive enforcement aimed at legitimate trade out of a desire to strengthen the position of IP rights holders. That would entirely undermine the balance of interests envisioned by the EU legislator. Third, there is nothing in the ECJ's case law interpreting the Enforcement Directive to suggest that infringer safeguards contained therein are optional. To the contrary, the ECJ consistently emphasises that these safeguards must be observed at all times.[23] Clearly, then, the Enforcement Directive sets not just minimum standards for, but also binding ceilings to, enforcement measures, including in Article 3.

In sum, Article 3 of the Enforcement Directive sets mandatory limits on patent enforcement that are distinct from general limitations on rights enforcement found in the laws of the Member States. It does not, however, follow that proportionality should be a free-standing test. Courts could also rely on conforming interpretation to imbue open-ended national principles or provisions with the standards set by the Enforcement Directive, even disregarding settled national case law.[24] I do not favour that approach because it needlessly introduces ambiguity on two levels. On the national level, relying on abuse provisions or general principles of fairness to ensure patent injunctions are proportionate risks creating inconsistencies with the application of these provisions or principles in other fields of law, where traditional, more stringent standards likely apply. On the European level, it hinders judicial dialogue between courts and critical engagement by scholars because it would remain unclear to what extent the decision is driven by the EU proportionality standard and to what extent by the idiosyncrasies of the

[21] ibid para 26.

[22] In his opinion, Advocate General Bobek took the view that the ruling's effect should extend to other secondary EU legislation requiring that remedies be effective, proportionate, and dissuasive: Opinion of AG Bobek ECLI:EU:C:2021:759, paras 55–57.

[23] See, eg *NovaText* (n 8) para 52; *MICM* (n 6) paras 94–95; *Bayer Pharma* (n 8) para 68.

[24] *Phoenix Contact* (n 8) para 52.

national provision. To be sure, these drawbacks can be overcome, and conforming interpretation certainly is to be preferred over excluding proportionality considerations by relying solely on external limitations in their traditional interpretation. But this ambiguity can easily be avoided by explicitly applying a proportionality test and articulating, where necessary, how it differs from proportionality in other fields of IP or law more generally.

Having established that the proportionality test deriving from the Enforcement Directive sets independent restraints on the patentee's entitlement to injunctive relief, it is time to examine them in detail. The next section explains how the Directive weaves together the various parties' primary law entitlements and treaty-derived obligations to create a balanced framework for patent enforcement.

5.2. Anatomy of Article 3: Conditions, Charter Rights and Fair Balance

5.2.1. The Enforcement Directive's Two-Tiered Balance of Charter Rights

Our inquiry starts with Article 17(2) CFR, which states that 'intellectual property shall be protected'. In the context of patents, this provision first and foremost guarantees the patent owner's exclusive right to use an invention either by manufacturing industrial products or licensing others to do so, as well as their right to oppose infringements, all to reward the patentee's creative effort.[25] Arguably, this guarantee constitutes the 'social function' of the patent. The protection patents afford is not absolute but must be exercised in accordance with this function.[26] Unfortunately, not much is known about the scope and content of Article 17(2) CFR as it applies to patentees beyond these general observations. As a consequence, a patentee's entitlements under secondary EU law are underpinned by a Charter right that we know is functionally bound but otherwise remains opaque. Furthermore, patentees enjoy a constitutional guarantee to effective enforcement of their rights under Article 17(2) CFR, which is laid down in Article 47, first paragraph CFR. This latter provision protects against violations of any right arising from EU law and is thus accessory in nature to other rights, such as Article 17(2) CFR in the case of patents.[27]

These rights of the patentee must be brought into harmony with the rights of those affected by patent exclusivity: infringers and third parties. On the part

[25] *Huawei* (n 7) Opinion of AG Wathelet ECLI:EU:C:2014:2391, fn 34 (with references to case law).

[26] See, by analogy, *Metronome Musik* (n 15) para 21.

[27] H Hoffmann, 'Article 47' in S Peers et al (eds), *The EU Charter of Fundamental Rights: A Commentary*, 2nd edn (Hart Publishing, 2021) 47.69.

of infringers, IP rights enforcement measures implicate at least Articles 16 and 47 CFR. In addition to laying down the aforementioned right to an effective remedy, Article 47 CFR entitles everyone to a fair trial. The Charter's explanations indicate that the intention of the second paragraph of Article 47 CFR is to ensure that the guarantees of Article 6 of the European Convention on Human Rights (ECHR) apply in a similar way in the EU. It follows that the various procedural safeguards for infringers in the Enforcement Directive, characterised by the ECJ as a 'counterweight' to the remedies afforded to rights holders, must at a minimum provide the protection that Articles 47 CFR and 6 ECHR afford them.[28] Furthermore, because injunctions can (severely) affect an infringer's capacity to do business, they will almost always affect the infringer's rights under Article 16 CFR.[29] The right to engage in an economic or commercial activity that this provision protects derives from the principle of free competition, enshrined in Article 119(1) TFEU. In *Sky Österreich*, the ECJ suggested that the 'core content' of Article 16 CFR is to carry out a business activity 'as such' and to exploit rightfully acquired entitlements, such as exclusive broadcasting rights.[30] According to *UPC Telekabel Wien*, it also protects 'the right for any business to be able to freely use, within the limits of its liability for its own acts, the economic, technical and financial resources available to it'.[31] All in all, Article 16 CFR is commonly understood to cover, at a minimum, a business's freedom to conduct any activity allowed by the relevant laws.[32] As regards third parties, a range of Charter rights could be affected depending on the technology at stake. For instance, an injunction on encryption technology could encroach on the right to liberty and security (Article 6 CFR); exclusivity claims threatening public–private research alliances formed by the infringer could have repercussions for the freedom of the arts and sciences (Article 13 CFR); and where enforcement results in layoffs, employees' right to engage in work (Article 15 CFR) might be at stake.

The conflict between the patentee's rights and those of others permeates all of patent law. It is not controversial that in enacting patent statutes, the legislator strikes a calculated balance between these various rights (section 1.1.2). Thus, the expansion of patentable subject matter may constitute an impermissible encroachment on the rights of others if it would too severely restrict the public domain.[33] Conversely, a compulsory licensing provision will interfere with the patentee's right to property, but the interference will be permissible if

[28] *Phoenix Contact* (n 8) para 48.

[29] Wathelet opinion (n 25) para 59.

[30] Case C-283/11 *Sky Österreich* ECLI:EU:C:2013:28, para 49.

[31] *UPC Telekabel Wien* (n 5) para 49.

[32] E Gill-Pedro, 'Freedom to Conduct Business in EU Law: Freedom from Interference or Freedom from Domination?' (2017) 9 *European Journal of Legal Studies* 103, 113; M Everson and R Correia Goncalves, 'Article 16' in Peers et al (n 27) 16.56.

[33] Case C-377/98 *Netherlands v Parliament and Council* ECLI:EU:C:2001:523, [2001] ECR I-07079, para 77 (finding that the right to human dignity was safeguarded where the directive is framed in a manner 'sufficiently rigorous to ensure that the human body effectively remains unavailable and inalienable').

it is lawful, in accordance with the general interest, and pursues a legitimate aim in a proportionate manner.[34] In much the same way but in the specific context of infringement proceedings, the Enforcement Directive also strikes a balance between the rights of patentees and others. On the patentees' side, the Directive's key provisions 'apply and implement' Articles 17(2) and 47 CFR.[35] On the infringers' side, the Directive lays down various 'guarantees' that act as a 'counterweight' against measures that affect their interests.[36] Although the ECJ has not expressly traced these guarantees to the infringer's Charter rights, it has held that the Directive and national implementing measures must not be interpreted in a way that would conflict with the various fundamental rights protected by the EU legal order, which ostensibly includes the infringer's rights.[37] On the side of third parties, their interests are mentioned specifically only in Article 10(3) of the Enforcement Directive (on corrective measures) and otherwise generally acknowledged in Recital (32), which states that the Directive 'respects' fundamental rights. The Enforcement Directive sets boundaries on all these affected rights in accordance with Article 52 CFR.

More controversial is the argument that the Enforcement Directive does not just strike a static balance between the various rights at stake, but additionally requires tailored remedies based on a case-by-case assessment to ensure the balance is not upset.[38] This finds clear illustration in *Promusicae*, where the ECJ addressed whether information requests as provided for in (inter alia) Article 8 of the Enforcement Directive could upset the privacy safeguards laid down in Directive 2002/58. The Court held that such information requests created 'the need to reconcile the requirements of the protection of different fundamental rights', ie the respect for private life on the one hand and Articles 17(2) and 47 CFR on the other.[39] In line with our inquiry so far, the Court identified the 'rules' contained in the relevant directives as a first mechanism 'allowing those different rights and interests to be balanced'. Second and additionally, it pointed to 'the application by the national authorities' of the directives' provisions as another source of

[34] *Smith Kline and French Labs v Netherlands* App no 12633/87 (Commission Decision, 4 October 1990).

[35] The ECJ held this expressly in relation to Art 8, laying down a right to information: *Coty Germany* (n 3) para 29; Case C-427/15 *New Wave CZ* ECLI:EU:C:2017:18 para 25. As far as injunctions (Arts 9 and 11) are concerned, the ECJ held that they fall 'within the scope of the protection of the fundamental right to the protection of intellectual property' laid down in Art 17(2) CFR: *McFadden* (n 5) para 81.

[36] *Phoenix Contact* (n 8) para 48; Case C-681/13 *Diageo Brands* ECLI:EU:C:2015:471, para 74 (in the context of provisional measures). The Enforcement Directive contains various other guarantees for infringers, most notably in Art 3.

[37] *Promusicae* (n 3) para 68. *cf* Case C-452/20 *Agenzia delle dogane e dei monopoli en Ministero dell'Economia e delle Finanze* ECLI:EU:C:2022:111, para 51 (linking the proportionality requirement for national penalties to the affected party's rights under Art 16 CFR).

[38] *cf* recently Case C-433/20 *Austro-Mechana* ECLI:EU:C:2022:217, para 50 (finding, albeit in the context of Directive 2001/29, that excess compensation would not be compatible with the requirement 'that a fair balance must be *safeguarded* between the rightholders and the users of protected subject matter' (emphasis added)).

[39] *Promusicae* (n 3) para 66.

balance. The Court observed that the provisions of the directives implementing Articles 17(2) and 47 CFR are 'relatively general, since they have to be applied to a large number of different situations'; and that these rules are intended to be 'adapted to the various situations possible'.[40] That finding is followed by an oft-cited paragraph in which the ECJ establishes a duty for Member State courts, when interpreting national law transposing (inter alia) the Enforcement Directive, to 'take care to rely on an interpretation … which allows a fair balance to be struck between the various fundamental rights protected by the Community legal order'.[41] It is worth noting that nearly identical reasoning was applied in *Lindqvist*, an earlier case repeatedly cited in *Promusicae*, where the ECJ expressly added that 'it is, rather, at the stage of the application at national level of the legislation implementing Directive 95/46 in individual cases that a balance must be found between the rights and interests involved'.[42]

To be sure, *Promusicae* was an intermediary case and concerned the protection of personal data, which invariably requires a case-by-case assessment. But there are good grounds to conclude that *Promusicae*'s two-tiered balancing scheme – first on the legislative level, second on the level of actual application in practice – represents the Enforcement Directive's general structure and applies with equal force to permanent injunctions. In *Huawei*, the Court expressly referred to 'conditions which seek to ensure a fair balance between the interests concerned'.[43] At the same time, it seems unlikely that national courts should weigh the patentee's Charter rights against those of the infringer on a case-by-case basis and each time formulate the remedy that best reflects this balance. Although there are cases where the ECJ formulated a duty for courts along those lines, they were all cases concerning injunctions against intermediaries, ie measures that by definition affect third parties and quite possibly their legitimate behaviour.[44] In my view, the holding of these cases applies to patent cases only to the extent the injunction threatens to affect third parties, such as patients, as section 5.3.3 explains in more detail. After all, the Enforcement Directive lays down no 'guarantees' or 'counterweights' to protect third parties in the event of patent enforcement, whereas Recital (32) makes clear that these parties' Charter rights must be respected. The only exception – Article 10(3) of the Enforcement Directive – confirms this intuition as it merely requires that 'the interests of third parties shall be taken into account' when ordering the measure. The Directive itself provides no guidance on

[40] ibid para 67.
[41] ibid para 68.
[42] Case C-101/01 *Lindqvist* ECLI:EU:C:2003:596, [2003] ECR I-12971, para 85.
[43] *Huawei* (n 7) para 55. It should be noted that *Promusicae*'s fair-balance formula appears only in cases concerning information requests and permanent injunctions. It does not feature, for instance, in cases concerning Art 14 (on legal costs), where the Court appears merely to test for compliance with Art 14's specific safeguards and Art 3 of the Enforcement Directive: *United Video Properties* (n 8) para 27; Case C-559/20 *Koch Media* ECLI:EU:C:2022:317, para 56. The intriguing question whether this implies different legality tests depending on the measure invoked is outside the scope of this chapter but is certainly deserving of further attention.
[44] The classic examples are *UPC Telekabel Wien* (n 5) para 47; *L'Oréal and others* (n 4) para 143.

how those interests or rights might be considered within the measures provided and so courts will have to tailor patent injunctions to achieve a balanced result, for instance by including carve-outs in injunction orders.

Conversely, if patent courts would balance 'ad hoc' the interests of the patentee against those of the infringer, they would be substituting their own view on where that balance should lie for the EU legislator's. Given the various specific guarantees and safeguards contained in the Enforcement Directive for both the patentee and the infringer, it is not only unnecessary for courts to perform an additional balancing exercise, but this would also be inappropriate from a separation of powers perspective. The court's task is limited to ensuring all conditions the Directive sets for relief are met, failing which the balance struck by the EU legislator is distorted.[45] Of course, this latter task requires taking due account of the specific characteristics in each case, as Recital (17) and a variety of ECJ decisions remind us is necessary.[46] We also saw in section 1.3.1 that the need for case-by-case scrutiny was underscored by the EU legislator after the Enforcement Directive's scope was extended to cover all acts of IP rights infringement, rather than just piracy.[47] One could object that the discretion Member States have in implementing the Enforcement Directive's provisions means they have little bite in and of themselves. But cases like *OTK* and *NovaText* illustrate that these provisions nevertheless set concrete limits on the policy space left to Member States.[48] What is more, the ECJ held that the prohibition on imposing disproportionate penalties is stated sufficiently unequivocally and in sufficiently general terms to award it direct effect.[49] This necessarily implies that the proportionality requirement contains a precise obligation as to the result to be achieved, not subject to any condition or implementation decision on the part of the Member States, because under EU law those are preconditions for direct effect. It is for patent courts to scrutinise whether this obligation (like all others in the Enforcement Directive) is met before ordering the requested relief, but it bears repeating that this is not done by redoing the balance struck by the legislator. Rather, it requires vetting whether all conditions laid down in the Enforcement Directive are satisfied, including in particular those contained in Article 3. We turn now to a discussion of what those conditions entail.

[45] *cf* also Ohly (n 15) 156; Norrgård (n 3) 513.

[46] See, eg *NovaText* (n 8) para 52; *MICM* (n 6) para 95; *Bayer Pharma* (n 8) para 69.

[47] See esp EP Committee on Legal Affairs and the Internal Market, 'Report on the proposal for a directive on measures and procedures to ensure the enforcement of intellectual property (Janelly Fourtou)' A5-0468/2003 (5 December 2003) 41 (amendments proposed to 'ensure that the penalties and provisional measures will be applied in a graduated and proportionate way, taking into account whether or not the infringement was deliberate, so as to prompt judges to use their power of assessment when facing cases of infringement that are not properly acts of counterfeiting or piracy').

[48] *OTK* (n 8) para 31 (Art 3(2) precludes damages award that very clearly and substantially exceeds the loss actually suffered); *NovaText* (n 8) paras 51–52 (Arts 3(1) and 14 preclude shielding categories of expenses from any judicial review).

[49] *Bezirkshauptmannschaft Hartberg-Fürstenfeld* (n 16) para 27 (see discussion of this important decision in s 5.1.2).

5.2.2. The Guarantees and Safeguards of Article 3 of the Enforcement Directive

Because Article 11 of the Enforcement Directive does not set conditions for permanent injunctions beyond requiring that Member State courts may grant them, the most important conditions for their grant are found in Article 3. This provision sets requirements that all IP remedies must respect.[50] That includes injunctions in patent cases, both interim and final.[51] Article 3 reads as follows:

> Article 3
>
> **General obligation**
>
> 1. Member States shall provide for the measures, procedures and remedies necessary to ensure the enforcement of the intellectual property rights covered by this Directive. Those measures, procedures and remedies shall be fair and equitable and shall not be unnecessarily complicated or costly, or entail unreasonable time-limits or unwarranted delays.
> 2. Those measures, procedures and remedies shall also be effective, proportionate and dissuasive and shall be applied in such a manner as to avoid the creation of barriers to legitimate trade and to provide for safeguards against their abuse.

As noted above, the requirement that remedies shall be effective, proportionate and dissuasive (the EPD standard) is often considered the heart of Article 3 of the Enforcement Directive. In EU law, the EPD standard is intricately linked to the concept of procedural autonomy, according to which Member States are free in their choice of measures to ensure compliance with Union law provided that the requirements of equivalence and effectiveness are met.[52] In an early case, the ECJ seemingly inferred from the requirements of equivalence and effectiveness that national enforcement measures must 'in any event' be effective, proportionate and dissuasive.[53] Since then, the EPD standard has been incorporated in many EU directives as conditions for national enforcement measures. Importantly, in most cases, the EPD standard governs non-harmonised procedural measures to enforce a directive's harmonised substantive measures. In the Enforcement

[50] *IT Development* (n 8) para 45; *OTK* (n 8) para 21; *Bayer Pharma* (n 8) para 66 ('Article 3 of that directive … sets out a "general obligation" governing all of Chapter II of that directive'); *Tommy Hilfiger* (n 4) para 36 ('It follows from the wording of Article 3 of the directive that it applies to any measure referred to by that directive').

[51] *Warner-Lambert Co v Sandoz* [2016] EWHC 3317 (Pat), paras 74–76.

[52] R Widdershoven, 'National Procedural Autonomy and General EU Law Limits' (2019) 12 *Review of European Administrative Law* 5, 7. For an example of application of the EPD standard in an IP case in the context of national procedural autonomy, rather than Art 3 of the Enforcement Directive, see Case C-348/04 *Boehringer Ingelheim* ECLI:EU:C:2007:249, [2007] ECR I-3391, para 59.

[53] Case C-68/88 *Commission v Greece* ECLI:EU:C:1989:339, [1989] ECR 2965, para 24. In fn 63 of its original proposal for the Enforcement Directive ('Proposal for a directive of the European Parliament and of the Council on measures and procedures to ensure the enforcement of intellectual property rights' COM(2003) 46 final), the Commission refers to this case and two others, which also concerned national law penalties for failure to respect EU law.

Directive, this scenario is reversed: here, the EPD standard governs harmonised procedural measures for the enforcement of non-harmonised substantive law. Because the procedural measures themselves are being harmonised, the EPD standard acts not as an outer limit on national procedural autonomy, but as a substantive norm for the subject matter the EU legislator is seeking to harmonise. Additionally, the contexts in which the EPD standard is often applied (criminal or administrative penalties, or to aid weaker parties such as consumers or employees) are somewhat different from patent disputes, ie civil proceedings between parties that are generally equally sophisticated. In my view, this justifies a more functional interpretation of the EPD standard than in classic procedural autonomy scenarios.[54] In the context of the Enforcement Directive, therefore, the EPD standard must be interpreted and applied in light of the Directive's objectives (*cf* Recital (10)), the specific features of the IP right enforced (*cf* Recital (17)) and the specific subject matter of the underlying Charter rights at stake.

Article 3's other requirements derive from Article 41(1)–(2) of the Agreement on Trade-Related Aspects of Intellectual Property Rights (TRIPS). It is worth noting that while Article 41 TRIPS sets conditions for enforcement *procedures*, Article 3 of the Enforcement Directive extends these same conditions to specific *measures* and *remedies*. The ECJ's interpretation of 'unnecessarily complicated or costly' illustrates well the effects of the shift. In *Scarlet Extended* and *SABAM*, a blocking injunction was considered unnecessarily complicated and costly for an internet service provider to implement, whereas in *United Video Properties* and *NovaText*, this condition justified limiting cost awards under Article 14 of the Enforcement Directive only to reasonable legal costs.[55] Thus, language that in Article 41(2) TRIPS sets standards for the costs and efficiency of enforcement proceedings in favour of right holders becomes, in Article 3(1) of the Enforcement Directive, a limitation on the allowable scope and content of enforcement measures in favour of their addressees. As a consequence, even conditions that originate directly from Article 41 TRIPS must be interpreted autonomously in the context of Article 3 of the Enforcement Directive.

Together with unnecessary complications and costs, 'unreasonable time-limits' or 'unwarranted delays' principally seem illustrations of how either party's rights may be affected in a given case. Although the first condition so far has been interpreted as a safeguard for infringers, it is easy to see what kind of guarantees it might require for patentees, in line with its original purpose in the TRIPS agreement. When it comes to injunctions, granting an indefinite stay could qualify as an

[54] The ECJ interprets the Enforcement Directive's provisions in light of 'the objectives pursued by the measure of which [they form] part': eg *Perfumesco.pl* (n 8) para 39. *cf* F Cafaggi and P Iamiceli, 'The Principles of Effectiveness, Proportionality and Dissuasiveness in the Enforcement of EU Consumer Law: The Impact of a Triad on the Choice of Civil Remedies and Administrative Sanctions' (2017) 25 *European Review of Private Law* 575, 583 (arguing that effectiveness 'operates differently depending on whether redress is individual or collective and on the status and identity of the claimant').

[55] Case C-360/10 *SABAM* ECLI:EU:C:2012:85, para 46; *Scarlet Extended* (n 6) para 48; *United Video Properties* (n 8) para 24; *NovaText* (n 8) para 45.

unwarranted delay, but not granting any stay could be considered an unreasonable time limit for the infringer to cease infringement. All these conditions seem to lack specific substance because each begs the question when complications or costs are unnecessary, delays unwarranted or time limits unreasonable. Those questions can only be answered by applying the other conditions of Article 3.

The same could be said of the requirement that remedies shall be fair and equitable.[56] In my view, however, fairness should be understood as a reference to the parties' right to a fair trial (Articles 47 CFR and 6 ECHR), as it was also intended in the TRIPS agreement.[57] On the infringer's side, this condition is a safeguard against injunctions that are proportionate in principle but suffer from a procedural defect.[58] As I have argued elsewhere, that could particularly be the case where a permanent injunction is issued without verifying the validity of the patent, as can happen in bifurcated systems.[59] Regarding equity, the ECJ recently held that the cost allocation rule of Article 14 of the Enforcement Directive 'does not apply if equity prevents [it]', even if the costs are 'reasonable and proportionate'.[60] That would suggest equity sets some limitations independent of proportionality, but it should be borne in mind that Article 14 of the Enforcement Directive explicitly states that it applies only 'unless equity does not allow this'. Indeed, in the context of cost awards, a separate equitable test makes sense given the Directive's concern for inadvertent infringement – see Recital (17) – and especially where infringers may be individuals, as can happen in copyright cases. On the other hand, the case for a general equitable test applicable to all remedies and derived from Article 3 of the Enforcement Directive is much weaker, not least because the ECJ has never hinted at such a test and it would be hard to reconcile with the balance struck by the legislator. I therefore assume that, at least in the context of patent injunctions, the requirement in Article 3 that remedies shall be 'equitable' has no independent effect and is subsumed in the requirements of the article's second section.

It follows that, barring situations that raise issues concerning the parties' fair trial rights, the key guarantees for patentees and safeguards for infringers when it

[56] Ohly (n 2) 258 (arguing that 'proportionality is a function of fairness and equity'). There is some support for this view in the case law, eg in *L'Oréal and others* (n 4) para 139, where the ECJ dismissed a general monitoring obligation as not fair and proportionate, without further distinction.

[57] See WTO Appellate Body 2 January 2002, WT/DS176/AB/R *United States – Section 211 Omnibus Appropriations Act of 1998*, para 221 (rights laid down in Art 42 TRIPS 'are *procedural* in nature'); see also C Correa, *Trade Related Aspects of Intellectual Property Rights: A Commentary on the TRIPS Agreement*, 2nd edn (Oxford University Press, 2020) 397 ('Article 42 details several aspects of due process of law'); Norrgård (n 2) 511.

[58] For an example, see GH The Hague 2 December 2019, ECLI:NL:GHDHA:2019:3709 (*VG Colours v HE Licenties*), para 4.6, where the Court of Appeal stayed an injunction pending appeal because the lower court had overlooked one of the defendant's critical arguments.

[59] L Dijkman, 'Does the Injunction Gap Violate Implementers' Fair Trial Rights under the ECHR?' (2021) 70 *Gewerblicher Rechtsschutz und Urheberrecht International* 215; L Dijkman, 'Does the Injunction Gap Violate Implementer's Fair Trial Rights under the Charter?' [2022] *Gewerblicher Rechtsschutz und Urheberrecht* 857.

[60] *NovaText* (n 8) para 39.

comes to injunctive relief are found in Article 3(2) of the Enforcement Directive: the injunction must be effective, proportionate and dissuasive; it must not create barriers to legitimate trade; and courts must not allow abuse.[61] As argued above, where injunctions would affect the fundamental rights of third parties, those must be taken into account when deciding on the appropriate form of relief. The next section provides a detailed analysis of these guarantees and safeguards.

5.3. The Conditions for Patent Injunctions in Article 3 of the Enforcement Directive

5.3.1. Effective, Proportionate, Dissuasive Remedies; No Barriers to Legitimate Trade

5.3.1.1. Effectiveness: The Patentee's Basic Entitlement to an Injunction

In EU law, effectiveness can require a broad range of things depending on the penalty or remedy at stake and the context in which it applies, but at its most abstract it seeks to ensure compliance with EU law.[62] When applied to Article 11 of the Enforcement Directive, effectiveness thus requires attainment of a high, equivalent and homogeneous level of protection for patentees; and it drives the enjoyment of the patentee's rights under Article 17(2) CFR, ie their exclusive right to use an invention either by manufacturing industrial products or licensing others to do so. In my view, effectiveness thus establishes a comprehensive entitlement to an injunction for all patentees.[63] Rules that would categorically limit this entitlement likely run afoul of the effectiveness requirement.[64] In my view, the effectiveness principle is best read as precluding an outright denial of injunctive relief with an award of damages in lieu. True, the EPD standard can be likened to 'three sisters' that must be 'treated equally', ie without adopting a 'simple presumption in favour of effective enforcement'.[65] But it seems unlikely that one 'sister', proportionality, could ever neuter another, effectiveness. Rather, achieving harmony between the different elements of the EPD standards presumably requires that the essence of each is respected. It strikes me as implausible that

[61] The English court accepted this in *HTC* (n 11) para 26.

[62] Case C-81/12 *Asociaţia Accept* ECLI:EU:C:2013:275, para 63 (sanctions must ensure 'real and effective legal protection of the rights' deriving from EU law). *cf* Cafaggi and Iamiceli (n 54) 581, 583.

[63] *cf UPC Telekabel Wien* (n 5) para 62 (measures sufficiently effective if they 'ensure genuine protection of the fundamental right at issue', by 'preventing unauthorised access to the protected subject matter' or at least 'making it difficult to achieve').

[64] *cf Phoenix Contact* (n 8) para 40; *Bastei Lübbe* (n 3) para 52. That includes limiting injunctions for non-practising entities: *cf MICM* (n 6) paras 74–75.

[65] Ohly (n 2) 274.

an award of damages in lieu could ever qualify as an effective remedy because that would fundamentally alter the nature of the patent entitlement. As we saw, Article 17 CFR guarantees to patentees an exclusive right to an invention. It can hardly be said that allowing infringers to use the invention indefinitely at a court-set damages rate constitutes an effective means to ensure that exclusive right is respected.

Additional support for this view can be found in Article 12 of the Enforcement Directive. Initially introduced to 'protect the interests of a defending party who has acted without fault of negligence', it ended up an optional provision that very few Member States chose to implement.[66] Article 12 of the Enforcement Directive would allow courts to substitute an injunction for a damages payment if (i) the infringer acted unintentionally and without negligence, (ii) the injunction would cause them disproportionate harm and (iii) monetary damages appear reasonably satisfactory to the right holder. It has been argued that this provision offers 'no more than an example' of a case where patent courts may withhold an injunction.[67] I do not consider that argument compelling. It is clear that Article 12 derogates from the general rules set by the Enforcement Directive, which strongly suggests that, absent voluntary implementation by Member States and outside its narrow scope of application, an injunction may not be substituted for damages in lieu. Additional support for this position is found in the Commission's proposal for the Directive, where it stated that 'this provision *permits* reparation in the form of a fixed-rate remuneration instead of the application of the penalties referred to in the same section' (emphasis added).[68] If Article 3 of the Enforcement Directive allowed the outright denial of injunctive relief, it would seem superfluous to give a very specific example in Article 12, nor would courts need 'permission' to deny injunctive relief. The better view, which is also in line with the plain meaning of effectiveness and its interpretation by the ECJ, is that EU patent courts may not deny an injunction and award damages in lieu except where Article 12 of the Enforcement Directive was implemented and its conditions met.[69]

At the same time, the injunction need not always have immediate effect. In a recent decision on notice-and-takedown rules, the Court considered such rules effective so long as they require 'expeditious', not immediate, removal of infringing content.[70] Non-immediate removal would impair effectiveness only if 'the actual cessation of the infringement [would be] delayed in such a way as to cause

[66] Commission proposal (n 53) 23.

[67] A Ohly, 'Injunctions in the UPC and the Principle of Proportionality' (2022) 5 *Stockholm Intellectual Property Law Review* 58, 61. *cf* P Blok, 'A Harmonized Approach to Prohibitory Injunctions: Reconsidering Article 12 of the Enforcement Directive' (2016) 11 *Journal of Intellectual Property Law & Practice* 56, 60 (arguing that Art 12 'offers a basis for a harmonized European approach' to proportionality).

[68] Commission proposal (n 53) 23.

[69] W Tilmann, 'Article 63' in W Tilmann and C Plassmann (eds), *Unified Patent Protection in Europe: A Commentary* (Oxford University Press, 2018) no 39.

[70] *YouTube and Cyando* (n 5) para 141.

disproportionate damage to the rightholder'.[71] The decision illustrates that delayed cessation may constitute an effective remedy and even appears to provide courts with considerable leeway when determining the duration of the stay by setting the upper limit at 'disproportionate damage to the rightholder'. Some leeway in this respect is not surprising, given the great variance in the duration of infringement proceedings across Member States, as well as the different formalities they set for the effective enforcement of a court order. Those differences, as well as practical difficulties faced by addressees of cessation orders (such as YouTube in the case here cited), make an effectiveness standard that requires 'immediate' termination in each and every case untenable. A stay of the injunction must therefore be considered allowable under the effectiveness principle. Indeed, a stay is the most evident way in which this 'sister' can accommodate the requirements of proportionality, while still respecting the patentee's exclusive right.

5.3.1.2. Dissuasiveness and Proportionality: Remedies Commensurate with the Infringement

The requirements of dissuasiveness and proportionality warrant joint analysis because they coalesce into a commensurability standard: the severity of sanctions must be commensurate with the underlying violation. Thus, while sanctions should not go beyond what is necessary for the objectives pursued (proportionality), graver violations warrant more severe measures (dissuasiveness). These are two sides of the same coin, and the ECJ often mentions them in the same breath.[72] The baseline for any sanction is that it must deprive the infringer of the economic benefits of infringement; if the infringement is liable to confer an advantage on the infringer despite the penalty, it will not be genuinely dissuasive.[73] Proportionality generally caps the severity of sanctions at this baseline level and requires that they go no further, as this is generally not necessary for the objectives pursued.[74] In this respect, the ECJ often compares the benefit generated by the infringement with the loss penalties would cause.[75] But the specific circumstances under which the infringement occurred can move the needle towards more severe penalties to ensure they remain dissuasive. Such circumstances include, in particular, the

[71] ibid para 142.

[72] eg *Agenzia delle dogane* (n 37) para 44; Case C-565/12 *LCL Le Crédit Lyonnais* ECLI:EU:C:2014:190, para 45.

[73] eg Case C-77/20 *KM* ECLI:EU:C:2021:112 para 45, 48; *Le Crédit Lyonnais* (n 72) para 51. *cf* Art 68 of the UPC Agreement: 'The infringer shall not benefit from the infringement.'

[74] Norrgård (n 2) 512.

[75] eg Case C-655/18 *Schenker* ECLI:EU:C:2020:157, para 44 (penalty corresponding to 100% of the value of goods removed from customs supervision is disproportionate); Joined Cases C-497/15 and C-498/15 *Euro-Team* ECLI:EU:C:2017:229, para 65 (fine 87 times greater than amount of unpaid toll is disproportionate); Case C-255/14 *Chmielewski* ECLI:EU:C:2015:475, para 30 (fine equivalent to 60% of undeclared cash is disproportionate).

frequency with which infringements occur;[76] whether or not infringement was intentional;[77] and the harm caused by the infringement.[78]

We should be careful not to read too much into the cases cited in the previous paragraph as they arose in contexts very different from patent litigation. But the ECJ seems to interpret the EPD standard consistently across legal domains and some of the overarching principles can illuminate its application in patent cases as well. First, in assessing proportionality, the ECJ primarily looks at how the penalty relates to the severity of the underlying offence. The inquiry, therefore, is not about how the affected party's interest in enforcement relates to the infringer's interests, as proportionality has sometimes been interpreted in the context of patent injunctions.[79] The closest the ECJ has come to interpreting proportionality this way is stating, on occasion, that remedies must not be disproportionate to the objectives pursued by the legislation enforced.[80] But that does not necessarily imply a weighing of interests, and the ECJ did not instruct national courts to do so on any occasion. Second, particularly where infringements are a regular occurrence, the threat of severe penalties may be necessary to dissuade prospective infringers from committing violations in the first place.[81] Dissuasiveness thus seems to require general, not just specific, deterrence. If this finding carries over to Article 11 of the Enforcement Directive, it suggests that the occasional costly injunction is a feature, not a bug, of the Directive and the threat thereof plays an important role in deterring holdout tactics.[82] Third, while proportionality is essentially an objective test, its application may be limited by subjective circumstances. The emphasis on the infringer's behaviour, in particular, dovetails with observations in the literature that the parties' 'relative blameworthiness' is an important aspect of the proportionality assessment for patent injunctions.[83]

5.3.1.3. *Barriers to Legitimate Trade: The Importance of 'Collateral Damage'*

Although barriers to legitimate trade are not part of the EPD standard, they help interpret the proportionality requirement in the specific context of remedies for IP rights infringement. In the ECJ's case law, legitimate trade refers simply to

[76] *KM* (n 73) para 43 (infringements common and hard to detect); *Agenzia delle dogane* (n 37) para 56 (repeat offenders).

[77] *Euro-Team* (n 75) para 63; Case C-148/14 *Nordzucker* ECLI:EU:C:2015:287, para 44; Case C-388/13 *UPC Magyarország* ECLI:EU:C:2015:225, para 58.

[78] Case C-537/16 *Garlsson Real Estate* ECLI:EU:C:2018:193, para 59; *Euro-Team* (n 75) paras 62–63; Case C-42/15 *Home Credit Slovakia* ECLI:EU:C:2016:842, para 72.

[79] eg Sikorski (n 10) 37.

[80] *Schenker* (n 75) para 43; *Euro-Team* (n 75) para 58.

[81] *KM* (n 73) para 49. *cf United Video Properties* (n 8) para 27 (suggesting that under the Enforcement Directive, the prospect of a potential infringement action as such should have 'dissuasive effect').

[82] This would appear true of the EU law on remedies more broadly: Cafaggi and Iamiceli (n 54) 606.

[83] N Siebrasse et al, 'Injunctive Relief' in CB Biddle et al (eds), *Patent Remedies and Complex Products: Toward a Global Consensus* (Cambridge University Press, 2019) 147.

non-infringing conduct.[84] Ruling on an injunction against an online marketplace, the Court held that 'the injunction obtained against that operator cannot have as its object or effect a general and permanent prohibition on the selling, on that marketplace, of goods bearing those trade marks'.[85] In an English patent case, the court considered (in obiter dictum) that an injunction targeting two million widgets, only 2000 of which infringe, would not be allowable under Article 3 of the Enforcement Directive (inter alia) because it would constitute a barrier to legitimate trade.[86] In my view, this requirement brings into focus the proportionality inquiry as it applies to patent injunctions. It seems clear that effectiveness and dissuasiveness require termination of any infringing conduct. So long as the practical effects of the injunction are limited to the cessation of infringing conduct only, it does not affect legitimate trade and proportionality, at least as interpreted by the ECJ. After all, the injunction would not do more than is necessary to deprive the infringer of the benefits of the violation: here, the use of patented technology. Only where, in practice, the injunction would *also* affect non-infringing technology – collateral damage, so to speak – can proportionality play a role, because in such cases the relation between the infringement and the damage caused by the remedy becomes an important inquiry.

5.3.1.4. Synthesis

The analysis in the preceding paragraphs shows any patentee has a right to termination of infringement of their rights, but that termination does not have to be immediate, and the infringer may need to be allowed time to design around the patented technology before an injunction takes effect. Whether that is the case will depend on whether the effects of the injunction are proportionate to the act of infringement it seeks to stop, a question whose answer, in turn, will be influenced by subjective considerations, particularly the infringer's good or bad faith. This outline provides the basis for what I will call, in the next chapter, cases of 'overreach', a concept that fits particularly well with component patent cases. My analysis in this section shows that the EPD standard is particularly concerned with remedies that affect, as a practical matter, non-infringing technology falling outside the scope of the patent's claims. Specifically, I see two limitations to the reach of the EPD standard that make its application outside component cases rare.

First, a patentee's specific interest in injunctive relief seems irrelevant to the proportionality inquiry because the effectiveness and dissuasiveness requirements, interpreted in light of Article 17(2) CFR, entitle every patentee to an

[84] That is consistent with the WTO Panel's interpretation of 'legitimate' in its decision of 17 March 2000, WT/DS114/R *Canada-Pharmaceutical Products*, para 4.69. For a different view, not substantiated by case law, that 'barriers to legitimate trade' refers to the EU's 'rules of the single market' and 'competition rules', see Tilmann (n 69) no 15.

[85] *L'Oréal and others* (n 4) para 140.

[86] *Napp Pharmaceutical Holdings v Dr Reddy's Laboratories* [2016] EWHC 1517 (Pat), para 170.

injunction. After all, real and effective protection of the patentee's exclusive right to use an invention either by manufacturing industrial products or licensing others to do so can only be realised with an injunction. The patentee's interest in an injunction therefore cannot be called into question; it is simply a given that flows logically from the substantive entitlement enshrined in Article 17(2) CFR and the guarantee of effective enforcement attached to it. In this respect, the EU framework for proportionality differs critically from its US counterpart, where the patentee's interest in an injunction not only is the most important consideration in practice, but also must be proven by the patentee. In the EU, requiring the patentee to furnish evidence of their interest in an injunction would likely be unallowable.[87] In fact, limiting a patentee's entitlement to injunctive relief based on findings concerning their interest in an injunction may not be compatible with the Enforcement Directive as it would fail to meet the minimum level of protection it guarantees to right holders.[88]

Second, even 'substantial negative economic consequences' do not necessarily render a penalty disproportionate.[89] In my view, it will all depend on how substantial they are in relation to the infringing act. If damage threatened to the infringer is caused primarily by the loss of sales of non-infringing technology effectively targeted by the injunction, that may be suggestive of a disproportionate remedy liable to create barriers to legitimate trade. Conversely, where negative economic consequences for the infringer follow exclusively from having to cease infringement (eg by having to cease the lucrative sales of an infringing generic pharmaceutical), proportionality has no role to play. It is worth noting that there is no case on the EPD standard where the ECJ relied on proportionality to condone illegal conduct just because prohibiting it would cause the culprit great harm. This is consistent with Article 16 CFR, the scope of which is limited to legal activity; there is no fundamental right to infringe a patent, as follows clearly from the official explanation of this provision.[90] A senior German patent judge expressed to me his doubts that this is correct, pointing out that fundamental rights often protect otherwise infringing conduct.[91] It is certainly true that *legislators* balance patent protection against competing rights and interests. The result is either a proportionate limitation of those competing rights or an exception to patent exclusivity; in neither case is infringing conduct covered by

[87] Case C-316/05 *Nokia* ECLI:EU:C:2006:789, para 32.

[88] *cf Perfumesco.pl* (n 8) para 48 ('restricting the application of the measures provided for by [the Enforcement Directive] to certain types of infringement' not allowable); *MICM* (n 6) para 77.

[89] *cf Agenzia delle dogane* (n 37) para 50 (depending on the public policy objective pursued, measures that cause such consequences may be justified).

[90] Explanations relating to the Charter of Fundamental Rights [2007] OJ C303/17, Explanation on Article 16: 'Of course, this right is to be exercised with respect for Union law and national legislation.'

[91] *cf* BVerfG GRUR 2001, 43; 1 BvR 1864/95 *Nutzung eines Patents für Arzneimittel* (finding that the general interest in scientific progress justifies limiting the patentee's rights by excluding from a patent's scope use for the purpose of clinical studies); for copyright, see *Ashby Donald v France* App no 36769/08 (ECtHR, 10 January 2013).

the countervailing right. Under EU law, it is doubtful that additional uncodified exceptions to exclusive rights are acceptable.[92] To the extent they are, or insofar as countervailing rights are considered at the remedies stage, these rights represent some general interest that is exceptionally affected in the case at hand in a manner not contemplated by the legislator. In the case of Article 16 CFR, as we saw, that interest is free competition. But the very point of patents is that they limit that competition so that it is hard to imagine scenarios where infringing conduct raises legitimate concerns under Article 16 CFR without asking the court to redraw the balance already struck by the legislator.[93] Thus, while other fundamental rights might justify tolerating infringing conduct (as is further addressed in section 5.3.3 below), this seems impossible for Article 16 CFR because of its specific content. The situation is different for non-infringing conduct because here there is a conflict between the patentee's right to terminate infringing conduct and the infringer's right to proceed with non-infringing conduct. In my view, this is the conflict that the EPD standard, coupled with the prohibition on barriers to legitimate trade, primarily seeks to resolve.

These two limitations mean that two archetypal enforcement cases that the literature generally considers problematic – non-practising entities (NPEs) and substantial hardship for the infringer – are outside the remit of Article 3(2) of the Enforcement Directive. Consequently, they cannot be addressed by a proportionality test, but that need not concern us here. NPE and hardship cases do not necessarily pose problems with exclusivity going beyond the scope of the patent claim; they are not new phenomena that courts should find a way to tackle; and it is simply unclear how courts could do so in a predictable manner, given the inevitably subjective judgement calls such cases require. It goes without saying that enforcement in these cases could still be limited on other grounds, such as competition law or general doctrines of good faith and abuse of rights. But to keep the scope and function of the proportionality test distinct from these instruments, they should not be conflated, and I have demonstrated here that EU law does not so require.

5.3.2. Safeguards against Abuse

In the EU, the concepts of abuse of a dominant market position (Article 102 TFEU) and abuse of rights have a long track record in curtailing patent abuse. The EU courts have repeatedly addressed the limits that competition law sets to enforcement of IP rights. Competition law was also invoked against more subtle,

[92] *cf* Case C-476/17 *Pelham* ECLI:EU:C:2019:624, para 63.

[93] The Dutch Supreme Court held that the limitation of competition that results from patent enforcement is justified by patent law itself: HR 17 April 2017, ECLI:NL:HR:2017:692 (*Novartis v Sun*), para 3.6.2. Presumably the reference is (also) to patent law's underlying policy objectives.

context-specific behaviour, such as patent ambush strategies, misrepresentations to the patent office and pay-for-delay agreements.[94] Unusual cases escaping scrutiny by competition law, yet resulting in flagrantly unfair outcomes, could be tackled as abuses of rights. In a comprehensive study, Amandine Léonard concluded that abuse of rights is a 'pervasive legal concept' in Europe that is used to curtail rights enforcement considered 'imbalanced' and realise 'a right of exercise considered normal by the deciding authority'.[95] In what follows, I refer to conduct that these two doctrines seek to prevent as 'sanctionable abuse' because engaging in such conduct will normally lead to civil or even criminal liability.[96]

In my view, the abuse that Article 3(2) of the Enforcement Directive is concerned with is distinct from sanctionable abuse. Of course, enforcement efforts that are so egregious as to constitute sanctionable abuse must be prevented in any case. However, if 'safeguards against abuse' were to refer only to Article 102 TFEU and abuse of rights doctrines, its inclusion in Article 3(2) of the Enforcement Directive would be superfluous.[97] It is important to note that while the Commission's first proposal for the Enforcement Directive already contained a 'General obligation' in Article 3 modelled on the TRIPS agreement, it did not require the provision of safeguards against abuse.[98] That requirement was added only after the scope of the Directive was extended to all acts of IP rights infringement, not just counterfeit. The quid pro quo for this extension was case-by-case scrutiny of remedies by courts, as we saw in section 1.3, and a specific requirement for safeguards against abuse. And as we saw in section 3.1.4, concerns that the unusually strong suite of remedies offered by the Enforcement Directive would invite gamesmanship have not proven unfounded. Such gamesmanship do not need to rise to the level of sanctionable abuse to be potentially problematic, especially vis-à-vis targets of enforcement who pay the price.[99] Thus, a stringent abuse standard is a necessary check on myriad possibilities for strategic acquisition, obfuscation and enforcement that intellectual property rights in general and patents in particular afford their owners.

[94] See, respectively, *RAMBUS* (Case COMP/38.636) Commission Decision C(2009) 7610 [2010] OJ C30/17; Case C-457/10 P *AstraZeneca v Commission* ECLI:EU:C:2012:770; Case C-307/18 *Generics (UK)* ECLI:EU:C:2020:52.

[95] A Léonard, 'Abuse of Rights in European Patent Law – Reconsidering the Principle of the Prohibition of Abuse of Rights as an Internal Correction Mechanism against Over-enforcement Practices by Right Holder' (Dissertation, KU Leuven, 2019) 398.

[96] ibid ch 1 finds that in Belgium, France, Germany and the Netherlands, a finding of abuse entitles the affected party to damages at least in theory. As the cases in n 94 above show, violation of Art 102 TFEU results in a fine.

[97] Wathelet opinion (n 25) fn 37 (abuse within the meaning of Art 3(2) of the Enforcement Directive 'necessarily, though not exclusively, encompasses infringements of Articles 101 TFEU and 102 TFEU').

[98] Commission proposal (n 53) 34.

[99] Tilmann (n 69) no 14 gives the example of patentees giving different interpretations of a claim before the EPO and the UPC. See further J Vesala, 'Misuse of Patent Application Procedures: A Case for Condemning Non-misleading Strategies?' in R Ballardini et al (eds), *Transitions in European Patent Law: Influences of the Unitary Patent Package* (Kluwer, 2015) 275.

This hypothesis finds support in the ECJ's numerous references to safeguards against abuse, which often accompany interpretations of the Enforcement Directive's provisions favourable to rightsholders. Thus, the ECJ justified its infamous decision in *Bayer* by finding that a patentee must not be 'discouraged' from availing itself of preliminary relief, but stressed it must not abuse that possibility.[100] In *Oławska Telewizja Kablowa*, the Court held that it would be abusive for rights holders to claim twice the amount of a hypothetical royalty, even if normally allowed, when that amount 'clearly and substantially' exceeds the loss actually suffered.[101] Most recently in *NovaText*, the ECJ cautioned against the 'misuse' of a rule that required no more than a 'declaration on honour' by a party's representative for a full-cost award.[102] But the clearest example is *Mircom*, where a 'copyright troll' tracked down and sought out-of-court settlements with individuals who illegally downloaded pornographic content. In other proceedings involving the same plaintiff, the English court characterised it as 'a money-making scheme designed to embarrass and coerce as many people as possible (regardless of whether they were actual infringers) into making the payments demanded'.[103] The referring court asked whether information requests to Belgian internet service providers made for this purpose might be abusive. The ECJ answered that relevant considerations to establish abuse include 'the way in which Mircom offers amicable solutions to alleged infringers', 'whether it actually brings legal proceedings in the event of a refusal to reach an amicable solution' and whether Mircom was attempting 'to extract economic revenue from the very membership of the users concerned in a peer-to-peer network such as the one at issue, without specifically seeking to combat the copyright infringements caused by that network'.[104] In all these cases, the ECJ is telling us that it might be abusive for a right holder to request measures that the Enforcement Directive formally entitles it to, but in the specific context of the case would result in benefits not contemplated in the Directive (*Bayer*, *NovaText*, *OTK*) or falling outside the scope of the underlying right (*Mircom*).

If *Mircom* shows how easily remedies included in the Enforcement Directive can be used to obtain undue advantages, practices such as patent ambush or reliance on divisional shields show that the same is true for other intricate rules in the patent ecosystem.[105] The patentee is naturally entitled to benefit from these

[100] *Bayer Pharma* (n 8) paras 65, 69; repeated in *Phoenix Contact* (n 8) para 43.
[101] *OTK* (n 8) para 31.
[102] *NovaText* (n 8) para 54.
[103] *Mircom v Virgin Media* [2019] EWHC 1827 (Ch), para 59.
[104] *MICM* (n 6) para 95.
[105] *cf* A Ohly, '"Patenttrolle" oder: Der patentrechtliche Unterlassungsanspruch unter Verhältnismäßigkeitsvorbehalt? Aktuelle Entwicklungen im US-Patentrecht und ihre Bedeutung für das deutsche und europäische Patentsystem' (2008) 57 *Gewerblicher Rechtsschutz und Urheberrecht International* 787, 795 (qualifying 'anti-functional' (*funktionswidrige*) use of injunctive relief as abuse and citing as possible examples habitual enforcement efforts, withdrawal of previous commitments to license and delaying enforcement to create lock-in effects).

rules and use them in a way that best serves their interests. But a patent's intangible nature coupled with the extraordinary complexity of the patent ecosystem mean that, in a specific case against a specific patentee, a requested remedy might become disproportionate. In other words, the abuse standard in Article 3(2) of the Enforcement Directive is relative and situational, its application tied to the remedies inquiry, and its effects limited to delaying an injunction's effects or, at the very worst, replacing it with a damages entitlement. It thus differs considerably from sanctionable abuse, which penalises behaviour in the abstract, thereby limiting the perpetrator's material entitlement, and results in liability for the owner, not the infringer, of the right enforced. If the particularly invasive nature of patent remedies justifies the more stringent abuse standard I advocate for, this difference with sanctionable abuse mitigates its consequences to assuage possible concerns about devaluing patents or legal uncertainty.[106]

In sum, 'abuse' in Article 3(2) of the Enforcement should be understood as distinct from abuse of law or abuse within the meaning of Article 102 TFEU. One could argue, as Léonard does, that the malleability of the abuse of rights doctrine makes it suitable to address instances of 'imbalanced' enforcement. Léonard would thus rely on abuse of rights to 'provide courts with some leeway to determine whether they should grant or deny injunctive relief without having to refer to the principle of proportionality as an all-encompassing principle'.[107] While certainly possible, my concerns with this approach are the same as with conforming interpretation of existing limitations, as outlined in section 5.1.2 above. Applying a proportionality test under the guise of abuse of rights would significantly alter this doctrine, creating problems of coherence with its application in other fields of law. The better solution is to apply a free-standing proportionality test, part of which is a specific inquiry into potentially abusive conduct.[108]

5.3.3. Conflicts with Third Party Rights

The third part of the Enforcement Directive's proportionality test concerns conflicts with the rights of third parties. While lacking support in Article 3(2), it is clear from Recital (32) and the ECJ's fair balance case law that courts must consider any affected third-party rights when ordering remedies for IP rights infringement. Some constitutional courts consistently follow a specific balancing methodology to make their reasoning on the ultimately subjective estimation this requires more transparent. Unfortunately, the ECJ has not articulated

[106] The revised § 139 of the German Patent Act explicitly clarifies not only that limiting injunctive relief does not affect the patentee's claim for damages, but also that a separate claim for damages arises to compensate for the delay before the injunction takes effect. It is doubtful that this outcome could be achieved under the doctrine of *Rechtsmisbrauch*.

[107] Léonard (n 95) 219, 229.

[108] For a similar view, see Vesala (n 99) 288.

any guidance for the fair balance test in its IP jurisprudence. In principle, Article 52 CFR provides a balancing mechanism and the ECJ has occasionally referred to it when determining whether a national measure struck the necessary fair balance.[109] In practice, however, the ECJ often omits references to Article 52 CFR in its IP case law, citing no more than the fair balance test and jumping to the outcome without a clear justification, much less a structured justification that could make the application of the fair balance test more predictable. Nevertheless, some common threads can be distinguished in the Court's case law. These are the subject of this section, which first addresses the preliminary question of the reach of the ECJ's fair balance cases.

5.3.3.1. Does the Fair Balance Requirement Apply in Horizontal Infringement Cases?

Most of the ECJ's fair balancing cases to date concern injunctions against intermediaries, and some commentators believe the outcome in these cases does not mean a fair balance test is also required in ordinary, horizontal infringement cases.[110] Indeed, the ECJ has expressly held that the types of injunctions referenced in Article 11 of the Enforcement Directive – those against infringers aimed at preventing them from continuing the infringement and those against intermediaries – 'cannot be equated'.[111] That distinction was made in a case where the ECJ, for the first time, set parameters for an injunction against an intermediary, a situation it considered 'more complex' and lending itself 'to other kinds of injunctions' than injunctions merely aimed at prohibiting the continuation of an infringement.[112] It is certainly true that injunctions against intermediaries raise special balancing concerns, particularly because the intermediaries themselves are not infringers and facilitate lawful activities by users. Special scrutiny is thus required to ensure the injunction is not too burdensome for the intermediary.[113] As was argued in section 5.2.1 above, that is not the case where the injunction targets an infringer, because the Enforcement Directive already contains the necessary safeguards for them.

From the perspective of affected third parties, however, it makes no difference whether the injunction's addressee infringes or not. The ECJ has been crystal clear that any time a measure is liable to affect the rights of third parties – be it their right to privacy following an information request or their freedom of information following a blocking injunction – these rights should be taken into consideration when imposing the measure. I therefore see no reason to disregard third-party

[109] S Peers and S Prechal, 'Article 52' in Peers et al (n 27) 52.56 suggest the fair balance test stands in for Art 52 CFR in many cases; the Court mentioned both, eg in *Coty Germany* (n 3) para 35.
[110] Schellhorn (n 12) 271.
[111] *L'Oréal and others* (n 4) para 130.
[112] ibid para 129.
[113] *UPC Telekabel Wien* (n 5) para 47; *Scarlet Extended* (n 6) para 48.

rights in ordinary patent disputes if deprivation of access to infringing technology would affect those rights. The Court's reference to a fair balance in *Huawei*, a horizontal patent enforcement case, seemingly confirms this intuition.[114] And in its other fair balance cases, the ECJ certainly made no effort to restrict its rulings specifically to intermediary cases.[115] In sum, it is reasonable to assume that third-party rights must be taken into account any time a measure imposed under the Enforcement Directive would affect them, as Recital (32) also suggests. Certainly, after the inclusion of third-party rights in the amended § 139 of the German Patent Act, that no longer seems to be a controversial position.

5.3.3.2. The Threshold for Finding Interference with a Countervailing Right

A salient feature of the ECJ's cases involving third-party rights is the low threshold for their applicability. This is apparent most clearly from *McFadden*, which concerned a shopkeeper whose WiFi network was being used to infringe Sony's copyrights. Even though provision of a WiFi network was secondary in nature to McFadden's business, the ECJ required minimal encroachment with his rights under Article 16 CFR.[116] Although that can be explained by McFadden's status as an intermediary, the Court's striking concern for his customer's right to access the internet through the store's WiFi, which it considered protected by Article 11 CFR, cannot. It would be fanciful to suppose that the freedom of information of McFadden's customers would be materially affected by cutting off access to his WiFi network, and the ECJ in fact noted that it constituted 'only one of several means of accessing the internet' for them.[117] Still, the Court not only considered Article 11 CFR relevant to the fair balance test in this case, but also reiterated that any measure affecting it should be 'strictly targeted' to ensure users remain able to access lawful information.[118] If the threshold for engaging third-party rights is so low, it is easy to imagine a range of fundamental rights being affected by a patent injunction, depending on the technology at stake. To be sure, none of these rights will normally outweigh the patentee's rights under Articles 17(2) and 47 CFR. But *McFadden* and the ECJ's other cases in this area at least require consideration and, in appropriate cases, may necessitate stays or carve-outs to achieve the required fair balance.

As with Article 16 CFR, the ECJ has so far limited the scope of other Charter rights to lawful, ie non-infringing, activities.[119] This is understandable in the

[114] *Huawei* (n 7) para 55. The same can be said of *Bastei Lübbe*, which also targeted an infringer and not an intermediary: (n 3) para 44.
[115] The wording in *Tommy Hilfiger* (n 4) para 36 rather suggests the opposite.
[116] *McFadden* (n 5) paras 89–90.
[117] ibid para 92.
[118] ibid para 93.
[119] eg ibid para 94 (measure does not affect the possibility of customers 'to access information lawfully'); *UPC Telekabel Wien* (n 5) para 56 (injunction must not affect internet users 'who are using

copyright context, where peer-to-peer file sharing poses serious problems for rights holders and individuals may themselves be liable for copyright infringement. Also in the patent context, it is reasonable to assume that Charter rights will weigh heaviest where an injunction would have the effect of blocking non-infringing technology. However, due to the specific nature of patents, the Charter may well afford end users a claim also against infringing technology. To start, consumers' use of patent technology, even if infringing, will normally be 'lawful' in that, contrary to the copyright context, they themselves are not liable for patent infringement (which requires acts done for commercial purposes). More fundamentally, deprivation of access to infringing technology may have much more profound effects than deprivation of unlawful access to copyrighted works. The oft-discussed case of life-saving medicines illustrates this well and it should not surprise us that patients' dependence on critical, but infringing, drugs or medical devices has been accepted as grounds to limit an injunction and even to grant a compulsory licence.[120] But it may also not be appropriate in other situations to deprive non-parties of access to infringing technology, at least not without a transition period; an example that is sometimes mentioned is where an injunction would affect the telecommunications network.

5.3.3.3. The Threshold for Impermissible Interferences

There are three degrees of interference with Charter rights: a proportionate restriction of the right; a disproportionate restriction of the right; and infringement of the essence of the right. Essence restrictions are never allowed and obviate the need for further balancing.[121] So far, the ECJ has not found essence violations in any IP cases and it is not easy to imagine them occurring. This section therefore focuses on the dividing line between proportionate and disproportionate restrictions.

A measure will restrict Charter rights as soon as it limits the activity covered by its scope, but that need not mean it is prohibited. Thus, in *UPC Telekabel Wien*, the Court approved an injunction, although it restricted the addressee's rights under Article 16 CFR, even imposing on it 'a significant cost' and having 'considerable impact on the organisation of his activities'.[122] On the other hand, some measures are so invasive that they constitute an impermissible interference. In its IP case law, the Court calls these 'serious infringements'. A serious infringement can be found for rights of affected parties if the measure is too invasive, or conversely for

the provider's services in order to lawfully access information'). Because of the presumption of innocence, the right to privacy is perhaps a special case: *Bastei Lübbe* (n 3) para 49. Note that the ECJ avoided explicitly weighing Art 7 CFR against Art 17(2) CFR in that decision.

[120] *Edwards Lifesciences LLC v Boston Scientific* [2018] EWHC 1256 (Pat); TO Torino 16 June 2021, 10009/2020 (*Edwards Lifesciences v Meril Life Sciences*) at 3; BGH GRUR 2017, 1017; X ZB 2/17 *Raltegravir*.

[121] K Lenaerts, 'Limits on Limitations: The Essence of Fundamental Rights in the EU' (2019) 20 *German Law Journal* 779, 786.

[122] *UPC Telekabel Wien* (n 5) para 50.

Articles 17(2) and 47 CFR, where the national implementing measure is insufficiently effective. For instance, in *Bastei Lübbe*, national legislation that shielded from copyright infringement individuals who share their internet connection with others without compelling them to disclose information about potential other users was considered to seriously infringe Articles 17(2) and 47 CFR.[123] In *Scarlet Extended*, an injunction that would require an internet service provider to install a complicated, costly and permanent monitoring system seriously infringed Article 16 CFR.[124]

Neither these nor other cases where a serious infringement of a Charter right was found have applied a proportionality test in line with Article 52 CFR. It therefore remains unclear what, exactly, renders an interference 'serious'. Third parties will have to accept occasional inconvenience or even hardship to ensure the patentee's rights under Articles 17(2) and 47 CFR are respected, but a fair balance may require a middle ground that also modestly limits the patentee's rights. The Court's meticulous balancing in cases like *McFadden* suggest fair balance means the single solution that best balances all applicable rights, not a broader range of outcomes that can each be considered fair. It remains an open question whether it would be so strict in a horizontal patent infringement case. Even if it were not, under the case law as it stands, third-party rights are an important counterweight to the patentee's rights under Articles 17(2) and 47 CFR, particularly where a short stay could significantly mitigate consequences for third parties.

5.3.3.4. Two Intriguing Questions

I end this section with two consequential questions on the fair balance test that, to my knowledge, have not yet been answered. The first is if and how various countervailing rights might be combined to justify an interference with Articles 17(2) and 47 CFR. Striking a fair balance between all rights at stake necessarily requires that none of these rights are seriously infringed, whereas serious infringement of just a single right suffices to upset the balance.[125] But if multiple rights are infringed to a modest degree, does that add up to a sufficiently serious infringement for the purposes of the fair balance test? Suppose that an injunction would require over five million consumers to be refitted with alternative contact lenses, each incurring a cost of €100 for this service. A US court held that such 'deleterious effects of the injunction on the general public' were 'simply too great to permit'.[126] How such a case should be dealt with under the EU's fair balance test is unclear. On the one hand, and assuming a payment of €100 is not a serious infringement of a consumer's fundamental rights, the ECJ's emphasis on serious infringements would

[123] *Bastei Lübbe* (n 3) para 51.
[124] *Scarlet Extended* (n 6) para 48.
[125] eg *McFadden* (n 5) paras 88–89.
[126] *Johnson & Johnson Vision Care Inc v CIBA Vision Corp* 712 FSupp2d 1285, 1292 (MD Fla 2010).

suggest the injunction should be granted. It is uncontroversial that at least some inconvenience to others is an acceptable price for the patent system, and so long as that inconvenience does not rise to unacceptable levels (ie a serious rights violation), it seemingly makes no difference whether it is experienced by 10, 1000 or 10,000 individuals. They all enjoy the benefit of the patent bargain without anyone being inconvenienced to such a degree as a serious rights violation. On the other hand, if fair balance means a single solution that best balances all applicable rights, the implication is that non-serious infringements also count. In the lens case, that would mean the injunction may need to be tailored so as to achieve the lowest overall costs for all affected parties. If all fundamental rights affected are of equal rank and status, this might be the outcome the Charter envisions. The admonition, in Article 3(1) of the Enforcement Directive, against unnecessarily costly remedies lends further support to this view. If the overall costs that IP remedies impose on addressees are a relevant factor to consider (as confirmed in *Scarlet Extended* and *SABAM*), then it would make sense that these costs need to be considered in the aggregate.

The second question was put to me by a colleague, who asked me to hypothesise the nature of the legal relation between the patentee and third parties whose rights are considered in the fair balance test.[127] Suppose a patentee obtains an injunction that results in the removal from the market of a medicament. Would affected patients then have recourse against the patentee and, if so, what might be the basis of their claim? Tort-based claims are highly unlikely to succeed, as the patentee is doing no more than exercising their right of property.[128] In cases of very severe disparity between the patentee's interests and those of patients, an abuse of rights claim could be plausible. A claim for exclusionary conduct might succeed if the patentee sets excessive prices.[129] Either way, the threshold for a successful claim would be very high. As we saw, however, the ECJ's fair balance cases imply a lower threshold for taking into account third-party rights. That would lead to the incongruous result that third-party rights are more easily vindicated by an infringer than if those third parties were to vindicate their own rights. This seems to be the outcome of *McFadden*: if Sony had succeeded in shutting down Mr McFadden's WiFi network, would his customers have had recourse against Sony for violation of their rights under Article 11 CFR? I doubt it. Of course, my reading of the cases

[127] The issue was recently taken up in M Nieder, 'Eingeschränkter Unterlassungsanspruch im europäischen Patentrecht: Folgen auf der Abnehmerseite' [2023] *Gewerblicher Rechtsschutz und Urheberrecht* 995, 996 (finding no 'overall satisfactory' theory to ground the relationship between the patentee and third parties).

[128] Compare GH The Hague 18 December 2021, ECLI:NL:GHDHA:2021:2535 (*AstraZeneca v Menzis*), where the court rejected claims based on tort and unjustified enrichment brought by a healthcare insurer against a patentee whose patent was invalidated. That conclusion would apply a fortiori in case the patent was upheld.

[129] For a recent example, see Netherlands Authority for Consumers and Markets 1 July 2021, ACM/20/041239 (*Laediant*), which imposed a fine of almost €20 million on a pharmaceutical company for excessive pricing.

could be wrong and the ECJ may go a different way if it is ever asked to provide guidance on the fair balance test in a patent dispute. For its part, the English High Court has confirmed the intuition that a carve-out on third-party grounds is allowable only in the case of a threat to patient's lives or very severe health consequences, while during the reform of the German Patent Act some expressed the view that third-party interests are only relevant for proportionality if they would also justify the grant of a compulsory licence.[130] Those positions would place the fair balance test more in line with the legal claims the third parties concerned have against the patentee.

5.4. The Conditions for Patent Injunctions before the UPC

According to Article 71a of Regulation 1215/2012, the UPC is a court common to several Member States.[131] Article 20 of the UPC Agreement states that the UPC 'shall apply Union law in its entirety and shall respect its primacy'. EU courts are under an obligation 'to ensure the full application of European Union law in all Member States and to ensure judicial protection of an individual's rights under that law'.[132] The conditions and requirements that EU law sets for patent injunctions, outlined in this chapter, therefore bind the UPC in the same manner as they do Member State courts. As we saw in section 1.3.3, the drafting committee for the UPC's Rules of Procedure acknowledged this and clarified, in response to a public consultation, that 'the general rules of Article 3(1) and (2) of the Enforcement Directive are applicable and allow for alternative relief to injunctions'.[133] Largely in line with my argument here, the leading commentary on the UPC states that it may grant a stay based on Article 3(2) of the Enforcement Directive (and cannot altogether deny the injunction and award damages in lieu).[134]

How the UPC will interpret and apply the restrictions that the Enforcement Directive sets on patent injunctions will be extremely consequential for the future

[130] *Evalve v Edwards Lifesciences* [2020] EWHC 513 (Pat), para 87; German Federal Parliament, Transcript (*Wortprotokoll der 132. Sitzung*) of 24 February 2021, BT-Drs 19/2581, 39 (Fabian Hoffmann).

[131] Regulation (EU) No 1215/2012 of the European Parliament and of the Council of 12 December 2012 on jurisdiction and the recognition and enforcement of judgments in civil and commercial matters (recast) [2012] OJ L351/1.

[132] Opinion 1/09 *Accord sur la création d'un système unifié de règlement des litiges en matière de brevets* ECLI:EU:C:2011:123 [2011], ECR I-01137, para 68.

[133] Legal Group of the UPC Preparatory Committee, 'Responses to the Public Consultation of the Rules of Procedure of the UPC' (31 January 2014) 95, www.veron.com/upc/various-documents/?lang=en.

[134] Tilmann (n 69) no 35. It is not clear why Tilmann appears to believe the stay can only be based on the 'second half-sentence' of Art 3(2) (cf no 12); that position seems untenable, certainly since the ECJ's decision in *Bezirkshauptmannschaft Hartberg-Fürstenfeld* (n 16).

of the proportionality doctrine in European patent law. Though it is clear that the UPC's Court of Appeal will have to address the issue sooner or later, at the time of writing not much is known about which way it will lean. For what it is worth, the members of the drafting committee of the Rules of Procedure reportedly held differing views on the issue but compromised on the observation that 'Only under very exceptional circumstances [the UPC] will use its discretion and not [issue an injunction] ... When exercising this discretion the Court can also consider the use of alternative measures'.[135] Diverse views also exist among judges appointed to the Court of Appeal, at least judging by their academic writing.[136] What these statements suggest about stays of injunctions, particularly shorter ones, is difficult to predict. Some scholars take a sceptical view and argue for legislative intervention by the EU.[137] In my view, it is too early to give up hope as a properly delineated and sensible proportionality test may yet be looked upon favourably by the UPC. The issues it must address are pressing, the guidance from EU law is clear and the UPC's sister court across the Atlantic, the Court of Appeals for the Federal Circuit, has demonstrated that judicial solutions to specific problems with injunctive relief are possible through its development of the causal nexus test. Thus, with all building blocks in order, the next and final chapter outlines what a European solution might look like.

[135] Legal Group of the UPC Preparatory Committee, 'Table with Explanatory Notes to the Changes Made by the Legal Group of the Preparatory Committee in the 17th Draft of the Rules of Procedure' (31 October 2014) 11, www.veron.com/upc/various-documents/?lang=en.

[136] Compare Grabinski (n 12) 203 (arguing that German law is compliant with Art 3(2) of the Enforcement Directive without granting courts any remedial discretion) and Blok (n 67) 60 (seemingly sympathetic towards greater court discretion, to be exercised with a view to the 'factors' contained in Art 12 of the Enforcement Directive).

[137] L Van Dongen, 'Proportionality and Flexibilities in Final Injunctive Relief' in L Desaunettes-Barbero et al (eds), *The Unitary Patent Package & Unified Patent Court: Problems, Possible Improvements and Alternatives* (Ledizioni 2023) 374, 385.

6

A Proportionality Test for European Patent Law

This chapter ties together the strands of the previous chapters and proposes a legal test to determine when a patentee's entitlement to injunctive relief should be limited on proportionality grounds. Its tripartite structure mimics the limitations imposed by EU law that were outlined in the previous chapter, but it interprets and applies these limitations in the specific context of patent law and with the insights from earlier chapters in mind. It thus starts from the assumption that the patentee is entitled to an injunction with immediate effect (section 6.1), but allows for limitations to that entitlement – primarily in the form of stays – in three sets of cases, generally introduced in section 6.2. The majority of this chapter is devoted to elaborating on these cases and is schematically summarised in Figure 6.1. Section 6.6 ends this final chapter by addressing the payment due to the patentee for the duration of the stay.

Figure 6.1 A European Framework for Proportionality

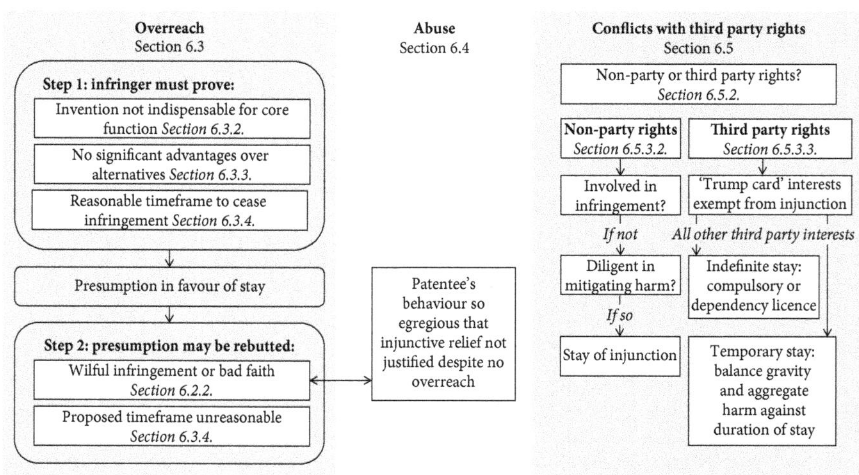

In a nutshell, a limitation of injunctive relief on proportionality grounds is appropriate only in one of three circumstances: where the injunction would overreach; where the patentee engaged in abusive behaviour; and where the injunction would impermissibly interfere with the rights of third parties. Crucially, these three aspects are not weighed together with other circumstances of the case as part of a balancing test. Instead, each aspect stands on its own and jointly they provide an exhaustive catalogue of situations where the proportionality test may lead to a limitation of the patentee's entitlement to a permanent injunction.

6.1. The Patentee's General Entitlement to Immediate Injunctive Relief

A patentee that succeeds on the merits is entitled to a permanent injunction. By default, the injunction should have immediate effect, discounting limited delays to avoid enforcement problems. This point of departure derives, first and foremost, from the respective laws and civil codes of Europe's jurisdictions, most of which stipulate that a successful patentee is entitled to a permanent injunction as a matter of right.[1] It is also consistent with the principal effect of a patent, which is to confer on the patentee an exclusive right to use the invention and the right to prevent any third party from committing acts against which the patent provides protection.[2]

As we saw in chapter five, a presumptive entitlement to injunctive relief is also in line with EU law. I would go even further and argue that under EU law, a patentee's interest in injunctive relief is a given in each case. The European Court of Justice (ECJ) has held that requiring a trademark holder to furnish evidence of their need for an injunction risks 'undermining the exclusive right'.[3] It also held that a court *must* take measures that are appropriate in the circumstances of the case upon finding infringement of a trademark, stressing the importance of an injunction to attain genuine and effective protection.[4] In one copyright case, it seemed to imply that the specific prejudice suffered by the right holder was irrelevant for their entitlement to remedies under the Enforcement Directive.[5] Further, Attorney-General Cruz Villalón considered it 'clear' that a 'frustration of the right of any holders of intellectual property (IP) rights to obtain protection from the courts' would violate the essence of these rights.[6] As we saw in the previous chapter, not much is known about the scope and content of Article 17(2) of the Charter of Fundamental Rights (CFR). We do, however, know that the owner of a patent is guaranteed an 'exclusive right', as well as a 'right to oppose infringements'.[7]

[1] J Contreras and M Husovec, 'Issuing and Tailoring Patent Injunctions: A Cross-Jurisdictional Comparison and Synthesis' in J Contreras and M Husovec (eds), *Injunctions in Patent Law: Trans-Atlantic Dialogues on Flexibility and Tailoring* (Cambridge University Press, 2022) 316.

[2] Case C-15/74 *Centrafarm BV v Sterling Drug* ECLI:EU:C:1974:114, [1974] ECR I-1147, para 9.

[3] Case C-316/05 *Nokia* ECLI:EU:C:2006:789, [2006] ECR I-12083, para 32.

[4] Case C-145/05 *Levi Strauss* ECLI:EU:C:2006:264, [2006] ECR I-3703, para 24.

[5] Case C-597/19 *MICM* ECLI:EU:C:2021:492, paras 70, 76.

[6] Case C-580/13 *Coty Germany* ECLI:EU:C:2015:485, para 39.

[7] *Centrafarm v Sterling Drug* (n 2) para 9.

Read in light of the ECJ's cases here cited, it seems reasonable to infer that under EU law each patentee has an undeniable interest in injunctive relief. If that is correct, it would violate EU law to require patentees to demonstrate their interest in an injunction, let alone to establish a practice whereby a special class of patentees is generally precluded from making this showing. It may not even be allowable to accept an infringer's evidence that a patentee has no interest in an injunction, as proponents of the innovation paradigm seem to assume is possible. While this is an open question of EU law, I believe the best interpretation of the current *acquis* is that every patentee has an interest in an injunction by default that is not subject to evidence to the contrary.

This is not to say that a permanent injunction must be granted in every case, since we know that there are circumstances where it is not.[8] It is merely to suggest that under EU law, it may not be valid to argue that the injunction should be denied or limited because the patentee can be made whole just as well through a damages award. That argument derives from the first two *eBay* prongs in US law and has gained substantial traction in the literature, including in Europe.[9] But there is no suggestion whatsoever in the Enforcement Directive or the ECJ's case law that irreparable harm is a relevant factor when deciding to grant permanent injunctive relief. This is notably in contrast to provisional measures, which are 'particularly justified where any delay would cause irreparable harm' according to Recital (22) of the Enforcement Directive. The cases cited in the previous paragraph, although admittedly not concerning patent law, rather suggest the opposite for permanent injunctions. Indeed, to the extent that the ECJ considers the interests of rights holders, it simply equates them with their underlying rights. *Coty Germany* and *Bastei Lübbe* are illustrative examples, as the ECJ assumed an abstract right to information and enforcement, even though both were fair balance cases with fact patterns where the right holder's specific interest in relief might have been questioned.[10] Scrutiny of the right holder's motives has occurred only in cases concerning allegations of abuse.[11] It does not seem necessary or appropriate in non-abuse cases, at least under the ECJ's case law so far.

In my view, then, whether a patentee practices the invention or other considerations relating to their interest in exclusivity should be irrelevant for the proportionality test. Instead, the test should be limited to considerations derivable from Article 3 of the Enforcement Directive and the CFR, which I have here distilled into three categories: overreach; abuse; or conflicts with third-party rights. It appears that the limits these provisions set on the entitlement to injunctive relief

[8] eg where requesting it would violate competition law: Case C-170/13 *Huawei Technologies* ECLI:EU:C:2015:477, paras 47, 55.

[9] eg M Stierle and F Hofmann, 'The Latest Amendment to the German Law on Patent Injunctions: The New Statutory Disproportionality Exception and Third-Party Interests' (2022) 71 *Gewerblicher Rechtsschutz und Urheberrecht International* 1123, 1128; A Ohly, 'Injunctions in the UPC and the Principle of Proportionality' (2022) 5 *Stockholm Intellectual Property Law Review* 58, 62.

[10] *Coty Germany* (n 6) para 38; Case C-149/17 *Bastei Lübbe* ECLI:EU:C:2018:841, para 51.

[11] *MICM* (n 5) para 95.

need to be applied by courts *ex officio*.[12] It is nevertheless difficult to imagine how courts could do so, and in any event the problem seems largely academic since, in cases where the defence might succeed, infringers can be expected to present a proportionality argument.

6.2. Application of the Proportionality Test: General Remarks

6.2.1. Outline

Section 5.3 analysed the requirements in Article 3(2) of the Enforcement Directive that injunctive relief in patent cases be effective and dissuasive, yet proportionate and not liable to create barriers to legitimate trade; and that Member States shall provide for safeguards against the abuse of the measures provided by the Directive. These requirements must be interpreted in light of the underlying Charter rights of the patentee, the infringer and affected third parties. As we saw, both the safeguards of Article 3 of the Enforcement Directive (proportionality, barriers to legitimate trade) and the Charter right that protects infringers in patent enforcement cases (Article 16 CFR) emphasise that the effects of an injunction should not extend beyond what is necessary to ensure patent exclusivity is respected. It follows that the case for limiting the patentee's entitlement to injunctive relief is strongest where the injunction would severely affect the infringer's capacity to produce or market non-infringing technology.

This problem is addressed in the first element of the proportionality test proposed here: overreach. The concept of overreach seeks to reconcile the patentee's entitlement to an injunction with the infringer's constitutional guarantee, in Article 16 CFR, to freely use 'the economic, technical, and financial resources available to it', so long as such use is not illegitimate.[13] Clearly, tension between these two precepts is most likely to arise in component patent cases. In such cases, the injunction can have a high threat value caused by the long time and/or high costs of redesigning the infringing product to omit the infringing element. That is an old problem, but if the analysis in chapter three is correct, it is much more prevalent today than it has been historically due to the rise in patent density.[14]

[12] This seems to be implicit in the ECJ's case law: see, eg Case C-666/18 *IT Development* ECLI:EU:C:2019:1099, para 44 ('it is essential that in all cases the requirements of Directive 2004/48 are respected'); Case C-531/20 *NovaText* ECLI:EU:C:2022:316, para 52 (considering 'automatic application' of national provision contrary to Art 3(1) of the Enforcement Directive, possibly implying that ex officio scrutiny is necessary).

[13] Case C-314/12 *UPC Telekabel Wien* ECLI:EU:C:2014:192, para 49.

[14] *Hoe v Boston Daily Advertiser Corp* 14 F 914 (CCD Mass 8 February 1883) (injunction denied where the 'improvement in question is but part of a large machine').

US courts have developed the causal nexus test to resolve this problem.[15] The concept of overreach can be seen as the European counterpart to the causal nexus test and I expect it will be the most important aspect of the proportionality test in practice.

The second element of the proportionality test is abuse and can be traced clearly to Article 3(2) of the Enforcement Directive and the ECJ's case law.[16] The Byzantine complexity of patent prosecution rules, coupled with the European Patent Office's heavy workload stemming from the ever-growing number of patent filings, create ample opportunities for strategic manoeuvring when applying for patent protection. Such tactics are legitimate in principle. In certain contexts, they can result in a strategic advantage for the patentee not contemplated by the Enforcement Directive. I argue that these are precisely the types of behaviours that courts must provide safeguards against as per Article 3(2) of the Enforcement Directive, even if they do not rise to the level of sanctionable abuse. In those situations, which can be expected to be rare occurrences, the proportionality test may be relied upon to limit the patentee's entitlement to injunctive relief.

Conflicts with third-party rights form the third element of the proportionality test. This part of the test stems from Recital (32) of the Enforcement Directive, which guarantees respect for Charter rights, and particularly from the ECJ's fair balance jurisprudence. Patents are embedded in the constitutional structure of the European Union and their enjoyment is protected through Article 17(2) CFR. This provides protection to rights holders, but also means that their rights must be limited if that is necessary to protect the rights and freedoms of others, as per Article 52 CFR. The ECJ has made clear that the enforcement of IP rights must proceed in a manner that ensures a fair balance is struck between all fundamental rights at stake. While the fundamental rights of the infringer are embedded in the Enforcement Directive's safeguards, those of third parties are not. It is therefore necessary to consider them as part of the proportionality test.

In my view, these three categories cover exhaustively all cases where the patentee's entitlement to injunctive relief may be limited on proportionality grounds. This has an important consequence: just like the patentee's status or motives for enforcement are irrelevant, so too is the financial hardship it would cause on the infringer. Thus, absent a finding of overreach, abuse or conflict with third-party rights, harms threatened to the infringer do not justify limiting injunctive relief even in the case of potential bankruptcy. Such hardships have captured the imagination in the debate over patent injunctions, but it can seriously be questioned whether they should have any role to play in the proportionality test. First, it would mean that courts decide when the social costs imposed by patent

[15] *Apple Inc v Samsung Electronics Co Ltd* 735 F3d 1352, 1361 (Fed Cir 2013) (holding that the causal nexus test serves to distinguish between 'irreparable harm caused by patent infringement and irreparable harm caused by otherwise lawful competition').

[16] eg Case C-688/17 *Bayer Pharma* ECLI:EU:C:2019:722, paras 68–69 (Member States and national courts must ensure measures and procedures provided in Enforcement Directive are not abused).

protection are unacceptable. However, as argued in chapter two, those costs are difficult for them to oversee, and placing them at the heart of the proportionality test would make it unpredictable at best and arbitrary at worst. Second, hardship caused by having to cease infringement falls outside the guarantees that EU law lays down for infringers. Article 16 CFR does not cover infringing conduct and the standard, in Article 3(2) of the Enforcement Directive, that remedies be effective, proportionate and dissuasive requires at a minimum that the infringer is deprived of the economic benefits of infringement.[17] It should not matter that those economic benefits are big or small. Accepting otherwise would mean raising the threshold to enjoin larger firms when we know that patents play a crucial role in enabling competition between R&D-focused newcomers and established incumbents.[18] Third, in the event the balance of hardships is so skewed that enforcement can be considered grossly disproportionate, there already exist legal doctrines or provisions that prevent it. It is not clear why more allowance should be made for defendants' interests in the specific context of patent law through a more lenient balancing exercise comprised in the proportionality test.

In sum, contrary to how proportionality is sometimes perceived in the literature, in my view, it should not be a balancing exercise that weighs the patentee's interest in injunctive relief against the hardship it would cause the infringer in light of an open-ended catalogue of potentially relevant circumstances.[19] That also means the three elements of the test outlined here should not be considered jointly, in that a close case on overreach does not lower the bar to assume conflicts with third-party rights. Joint consideration of factors makes sense in the context of an overall balancing exercise, but not where each element of the proportionality test checks for a specific type of disproportionate outcome. Court practice in the years to come will demonstrate whether grounds of disproportionality beyond the three outlined here are accepted in Europe. In my view, there presently exists no need for them.

6.2.2. The Parties' Relative Blameworthiness

The proportionality analysis cannot be seen separately from the parties' conduct, aptly referred to as their 'relative blameworthiness' by a group of leading patent scholars.[20] As they point out, 'Even a "small sliver" case of infringement might be

[17] *cf Windsurfing Int'l Inc v AMF Inc* 782 F2d 995, 1003, n 12 (Fed Cir 1986) ('one who elects to build a business on a product found to infringe cannot be heard to complain if an injunction against continuing infringement destroys the business so elected').

[18] J Barnett, *Innovators, Firms, and Markets: The Organizational Logic of Intellectual Property* (Oxford University Press, 2021) 154.

[19] For the balancing view, see, eg N Siebrasse et al, 'Injunctive Relief' in CB Biddle et al (eds), *Patent Remedies and Complex Products: Toward a Global Consensus* (Cambridge University Press, 2019) 152.

[20] ibid 147.

viewed as substantially problematic if the infringement in question is willful and malicious'.[21] Infringers should not be incentivised to refuse good faith engagement in licensing negotiations, preferring to take their chances in litigation because even losing would not make them worse off. Indeed, Recital (17) of the Enforcement Directive singles out 'the intentional or unintentional character of the infringement' as a particularly relevant circumstance to be considered when imposing remedies for infringement. The possible need for a proportionality correction in case of non-deliberate infringement was also emphasised during the adoption of the Directive (section 1.3.1). At the same time, there exist plenty of opportunities for strategic prosecution or enforcement of patents which can substantially alter the balance of power between parties. Thus, integrated into the overreach analysis should be considerations of the parties' respective behaviour, and a critical issue in this respect is where the burden of proof should lie.

It goes without saying that the infringer must prove allegations of harmful strategic behaviour on the part of the patentee. However, contrary to what some authors have suggested, the infringer should not be required to prove good faith or reasonable search efforts as part of their proportionality plea. This issue featured prominently during the reform of the German Patent Act (GPA) and, just before the final vote, an amendment was even proposed to allow proportionality arguments only 'to the extent the infringer carried out its search duties' to prevent infringement.[22] Ansgar Ohly and Martin Stierle have since argued that infringers advancing a proportionality plea should generally demonstrate they conducted a freedom-to-operate (FTO) analysis prior to launching the infringing product.[23] That position was seemingly embraced by the German legislator.[24]

Such a rule would create more problems than it solves. First and foremost, it risks turning every proportionality argument into an ex post discussion of whether the FTO analysis was performed properly. There is no end to the issues that could come up: does a report by an in-house attorney suffice? How recent must the report be to be taken into account? Can overlooking a direct competitor's patent ever be justified? In addition, affording a key role to the FTO analysis in the proportionality test may incentivise excessive (and hence wasteful) searches or even strategic behaviour, for instance commissioning several FTO reports, each omitting one or two key patents, to submit the most favourable in the event of a later infringement suit.

In addition, an FTO rule conflates proportionality with innocent infringement, which, in my view, is incorrect. Patent density may make innocent

[21] ibid.

[22] German Federal Parliament, Final Recommendation and Notice (*Beschlussempfehlung und Bericht*) of 9 June 2021, BT-Drucksache 19/30498, 51. It was not adopted.

[23] A Ohly and M Stierle, 'Unverhältnismäßigkeit, Injunction Gap und Geheimnisschutz im Prozess' [2021] *Gewerblicher Rechtsschutz und Urheberrecht* 1229, 1232.

[24] German Federal Parliament, Proposed Bill (*Gesetzentwurf: Entwurf eines Zweiten Gesetzes zur Vereinfachung und Modernisierung des Patentrechts*) of 31 January 2021, BT-Drucksache 19/25821, 54.

infringement more likely, but the proportionality test is fundamentally about observance of the commensurability principle at the remedies stage, not about protecting innocent infringers.[25] Making an FTO analysis an entry requirement for a proportionality plea implies that any awareness of the patent suffices to defeat it, but this may not always be warranted. What if the claims pending at the time of the FTO analysis differed from the claims in the patent as granted? What if the infringer could not reasonably estimate whether it would operate within the claim scope? What if it had reason to believe the patent was invalid, for instance because it had been revoked in opposition or by a foreign court? Over-reliance on the FTO analysis may create a chilling effect and, particularly in light of the high invalidity rates of patents granted today, it would be undesirable if a company halted an innovation just because a potentially relevant patent showed up in one. And an FTO rule assumes a highly stylised view of innovation whereby a new product is conceived on paper, an FTO analysis is performed and only then is the green light given for investments in production. It may work that way in some cases, but more often than not the innovative process is far messier: production parameters may require modifications to the original design, existing products are constantly improved, new versions are introduced, products for local markets slip by global IP departments … Cases may arise where a party is excused for not performing an FTO analysis at all, perhaps where a small company lacked the funds to perform a Europe-wide clearance search before scaling up, or where patent density is simply too high to oversee all potentially relevant patents.[26] Ohly and Stierle concede some of these points, and to be fair they seem to have in mind a rule of thumb rather than a hard requirement, where the availability of an FTO analysis is one factor among others in the proportionality test.[27] But this nuance may not help much. More likely than not, the FTO analysis will become a de facto requirement, as failure to submit it will immediately raise suspicions and the justification Ohly and Stierle propose, that the 'patent situation' in the relevant field is 'hard to navigate', seems very hard to establish.[28]

None of this is to say that it makes no difference if companies perform FTO analyses: they should and they do, if only to avoid director liability in case of a later infringement suit.[29] But submitting an FTO analysis, or satisfying a diligence standard in another way, should not be a threshold requirement for a

[25] If protection of innocent infringers were the purpose of the proportionality test, one wonders why they should not be shielded from liability altogether, as proposed in P Goold, *IP Accidents: Negligence Liability in Intellectual Property* (Cambridge University Press, 2022) 59.

[26] *cf Halo Electronics Inc v Pulse Electronics Inc* 136 SCt 1923, 1936 (2016) (Breyer J concurring) ('Such costs can prevent an innovator from getting a small business up and running').

[27] Ohly and Stierle (n 23) 1232.

[28] ibid (it 'works in the infringer's favour' '*wenn die Patentlage auf dem betreffenden Gebiet der Technik sehr unübersichtlich ist*').

[29] BGH GRUR 2016, 257; X ZR 30/14 *Glasfasern II* established liability for directors if they fail to take reasonable precautions to avoid IP infringements.

proportionality defence.[30] Instead, the onus should be on the patentee to prove that the infringer was or should have been aware of the patent, for instance following contacts between parties or the patentee's efforts to raise industry awareness of its patent portfolio. Such a rule places the evidentiary burden with the party best situated to provide relevant evidence, ie capable of demonstrating that this specific infringer was aware of this specific patent. It also creates incentives to provide early notice of patents, which is commonly considered desirable.[31] If the patentee proves wilful infringement, the proportionality defence should be rejected.[32] To so penalise opportunistic conduct is justified and consistent with EU law. It goes without saying that an FTO analysis (or any other clearance effort) will be an important argument for infringers when defending against allegations of wilfulness. However, in the considerable grey area between wilful infringement and demonstrable diligence, a proportionality plea should remain open to the infringer. That makes the test more workable and achieves parity between the parties' evidentiary positions: effectively, good faith is presumed on both sides and the onus is split between them to show the other acted opportunistically or negligently. The availability of a proportionality defence (excluding cases where third-party rights are at stake, see section 6.5 below) is summarised in Table 6.1.

Table 6.1 The availability of the proportionality defence

	Infringer acted wilfully, negligently or in bad faith: *patentee bears burden of proof*	**Neither party acted in bad faith: *default scenario***	**Patentee acted opportunistically or in bad faith: *infringer bears burden of proof***
Overreach	–	section 6.3	section 6.3
No overreach	–	–	section 6.4

As the table shows, by default, the availability of the proportionality defence turns on a finding of overreach: section 6.3 explains this concept in detail. A showing that infringement was wilful or the infringer otherwise behaved in bad faith (eg by employing holdout tactics) will defeat the proportionality defence, even if overreach is established. Conversely, a showing by the infringer that the patentee acted opportunistically or in bad faith (eg by delaying enforcement to create lock-in effects) is, in principle, irrelevant once overreach is established. Such opportunistic behaviour may, however, be sufficiently egregious to support a proportionality defence even in non-overreach cases, in which case the injunction may be limited on grounds of abuse. That scenario is discussed further in section 6.4.

[30] *cf Halo* (n 26) (Breyer J, concurring) (supporting US Congress's decision not to allow 'failure of an infringer to obtain the advice of counsel' as evidence of wilful infringement).

[31] Goold (n 25) 26–29.

[32] The standard for wilfulness is a delicate question. Recital (9) of Council Regulation (EU) No 1260/2012 implementing enhanced cooperation in the area of the creation of unitary patent

6.2.3. The Consequences of Applying the Proportionality Test

What should be the consequences of a successful proportionality defence? Under the test proposed here, it would lead to a stay of the injunction or a limitation of its scope, not to an outright denial (as may occur in the USA). This is in line with the majority view in the literature. Most authors consider an outright denial of the injunction a possibility in very exceptional cases. In my view, it is appropriate only in two situations. The first is where it is necessary to respect third-party rights, in situations that should be treated analogously to a compulsory licence request (see section 6.5.3). The second is where the stay to which the infringer is entitled exceeds the remaining lifespan of the patent, which comes down to a de facto denial of injunctive relief. Although patentee conduct that rises to the level of sanctionable abuse (Article 102 of the Treaty on the Functioning of the European Union (TFEU), national abuse doctrines) could be a ground to deny them injunctive relief altogether, in my view, this should not be possible within the context of the proportionality test outside these two cases. While the patentee's exclusive right is respected in the case of a stay, a denial converts the patent from a property right into a damages entitlement. That is a normative shift the proportionality test cannot justify because neither Article 16 CFR nor the proportionality principle in Article 3(2) of the Enforcement Directive can be relied upon to condone illegitimate behaviour.[33] Such a conversion was contemplated in Article 12 of the Enforcement Directive, but, outside the narrow set of cases where that provision applies, outright denial is inconsistent with the Directive – and is more so in jurisdictions that opted not to implement Article 12.

Stays should be for a specified time, and section 6.3.4 below addresses how that time should be determined. Stays for indeterminate periods of time, for instance pending appeal proceedings, should be avoided. Because such stays considerably limit the patentee's enjoyment of an entitlement validated by a court, most jurisdictions set stringent requirements for their grant. I see no reason why the proportionality test should depart from these established standards for stays pending appeal; in my view, they should be allowable only in atypical cases where key prior art could not be taken into consideration or procedural defects impaired the infringer's possibility to make their case.[34] Limits to the injunction's scope

protection with regard to the applicable translation arrangements may imply that wilfulness should not be assumed before the infringer has been provided with the patent translated in their own language.

[33] Of course, strictly speaking, a proportionality test never 'condones' infringement: Stierle and Hofmann (n 9) 1129. But the denial of an injunction comes dangerously close to the practical equivalent of condoning infringement, certainly without a supracompensatory damages award.

[34] *cf* GH The Hague 2 December 2019, ECLI:NL:GHDHA:2019:3709 (*VG Colours/HE Licenties*), paras 4.5–4.6 (staying injunction pending appeal because key argument was overlooked by first instance court). In my view, stays are also appropriate in bifurcated systems where a so-called 'injunction gap' can occur: L Dijkman, 'Does the Injunction Gap Violate Implementer's Fair Trial Rights under the Charter?' [2022] *Gewerblicher Rechtsschutz und Urheberrecht* 857.

should be construed as narrowly as possible, for instance by allowing only supplies to a specific customer under a specific contract.[35] This is in accordance with the general principle of EU law that 'exceptions are to be interpreted strictly so that general rules are not negated'.[36]

The stay creates a window of opportunity for the parties to settle on reasonable terms. On the one hand, the conclusion of a licence agreement is frequently the end goal of enforcement proceedings. If the infringer successfully redesigns their product, there is no longer any ground for a licence and so the patentee will remain incentivised to come to an agreement. On the other hand, the infringer is also incentivised to come to an agreement. True, the threat value associated with an immediate sales ban can no longer be leveraged by the patentee. The cost to any business of an immediate sales ban or production stop is often so high that they have no choice but to settle on the patentee's terms.[37] During the GPA reform, Siemens appeared to take the position that this is precisely the point of the injunction: its threat value is 'the appropriate and sometimes only way for independent inventors and smaller businesses to effectively defend against bigger companies'.[38] There is certainly some truth to this.[39] But it does not follow that the threat value should materialise in every case. It seems appropriate primarily where the infringer acted negligently or in bad faith, since those are the behaviours that the threat value seeks to discourage. It is harder to justify outside these cases. Relying on patents to foster innovation has the benefit that the market decides on an appropriate reward for the inventor. Bargaining power accruing from the context of enforcement is not part of a patent's guarantee and in fact distorts its market-based reward logic.

Nevertheless, the infringer still faces (i) the loss of access to the patented technology, (ii) the costs of redesigning their product and (iii) the payment of compensation for the duration of the stay. Those costs may be high, and the idea of a redesign that is not 'economically feasible' was also a concern for the German legislator during the GPA reform.[40] However, the infringer has complete control over its production processes and adopting supply and production chains where changes are costly comes at its own risk. That is also the default in other fields of law, such as product liability or environmental regulation: to the best of my knowledge, neither exempts manufacturers from liability just because changing their production lines would be expensive. In addition, I am not convinced that

[35] *Virgin Atlantic v Premium Aircraft* [2009] EWCA Civ 1513, para 38 (allowing the delivery of a specific number of aircraft seats to a specific client to avoid significant contractual penalty).

[36] Case C-346/08 *Commission v UK* ECLI:EU:C:2010:213, [2010] ECR I-3491, para 39.

[37] These costs are what drove the settlement following the *Wärmetauscher* case, BGH GRUR 2016, 1031; X ZR 114/13: see s 3.3. They were also emphasised by the automotive industry's representative during the parliamentary hearing in Germany: German Federal Parliament, Transcript (*Wortprotokoll der 132. Sitzung*) of 24 February 2021, BT-Drucksache 19/2581, 11–12 (Kurt-Christian Scheel).

[38] Siemens, Position Paper of 2 March 2020 at 2; see Annex I.

[39] Barnett (n 18) 162.

[40] Proposed Bill (n 24) 54.

there are so many cases where the economic value of the invention is trivial but switching costs are high. They surely exist, but more often than not the assumption seems reasonable that high switching costs correlate with high economic value of the patented technology, certainly where it is not standard essential. To the extent economic value and switching costs are correlated, pressure to settle caused by high switching costs would in fact be justified by the invention's merits. Limitation of the injunction on proportionality grounds, then, is not a free pass for infringers, nor should it be. The costs associated with redesigning their product ought to offer sufficient incentives to come to an agreement with the patentee on reasonable terms.

Conversely, the patentee should bear the risk of losing its entitlement to injunctive relief because enforcement was initiated only shortly before expiry of the patent. As noted above, this is the only scenario, apart from compelling third-party rights, where an injunction might be denied altogether, namely where a reasonable period to design around the patent would last longer than the remaining lifespan of the patent. It is important to keep in mind that in these cases, the balance between parties shifts dramatically as the infringer will not need to make any redesign efforts at all and will thus have less of an incentive to settle. That is hard on the patentee, but this is one instance where proportionality cannot craft a compromise position and courts therefore face a binary, everything-or-nothing choice. After all, granting the injunction would be disproportionate vis-à-vis the infringer who established overreach, and the fact that the injunction will only last for a short period of time often will not help them, since they must settle anyway.[41] Just as high redesign costs are a risk for the infringer to bear, so is a short remaining lifespan of the patent a risk for the patentee to bear, at least in those cases where enforcement could have been initiated earlier. In these types of cases, courts might consider awarding additional compensation for 'other than economic factors' (Article 13(1)(a) of the Enforcement Directive).

6.3. Overreach

6.3.1. Justifying Overreach

Overreach is the central element of the proportionality test proposed in this book. The overreach inquiry starts from the patented invention, understood here as the claimed subject matter to the extent that it is novel, inventive and sufficiently

[41] The reasoning in LG Düsseldorf OpenJur 2022, 14333; 4b O 7/22 *Fahrzeugdächer*, III.1(bb)(3) therefore cannot be accepted. Note that a short remaining lifespan of the patent can cut both ways: *cf* RB Amsterdam 3 May 2022, ECLI:NL:RBAMS:2022:2418 (*Boston Scientific v Cook*), para 4.22 (denial of provisional injunction, inter alia because forcing medical staff to retrain only for a few months is disproportionate).

disclosed. The wording of the patent claims is irrelevant, especially where they nominally cover an object of which the invention is only a part, as is common claiming practice.[42] Patent courts will develop a clear understanding of the invention over the course of infringement proceedings, especially in non-bifurcated systems, as it is a central concept during claim construction and when deciding on validity. The injunction they issue upon finding infringement will normally be limited only to the use of the invention, by specifying either the patent or infringing acts. Ceasing use of the invention may, however, necessarily require ceasing use of other technology not falling within the scope of the invention. The next step within the overreach inquiry is therefore to establish what, if any, additional technology will be affected by the injunction. I refer to this as the injunction's effective scope, to be substantiated by the infringer. The overreach test applies the commensurability principle at the remedies stage and thus revolves around the question of how the inventive contribution relates to the effective exclusivity achieved by the injunction. Overreach is established when the effective scope is not warranted by the invention. I propose three questions to guide that determination: first, is the invention indispensable for the core functionality of the technology caught by the injunction? Second, if not, is the invention nevertheless highly inventive? Third, how much time does the infringer need to design around the invention? These limbs are discussed further in the sections that follow.

As noted above, the concept of overreach seeks a compromise between the patentee's entitlement to an injunction and the infringer's equally legitimate entitlement to maintain access to its non-infringing technology, an issue with particular salience in component patent cases. Rather than looking at the commercial value of the technology, as the American causal nexus test does, overreach is concerned with the technological value of the invention for the infringer's product. Evaluating the technology's commercial value fits well with the centrality afforded to irreparable harm in the *eBay* framework, but, as we saw above, irreparable harm is irrelevant under EU law and the attractiveness of technology for customers is difficult for courts to determine, especially without the benefit of disclosure. Furthermore, there are several other reasons why technological significance seems to be an appropriate criterion. It offers a neutral and objective criterion to determine potential limitations on the patentee's sphere of exclusivity. To be sure, evaluating the significance of the patented technology for the infringing device is difficult and turns on an ultimately subjective assessment in that reasonable minds may differ over the correct outcome, but at least it is easier to formulate objective guidance for a technologically oriented evaluation than for a value-oriented evaluation. Such guidance may introduce a measure of objectivity into the assessment and foster the development of a

[42] This is known in the UK as the 'tin whistle' problem, where it is established that the form of the claim should not alter a damages entitlement or an injunction: *Celanese International Corp v BP Chemicals Ltd* [1999] RPC 203, para 51; *Stena Rederi AB v Irish Ferries Ltd* [2002] EWHC 737 (Ch), para 82.

predictable legal test, much like the problem solution approach boosts the objectivity and predictability of the inherently subjective assessment of inventive step. The approach is reminiscent of indirect infringement in patent law, where the question is whether the infringer offers a means relating to an essential element of the invention. That criterion serves to prevent extending the patent monopoly to activities too far removed from the actual invention. Just so, overreach checks that the patent does not afford a measure of exclusivity that in practice reaches far beyond the patented invention.

One way or another, it seems unavoidable that European patent law must grapple with the problems posed by component patents in the years to come.[43] The overreach test proposed here offers a workable and predictable solution, at least relative to an open-ended test in which component patent status is only one of many factors to consider. Overreach not only delineates the inquiry from other proportionality considerations, but also matches it with the expertise par excellence of patent judges and requires comparatively little evidence on the side of parties. A focus on the technological significance of the invention in relation to the invention's effective scope seems attractive to courts staffed with judges having a technical background (as in England) or long-term experience with patent cases (as in the Netherlands and France), or complemented with technical judges (as in the Unified Patent Court (UPC)). Especially the first two limbs of the overreach test would be defined through their application in different fact patterns, much like the European Patent Office's Boards of Appeal refine the general rules laid down in the European Patent Convention (EPC) through their decision-making practice. Through this process, courts would calibrate the overreach test as a filter for cases where granting immediate injunctive relief would be undesirable. As we saw, a similar process took place in the USA, where the Courts of Appeals for the Federal Circuit (CAFC) 'calibrated' the causal nexus test in a back-and-forth with the district court in proceedings between Apple and Samsung, moving from a strict standard to a lenient standard to a compromise position.[44] Evidently, the calibration process is still ongoing, but the CAFC's guidance so far has clarified the appropriate treatment of component patents in US patent law significantly. In Europe, the UPC could lead the way in these efforts, which may well reveal that findings of overreach need not be limited to exceptional cases. Indeed, why should they be, when there are clear indications that component patents are much more prevalent today? There are good reasons why a proportionality test that turns on a balance of the parties' interests should apply only very rarely.[45]

[43] Early examples include *HTC Corp v Nokia Corp* [2013] EWHC 3778 (Pat), para 26; *Fahrzeugdächer* (n 41) III.1.aa.

[44] See, respectively, *Apple Inc v Samsung Electronics Co Ltd* 695 F3d 1370, 1375 (Fed Cir 2012) (*Apple II*: infringing feature must drive consumer demand); 735 F3d 1352, 1364 (Fed Cir 2013) (*Apple III*: there must be some connection between consumer demand and infringing feature); 809 F3d 633, 644 (Fed Cir 2015) (*Apple IV*: infringing feature must be important to customers).

[45] *HTC* (n 43) para 32. See further s 2.3.

Conversely, there is no reason for overt caution when the test is narrowed down to a phenomenon on which there is at least tentative consensus that it can be problematic.

6.3.2. First Limb: Patented Technology Indispensable for Core Functionality?

To establish overreach, an infringer must first prove that the patented technology is not indispensable for the core functionality of the products falling within the effective scope of the injunction. The intuition behind this limb is that a patented invention's sphere of exclusivity may reasonably extend to subordinate features in a device it enables. Notably, the German legislature takes precisely the opposite approach in the explanatory memorandum to the revised § 139 GPA by suggesting that a proportionality defence will be less likely to succeed if it relates to technology not 'essential to the functioning' (*funktionswesentlich*) of the overall device.[46] This would appear to be premised on the assumption that the proportionality test may be relied upon to foster access to enabling technologies, but that exact function is performed by Article 102 TFEU. With respect, as a general rule, the German Federal Supreme Court's view cannot be right as this would suggest exclusivity is more readily limited the greater the importance of the underlying technology, turning the idea of commensurate reward on its head.

'Core functionality' refers to the functionality that defines the product as a whole: in a pharmaceutical this would be the active substance, in speakers it would be the sound system and in clocks it would be the time-tracking functionality, to name but some examples. It is possible for a device to possess multiple core functionalities. For a mobile phone, these may include the battery, the screen and its connectivity; for a car, these may include the engine, the body and the driving system. Far from provoking philosophical discussions about the essence of objects, the purpose of this first requirement is to single out technologies that are manifestly subordinate to the functionality of the overall device, such as the steps tracker in a mobile phone or windshield wipers in a car. 'Core functionalities' should thus generally be construed broadly. Additionally, the technology should be 'indispensable' for a core functionality to avoid overreach. The fact that the functionality would not operate without the patented technology does not make it indispensable, as that is true for any component of a complex device. Generally speaking, the 'bigger' the patented component, the likelier it is to be indispensable for the overall device's core functionality: a good rule of thumb that aligns with US practice might be to ask whether the product would be commercially viable without the technology.

[46] Proposed Bill (n 24) 54. This follows the decision in *Wärmetauscher* (n 37) para 52.

I discuss two examples to clarify. In one of the first post-reform German cases to reject a proportionality defence, an injunction was issued against panoramic sunroof for motorised vehicles (the infringer specialised in their production). The patented invention provided a simple, reliable and low-wear mechanism for locking and unlocking the parts of the sunroof that open.[47] Such a mechanism clearly relates to the core functionality of panoramic sunroof, since their very purpose is to open and close while driving. A locking mechanism is surely indispensable for a panoramic sunroof, but such sunroofs have been around for decades. Thus, the question is not whether a locking mechanism as such is indispensable, but whether the specific features of the patented invention contribute indispensably to the locking mechanism in the infringer's panoramic sunroof. It is impossible to tell from the decision, which is anonymised and does not address the validity of the patent, but it seems plausible the answer could go either way.

The *Fahrzeugdächer* case also touches on the different role a proportionality test might play depending on the level of the production chain where enforcement takes place, a problem that received some attention in the German literature after the GPA reform.[48] One of the strengths of looking at how the inventive contribution relates to the effective sphere of exclusivity is that it naturally differentiates between production chain levels. Thus, when the injunction would target the entire car, overreach may well be established if the patent is only to a locking mechanism for the opening parts of the sunroof. Conversely, where the injunction would only target sunroofs, a finding of overreach may be denied as the effective sphere of exclusivity is concomitantly smaller. In rare cases involving highly specialised suppliers, a proportionality defence may still be plausible on the grounds that the injunction will disproportionately affect downstream (or upstream) partners, as discussed further in section 6.5.2.

The second example involved the popular streaming service Netflix, which was sued over a feature called TrickPlay, allowing faster rewinds, fast-forwards or jumps to other parts of the show. The Mannheim regional court issued an injunction and the Karlsruhe appeal courts declined to stay it pending appeal, despite Netflix claiming that it would be forced to shut down its services in its largest European market.[49] In my view, a feature like TrickPlay cannot be considered related to the core functionality of a streaming service like Netflix because that core functionality – streaming films – does not appear to relate to the TrickPlay feature. Arguably, then, Netflix might succeed on the first limb of the overreach test proposed here. But the example also illustrates that doing so is not enough, as the feature may nevertheless be highly inventive and for that reason would preclude a finding of overreach. That is what the second limb seeks to address.

[47] *Fahrzeugdächer* (n 41) I.2.
[48] Stierle and Hofmann (n 9) 1133.
[49] OLG Karlsruhe GRUR 2023, 51; 6 U 131/22 *Trick-Play*.

6.3.3. Second Limb: No Notable Commercial or Technical Advantages

Even inventions unrelated to core functionality may be trailblazing and commercially valuable. TrickPlay offers a good example: users can still stream content without it, but much less conveniently. Such differences can have an enormous impact in competitive markets like the one for streaming services, and more likely than not explain Netflix's coyness about the possibility of a design-around in the aforementioned proceedings.[50] The most famous example from recent years is probably Apple's victory over Samsung regarding its 'slide to unlock' feature, which enables users to unlock their phones by sliding their finger over the screen.[51] This feature is not related to the core functionality of mobile phones, yet has considerable commercial value, as also becomes apparent from evidence that Samsung had deliberately copied it.[52] The intuition behind this limb is twofold. First, these types of inventions are entitled to broader protection, as is also commonly assumed for so-called 'pioneer inventions'. Second, their commercial value makes it likely that a diligent search would have revealed the relevant patent.

Thus, to establish overreach, an infringer must further demonstrate that the patented technology offers no notable commercial or technical advantages over alternative technologies. Of course, in most cases, the infringer will dispute that the patent has any inventive merits at all in the course of proceedings. In line with that argument, under the second limb of overreach, it should additionally show that the patented invention is one of several non-infringing alternatives available at the time of infringement.[53] Those alternatives set the stage for this limb of the overreach test as the infringer must demonstrate that the advantages the patented invention has over those alternatives, if any, are modest – an allegation the patentee will obviously dispute. Established case law on secondary indicia of inventive step, which evaluates such factors as a long-felt need, commercial success and industry adoption, is likely to provide guidance in this respect.

6.3.4. Third Limb: Suggesting a Reasonable Limitation of the Patentee's Entitlement

6.3.4.1. *The Duration of a Stay*

The third limb in establishing overreach is that the infringer must substantiate how the patentee's entitlement to injunctive relief ought to be limited and why their

[50] The higher regional court considered the lack of any information on this 'astonishing': see ibid 18.

[51] *Apple Inc v Samsung Electronics* 839 F3d 1034 (Fed Cir 2016).

[52] ibid 1054.

[53] T Cotter et al, 'Reasonable Royalties' in CB Biddle et al (eds), *Patent Remedies and Complex Products: Toward a Global Consensus* (Cambridge University Press, 2019) explain that this is common in damages calculations, but also that problems arise when those alternatives are also patented. For the

proposal is reasonable. In most cases, that will mean demonstrating how much time is required to cease infringement, for instance by redesigning the infringing product, switching to non-infringing alternatives or phasing out infringing sales. Although this may seem a merely pragmatic aspect of the proportionality test, it is a crucial element thereof because the timing of efforts to cease infringement is a delicate issue. On the one hand, it is clear that infringers cannot in good faith start considering their options only after the court confirms the patentee's claims.[54] In addition, an injunction is unlikely to be disproportionate if the infringer can readily switch to non-infringing alternatives.[55] Courts must therefore be informed of how long cessation of infringement would take when considering the proportionality plea. On the other hand, the Munich regional court has faulted infringers for failing to start redesign efforts as soon as they received the summons in the infringement case.[56] If that were expected of infringers, the proportionality test would become meaningless and the mere act of issuing summons would obtain an undesirable chilling effect. So strict a standard would therefore go too far in the other direction.

An acceptable middle ground is to require infringers to submit, as part of their proportionality argumentation, a substantiated estimate of how long it would take them to cease infringement. Infringers are thus required to develop a 'backup plan' in case the patentee's claims are granted, but not yet to initiate its implementation. The backup plan should reflect best efforts to terminate infringement in the shortest time reasonably possible, even if cheaper alternatives exist that would take longer.[57] Estimated timelines can be based on the claim construction put forward by the patentee in the writ of summons, even if challenged in the context of the infringement; if necessary, alternative plans could be proposed depending on how the court will determine the claim's scope. Making the infringer thus responsible to first suggest the duration of the stay absolves the court from having to estimate a reasonable time period and instead leaves it up to the party most knowledgeable on this point. If the court is satisfied that the proposed timeline is reasonable and accepts the case for delay, the timeline would start running from the date of decision with the infringer well prepared to start the redesign process straight away. While some might fear this gives infringers too much of an opportunity to obtain longer stays than necessary, I believe such fears are unfounded for two reasons. First, because failure to propose a reasonable timeline will lead to the rejection of the proportionality defence – and the patentee will therefore heavily scrutinise the infringer's proposed timeline – infringers have a clear incentive to propose a

purposes of overreach, that should not matter, since either way these alternatives lie beyond the scope of the patented invention.

[54] *cf SynQor Inc v Artesyn Technologies Inc* 2011 WL 238645, *9 (ED Tex Jan 24 2011) ('The Court will not reward Cisco and Defendants for their inaction').

[55] *HTC* (n 43) para 67; Siebrasse et al (n 19) 154–55.

[56] LG München BeckRS 2019, 11305; 7 O 10261/18 *Steuerventil*, para 67.

[57] *cf Callaway Golf Co v Acushnet Co* 585 FSupp2d 600, 622 (D Del 2008) ('The court is not in the business of making defendant's infringements easier to unravel').

credible timeline. Second, a longer stay will also mean that the compensation owed to the patentee is due over a longer period of time. Especially before the UPC, where the compensation will accrue over sales in all participating states combined, that may be a significant reason not to request overly long stays.

Like the other limbs of the overreach test, the calculation of the duration of the stay will doubtlessly give rise to various issues in practice (though, at least in US practice, they have rarely proved to be insurmountable). Here, I discuss two that are likely to arise. The first is where the requested period proves insufficient to cease all infringement. In such cases, the infringer should be able to petition for an extension, as one court already accepted.[58] The extension could be accompanied by an increase in the compensation due to the patentee for the remainder of the stay. The second situation is where implementing an alternative to the infringing product depends on third parties. If the infringer depends on supplies from third parties, it seems reasonable to assume that the infringer can coordinate the estimated timeline with them. A more complicated scenario is where the infringer requires regulatory approval of an alternative or redesigned product. This scenario is especially plausible for medical devices, where third parties are likely to depend on the continued availability of the infringing device until approval of a new variant. In these cases, it seems reasonable to extend the stay for the duration of the approval process, though much will depend on the specifics of the case and particularly the infringer's diligence in pursuing the approval process.

6.3.4.2. Carve-Outs, Infringing Stock and Recalls

Although, in most cases, infringers will request a stay of the injunction, this will not always be adequate. *Wärmetauscher*[59] presents a good illustration: the hardship for the infringer was caused not so much by having to redesign (though that would also have been costly), but by its inability to sell its existing fleet of cars. In these types of cases, courts may refuse a stay but limit the injunction in other ways. In *Wärmetauscher*, the infringing feature was an optional add-on for convertible cars. The court might thus have ordered an immediate stop of the production of new cars, while allowing sales of those already produced (as Mercedes had in fact requested). Such solutions may be appropriate any time where the infringer shows it can implement a redesign for new products quickly but requires more time to phase out existing products. This is where overreach and conflicts with third-party rights may typically intersect. The court could also impose limitations on ongoing sales, for instance by restricting them to existing customers or excluding potential customers for whom parties compete, as may happen in 'design wins' markets or when contracts are awarded by tender.[60] When it comes to delivery

[58] *Edwards Lifesciences v Boston Scientific* [2018] EWHC 1256 (Pat), para 67.

[59] Above n 37.

[60] See, eg *Presidio Components Inc v American Technical Ceramics Corp* 2013 WL 4068833, *8 (CD Cal 12 August 2013) (allowing shipment of orders placed before hearing); *Broadcom Corp v*

up of infringing stock and ordering recalls, these are already subject to broader court discretion. Even in jurisdictions hesitant to adopt a proportionality test, such orders are regularly limited or refused.[61] Such discretion would, when combined with the proportionality test proposed here, give courts ample freedom to reach a solution that is tailored to the specifics of the case and strikes a fair balance between all rights at stake.

6.3.5. Rebutting the Presumption in Favour of a Stay

A finding of overreach implies that an immediate injunction would create unacceptable barriers to legitimate trade and would therefore be disproportionate. Consequently, a stay of the injunction should presumptively be granted for the requested duration. The onus then shifts onto the patentee to rebut the presumption in favour of a stay. To make this possible, the proportionality defence should be included in the first written statement submitted by the infringer. Thus, taking proceedings before the UPC as an example, the infringer must satisfy their initial burden under all three limbs in their statement of defence, to be lodged within three months after service of the statement of claim (UPC Rules of Procedure, Rule 23). The patentee may respond to the defence in its Reply, after which each party is afforded another written round (Rule 29). Under this timeline, the proportionality defence will have been debated by parties in two written rounds before the hearing (and, in the case of the UPC, in an interim conference, where additional evidence may be requested). In all but the most extreme cases, the court should thus be in a position to decide on the proportionality defence and, if appropriate, the duration of the stay in the same opinion that contains the decision on the merits. If thus integrated into the procedural regime, the proportionality defence will not slow down the overall proceedings, as some opponents fear and as may be the case in the USA, where remedies are often the subject of post-trial motions and possibly a separate hearing.

In addition to rebutting the arguments put forward by the infringer under the first two limbs, the patentee may overcome the presumption in favour of a stay primarily by demonstrating, as per section 6.2.2 above, that the infringer's conduct bars a proportionality defence. This is an open-ended inquiry that can include all manner of behaviour, but particularly common examples are likely to include showing wilful infringement, prior refusal of a reasonable licensing offer or hold-out tactics. Contrary to US law, the doctrine of wilful infringement is hardly developed in European jurisdictions because wilfulness is rarely relevant, but wilfulness will in any event be established if the infringer knew of the patent or was grossly negligent. In this context, efforts by the patentee to raise awareness of

Qualcomm Inc No SACV 05-467 JVS, *19, *13 (CD Cal 31 December 2007) (excluding specific pitch from scope of carve-out). For more examples, see Siebrasse et al (n 19) 155.

[61] Contreras and Husovec (n 1) 335.

its patent or the portfolio it belongs to will be relevant, as will clearance efforts by the infringer, and the court could question either party on these points. A proportionality defence may also be excluded where the infringer was previously offered a licence but declined to take it.[62] In my view, however, the onus should be on the patentee in such cases to demonstrate that the terms offered were reasonable, because otherwise any licensing offer prior to proceedings, no matter on what conditions, would suffice to defeat a potential proportionality plea. A common argument in practice is likely to be that the infringer refused to engage in good faith negotiations over a licence or employed delaying tactics, behaviour known as holdout in the standard essential patent (SEP) literature.[63] The burgeoning SEP case law across Europe's patent courts is likely to be instructive in evaluating these allegations. It is possible that bad faith allegations against the infringer will have to be weighed against allegations of bad faith levelled against the patentee, so that ultimately the 'relative blameworthiness' of parties will determine whether a proportionality defence can be accepted.[64] In sum, the bad faith inquiry will be highly context-specific, but courts can likely rely on their experience in SEP cases and, more generally, on traditional maxims common to most jurisdictions that penalise opportunistic behaviour.

6.3.6. Other Cases of Overreach

So far, the analysis has focused on component patent cases, and I expect that these will far and away be the most likely candidates for application of the proportionality test. But the principle of technical commensurability has broader application, and it is conceivable that the inventive contribution does not justify the effective scope of the injunction even in non-component patent cases. In addition, the requirement to 'take due account of the specific characteristics' of a case (Recital (17) of the Enforcement Directive) makes some open-endedness in the overreach assessment necessary. That requirement exists precisely because all possible enforcement constellations cannot presently be foreseen and it would therefore be ill-advised to try to capture all of them in the overreach test outlined here. At the same time, such cases should be rare exceptions in order to preserve the legal certainty promised by a more structured approach to proportionality such as the one in this book. I discuss some possible scenarios here.

An often-discussed example is the mirror image of the first limb discussed above, ie where the patented technology is, in the patois of the patent community, 'de facto essential'.[65] Such technology is not part of a formal

[62] *cf Omega Patents LLC v Fortin Auto Radio Inc* 2007 WL 9719177, *6 (MD Fla 4 April 2007).

[63] I Nikolic, *Licensing Standard Essential Patents: FRAND and the Internet of Things* (Hart Publishing, 2021) 40–55.

[64] Siebrasse et al (n 19) 147.

[65] Nikolic (n 63) 14.

standard and the patent is therefore unencumbered by a fair, reasonable and non-discriminatory commitment, but is nevertheless indispensable. As discussed above, the German Federal Court of Justice's decision in *Wärmetauscher* was premised in part on the (incorrect) assumption that necessity of the technology for the device to function is an indication that a proportionality exception might be warranted. But if technical commensurability is to guide the proportionality test, then surely the fact that the patent reads on enabling technology suggests a broad scope of exclusivity is warranted, not that it ought to be limited. Pleas for permission to use technology because it is indispensable are traditionally evaluated under competition law, and there are indications that competition authorities are becoming more lenient towards implementers at least in some industries. Such pleas are a more problematic fit for the proportionality test, at least if understood as a temporary limitation of the patentee's rights to mitigate disproportionate consequences. After all, if the patented technology is de facto essential, then by definition a design-around or non-infringing alternative will not be available and a stay will be of no avail to the infringer. The infringer must therefore ask for a denial of the injunction or a court-imposed ceiling on royalties, but competition law (and, in some jurisdictions, compulsory licensing rules) already provides a material entitlement to this outcome, subject to very strict conditions. It seems to me that the proportionality test should not be utilised to circumvent these conditions at the remedies stage.

A variant of de facto essentiality is where technical alternatives exist – and there may even be a case of overreach as defined here – yet designing around them is not economically feasible. As noted above, this scenario played a vivid role during the German reform process as the automotive industry in particular argued that designing around patented technology, even when it is 'subordinate' in terms of technical functionality and economic value, can be prohibitively costly due to the complexity of the product design- and approval processes and intricate supply chains. First and foremost, there is nothing to suggest that the duration stays should be limited to a few weeks or even months. In an English case, a stay was granted for a year, with the possibility of extension, and US courts have on several occasions ordered stays for over a year.[66] So long as the infringer can demonstrate that the requested stay is reasonable, ie reflects best efforts to cease infringement in the shortest time possible, the duration of the stay should not preclude the proportionality defence. An infringer's unwillingness to implement an alternative that is technically feasible because of the costs this would incur is another matter. I view this as a business risk borne by the infringer whose choice it is to source parts from a complicated web of worldwide suppliers. Here, too, the proportionality test would simply come down to permission to keep infringing on court-ordered terms. I see no reason such requests could not

[66] *Edwards v Boston* (n 58) para 67. For examples from US practice, see s 4.4.2.

be addressed under existing provisions intended specifically for this purpose.[67] One could argue, of course, that the stringent conditions set by these existing provisions are incapable of preventing the social losses these types of scenarios cause, ie overpayment for patent licences or wasteful redesign processes. That may well be true, but I do not believe it is possible to address these issues with a proportionality test without creating social losses in different enforcement contexts, for instance by incentivising holdout tactics. If it were established that patent enforcement or certain aspects thereof systematically cause social losses, the proper course of action might be to make patent infringement subject to negligence liability or to re-evaluate the need for patent protection altogether.

Another case concerns broad claims, discussed in section 3.2.7. As we saw, it is sometimes difficult, if not impossible, to establish whether a product falls within the scope of a functionally defined claim. Could an injunction against a product there was no way of knowing would fall within the claim scope constitute overreach? While there are indeed good grounds to argue that this would extend the patentee's sphere of exclusivity beyond what is warranted by their inventive contribution, substantive patent law seems capable of addressing this concern. The English courts have held that a claim must be invalidated for insufficiency if it 'does not enable the skilled person to know whether they are within the claim or outside'.[68] Even if a broad claim as here discussed would survive a sufficiency challenge, there might be a plausible argument for non-infringement if the accused product's functionality is sufficiently far removed from the inventive concept disclosed in the patent.[69] In my view, there is little a proportionality test could credibly add to these defences. Here, too, the best approach to addressing residual problems, or systematic social losses in industries where they are especially likely to occur, is through better calibration of doctrines of substantive law, not meddling through the back door of remedies.

In sum, it is unlikely that there will be many cases where overreach occurs outside those where the first two limbs outlined above are satisfied. In line with the technical commensurability principle, a finding of overreach would require an effective injunction scope that extends well beyond the patented invention. An example might be where the injunction affects the infringer's capacity to compete with non-infringing products.[70] This could occur where the infringing product is part of a broader ecosystem of non-infringing products that nevertheless depend

[67] *cf* U Scharen, 'The Practice of Claiming Injunctive Relief for Patent Infringement in Germany' (2019) 14 *Journal of Intellectual Property Law & Practice* 112, 116 (discussing examples under German law).

[68] *Akebia Therapeutics v Astellas Pharma* [2020] EWHC 866 (Pat), para 347.

[69] *cf* HR NJ 1942/519; ECLI:NL:HR:1942:170 (*Handley Page v KLM*) (no infringement if accused product does not attain the 'purpose' of the patented invention, despite falling within literal scope of the claim). In US law, this might be addressed by the doctrine of reverse equivalents: R Merges and R Nelson, 'On the Complex Economics of Patent Scope' (1990) 90 *Columbia Law Review* 839, 911.

[70] *cf Veracode Inc v Appthority Inc* 137 FSupp3d 17, 96 (D Mass 2015) (refusal to enjoin database obtained with infringing technology but now no longer infringing).

on availability of the infringing product to function, or where the infringing technology is necessary to service non-infringing products or has interoperability with other devices with non-infringing uses. For instance, in a US case, an infringing blood collection kit was used in a machine that offered a platform to use the kit, but did not itself fall within the scope of the patent claims. Even though, when the case was decided, the machine's only use was to provide a platform for the infringing kit, the court excluded the machines from the scope of the injunction, accepting that they might also be compatible with a future non-infringing version of the kit.[71] Lastly, doubts concerning the validity of the patent may also be suggestive of overreach, especially in bifurcated systems.[72] This is harder to imagine in non-bifurcated systems, and most legal systems have procedural safeguards to stay infringement if revocation of the injunction is likely for whatever reason.[73] All in all, while it cannot be excluded that courts might identify other cases of overreach, I imagine such cases will be rare.

6.4. Abuse

As was addressed above, the parties' relative blameworthiness is an integral part of the proportionality test. In cases where the infringer makes out a case of overreach, the patentee's blameworthiness is generally irrelevant (but the proportionality defence may still be rejected if the infringer acted in bad faith: section 6.3.5). However, there may be grounds to limit injunctive relief even where no overreach is established if the patentee's conduct amounts to abuse. This follows from Article 3(2) of the Enforcement Directive, which requires that courts provide safeguards against abuse of the remedies provided by the Directive.[74]

Section 5.3.2 argued that abuse within the context of the proportionality test is distinct from, and sets a lower threshold for application than, sanctionable abuse as prohibited by Article 102 TFEU and abuse of rights doctrines. Rather, it checks against behaviour that seeks to exploit for unintended advantage the remedies the Enforcement Directive provides. The abuse inquiry must thus be sensitive to the goal pursued by the enforcement measures and the specifics of the underlying right invoked. European trademark law, for instance, contains an open-ended prohibition on applications made in bad faith recently reinvigorated by the ECJ

[71] *Haemonetics Corp v Baxter Healthcare Corp* 2009 WL 10692802, *5 (D Mass 1 June 2009).

[72] Ohly and Stierle (n 23) 1231. *cf* CoA Paris 15 June 2021, 20/12617 (*Allergan/Mylan*), 13 (considerable chance that patent will be revoked renders injunction disproportionate, though in interim relief proceedings).

[73] *VG Colours* (n 34) paras 4.5–4.6 (injunction stayed pending appeal because of clear indications the appeal would succeed).

[74] R Hilty, 'Legal Remedies against Abuse, Misuse and Other Forms of Inappropriate Conducts of IP Right Holders' in R Hilty and K Liu (eds), *Compulsory Licensing: Practical Experiences and Ways Forward* (Springer, 2015) 270.

and precluding, inter alia, registrations 'with the intention of undermining, in a manner inconsistent with honest practices, the interests of third parties'.[75] That sets a threshold that is high, but arguably lower than sanctionable abuse, and in any event is tailored to the specifics of trademark law.[76] In my view, the proportionality test should set similar limits on patent remedies. For comparison, US law expressly provides for a prohibition against 'patent misuse' and further contains various court-made doctrines to target opportunistic behaviour specific to the patent system.[77] This important difference with European patent law is rarely mentioned in the literature.[78] It is worth noting that the Federal Circuit's approach to patent misuse adopts a technical commensurability logic: according to this approach, courts must decide whether behaviour is 'reasonably within the patent grant, ie that it relates to subject matter within the scope of the patent claims'.[79] In contrast, most European jurisdictions do not appear to have misuse doctrines specific to patents beyond the recognition that fraudulent representations to the patent office may constitute abuse.[80] Because of its sensitivity to context and the circumstances in which enforcement takes place, as well as strong textual support in the Enforcement Directive, the proportionality test would seem an ideal candidate to incorporate a European counterpart to the patent misuse doctrine. The nature of patents and the intricacies of prosecution afford patentees plenty of opportunities to obtain a strategic advantage. Sometimes, these advantages might be unfair even if they do not amount to a violation of competition law or abuse of law. Limiting the patentee's entitlement to injunctive relief is an 'easy, time- and cost-efficient' way to address such cases.[81]

A finding of abuse without overreach requires a high threshold, but there are certainly examples that would qualify. Patent ambush, discussed in section 4.3.5, is a case in point. Another example is a divisional shield, where a patentee abandons a patent every time it threatens to be invalidated but re-files a new divisional application, all the while threatening strict enforcement in case of infringement.[82] In both cases, the patentee takes advantage of some particular feature of the patent system (technical standards and divisional applications, respectively) and seeks to capitalise on it through the threat of injunctive relief. Notably, neither scheme so

[75] Case C-104/18 P *Koton* ECLI:EU:C:2019:724, para 46.

[76] For instance, bad faith may limit the possibilities – unique to trademark law – of performing repeat filings or setting 'priority traps': Case T-663/19 *Hasbro v EUIPO* ECLI:EU:T:2021:211, para 57; Case T-82/14 *Copernicus-Trademarks v EUIPO* ECLI:EU:T:2016:396, para 138.

[77] Thus, various types of misconduct during prosecution and litigation may form the basis of limiting injunctive relief: *Gilead Sciences Inc v Merck & Co* 888 F3d 1231, 1247 (Fed Cir 2018).

[78] Notable exceptions are found in Hilty (n 74) 268; J Vesala, 'Misuse of Patent Application Procedures: A Case for Condemning Non-misleading Strategies?' in R Ballardini et al (eds), *Transitions in European Patent Law: Influences of the Unitary Patent Package* (Kluwer, 2015) 275.

[79] *Virgina Panel Corp v MAC Panel Co* 133 F3d 860, 869 (Fed Cir 1997).

[80] Case C-457/10 P *AstraZeneca v Commission* ECLI:EU:C:2012:770.

[81] Hilty (n 74) 268.

[82] *Fujifilm Kyowa Kiring Biologics v AbbVie Biotechnology* [2017] EWHC 395 (Pat) para 396.

far has been qualified as sanctionable abuse. Because of Rambus's settlement with the European Commission, the status of patent ambush under EU competition law remains uncertain, while US courts so far have not considered it an antitrust violation.[83] As for divisional shields, the English court considered whether they constitute abuse of process 'an important and complex one', but has yet to rule on the matter.[84] The European Commission is currently investigating this practice under competition law, but it may take a while for guidance to be provided by the European courts.[85] Yet another example, often cited in the literature, is a strategic delay in bringing proceedings to create a lock-in effect. At least on one occasion, a US court has denied the patentee injunctive relief on this ground.[86] A final possibility that has received little to no attention in the literature is where the patentee strategically delays the grant of the patent to write the claims more closely to a competitor's product. While Article 123 EPC sets strict limits on this possibility, that does not mean shifts in claim scope are always foreseeable to the infringer. These examples are not exhaustive, and further (empirical) research on how patentees do or may weaken the notice function of patents for strategic advantage would be worthwhile.

All these examples have in common that they concern behaviour that is, in principle, legitimate (opting out of standardisation, filing divisional applications, timing enforcement proceedings, amending claims during prosecution). However, it should be clear that any one of these behaviours – and certainly a combination – may mean enforcement of the patent takes the infringer completely by surprise. Where that results from a deliberate strategy by the patentee, application of the proportionality test to deny them an unfair advantage is appropriate.

6.5. Conflicts with Third Party Rights

6.5.1. Definitions and Practical Issues

6.5.1.1. Definitions

How to address third- and non-party interests is possibly the most difficult element of a proportionality test, because it requires balancing something as abstract as patent exclusivity against concrete harms of others or, worse, some equally abstract public policy goal. Section 5.2.1 demonstrated that the Enforcement Directive

[83] Nikolic (n 63) 78–79.
[84] *Neurim v Generics* [2022] EWHC 109 (Pat), para 160.
[85] Commission, 'Antitrust: Commission Sends Statement of Objections to Teva over Misuse of the Patent System and Disparagement of Rival Multiple Sclerosis Medicine' IP/22/6062.
[86] *Hynix Semiconductors Inc v Rambus Inc* 609 FSupp2d 951, 985 (ND Cal 2009).

is unlikely to require 'ad hoc' balancing of the interests of the patentee and the infringer, but the ECJ's case law shows that such balancing cannot be avoided when third-party rights are at stake. This opens the door to the problems with remedial balancing addressed in chapter two, which is perhaps the reason why European patent courts to date have shown great reserve when considering third-party interests in the context of a proportionality test. And yet, as the revised wording of § 139 GPA also shows, an adequate proportionality test must account for the effects that patent injunctions may have on others. This section offers some suggestions on how it may do so.

Although I refer generally to third-party interests throughout the book, I make some distinctions here. Non-parties are financially dependent on the infringement: suppliers and customers, resellers and distributors, but also employees. Third parties depend on the infringing technology: for instance, patients, consumers or scientific partners. Both non- and third-party interests can be traced to specific individuals or entities; in this section, I refer to them jointly as 'external interests'. In the literature, third-party interests are sometimes referred to in the aggregate as the 'public interest', but this term can also refer to more abstract interests, such as regional employment and innovative competitiveness. Here, I use 'public interest' only in the latter sense to distinguish it from specific harms to identifiable individuals. Non-party and third-party interests may overlap, but I discuss them separately because they present different considerations.[87] Conflicts between patent exclusivity and public interests raise yet other issues and are also discussed separately.

External interests raise special evidentiary concerns. First, since the relevant persons are not themselves a party to the proceedings, these interests are represented by the infringer. Because the infringer may be tempted to paint a bleak picture of the injunction's effects to boost their proportionality case, their representation of external interests probably warrants special scrutiny. Second, external interests suffer the effects of an injunction vicariously, ie through the infringer and potential interagents, making a causal link between the injunction and any harm suffered harder to establish. The problem will be especially pressing before the UPC, where differences between countries may make a profound difference in how third parties are affected, and proving those effects is costly and complicated. For these reasons, it may be difficult to establish the occurrence of harms to external interests beyond the realm of speculation. At the same time, affected parties often have no way of independently asserting their interests vis-à-vis the patentee and must therefore rely (often unwittingly) on the infringer as their representative. This might be best resolved by having a court-appointed expert providing an assessment of expected harms.

[87] *cf* Stierle and Hofmann (n 9) 1132–33 (distinguishing between infringing and non-infringing third parties).

6.5.1.2. *Threshold Requirements*

Although this is sometimes overlooked in the literature, not every case involving technology on which third parties rely will raise potential conflicts with the rights of those third parties. In my view, external interests may only be considered as part of the proportionality test if they would actually be affected by the injunction. There are three threshold requirements that must be satisfied for this to be the case.

First, enforcement should be pursued for exclusivity, not with a view to licensing. Harm to third- and non-parties will not materialise if it is clear the case will end in a licence, even if the injunction would force payment of excessive royalties. After all, the infringing technology will remain available in this case. There is at least one example of a European court declining to consider external interests on this ground.[88] Even if the infringer declines to accept the licence because of its extortionate terms, it could be argued that this business decision (understandable though it might be) and not the patent as such is the cause of the harm to external interests.[89] To the best of my knowledge, this difficult issue has not been addressed in the literature so far, but, given widespread enforcement following unsuccessful licensing negotiations, it will need to be addressed sooner or later. A relevant factor to consider in this context might be whether the infringer owes legal duties to third- or non-parties. For instance, if an infringer has contracted with hospitals to supply medical devices, the hospitals' interests will arguably have greater influence on the infringer's decision to accept the licence or not than where it bears no legal responsibility for continued supplies.[90]

Second, if there are readily available alternatives for the infringing technology, external interests are also unlikely to be affected.[91] As was observed in section 4.4.5.1, that is the starting point for US courts under *eBay*'s public interest prong, and many pleas for denial of injunctive relief fail because the patentee, competitors or the infringer itself can readily supply alternative products. Thus, where third parties have access to replacement technologies, their interests will not justify a limitation of the entitlement to an injunction. Similar reasoning governs non-party interests. If employees can easily switch jobs, or customers can switch suppliers and vice versa, their interests will not carry weight in the proportionality test.

Third, the various parties involved may be subject to duties of care before their interests can be considered. Starting with the infringer itself, German courts have declined to consider third-party interests as part of the proportionality test where the infringer did not timely apply for a compulsory licence, even after

[88] RB The Hague 18 July 2018, ECLI:NL:RBDHA:2018:8777 (*Nikon v ASML*), para 4.51.

[89] GH Leeuwarden NJF 2005, 446; ECLI:NL:GHLEE:2005:AU4338 (*Schneider v Cordis*), para 13.

[90] *cf* TO Torino 16 June 2021, 10009/2020 (*Edwards Lifesciences v Meril Life Sciences*), 3 (carve-out on public interest grounds for deliveries to hospitals on the basis of prior contracts, but not for devices in storage not subject to contractual obligations).

[91] *HTC* (n 43) para 56; *Nikon v ASML* (n 88) para 4.50.

the reform.[92] Such a requirement elides the distinction between third- and non-parties (the latter are unlikely to be covered by compulsory licensing provisions) and, more generally, the distinction between consideration of third-party interests as part of the proportionality test and compulsory licences. In any event, the requirement seems untenable in those Member States where compulsory licences cannot be granted on an expedited basis and before the UPC, because at the time of writing there is no compulsory licence regime to match the territorial scope of its jurisdiction. Conversely, it has been argued that third-party interests should be considered even if the infringer was negligent.[93] This seems correct in that both sets of interests are distinct and merit consideration on different grounds, but only up to a point. It seems disingenuous for a wilful infringer to argue infringement should proceed for the benefit of others. While hypothetically possible, it would have to be a very extreme case – for example if, during a health emergency, a pharmacy chain were to dispense infringing treatments that the patentee is incapable of supplying in sufficient quantities. It certainly seems reasonable that an infringer seeking to rely on third-party interests would show diligence in protecting those interests before the injunction were issued, for instance by preparing customers for a potential interruption of service. Furthermore, in cases where the parties' relative blameworthiness favours the patentee, only third-party, not non-party, interests should be cognisable. It is one thing to argue that wilful infringement was necessary for those dependent on the technology; it is quite another to argue that those profiting from the infringement should also be shielded from an injunction.

Indeed, non-parties are themselves subject to a duty to mitigate the damage an injunction would cause. In many cases, they are not 'innocent bystanders', as one US court held, but actively profit from the infringement.[94] Where supply chains are closely integrated, the 'backup plan' for a design-around that the infringer must submit will often require a joint effort as suppliers and customers may also need to prepare to phase out infringement on short notice. Thus, as a general rule, where implementing a design-around requires collaboration with non-parties, their best efforts must also be reflected in the timeline presented to the court for the proportionality defence to succeed. But non-parties may also be required to make independent efforts to mitigate the potential damage from an injunction. For instance, wholesalers may need to lower their stocks of the infringing product; clients may need to engage with the patentee or other providers to ensure uninterrupted support; and specialised suppliers may need to initiate certification processes for non-infringing alternatives. What can be

[92] LG Düsseldorf GRUR 2022, 1665; 4c O 18/21 *Gilead*, C.II. In defence of this approach, see K Grabinski, 'Injunctive Relief and Proportionality in Case of a Public Interest in the Use of a Patent: Different Ways – Same Result' [2021] *Gewerblicher Rechtsschutz und Urheberrecht* 200, 202.

[93] Transcript (n 37) 25 (Fabian Hoffmann).

[94] *SynQor v Artesyn* (n 54) *8. The argument was extended to retailers in *Apple Inc v Samsung Electronics Co Ltd* 909 FSupp2d 1147, 1162 (ND Cal 2012).

expected of non-parties will strongly depend on the circumstances of the case and should be determined in accordance with general duties to mitigate losses. While it cannot be entirely excluded that similar duties could arise for third parties – as when university partners fail to prepare in any way for a potential loss of access to the technology – this is generally unlikely as classic examples of third parties (eg patients and consumers) normally have no way to prepare themselves for the impact of an injunction.

After verifying these threshold conditions, patent courts face the difficult question of deciding whether these interests justify limiting the patentee's claim to injunctive relief. This is a classical balancing exercise that resists theorisation, but I make some suggestions below separately for non- and third-party interests.

6.5.2. Which Interests are Cognisable for the Proportionality Test?

6.5.2.1. Non-party Interests

In complex supply chains, an injunction may have spill-over effects on up- or downstream parties. The extent to which these parties' interests are cognisable in the proportionality test largely follows between infringing and non-infringing technology. Thus, the interests of the supplier of an infringing component ought to be irrelevant, because proportionality cannot be relied upon to legitimise their infringement any more than the infringer's own. The same is true for employees, whose potential job loss is not a cognisable interest for purposes of proportionality if directly related to the infringement. Holding differently would lead to the counterintuitive result that infringements are harder to enjoin the larger the scale on which they occur. It could also mean that the strength of a party's proportionality defence would depend in part on its geographical location and on when the suit is brought, as job losses will surely weigh heavier in the minds of courts if they occur in less-developed regions or during a recession.[95] This is not to suggest that unemployment is not a pressing social issue: it certainly is, but the proportionality test is not the correct means to address is it. The better way to do so, in appropriately extreme cases, is through the grant of a compulsory licence, and there is some historical precedence for this.[96] It will therefore be a rare case where non-party interests warrant consideration because this requires them to operate outside the scope of the patent and yet be dependent on infringement thereof by another entity threatening to be shut down, without alternative commercial options or

[95] *cf Illinois Tool Works v Autobars Company* [1972] FSR 67, 74 (having 200 employees lose their jobs immediately 'would be a most unfortunate thing … when everything should be done … to avoid increasing the existing unemployment').

[96] Reichtsgericht Blatt 1917, Jg 40, 110; I 37/33 *Tonaufnahme*; Reichsgericht GRUR 1937, 676; I 26/36 *Graugussverfahren*.

meaningful ways to mitigate potential losses stemming from an injunction. The classical (and possibly only) case would be specialised suppliers of highly advanced technology, either for unique products such as lithography machines or subject to long production cycles, as in the automotive industry. In the former case, the supplier may not have any viable alternatives simply because their entire business is built around supplying the composite product targeted by the injunction; in the latter case, switching supplies to products not affected by the injunction or other customers may be possible but difficult in practice as this requires certification and coordination with other suppliers. The interests of suppliers in this situation are plainly relevant to the proportionality analysis as they do not contribute to the infringement and usually have no realistic way of knowing about it.

Non-parties also raise the question of the extent to which proportionality defences 'spill over' to up- and downstream partners. During the GPA reform process, the concern was raised that patentees might strategically enforce the patent against parties other than the original equipment manufacturer (OEM) to circumvent a proportionality defence, while still disrupting the supply chain and so pressuring the OEM indirectly.[97] Reportedly, such strategic targeting is already taking place.[98] Infringement and proportionality of an injunction have to be assessed separately as against each entity in the supply chain, and infringing products allowed under a stay are not considered exhausted for downstream users.[99] In my view, a successful proportionality defence at any level in the supply chain should nevertheless be considered to enable downstream (re)sales: an attempt to circumvent the stay by targeting clients could be considered abusive, as per section 6.4.

The matter is more complicated for upstream suppliers, since a finding of overreach becomes less likely as enforcement targets the infringing component as such and not the device of which it is a part. Thus, as noted above, it may constitute overreach to enforce a patent on a sunroof-locking mechanism against a car manufacturer but not against the supplier of the infringing mechanism. After all, in the latter case, the patent exclusivity is commensurate with the scope of the invention. During the GPA reform, it was argued that in these situations the supplier should be able rely on the same proportionality arguments as the OEM.[100] I doubt, however, that this is right, as the injunction's effective scope is much more limited than in the case of an injunction against the OEM. Of course, the supplier might still advance a proportionality defence on the basis of third-party rights, citing the loss of access to non-infringing technology that the OEM and its customers would suffer. Such a scenario necessarily presupposes a specialised supplier of sophisticated technology; otherwise, the OEM could easily switch suppliers.

[97] See the position papers by Fabian Hoffmann and Ansgar Ohly: Transcript (n 37) 37, 62.

[98] D Geradin, 'European Union Competition Law, Intellectual Property Law and Standardization' in J Contreras (ed), *The Cambridge Handbook of Technical Standardization Law Competition, Antitrust, and Patents* (Cambridge University Press, 2018) 91.

[99] Stierle and Hofmann (n 9) 1133.

[100] Transcript (n 37) 8 (Fabian Hoffmann).

6.5.2.2. *Third Party Interests*

As noted above, third parties as intended here are individuals or institutions that have an interest in the continued availability of the infringing technology. The inclusion of these interests in the proportionality test is often defended by reference to the ECJ's fair balance case law. While correct in general, it is worth pointing out an important conceptual difference: the end user's cognisable interest in the ECJ's fair balance cases is not access to the infringing content, but rather access to other, non-infringing content which the requested injunction threatens to obstruct. Here, too, the commensurability logic underlying the EU framework for IP rights enforcement shines through as the balance is not one of restrictions versus access to, for example, copyrighted material.[101] Rather, these cases turn on whether these access restrictions are proportionate in light of the further-reaching restrictions to lawful content they threaten to imply.[102] Thus, transposed to patent law, third-party interests would weigh heaviest where the injunction would deprive them of non-infringing technology. That said, due to the potential importance of specific technology to individuals – life-saving drugs, for instance – I believe there is a good case to be made that interests in that technology find protection in the CFR. But we should be mindful that this is yet to be confirmed by the ECJ, and it is quite likely that the bar for interference with patent exclusivity will be high if the interest is in the patented technology as such.

A related question is whether third-party interests should be 'of a unique or socially valuable type' to warrant consideration, as US courts generally assume.[103] In my view, the ECJ's fair balance cases suggest the answer is no. As discussed in section 5.3.3.2, a case like *McFadden* – which held that the interest in accessing a WiFi network in a store is protected in the Charter – suggests the threshold for finding an interference with a Charter right is low; whether the interference is impermissible is another matter.[104]

6.5.2.3. *Public Interests*

The ECJ held that the 'public interest' should be considered as part of the fair balance test.[105] It is not clear what is meant here, but it seems ill-advised for courts to consider public interests in the abstract as part of the proportionality test. Courts' institutional constraints, discussed at the end of chapter one, make it difficult for them to weigh patent exclusivity against broader policy objectives.

[101] As was at issue in Case No 36769/08 *Ashby Donald v France* (ECtHR, 10 January 2013). It is doubtful that such a balancing exercise would be allowable under EU law: Case C-469/17 *Funke Medien* ECLI:EU:C:2019:623.

[102] This is most evident in Case C-324/09 *L'Oréal and others* ECLI:EU:C:2011:474, [2011] ECR I-6011, para 140.

[103] *ActiveVideo Networks Inc v Verizon Communications Inc* 827 FSupp2d 641, 652 (ED Va 2011).

[104] Case C-484/14 *McFadden* ECLI:EU:C:2016:689, para 92.

[105] Case C-264/19 *Constantin Film Verleih* ECLI:EU:C:2020:542, para 37.

An oft-cited example, also in the context of the GPA reform, is whether patent exclusivity should be limited to make the healthcare system more affordable.[106] In one case, a US court heard extensive evidence on the issue and concluded that, due to the practical realities of the US healthcare system, it could not be established that allowing a generic drug to stay on the market would in fact result in lowered prices.[107] It also concluded that 'separation of powers considerations' suggested courts should generally refrain from weighing patent exclusivity against competing policy considerations. In my view, these limitations are likely to constrain any court attempting to improve the patent equilibrium. Decisions of public policy are therefore best not left to courts and certainly not as part of their remedial discretion.

6.5.3. How Should the Balance be Conducted?

6.5.3.1. The Standard for Limitation: Non-party Interests

In line with my preference for tests with narrow scope but lower thresholds, I think the best approach would be for courts to evaluate strictly which non-parties qualify for consideration in the proportionality test, but not be overly cautious when considering the grant of stays to mitigate harms qualifying parties. Such harms are likely to be significant because to qualify for consideration in the first place, these non-parties must not have at their disposal an alternative clientele. Moreover, the technical commensurability paradigm clearly counsels against accepting such harms, even if not significant in absolute terms: they are suffered by entities unrelated to the infringer involved in acts that, by definition, lie outside the scope of the patent. An encroachment on the patent's rights in the form of a stay therefore seems justified to respect their evidently valid interest in conducting their business (Article 16 CFR). That stay will usually coincide with the time for a redesign requested by the infringer.

Another scenario that is sometimes referenced in the literature concerns employees. In my view, employees will almost always have at their disposal alternative options. Even highly specialised engineers can apply their skills elsewhere and will possibly be welcomed with open arms. Of course, there can still be important policy reasons to maintain such highly skilled workers, as the Dutch example of Organon shows (section 3.2.8). But these are not concerns that a proportionality test should address. It is even hard to imagine how it could: should courts stay the injunction until the employees are retrained and have

[106] During the reform, it was repeatedly emphasised that this would not be an appropriate ground to apply a proportionality test: Transcript (n 37) 38 (Fabian Hoffmann), 62 (Ansgar Ohly). According to Stierle and Hofmann (n 9) 1131, 'public interest' should be understood as 'cumulated interests' of specific third parties.

[107] *Amgen Inc v F Hoffman-La Roche Ltd* 581 FSupp2d 160, 223 (D Mass 2008).

found other work? The practical difficulties that such an order would entail already suffice to demonstrate that this is not an issue that courts in infringement proceedings should seek to address.

6.5.3.2. *The Standard for Limitation: Third Party Interests*

We saw that the ECJ's case law suggests that third-party interests need not be of a unique type or possess particular social value to warrant consideration. But that does not mean all third-party interests ought to be treated in the same way. Depending on the nature of the third-party interests (do they weigh sufficiently heavily at the individual level or are they to be considered in the aggregate?) and what respecting the interest requires (a short stay to accommodate transition to alternative products or longer term availability of the infringing product?), a variety of scenarios can arise.

In my view, courts should first consider whether the third-party interests at stake are so compelling that they justify a stay regardless of any other circumstances. I call these 'trump card interests' because they necessitate limiting the injunction even if they relate to just a handful of individuals and even if they require a long-term stay of the injunction. In these cases, there is no room for a balancing exercise since the interest simply trumps patent exclusivity and therefore courts must tailor the injunction order to accommodate it. Trump card status should thus be recognised very sparingly. Access to life-saving medicine has been accepted as an example.[108] National security might be another. As a rule, trump card interests should be so important that their protection would also justify the grant of a compulsory licence.[109] To accommodate them, the injunction should be limited to the minimum extent possible. Thus, where an alternative treatment is possible but not with immediate effect, a stay should be granted. Without alternatives, however, the injunction might be stayed indefinitely, with leave for the patentee to have it reinstated should circumstances change. Similarly, where only a subgroup of affected interests has trump card status, limitations to the injunction should be tailored to that subgroup as much as possible (a so-called carve-out). All these variants were present in the aforementioned *Edwards v Boston* case.[110]

All other third-party interests will require balancing against the patentee's interest in the issuance of an injunction. The relevant parameters when considering third-party interests are (i) the normative importance attached to the relevant interests; (ii) their weight in the aggregate; and (iii) the duration of the

[108] *Evalve v Edwards* [2020] EWHC 513 (Pat), para 87.

[109] ibid para 90; BGH GRUR 1996 190, 193; X ZR 26/92 *Polyferon*.

[110] *Edwards v Boston* (n 58) para 67 (stay for patients who could be treated with alternative); para 69 (exception for patients for whom infringing device was the only option); para 70 (how to determine which patients fall in the latter group). The reasoning in this case was expressly embraced in Italy in *Edwards v Meril* (n 90).

requested stay. The longer the stay, the more serious the interference with third-party interests should be, in terms of either their normative importance or their collective weight. Differently from US practice, non-trump card interests generally should not be relied upon to justify long-term stays or denials; a good rule of thumb might be that a stay of six months or more will require interests important enough to warrant the grant of a compulsory licence. But courts should keep in mind that short stays already have the capacity to do a lot of good. For instance, during the GPA reform network, operators argued that if an injunction were to cause interruptions to telecommunications infrastructure, this would affect millions of subscribers.[111] The burdens of having limited or no cell phone reception for a period of time do not have the same gravity as access to life-saving treatments. Still, when considered in the aggregate, these burdens can become considerate. It would cause very severe disruptions if, for instance, millions of subscribers could not access the internet for a week (let alone longer). Thus, if a stay of one month can prevent the immense damage that a long interruption of the cellular network would cause by allowing the network operator to switch to non-infringing technology, granting the stay may be justified. Alternatively, a short stay could be granted to fulfil orders already placed to prevent disruptions at customers.[112] Because this is a classical balancing exercise, everything will depend on the circumstances of the case.

A special case of third-party interests arises where alternatives exist to the infringing technology that are not perfect equivalents. A common example is where the infringer's product is superior to the patentee's product, for instance because it independently improved the relevant technology. This, too, was at issue in *Edwards v Boston*, where in fact several alternatives existed, but for a specific subset of patients only the infringing device was suitable.[113] Two years later, the English court held that exempting a superior alternative from the scope of an injunction would be allowable only where this would protect 'against serious risks of health'.[114] Indeed, in such a case, the interest would have trump card status and therefore the injunction should be limited. But I wonder whether third parties may not have a more general claim to technological improvements achieved by the infringer. From the perspective of the commensurability principle, an injunction that would deprive the public of significant advancements over the original invention reaches well beyond the patentee's original inventive contribution. This is an old problem in patent law that was historically resolved through dependency licences and, in my view, there is a lot to be said for its consideration as

[111] The need to consider 'important infrastructure' consequently made it into the explanatory memorandum: Proposed Bill (n 24) 55.

[112] Compare *Presidio Components Inc v American Technical Ceramics Corp* 2013 WL 4068833, *8 (CD Cal 12 August 2013) (in a case concerning capacitators for 'government, military, space, and infrastructure projects', granting a sunset period to allow shipping orders placed prior to oral argument).

[113] *Edwards v Boston* (n 58) para 22.

[114] *Evalve v Edwards* (n 108) para 87.

part of the proportionality test.[115] A good point of reference is Article 31(l) of the Agreement on Trade-Related Aspects of Intellectual Property Rights (TRIPS), which sets global minimum conditions for the grant of dependency licences. These conditions could be applied by analogy in the context of a proportionality test, where the infringer argues their product is superior to available alternatives and therefore must remain available to the public. As per Article 31(l) TRIPS, such a claim would require evidence that the infringing technology represents an important technical advance of considerable economic significance as compared to available alternatives, and a commitment to cross-license to the patentee any patents on the improved technology. Adopting these requirements in the context of the proportionality test is legitimate as they derive from the global wellspring of patent standards, while their stringency ensures that proportionality does not favour follow-on innovations over the patented invention too easily. A successful proportionality plea based on the superiority of the infringing technology may lead to a stay, for instance pending market approval for an improved product by the patentee, but it may also lead to a denial of the injunction where it is not clear a comparable alternative will become available. As noted above, that should be a rare outcome of the proportionality test, but because the conditions that TRIPS sets for a dependency licence are met, this is a situation in which a denial would be acceptable.

6.5.4. Relation to Other Elements of the Proportionality Test

The previous subsections assumed no finding of overreach or abuse. In such cases, the proportionality test's external interests limb operates standing alone and, as we have seen, there are certainly circumstances where it can result in a limitation of the patentee's entitlement to injunctive relief. Importantly, the different elements of the proportionality test are not communicating vessels. Thus, a defensible but ultimately unsuccessful case for overreach should not lower the standards under the external interests limb or vice versa. Accepting otherwise would to a large extent undo the benefits in terms of workability and the legal certainty offered by the structured test proposed here. In addition, because the consequences of an injunction for the infringer, for non-parties, for third parties and in the public interest are not just conceptually distinct but also different in nature, it is hard to credibly combine them into 'the expected negative effects of an injunction'.[116] The same is true for non-party and third-party interests: I believe these ought to be differentiated in the proportionality test because they raise distinct concerns. It would be anomalous if the interests of consumers would

[115] *cf Conceptus Inc v Hologic Inc* 2012 WL 44064, *3 (ND Cal 9 January 2012) (the public interest 'would undoubtedly be harmed by an injunction' where it would remove from the market 'an important alternative for patients').

[116] As is done, for instance, in Siebrasse et al (n 19) 152.

sooner justify interference with patent exclusivity just because the injunction also affects the interest of a supplier. In other words, patent injunctions may be disproportionate vis-à-vis infringers, non-parties or third parties, but in different ways, so each situation should be decided on its own merit.

By the same token, external interests may well require limiting injunctive relief in cases where overreach is also established. In these cases, the stay granted as part of the overreach assessment could also adequately safeguard the external interests, as will normally be the case with non-party interests. But this need not be so. For instance, an infringer might need two months to redesign a medical device and cease all infringing sales but four months to retrain staff already working with implemented devices. In such cases, the injunction order should reflect both limitations separately (as happened, for instance, in the aforementioned *Edwards v Boston* case). This shows once again that the interests protected by a proportionality test differ in nature and therefore should be assessed separately.

6.6. The Payment Due for the Duration of the Stay

It is more or less universally accepted in the European literature that the patentee is entitled to compensation for the use of their invention so long as the injunction is stayed. Because proportionality is such a recent development in European patent law, not much is known about the legal nature and calculation of this compensation, but in the wake of the GPA reform – where the entitlement to a compensation was codified in § 139 GPA, a doctrinal novelty – a debate on these issues took place in the German journal *Gewerblicher Rechtsschutz und Urheberrecht*.[117] Each of the four contributing authors assumed as the starting point a hypothetical royalty rate that parties would have agreed on prior to infringement. This represents the baseline compensation due to the patentee for the duration of the stay, with two authors suggesting courts ought to adjust the rate based on the circumstances of the case, eg upwards if the patented technology is valuable but possibly also downwards, even to zero, in other cases.[118] The two other authors instead suggested an upwards modification by default, respectively by a 'moderate surcharge' of 10–25 per cent or simply a factor of three to discourage strategic behaviour on the part of infringers.[119]

Before commencing the argument on the best way to arrive at a payment for the duration of the stay, it is useful to first consider the nature and legal basis of

[117] See issue 5 of the 2022 volume, with contributions by F Hoffmann, 'Der Ausgleichsanspruch Im Patentrecht: Die Leistungsgerechte Monetarisierung Eines Drohpotentials' at 286; G Wagner, 'Die Aufopferung Des Patentrechtlichen Unterlassungsanspruchs' at 294; C Osterrieth, 'Kriterien der Angemessenheit des Ausgleichs nach § 139 I 4 PatG' at 299; A Ohly, 'Der Ausgleichsanspruch gemäß § 139 I 4 PatG als Rechtsfortwirkungsanspruch' at 303.

[118] Ohly (n 117) 307; Osterrieth (n 117) 301.

[119] Wagner (n 117) 297; Hoffmann (n 117) 292.

this payment. The compensation provided for in the revised § 139 GPA has been characterised as a conversion right in that it converts one entitlement (the injunction) into another (monetary compensation).[120] It is thus conceptually distinct from the patentee's entitlement to damages, which § 139(1) GPA states explicitly remains unaffected by the conversion right to compensation. At the same time, both entitlements stem from one and the same act: the continued use of the invention for the duration of the stay. It has therefore been argued – rightly, in my view – that the conversion claim and the damages claim cannot cumulate.[121] After all, under Article 13 of the Enforcement Directive, damages are awarded 'appropriate to the actual prejudice suffered' by the patentee, but the conversion claim already compensates the patentee for that prejudice. It could be argued that cumulation should be allowed in order to discourage holdout or to compensate for the loss of exclusivity even after the decision on the merits. While I agree that the compensation should not simply be equivalent to a reasonable royalty (see further below), granting the patentee a conversion right to compensation on top of damages is problematic for two reasons. First, it can seriously be questioned whether it is appropriate to acknowledge a conversion right at all. The assumption underlying the conversion right is that there is something to convert, ie an entitlement to an injunction that did not materialise. But to the extent the injunction is disproportionate, the patentee is not entitled to it and there is nothing to convert (see section 5.3). Nevertheless, granting the patentee a right to compensation for the loss of an injunction seems at odds with the infringer's rights under Article 16 CFR because it imposes on them a liability for payment not corresponding to a legal entitlement on the part of the patentee. Second, while not precluding punitive damages, the ECJ has clearly signalled an aversion against monetary penalties that far exceed the damage actually suffered.[122] A duplicate entitlement to compensation for one and the same instance of infringement thus risks violating EU law. The situation is even clearer under the UPC Agreement, which provides, in Article 68(2), that damages 'shall not be punitive' but should serve to place the patentee 'in the position it would have been in if no infringement had taken place'. In sum, though the situation is admittedly uncertain, at the time of writing, the most compelling view appears to be that a separate entitlement to compensation for the duration of the stay, even if allowable, cannot result in a total compensation exceeding what the patentee would be entitled to in damages.

Apart from the issue of cumulation, there are two further reasons why a court might not set a specific amount of compensation when it stays the injunction on proportionality grounds. At the time the stay is ordered, the continued

[120] Ohly (n 117) 304 (referring to the compensation as a *Rechtsforwirkunganspruch*).

[121] Ohly (n 117) 308 (suggesting that the damages entitled is lowered by the amount awarded as compensation under § 139(1) GPA).

[122] Case C-367/15 *Stowarzyszenie Oławska Telewizja Kablowa (OTK)* ECLI:EU:C:2017:36, para 31; see recently Case C-522/21 *KWS Meridian* ECLI:EU:C:2023:218, para 49 (though in the context of Regulation 2100/94 on community plant variety rights).

infringement is yet to take place and it is unclear whether courts have the authority to award damages over future acts. Article 13 of the Enforcement Directive does not provide for the possibility of prospective damages. It would thus seem that Member States need to introduce this possibility, as Germany did in § 139(1) GPA, if it does not already follow from their law on damages. For its part, the UPC is unlikely to be able to award prospective damages as Article 68 UPC Agreement does not authorise it to do so (though the interim damages award, provided for in Article 119 of the Rules of Procedure, may effectively resolve this problem).[123] Thus, an initial requirement for the solutions offered in the *Gewerblicher Rechtsschutz und Urheberrecht* debate – all variations on a hypothetical royalty award issued together with the stay – is that the court is in fact authorised to order such an award. This will depend on each Member State's law on damages. More importantly perhaps than the question whether courts may order a compensation when they issue the stay is whether it is desirable that they do so. After all, this requires courts to determine (i) a hypothetical royalty and (ii) its appropriate upward or downward adjustment, if any, as part of their decision on the grant of the stay. These calculations are difficult and time-consuming to perform, as is well known from SEP litigation. Determining the appropriate adjustment introduces further complexities and subjectivity into this exercise. In other words, adopting the suggestions in the *Gewerblicher Rechtsschutz und Urheberrecht* debate would require labour-intensive and subjective assessments of the patent's value, which, as we saw in chapter two, courts are poorly situated to perform. I fear that requiring courts to determine a reasonable royalty for the duration of the stay will put another nail into proportionality's proverbial coffin. It is no wonder that in most cases where US courts deny or stay an injunction, they order parties to negotiate an appropriate royalty for future infringement.

There is another solution for courts either unable or hesitant to order a reasonable royalty for the duration of the stay. Courts could order the infringer to report periodically to the patentee the number of infringing sales as well as the turnover they generated, as was done in two early US cases.[124] The authority to do so is laid down in Article 8(1)–(2) of the Enforcement Directive and Article 67(1)(b) of the UPC Agreement.[125] These reports would be the basis for a later claim for the disgorgement of profits attributable to the infringement, a form of damages expressly provided for in Article 13 of the Enforcement Directive (as well as

[123] *cf* Ohly (n 9) 63 (arguing, however, that the possibility to grant compensation in lieu is comprised in the principle of proportionality).

[124] *z4 Technologies Inc v Microsoft Corp* 434 FSupp2d 437, 444 (ED Tex 2006); *Voda v Cordis Corp* 2006 WL 2570614, *6 (WD Okla 5 September 2006).

[125] It is not clear how the UPC's power to order the communication of information (Art 67 of the UPC Agreement) relates to its power to order the infringer to lay open books (Art 141 of the UPC Rules of Procedure), the latter order being available seemingly only upon request by the patentee following the decision on the merits. For our purposes, the authority to order disclosure of 'the price obtained for infringing products' (Art 67(1)(b) of the UPC Agreement) seems sufficient to give the patentee a general idea of the disgorgement award they may expect.

Article 68 of the UPC Agreement) and regularly awarded by some Member States' courts. Disgorgement of profits is a much more appropriate form of compensation for the duration of the stay than a reasonable royalty. The disgorgement remedy deprives the infringer of all financial benefits stemming from the infringement. It matches well with the nature of the proportionality defence, which exists to prevent disproportionate outcomes, not to allow continued used of the invention on commercially reasonable terms. The disgorgement remedy also obviates the need for an upwards adjustment of a royalty rate for dissuasive effect since no profits remain for the infringer. Going further than awarding all profits attributable to the infringement should be treated with caution as such an award would be punitive by definition. Nevertheless, in the rare case where the disgorgement remedy does not suffice to make the patentee whole, courts could additionally award damages for 'elements other than economic factors', as allowed by Article 13(1)(a) of the Enforcement Directive. Most importantly, an award of profits releases the court – and the parties – from establishing a reasonable royalty amount.

To be sure, there are also difficulties in establishing which profits are attributable to the infringement, particularly when it comes to component patents. But these difficulties would only need to be addressed in quantum damages proceedings, initiated after the infringement proceedings at a moment of the patentee's choosing. In this sense, my proposal aligns with standard practice in most continental European jurisdictions, where courts rarely decide on damages in the initial infringement proceedings and instead leave those for subsequent proceedings.[126] In most jurisdictions, those subsequent proceedings are hardly ever pursued as parties generally settle after the decision on the merits (and possible appeals). It is unlikely to be different in the case of compensation for proportionality-based stays, with two caveats. First, if it became commonly accepted that the patentee is entitled to disgorgement of profits for the duration of the stay and the infringer were ordered to give account of infringing sales, the parties would have a clear baseline for settlement negotiations which may help bring them together. Second, that baseline will become much more favourable for the patentee before the UPC, which, in the event of subsequent litigation, can order disgorgement of profits for all participating states (and possibly beyond, see Article 71b(3) of Regulation 1215/2012). In practical terms, the solution would thus be much like the practice of US courts to leave it up to the parties to negotiate an appropriate compensation, except with the clear indication that, as a default compensation, the patentee is entitled to all profits attributable to the infringement. To further boost the patentee's negotiation position, infringers could even be required to start making payments, which could be set, for instance, at a percentage of the proceedings value (*Streitwert*) and offset against a potential later damages award (provided, of course, that the court's law on damages allows for such an order).

[126] See also Rule 125 of the UPC's Rules of Procedure, which opens the possibility to order 'Separate proceedings for determining the amount of damages ordered'.

Conclusion

It is only fitting to end with tigers a book that shows one on its cover.[1] In 2008, Ms Katherine Lawrence brought a suit against the Fen Tigers, a speedway racing team in Mildenhall, for nuisance caused by racing events in the stadium close to her home. The dispute ended up before the UK Supreme Court, which ruled not just on the law of nuisance, but also on a trial court's capacity to award damages in lieu of an injunction.[2] Lord Neuberger held that the historical approach of English courts, whereby damages in lieu are awarded only in very exceptional circumstances, was 'simply wrong in principle'.[3] He added that 'where an injunction would in practice stop the defendant from pursuing [its] activities, an injunction may well not be the appropriate remedy'.[4] Lord Neuberger ultimately concluded that the historical practice was 'out of date', devised for times past when English society looked different, and 'will need one day to be reviewed in this court'.[5]

A decision issued in an English nuisance case may not have much guidance to offer for European patent cases. Even domestically, the High Court held that patent rights have a 'distinct rationale and are governed by a separate scheme' when it comes to injunctive relief and declined to take a more lenient approach to damages in lieu following *Coventry*.[6] But the *Fen Tigers* decision nevertheless has something to tell us: it signals an awareness of the drastic effects an injunction can have, which may no longer be palatable as societies grow more complex.[7] In my view, proportionality stands for precisely the same development in patent law. It seems that gone are the days when patent protection was absolute, in the sense that it would override any competing interest falling short of justifying a compulsory licence. That development should be welcomed. As technology permeates more and more aspects of our lives, patents become relevant in more and more sectors of the economy. This is not a plea to weaken patents, because this

[1] The painting, Henri Rousseau's *Fight Between a Tiger and a Buffalo* (1908), connects well to the rhinoceros we encountered at the start of this book: like Dürer, Rousseau had never seen the subjects of his jungle paintings. Both works nevertheless captivated their audience, and it is hoped that a book on proportionality in patent law may inspirit this doctrine even if its application remains virtually non-existent at the time of writing.

[2] *Coventry v Lawrence* [2014] UKSC 13.

[3] ibid 119.

[4] ibid 126.

[5] ibid 161.

[6] *Evalve v Edwards* [2020] EWHC 513 (Pat), para 50.

[7] A shift in German legal thinking along these lines is reported in M Stierle and F Hofmann, 'The Latest Amendment to the German Law on Patent Injunctions: The New Statutory Disproportionality Exception and Third-Party Interests' (2022) 71 *Gewerblicher Rechtsschutz und Urheberrecht International* 1123, 1124.

very development may just as well underline the importance of patent protection. It is only to observe, similarly to Lord Neuberger in the *Fen Tigers* case, that the contexts in which patent law operates have become more complex and that our thinking about appropriate remedies should evolve in tandem.

As noted in the Introduction, this latter observation is now broadly accepted in Europe. That becomes especially apparent from the recent revision of the German Patent Act (GPA), as well as other developments outlined in section 1.3. But we are still far from consensus as to when or why exceptions to the automatic injunction rule should be made. On the one hand, there is what might be called the conservative view, which holds that proportionality effectively adds nothing to existing safeguards against disproportionate enforcement efforts, like competition law and abuse of rights doctrines. On the other hand, the literature increasingly adopts what might be called the liberal view of proportionality, according to which courts should take stock of all relevant circumstances of the case and limit or deny the injunction where 'the expected negative effects of an injunction substantially outweigh … the expected noncompensable harm to the patentee is an injunction is not issued'.[8] What, then, will be the fate of the rhinoceros we encountered in the Introduction, where it served as a metaphor for proportionality in European patent law? Does it hibernate? Will it charge? I have argued neither view is correct. The conservative view is plainly incompatible with EU law (section 5.1.2), while the liberal view simply asks too much of courts, at least if the aim is to arrive at a proportionality test that is workable in practice and predictable for litigants (section 2.3.1). Caught between these two views, it is hardly surprising that, so far, the European patent bench has not been keen to apply any proportionality test. That is a shame, because it means European patent law will not adapt to the mismatch between the automatic injunction rule and the altered societal and technological context in which it operates today, so aptly articulated in the *Fen Tigers* case. Part II of the book has demonstrated that problems stemming from this mismatch also materialise in patent law.

This book offers a way out of this stalemate, and to that end makes two key points. The first is that the proportionality test requires more solid footing than the patent system's overall goals of fostering innovation and diffusing technology can offer. The journey towards a fully developed proportionality test starts with the purpose of this test and if we fail to define it, or rely on nebulous concepts like innovation and diffusion in doing so, we risk getting lost right out of the door. I advocate adopting the commensurability principle as the proportionality test's leitmotiv. On that view, the proportionality test serves to ensure that the patentee's effective sphere of exclusivity is justified by their inventive contribution to the art. Chapter two is devoted to defending this proposition and lists its various strengths. Commensurability is not just a foundational principle in all of patent

[8] N Siebrasse et al, 'Injunctive Relief' in CB Biddle et al (eds), *Patent Remedies and Complex Products: Toward a Global Consensus* (Cambridge University Press, 2019) 152.

law; it also fits perfectly with the nature of civil remedies, which seek to replicate a material entitlement in the form of a court order.[9] Evaluating a patent's inventive contribution is a familiar exercise for patent courts, so placing this inquiry at the heart of the proportionality test adapts it to their expertise and makes it easier to apply, at least relative to an open-ended balancing test. And it makes the test's outcome more predictable for litigants, because the assessment of technical importance lends itself to the formulation of an objectivised test, whereas determination of the point where one set of interests 'substantially outweighs' another does not.

The book's second key contribution is that it makes a proposal for what a proportionality test based on the commensurability principle might look like. As outlined in chapter six, such a test would apply in three sets of cases: overreach; abuse; and conflicts with third-party rights. The element that is likely to see most application in practice is overreach. It is effectively a translation of the commensurability principle into a legal test that asks three questions: how important is the invention relative to the technology to which the injunction would extend? How important is the invention in absolute terms? How much time does the defendant need to cease infringement? Armed with these questions, I believe the European patent judiciary can address an old problem in patent law that nevertheless has such salience today that it can no longer be ignored: component patents. The remaining issues – abuse and conflicts with third-party rights – are resolved through the other two elements of the proportionality test. Some form of check on litigation misconduct that exploits the complexities of the patent system is long overdue in Europe and I think the proportionality test offers courts the tools they need to perform it. Accommodation of third-party rights during patent enforcement is a necessary consequence of embedding patents in the constitutional architecture of the European Union and the ever-increasing penetration of technology into our daily lives.

What is gained and what is lost if proportionality were applied along the lines proposed here? Supporters of the liberal view as defined above might object that by restricting the proportionality test to an exhaustive list of three relatively narrow case types, the test loses the very flexibility that allows it to perform its function of a general safety valve.[10] But flexibility carries a cost for courts and litigants. It leaves to courts the decision when to use it and, given the multitude of potentially relevant factors and the difficulty of properly appraising them, that is no enviable situation to be in. For their part, litigants hardly know what to plead in support of their proportionality defence and risk being surprised should courts

[9] On this latter point, important work was done by a Dutch scholar of my generation who sadly passed away much too young. See T Nuninga, *Recht, plicht, remedie of: de belofte van de norm* (Wolters Kluwer, 2022) 34 (arguing that a private law remedy cannot compel the defendant to act beyond the legal duty owed to the plaintiff).

[10] A Ohly, 'Injunctions in the UPC and the Principle of Proportionality' (2022) 5 *Stockholm Intellectual Property Law Review* 58, 65.

decide to take up this or that circumstance to stay the injunction. The result is either unpredictable outcomes in a substantial number of cases, as in the USA, or a threshold for application so high that it practically makes proportionality a dead letter, as in Europe today. Neither outcome is desirable, especially if one agrees with Justice Kennedy in his famous concurrence that 'many' patent cases today 'present considerations quite unlike earlier cases'.[11] As noted in chapter three, it is very difficult to prove that claim, but there is likely some truth to it and a tentative consensus on this point seems to be emerging.[12] If we believe that the automatic injunction rule poses problems in 'many' cases, as per Justice Kennedy, or even with some regularity, then what good is a solution that applies only exceptionally?[13] A clearly delineated – if admittedly more narrow – proportionality test has the potential for more regular application because it sets boundaries to patent exclusivity that make manageable their discernment by parties and their enforcement by courts. Viewed in this way, a trimmed down proportionality test has the best chance of navigating the clash between traditional remedies and the modern world for which the *Fen Tigers* case stands. Certainly if coupled with traditional safeguards for cases of extreme hardship, it seems hard to think of cases falling outside its scope where good grounds exist to limit injunctive relief. And even if some potentially problematic cases remain, that is probably a price worth paying for the legal certainty and increased application that a circumscribed proportionality test can offer.

Perhaps it is folly to believe that Dürer – or anyone else – could ever draw a perfect rhinoceros. In fact, his woodcut went through several states and printings, each adding or omitting some detail. A similar process awaits the proportionality test. With the benefit of the pioneering scholarship that first coined proportionality in patent law, as well as the initial court decisions that grappled with it and the elaborate debate that preceded the reform of the GPA, my aim has been to move beyond the first sketches to a charted test. But we are still in the early stages. Though we cannot say what it will look like eventually, scholars, courts and other stakeholders will chisel and carve at our rhinoceros, each adding their own glosses. As they do so, the rhinoceros will come alive, and leave its mark on the European law of patents.

[11] *eBay Inc v MercExchange LLC* 547 US 388, 396 (2006) (Kennedy J concurring).

[12] See, eg the statements by the German Federal Parliament on the 'increasing complexity of many products' in the Proposed Bill (*Gesetzentwurf: Entwurf eines Zweiten Gesetzes zur Vereinfachung und Modernisierung des Patentrechts*) of 31 January 2021, BT-Drs 19/25821, 54; and, in the wake of the GPA reform, statements to similar effects by representatives of the Dutch and French governments: Dutch Minister of Economic Affairs and Climate, Letter of 20 June 2022, DGBI-I&K / 22257631; Assemblée Nationale, Rep min no 4621 JOAN 16 May 2023, p 4467 (Christophe Blanchet).

[13] Ohly (n 10) 62 ('[The entitlement to an injunction] is central, and should only be dislodged in exceptional cases').

POSTSCRIPT: A SIGN OF THINGS TO COME?

As was noted repeatedly in this book, the Unified Patent Court (UPC) will likely become Europe's pre-eminent patent law authority. After the manuscript was finished, but before the book went to press, the UPC issued its first decisions. One of these has been sufficiently important to warrant the inclusion of this postscript.[1] The case concerned machines for the rapid quantification of proteins and DNA-sequences in biological materials and the asserted patent disclosed a method that enabled the simultaneous detection of a (much) larger number of analytes than had previously been possible. Although at issue was a preliminary, not permanent, injunction the decision nevertheless contains several noteworthy considerations that may yet foreshadow the UPC's application of the proportionality test.

Article 62(2) of the Agreement on a Unified Patent Court (UPCA) provides that, when deciding on the grant of a preliminary injunction, the UPC has the discretion to weigh up the interests of the parties and particularly the potential harm for either of the parties resulting from the granting or the refusal of the injunction. Naturally, then, the balance of interests took centre stage in the decision. The court ultimately concluded the parties' threatened harms formed something of a mirror image: the patentee would likely suffer long-term loss of customers if infringement were permitted to continue, while the loss of business opportunities suffered by the infringer if enjoined would be hard to reverse even if the injunction were later lifted.[2] On balance, the court found that the patentee's interest in not having its rights infringed outweighed the defendant's interests (at VII.2). It did so even though one of the claimants was a non-practicing entity (NPE) and held that licensors, too, can suffer 'harm … with long-term consequences' from patent infringement (at VIII).[3]

In my view, this outcome is a perfect illustration of the argument in Section 2.3 and elsewhere in this book that we should be cautious to interpret proportionality as a 'broad-scope, high threshold'-balancing test. The argument that NPE status 'in itself has no significance' for the entitlement to an injunction will be all the

[1] Munich Local Division, *10x Genomics, Inc v NanoString (no.1)* (UPC CFI 2/2023), Zigann, Pichlmaier, Kupecz, Enderlin (19 September 2023).

[2] These considerations are reminiscent of the questions typically addressed by US courts when dealing with markets that are not easily contested, as outlined in Section 4.4.2.2. of this book.

[3] This finding departs from national practice, where courts have held that non-practicing entities' interest in an injunction is not sufficiently urgent to warrant a preliminary injunction (but in the context of standard-essential patents): GH The Hague 17 March 2020, ECLI:NL:GHDHA:2020:711 (*Sisvel v Xiaomi*), para 4.3; Tribunal Judiciaire de Paris 20 January 2020, 19/60318 *IPCom v Lenovo*, 16.

more compelling in the context of a permanent injunction, just like the court's implied finding that infringement will harm *any* patentee in a manner that is difficult to quantify. If this is accepted – as I think it should be: Section 6.1 – it will not be easy to argue the infringer's harm nevertheless outweighs that suffered by the patentee, much less to define a workable standard to make that determination. The court could hardly have been more meticulous in its assessment of the various harms that the injunction or lack thereof might cause and still the decision to grant the injunction ultimately came down to a judgment call. I believe that outcome is inevitable, and the judgment call will not be made easier if it is to be made by reference to the patent's value, the function(s) of the patent system, or hardship not warranted by the right to exclude.

However, the decision also shows us a viable alternative. When addressing NanoString's proportionality defence, the UPC seemed particularly receptive to the argument that the patent in suit was a component patent. It rejected NanoString's arguments because there was no showing (i) that the patented technology was subordinate to NanoString's own innovative technology in the infringing device; and (ii) that a design-around on short notice was not possible. Regardless of whether these findings were correct, the court certainly raised the right questions. Section 6.3 presents a detailed argument that overreach should be the heart of the proportionality test and that it revolves around these very issues. Significant investments in infringing technology cannot be the determining factor for the proportionality test, as the UPC aptly noted.[4] Instead, what matters is whether the injunction would deprive the infringer of access to its own non-infringing technology, protected by Article 16 Charter of Fundamental Rights and the safeguards in Article 3(2) of Directive 2004/48/EC (the Enforcement Directive). What matters, in other words, is whether the injunction would effectively extend patent exclusivity far beyond the patentee's inventive contribution to the art. Not hardships, but the principle of commensurate scope should guide the proportionality analysis. The UPC's first-ever injunction decision in *inter partes* proceedings holds out a hopeful prospect of future developments in that direction.

[4] See Section 6.2.1 and, for an oft-cited US precedent, *Windsurfing Int'l Inc v AMF Inc* 782 F2d 995, 1003, n12 (Fed Cir 1986).

ANNEX I: OVERVIEW OF POSITION PAPERS SUBMITTED DURING THE REFORM OF THE GERMAN PATENT ACT

Author	Position on discussion proposal	Position on draft bill
3M Deutschland GmbH	–	22 September 2020
AbbVie Deutschland GmbH	–	22 September 2020
ACT | The App Association	10 March 2020	23 September 2020
BASF Plant Science	–	18 September 2020
Bayer Intellectual Property GmbH	16 March 2020 (confidential)	21 September 2020
Bundesverband Deutscher Pflanzenzüchter (BDP)	–	22 September 2020
Bundesverband Deutscher Patentanwälte	10 March 2020	23 September 2020
Bundesrechtsanwaltkammer	1 February 2020	21 September 2020
BIO Deutschland eV	–	23 September 2020
Bitkom	10 March 2020	22 September 2020
Bundesverbands IT-Mittelstand (BITMi)	10 March 2020	22 September 2020 (with Patentverein)
Bundesverband mittelständische Wirtschaft (BVMW)	1 March 2020	22 September 2020
Canon Inc	10 March 2020	–
Deutsche Aktionsgesellschaft Bildung-Erfindung-Innovation (DABEI)	10 March 2020	22 September 2020
Deutscher Anwaltverein	–	23 September 2020
Deutsche Erfinderverband	6 March 2020	21 September 2020
Deutsche Telekom	16 March 2020 (confidential); 9 March 2020	23 September 2020

(continued)

(Continued)

Author	Position on discussion proposal	Position on draft bill
EPI (Patent attorneys)		5 October 2020
Ericsson GmbH	10 March 2020	23 September 2020
Die Familienunternehmer	–	23 September 2020
Fischer Group	–	2 October 2020
Fair Standards Alliance	10 March 2020	22 September 2020
Fraunhofer Gesellschaft	16 March 2020 (confidential)	1 September 2020 (confidential)
Prof Dr Heinz Goddar	10 March 2020	–
Deutsche Vereinigung für gewerblichen Rechtsschutz (GRUR)	16 March 2020	29 September 2020
Honda Motor Co Ltd	10 March 2020	–
IP Europe	10 March 2020	23 September 2020
IP2Innovate	10 March 2020	22 September 2020
Japan Automobile Manufacturer's Association (JAMA)	–	23 September 2020
Japan Business Machine and Information System Industries Association	10 March 2020	–
Mr Jost Lempert	–	2 October 2020
NVIDIA	9 March 2020	23 September 2020
Max-Planck-Institut	11 March 2020	–
Prof. Dr Ansgar Ohly	10 March 2020	23 September 2020
Patentanwaltskammer	9 March 2020	23 September 2020
Patentverein	1 February 2020	22 September 2020 (with BITMi)
Pro Generika	9 February 2020	23 September 2023
Sanofi-Aventis Deutschland	16 March 2020 (confidential); 9 March 2020	23 September 2023
Siemens	2 March 2020	22 September 2020
Dr Martin Stierle	–	23 September 2020
Prof. Dr Winfried Tilmann	–	2 September 2020
Verband des Automobilindustrie (VDA)	28 February 2020	22 September 2020

(continued)

(Continued)

Author	Position on discussion proposal	Position on draft bill
Verband der Chemischen Industrie	10 March 2020	22 September 2020
Vodafone	10 March 2020	–
VPP	9 March 2020	22 September 2020
Ms Renate Weisse	27 January 2020	–
Zentralverband Elektrotechnik- und Elektronikindustrie (ZVEI)	–	23 September 2020

All papers can be accessed via https://www.bmj.de/SharedDocs/Gesetzgebungsverfahren/DE/PatMoG_2.html.

ANNEX II: OVERVIEW OF US DISTRICT COURT CASES WHERE A PERMANENT INJUNCTION WAS DENIED, 2006–19

Case name	Court, date, citation	Patentee status (if known)	Irreparable harm	Balance of hardships	Public interest	Ongoing royalty (if included)
z4 Technologies Inc v Microsoft Corporation	ED Tex 14 June 2006, 434 FSupp2d 437	Non-practising entity	No: absence of causal nexus	Favours infringer	Favours infringer	Infringer ordered to file quarterly reports
Finisar Corporation v The DirecTV Group Inc	ED Tex 7 July 2006, 2006 WL 2037617		N/A	N/A	N/A	Court-set without upward adjustment
Paice LLP v Toyota Motors Corp[a]	ED Tex 16 August 2006, 2006 WL 2385139	Non-practising entity	No: willingness to accept licence	Favours infringer	Neutral	
Voda v Cordis Corporation[b]	WD Olka 5 September 2006, 2006 WL 2570614	Licensor to competitors	No: infringement does not affect patentee's market position	N/A	N/A	Infringer ordered to file quarterly reports
Sundance Inc v De Monte Fabricating	ED Mich 4 January 2007, n/a	Licensor to competitors	No: infringement does not affect patentee's market position	Favours infringer	Favours infringer	
IMX Inc v Lendingtree LLC	D Del 10 January 2007, 469 FSupp2d 203	Non-practising entity	No: willingness to accept licence	Neutral	Neutral	Determination deferred to subsequent proceedings

(continued)

(Continued)

Case name	Court, date, citation	Patentee status (if known)	Irreparable harm	Balance of hardships	Public interest	Ongoing royalty (if included)
Exergen Corporation v Wal-Mart Stores Inc	D Mass 12 January 2007, n/a		No: infringement does not affect patentee's market position	Neutral	N/A	
Amado v Microsoft[c]	CD Cal 13 March 2007, n/a	Non-practising entity	No: absence of causal nexus	N/A	Favours infringer	
Praxair Inc v ATMI Inc	D Del 27 March 2007, 479 FSupp2d 440	Competitor	No: infringement does not affect patentee's market position	N/A	N/A	
Heuft Systemtechnik GmbH v Industrial Dynamics Co Ltd	CD Cal 8 May 2007, n/a	Non-practising entity	No: infringement does not affect patentee's market position	Favours infringer	N/A	
MercExchange LLC v eBay Inc	ED Va 1 August 2007, 500 FSupp2d 556	Non-practising entity	No: willingness to accept licence	Neutral	Favours infringer	Determination deferred to subsequent proceedings
Respironics Inc v Invacare Corp	WD Pa 7 January 2008, 2008 WL 111983	Competitor	No: infringer unlikely to enter or remain on market	Favours infringer	Favours infringer	
ResQNetcom Inc v Lansa Inc	SD NY 1 February 2008, 533 FSupp2d 397		No: infringement does not affect patentee's market position	N/A	N/A	Court-set without upward adjustment
Ecolab Inc v FMC Corp[d]	D Minn 22 February 2008, n/a		N/A	N/A	N/A	

Avid Identifications Systems v Phillips Electronics North America Corp	ED Tex 25 March 2008, 2008 WL 2945476		Unclean hands bar injunction claim	N/A	N/A	Court orders supple-mental briefing
ORION IP LLC v Mercedes-Benz USA LLC	ED Tex 28 March 2008, 2008 WL 8856865	Non-practising entity	No: willingness to accept licence	N/A	N/A	Court-set without upward adjustment
Grantley Patent Holding Ltd v Clear Channel Communications Inc	ED Tex 10 June 2008, n/a		N/A	N/A	N/A	
Advanced Cardiovascular Systems Inc v Medtronic Vascular Inc	D Del 26 September 26, 579 FSupp2d 554	Competitor	No: infringement does not affect patentee's market position	N/A	Favours infringer	
American Calcar Inc v American Honda Motor Co	SD Cal 18 November 2008, 2008 WL 11337489		No: infringement does not affect patentee's market position	Favours infringer	Favours infringer	
Telcordia Tech Inc v CISCO Systems Inc	D Del 6 January 2009, 592 FSupp2d 727	Non-practising entity	No: willingness to accept licence	N/A	N/A	Court orders party negotiations
Hynix Semiconductor Inc v Rambus Inc	ND Cal 23 February 2009, 609 FSupp2d 951	Competitor	No: infringement does not affect patentee's market position	Favours infringer	Favours patentee	Court orders briefing on party preferences

(continued)

(Continued)

Case name	Court, date, citation	Patentee status (if known)	Irreparable harm	Balance of hardships	Public interest	Ongoing royalty (if included)
Bard Periphera v WL Gore & Associates[e]	D Ariz 31 March 2009, 2009 WL 920300	Competitor	No: horse has left the barn	N/A	Favours infringer	Court orders briefing on party preferences
Medtronic Sofamor Danek USA Inc v Globus Medical Inc	ED Pa 16 July 2009, 637 FSupp2d 290	Competitor	No: infringement does not affect patentee's market position	N/A	N/A	
Creative Internet Advertising Corporation v Yahoo! Inc	ED Tex 9 Decembet 2009, 674 FSupp2d 847		N/A	N/A	N/A	Court-set with upward adjustment
IGT v Bally Gaming International Inc	D Del 22 December 2009, 675 FSupp2d 487	Competitor	No: horse has left the barn	N/A	N/A	
Emcore Corp v Optium Corp	WD Pa 15 January 2010, 2010 WL 235126	Competitor	No: infringer unlikely to enter or remain on market	Neutral	Neutral	
Presidio Components Inc v American Technical Ceramics Corp[f]	SD Cal 13 April 2010, 723 FSupp2d 1284	Competitor	No: infringement does not affect patentee's market position	Favours patentee	Favours infringer	Court orders briefing on party preferences
Ricoh Co Ltd v Quanta Computer Inc	WD Wis 19 April 2010, 2010 WL 1607908	Formerly prac-tising entity	No: willingness to accept licence	Favours infringer	Neutral	Court orders party negotiations

Johnson & Johnson Vision Care Inc v CIBA Vision Corporation	MD Fla 27 April 2010, 712 FSupp2d 1285	Competitor	No: willingness to accept licence	Favours patentee	Favours infringer	Court orders supplemental briefing
Humanscale Corporation v CompX International Inc	ED Va 29 April 2010, 2010 WL 1779963	Competitor	No: infringement does not affect patentee's market position	Favours infringer	Neutral	Denied
Tyco Healthcare Group LP v Applied Medical Resources Corp	ED Tex 17 May 2010, 2010 WL 11469881	Competitor	No: infringer unlikely to enter or remain on market	Neutral	Favours patentee	Court orders party negotiations
LaserDynamics Inc v Quanta Computer Inc	ED Tex 22 June 2010, n/a	Non-practising entity	No: willingness to accept licence	Favours infringer	Neutral	Court orders supplemental briefing
***In re: Rosuvastatin Calcium Patent Litigation	D Del 13 July 2010, n/a	Competitor	N/A	N/A	N/A	
Cordance Corporation v Amazoncom Inc	D Del 23 July 2010, 730 FSupp2d 333	Competitor	No: infringement does not affect patentee's market position	Neutral	Favours patentee	Determination stayed pending appeal
Dow Chemical Company v Nova Chemicals Corp	D Del 30 July 2010, 2010 WL 3083023	Competitor	No: infringement does not affect patentee's market position	Favours infringer	Favours infringer	

(continued)

(Continued)

Case name	Court, date, citation	Patentee status (if known)	Irreparable harm	Balance of hardships	Public interest	Ongoing royalty (if included)
***Alcon Manufacturing Ltd v Teva Pharmaceuticals USA Inc	D Del 5 August 2010, 2010 WL 3081327	Competitor	No: infringer unlikely to enter or remain on market	Neutral	Favours infringer	
Soverain Software LLC v CDW Corp	ED Tex 11 August 2010, 836 FSupp2d 462	Non-practising entity	No: willingness to accept licence	Favours infringer	Favours infringer	Court-set with upward adjustment
***Altana Pharma AG v Teva Pharmaceuticals USA Inc	D NJ 13 August 2010, n/a	Competitor	N/A	N/A	N/A	
Robert Bosch LLC v Pylon Manufacturing Corp[g]	D Del 3 November 2010, 748 FSupp2d 383	Competitor	No: infringement does not affect patentee's market position	N/A	N/A	
Insituform Technologies Inc v AMerik Supplies Inc	ND Ga 4 January 2011, n/a	Licensor to competitors	No: willingness to accept licence	Favours infringer	Favours infringer	
Edwards Lifesciences AG v Corevalve Inc[h]	D Del 7 February 2011, 2011 WL 446203	Competitor	No: horse has left the barn	Neutral	Neutral	
Douglas Dynamics LLC v Buyers Products Co[i]	WD Wis 25 February 2011, n/a	Competitor	No: infringement does not affect patentee's market position	Neutral	Favours infringer	Court orders party negotiations

***Cephalon Inc v Watson Pharmaceuticals Inc	D Del 24 March 2011, n/a	Competitor	N/A	N/A	N/A	
WhitServe LLC v Computer Packages Inc[j]	D Conn 39 March 2011, n/a	Competitor	No: infringement does not affect patentee's market position	N/A	N/A	
3D Systems Inc v Envisiontec Inc	ED Mich 25 April 2011, n/a		No: infringement does not affect patentee's market position	N/A	N/A	
***Alcon manufac-turing Ltd v Apotex Inc	SD Ind 23 March 2011, 790 FSupp2d 868	Competitor	N/A	N/A	N/A	
LG Electronics USA Inc v Whirlpool Corp	D Del 1 July 2011, 798 FSupp2d 541	Competitor	No: horse has left the barn	Neutral	Neutral	
SOITEC SA v MEMC Electronic Materials Inc	D Del 13 July 2011, 2011 WL 2748725	Competitor	No: horse has left the barn	N/A	N/A	Determination stayed pending appeal
Belden Technologies Inc v Superior Essex Inc	D Del 12 August 2011, 802 FSupp2d 555	Competitor	No: infringement does not affect patentee's market position	Favours infringer	Favours patentee	
Lighting Ballast Control LLC v Advance Transformer Co	ND Tex 26 August 2011, 814 FSupp2d 665	Competitor	No: injunction pre-empted by damages award	N/A	N/A	Future infringement covered by damages award

(continued)

(Continued)

Case name	Court, date, citation	Patentee status (if known)	Irreparable harm	Balance of hardships	Public interest	Ongoing royalty (if included)
Bennett Marine Inc v Lenco Marine Inc	SD Fla 29 September 2011, n/a	Competitor	No: absence of causal nexus	Favours infringer	Favours infringer	
Accentra Inc v Staples Inc	CD Cal 19 December 2011, 851 FSupp2d 1205	Competitor	No: infringer unlikely to enter or remain on market	Neutral	N/A	
Conceptus Inc v Hologic Inc	ND Cal 9 January 2012, 2012 WL 44064	Competitor	Yes: infringement harms the core of patentee's business	Favours infringer	Favours infringer	Determination deferred to subsequent proceedings
Medtronic Sofamor Danek USA v Nuvasive Inc	SD Cal 26 January 2012, 2012 WL 12868478	Competitor	N/A	N/A	Favours infringer	Court orders supplemental briefing
***Pronova BioPharma Norge AS v Teva Pharamceuticals USA Inc	D Del 29 May 2012, n/a	Competitor	N/A	N/A	N/A	
Black Rapid Inc v Yall Inc	WD Wash 14 June 2012, n/a		No: infringer unlikely to enter or remain on market	N/A	N/A	
National Oilwell Varco LP v Pason Systems USA	D Colo 18 June 2012, 2012 WL 2291154		No: infringer unlikely to enter or remain on market	Favours infringer	Neutral	

Apple Inc v Motorola Inc[k]	ND Ill 22 June 2012, 869 FSupp2d 901	Competitor	No: infringement does not affect patentee's market position	Favours infringer	Favours infringer	Denied
Fractus SA v Samsung Electronics Co	ED Tex 26 June 2012, 876 FSupp2d 802	Formerly practising entity	No: willingness to accept licence	Favours infringer	Favours infringer	Court orders party negotiations
Hypoxico Inc v Colorado Altitude	SD NY 28 August 2012, 2012 WL 3705006		No: infringer unlikely to enter or remain on market	N/A	N/A	
Apple Inc v Samsung Electronics Co[l]	ND Cal 17 December 2012, 909 FSupp2d 1147	Competitor	No: absence of causal nexus	Neutral	Favours infringer	
***Allergan Inc v Sandoz Inc	MD NC 24 January 2013, n/a	Competitor	N/A	N/A	N/A	
VirnetX Inc v Apple Inc	ED Tex 26 February 2013, 925 FSupp2d 816	Non-practising entity	No: willingness to accept licence	Favours infringer	N/A	Court orders party negotiations
Tyco Healthcare Group LP v Ethicon Endo-Surgery Inc	D Conn 28 March 2013, 936 FSupp2d 30	Competitor	No: willingness to accept licence	Neutral	Neutral	
Unicom Monitoring LLC v Cencom Inc	D NJ 19 April 2013, 2013 WL 1704300		No: infringer unlikely to enter or remain on market	N/A	N/A	Denied
WBIP LLC v Kohler Co[m]	D Mass 12 August 2013, n/a	Competitor	N/A	N/A	Favours infringer	Court orders party negotiations

(continued)

(Continued)

Case name	Court, date, citation	Patentee status (if known)	Irreparable harm	Balance of hardships	Public interest	Ongoing royalty (if included)
Cardsoft Inc v Verifone Holdings Inc	ED Tex 30 October 2013, 2013 WL 5862762	Formerly practising entity	No: willingness to accept licence	Favours infringer	Neutral	Court orders party negotiations
***Takeda Pharmaceutical Co v Handa Pharmaceuticals LLC	ND Cal 1 November 2013, n/a	Competitor	N/A	N/A	N/A	
XpertUniverse Inc v Cisco Systems	D Del 20 November 2013, 2013 WL 6118447	Non-practising entity	No: horse has left the barn	Neutral	Favours patentee	Denied
KFX Medical Corp v Arthrex Inc	SD Cal 18 February 2012, 2014 WL 11961953		No: infringer unlikely to enter or remain on market	Favours infringer	Favours infringer	Denied
Apple Inc v Samsung Electronics Co	ND Cal 6 March 2014, 2014 WL 976898	Competitor	No: absence of causal nexus	Neutral	Favours infringer	
DePuy Synthes Products Inc v Globus Medical Inc	D Del 25 March 2014, 2014 WL 12716474	Competitor	No: willingness to accept licence	Favours patentee	Favours patentee	Court-set with upward adjustment
***Eli Lilly and Co v Teva Parenteral Medicines Inc	SD Ind 31 March 2014, n/a	Competitor	N/A	N/A	N/A	

Carnegie Mellon University v Marvell Technology Group Ltd	WD Pa 31 March 2014, 2014 WL 1320154	University	No: absence of causal nexus	Favours infringer	Favours infringer	Court-set without upward adjustment
Apple Inc v Samsung Electronics Co[n]	ND Cal 27 August 2014, 2014 WL 7496140	Competitor	No: absence of causal nexus	Favours patentee	Favours patentee	
***United Therapeutics Corp v Sandoz Inc	D NJ 29 August 2014, n/a	Competitor	N/A	N/A	N/A	
Riverbed Technology Inc v Silver Peak Systems Inc	D Del 12 September 2014, 2014 WL 4695765	Competitor	No: absence of causal nexus	Favours patentee	Favours patentee	
Power Integrations Inc v Fairchild Semiconductor International Inc	ND Cal 12 February 2015, 2015 WL 604582	Competitor	No: absence of causal nexus	N/A	N/A	
Server Technology Inc v Schneider Electric IT Corp	D Nev 31 March 2015, 2015 WL 1505654	Competitor	Yes: continued infringement will cause patentee to lose customers	Neutral	Favours infringer	Court-set with upward adjustment
Ameritox Ltd v Millennium Health LLC	WD Wis 19 June 2015, 2015 WL 3825499	Competitor	No: infringer unlikely to enter or remain on market	Favours infringer	Favours infringer	

(continued)

(Continued)

Case name	Court, date, citation	Patentee status (if known)	Irreparable harm	Balance of hardships	Public interest	Ongoing royalty (if included)
***Endo Pharmaceuticals Inc v Watson Laboratories Inc	ED Tex 22 October 2015, n/a	Competitor	N/A	N/A	N/A	
Nichia Corporation v Everlight Electronics Co[o]	ED Tex 25 January 2016, 2016 WL 310142	Competitor	No: infringement does not affect patentee's market position	N/A	N/A	
EMC Corp v Zerto Inc	D Del 31 March 2016, 2016 WL 1291757	Competitor	Yes: infringer markets patented features as advantages of its product	Favours infringer	Favours patentee	Court orders party negotiations
Texas Advanced Optoelectronic Solutions Inc v Intersil Corp[p]	ED Tex 22 April 2016, 2016 WL 1615741	Competitor	No: willingness to accept licence	Favours infringer	Favours infringer	Court orders party negotiations
Exergen Corp v KAZ USA Inc	D Mass 25 April 2016, n/a		No: infringer unlikely to enter or remain on market	N/A	N/A	
Cave Consulting Group LLC v OptumInsight Inc	ND Cal 7 September 2016, 2016 WL 4658979	Competitor	No: infringement does not affect patentee's market position	Favours infringer	Favours patentee	Determination stayed pending appeal
Genband US LLC v Metaswitch Networks Ltd[q]	ED Tex 9 September 2016, 211 FSupp3d 858		No: absence of causal nexus	N/A	N/A	

Bayer Pharma AG v Watson Laboratories Inc	D Del 28 December 2016, 2016 WL 7468172	Competitor	No: infringer unlikely to enter or remain on market	Favours patentee	Favours patentee	
Omega Patents LLC v Calamp Corp	MD Fla 5 April 2017, n/a	Formerly practising entity	No: willingness to accept licence	N/A	Favours infringer	Determination deferred to subsequent proceedings
Kaneka Corporation v SKC Kolon PI Inc	CD Cal 8 December 2017, 2017 WL 6343537	Competitor	No: infringer unlikely to enter or remain on market	N/A	N/A	
TCL Communication Technology Holdings Ltd v Telefonaktienbolaget LM Ericsson	CD Cal 22 December 2017, n/a	Licensor to competitors	N/A	N/A	N/A	Court-set without upward adjustment (SEP)
Huzu LLC v Nine Line Apparel Inc	SD Ga 1 March 2018, n/a		No: infringer unlikely to enter or remain on market	N/A	N/A	Future infringement covered by damages award
Verinata Health Inc v Ariosa Diagnostics Inc[r]	ND Cal 19 July 2018, 329 FSupp3d 1070	Licensor to competitors	No: infringement does not affect patentee's market position	Neutral	Neutral	Determination stayed pending appeal
ABS Global Inc v Inguran LLC	WD Wis 8 August 2018, n/a		N/A	N/A	N/A	Court-set without upward adjustment
EcoServices LLC v Certified Aviation Services LLC	CD Cal 26 October 2018, 340 FSupp3d 1004	Competitor	No: absence of causal nexus	Favours patentee	Favours patentee	Court orders party negotiations

(continued)

(Continued)

Case name	Court, date, citation	Patentee status (if known)	Irreparable harm	Balance of hardships	Public interest	Ongoing royalty (if included)
LF Centennial Ltd v Inovex Furnishings Corp	CD Cal 2 October 2019, 2019 WL 6655258	Licensor to competitors	No: infringement does not affect patentee's market position	N/A	N/A	
BASF Plant Science LP v Commonwealth Scientific and Industrial Research Organization[s]	ED Va 20 December 2019, 2019 WL 8108116	Competitor	No: infringement does not affect patentee's market position	Favours infringer	Favours infringer	Court-set with upward adjustment

[a]Injunction outcome affirmed in part on appeal: 504 F3d 1293.
[b]Injunction outcome affirmed on appeal: 536 F3d 1311.
[c]Injunction outcome affirmed on appeal: 517 F3d 1353.
[d]Injunction outcome reversed on appeal: 569 F3d 1335.
[e]Injunction outcome affirmed on appeal: 670 F3d 1171.
[f]Injunction outcome reversed on appeal: 702 F3d 1351.
[g]Injunction outcome reversed on appeal: 659 F3d 1142.
[h]Injunction outcome reversed on appeal: 699 F3d 1305.
[i]Injunction outcome reversed on appeal: 717 F3d 1336.
[j]Injunction outcome reversed on appeal: 694 F3d 10.
[k]Injunction outcome affirmed on appeal: 757 F3d 1286.
[l]Injunction outcome reversed on appeal: 735 F3d 1352.
[m]Injunction outcome reversed on appeal: 829 F3d 1317.
[n]Injunction outcome reversed on appeal: 809 F3d 633.
[o]Injunction outcome affirmed on appeal: 855 F3d 1328.
[p]Injunction outcome reversed on appeal: 895 F3d 1304.
[q]Injunction outcome reversed on appeal: 861 F3d 1378.
[r]Injunction outcome affirmed on appeal: 2020 WL 1970571.
[s]Injunction outcome affirmed on appeal: 28 F4th 1247.

BIBLIOGRAPHY

Academic Sources

Arnold, R, 'Injunctions in European Law: Judicial Reflections' in J Contreras and M Husovec (eds), *Injunctions in Patent Law: Trans-Atlantic Dialogues on Flexibility and Tailoring* (Cambridge University Press, 2022).

Baker, S, 'Can the Courts Rescue Us from the Patent Crisis?' (2010) 88 *Texas Law Review* 593.

Barnett, J, 'Has the Academy Led Patent Law Astray?' (2017) 32 *Berkeley Technology Law Journal* 1313.

Barnett, J, *Innovators, Firms, and Markets: The Organizational Logic of Intellectual Property* (Oxford University Press, 2021).

Barnett, J, 'Antitrust Mercantilism: The Strategic Devaluation of Intellectual Property Rights in Wireless Markets' (2023) 37 *Berkeley Technology Law Journal* 259.

Bechtold, S, Frankenreiter, J and Klerman, DM, 'Forum Selling Abroad' (2018) 92 *Southern California Law Review* 487.

Biagioli, M, 'Weighing Intellectual Property: Can We Balance the Social Costs and Benefits of Patenting?' (2019) 57 *History of Science* 140.

Birks, P, 'Three Kinds of Objection to Discretionary Remedialism' (2000) 29 *Western Australian Law Review* 1.

Blok, P, 'A Harmonized Approach to Prohibitory Injunctions: Reconsidering Article 12 of the Enforcement Directive' (2016) 11 *Journal of Intellectual Property Law & Practice* 56.

Borghetti, J-S, Nikolic, I and Petit, N, 'FRAND Licensing Levels under EU Law' (2021) *European Competition Journal* 1.

Burk, D and Lemley, M, *The Patent Crisis and How the Courts Can Solve It* (University of Chicago Press, 2009).

Cafaggi, F and Iamiceli, P, 'The Principles of Effectiveness, Proportionality and Dissuasiveness in the Enforcement of EU Consumer Law: The Impact of a Triad on the Choice of Civil Remedies and Administrative Sanctions' (2017) 25 *European Review of Private Law* 575.

Contreras, J, 'The Anticommons at 20: Concerns for Research Continue' (2018) 361 *Science* 335.

Contreras, J, 'Much Ado about Hold-Up' (2019) *University of Illinois Law Review* 875.

Contreras, J and Husovec, M, 'Issuing and Tailoring Patent Injunctions: A Cross-Jurisdictional Comparison and Synthesis' in J Contreras and M Husovec (eds), *Injunctions in Patent Law: Trans-Atlantic Dialogues on Flexibility and Tailoring* (Cambridge University Press, 2022).

Correa, C, *Trade Related Aspects of Intellectual Property Rights: A Commentary on the TRIPS Agreement*, 2nd edn (Oxford University Press, 2020).

Cotter, T, 'Patent Holdup, Patent Remedies, and Antitrust Responses' (2009) 34 *Journal of Corporation Law* 1151.

Cotter, T, 'On the Economics of Injunctions in Patent Cases' (2019) 11 *Zeitschrift für Geistiges Eigentum* 293.

Cotter, T et al, 'Reasonable Royalties' in CB Biddle et al (eds), *Patent Remedies and Complex Products: Toward a Global Consensus* (Cambridge University Press, 2019).

Cotter, T, Hovenkamp, E and Siebrasse, N, 'Demystifying Patent Holdup' (2019) *Washington & Lee Law Review* 1501.

Dijkman, L, 'Does the Injunction Gap Violate Implementers' Fair Trial Rights under the ECHR?' (2021) 70 *Gewerblicher Rechtsschutz und Urheberrecht International* 215.

Dijkman, L, 'Does the Injunction Gap Violate Implementer's Fair Trial Rights under the Charter?' [2022] *Gewerblicher Rechtsschutz und Urheberrecht* 857.

Dinwoodie, G and Dreyfuss, R, 'Injunctive Relief in Patent Law under TRIPS' in J Contreras and M Husovec (eds), *Injunctions in Patent Law: Trans-Atlantic Dialogues on Flexibility and Tailoring* (Cambridge University Press, 2022).

Dongen, L van, 'Proportionality and Flexibilities in Final Injunctive Relief' in L Desaunettes-Barbero et al (eds), *The Unitary Patent Package & Unified Patent Court: Problems, Possible Improvements and Alternatives* (Ledizioni 2023).

Drahos, P, *A Philosophy of Intellectual Property* (Dartmouth, 1996).

Drahos, P, 'Regulating Property: Problems of Efficiency and Regulatory Capture' in J Braithwaite et al (eds), *Regulating Law* (Oxford University Press, 2004).

Drahos, P, *The Global Governance of Knowledge: Patent Offices and Their Clients* (Cambridge University Press, 2010).

Drahos, P and Braithwaite, J, *Information Feudalism: Who Owns the Knowledge Economy?* (Earthscan, 2002).

Druedahl, L et al, 'A Qualitative Study of Biosimilar Manufacturer and Regulator Perceptions on Intellectual Property and Abbreviated Approval Pathways' (2020) 38 *Nature Biotechnology* 1253.

Epstein, R, 'The Disintegration of Intellectual Property – A Classical Liberal Response to a Premature Obituary' (2010) 62 *Stanford Law Review* 455.

Everson, M and Correia Goncalves, R, 'Article 16' in S Peers et al (eds), *The EU Charter of Fundamental Rights: A Commentary*, 2nd edn (Hart Publishing, 2014).

Foss-Solbrekk, K, 'The Divisional Game: Using Procedural Rights to Impede Generic/Biosimilar Market Entry' (2022) 53 *International Review of Intellectual Property and Competition Law* 1007.

Fusco, S, 'Markets and Patent Enforcement: A Comparative Investigation of Non-practicing Entities in the United States and Europe' (2014) 20 *Michigan Telecommunications and Technology Law Review* 439.

Galetovic, A, Haber, S and Zaretzki, L, 'An Estimate of the Average Cumulative Royalty Yield in the World Mobile Phone Industry: Theory, Measurement and Results' (2018) 42 *Telecommunications Policy* 263.

García Perez, R, 'Injunctions in Intellectual Property Cases: What Is the Power of the Courts?' (2016) *Intellectual Property Quarterly* 87.

Geradin, D, 'European Union Competition Law, Intellectual Property Law and Standardization' in J Contreras (ed), *The Cambridge Handbook of Technical Standardization Law Competition, Antitrust, and Patents* (Cambridge University Press, 2018).

Geradin, D, Layne-Farrar, A and Padilla, J, 'Elves or Trolls? The Role of Nonpracticing Patent Owners in the Innovation Economy' (2012) 21 *Industrial and Corporate Change* 73.

Gergen, M, Golden, J and Smith, H, 'The Supreme Court's Accidental Revolution? The Test for Permanent Injunctions' (2012) 112 *Columbia Law Review* 203.

Gill-Pedro, E, 'Freedom to Conduct Business in EU Law: Freedom from Interference or Freedom from Domination?' (2017) 9 *European Journal of Legal Studies* 103.

Gold, R, 'The Fall of the Innovation Empire and Its Possible Rise through Open Science' (2021) 50 *Research Policy* 104226.

Golden, J, '"Patent Trolls" and Patent Remedies' (2007) 85 *Texas Law Review* 2111.

Golden, J, 'Principles for Patent Remedies' (2010) 88 *Texas Law Review* 505.

Golden, J, 'Litigation in the Middle: The Context of Patent-Infringement Injunctions' (2014) 92 *Texas Law Review* 2075.

Golden, J, 'United States' in J Contreras and M Husovec (eds), *Injunctions in Patent Law: Trans-Atlantic Dialogues on Flexibility and Tailoring* (Cambridge University Press, 2022).

Goold, P, *IP Accidents: Negligence Liability in Intellectual Property* (Cambridge University Press, 2022).

Gorbatyuk, A and Kovács, A, 'Patent Notice (Failure) in the Era of Patent Monetization' (2022) 53 *International Review of Intellectual Property and Competition Law* 506.

Grabinski, K, 'Injunctive Relief and Proportionality in Case of a Public Interest in the Use of a Patent: Different Ways – Same Result' [2021] *Gewerblicher Rechtsschutz und Urheberrecht* 200.

Granstrand, O, 'Evergreening and Patent Cliff Hangers' (2019) 2 *Stockholm Intellectual Property Law Review* 4.

Gupta, K and Effraimidis, G, 'An Empirical Examination of Impact' (2019) 64 *The Antitrust Bulletin* 151.

Harbo, T-I, 'The Function of the Proportionality Principle in EU Law' (2010) 16 *European Law Journal* 158.

Harhoff, D and Wagner, S, 'The Duration of Patent Examination at the European Patent Office' (2009) 55 *Management Science* 1969.

Hatori, T, 'Restriction to an Injunctive Relief in Patent Infringement Proceedings under the Japanese Patent Act' (Master thesis, Max Planck Institute for Innovation and Competition, 2020).

Heiden, B and Petit, N, 'Patent "Trespass" and the Royalty Gap: Exploring the Nature and Impact of Patent Holdout' (2017) 34 *Santa Clara High Technology Law Journal* 179.

Heller, M and Eisenberg, R, 'Can Patents Deter Innovation? The Anticommons in Biomedical Research' (1998) 280 *Science* 698.

Hilgartner, S, 'Intellectual Property and the Politics of Emerging Technology: Inventors, Citizens, and Powers to Shape the Future' (2008) 84 *Chicago-Kent Law Review* 197.

Hilty, R, 'Legal Remedies against Abuse, Misuse and Other Forms of Inappropriate Conducts of IP Right Holders' in R Hilty and K Liu (eds), *Compulsory Licensing: Practical Experiences and Ways Forward* (Springer, 2015).

Hoffmann, F, 'Der Ausgleichsanspruch Im Patentrecht: Die Leistungsgerechte Monetarisierung Eines Drohpotentials' [2022] *Gewerblicher Rechtsschutz und Urheberrecht* 286.

Hoffmann, H, 'Article 47' in S Peers et al (eds), *The EU Charter of Fundamental Rights: A Commentary*, 2nd edn (Hart Publishing, 2021).

Hofmann, F, *Der Unterlassungsanspruch als Rechtsbehelf* (Mohr Siebeck, 2017).

Holte, R and Seaman, C, 'Patent Injunctions on Appeal: An Empirical Study of the Federal Circuit's Application of eBay' (2017) 92 *Washington Law Review* 145.

Kieff, FS and Layne-Farrar, A, 'Incentive Effects from Different Approaches to Holdup Mitigation Surrounding Patent Remedies and Standard-Setting Organizations' (2013) 9 *Journal of Competition Law and Economics* 1091.

Lee, W and Melamed, AD, 'Breaking the Vicious Cycle of Patent Damages' (2016) 101 *Cornell Law Review* 385.

Leistner, M and Pless, V, 'European Union' in J Contreras and M Husovec (eds), *Injunctions in Patent Law: Trans-Atlantic Dialogues on Flexibility and Tailoring* (Cambridge University Press, 2022).

Lemley, M and McKenna, M, 'Scope' (2016) 57 *William & Mary Law Review* 2197.

Lemley, M and Melamed, AD, 'Missing the Forest for the Trolls' (2013) 113 *Columbia Law Review* 2117.

Lemley, M, Richardson, K and Oliver, E, 'The Patent Enforcement Iceberg' (2019) 97 *Texas Law Review* 801.

Lemley, M and Shapiro, C, 'Patent Holdup and Royalty Stacking' (2007) 85 *Texas Law Review* 1991.

Lenaerts, K, 'Limits on Limitations: The Essence of Fundamental Rights in the EU' (2019) 20 *German Law Journal* 779.

Léonard, A, 'Abuse of Rights in European Patent Law – Reconsidering the Principle of the Prohibition of Abuse of Rights as an Internal Correction Mechanism against Over-enforcement Practices by Right Holder' (Dissertation, KU Leuven, 2019).

Love, B et al, 'Patent Assertion Entities in Europe' in DD Sokol (ed), *Patent Assertion Entities and Competition Policy* (Cambridge University Press, 2017).

Mellulis, K-J, 'Zur Notwendigkeit und Sinnhaftigkeit von Beschränkungen des Patentrechts' [2016] *Mitteilungen der deutschen Patentanwälte* 433.

Merges, R, 'Contracting into Liability Rules: Intellectual Property Rights and Collective Rights Organizations' (1996) 84 *California Law Review* 1293.

Merges, R, *Justifying Intellectual Property* (Harvard University Press, 2011).

Merges, R and Nelson, R, 'On the Complex Economics of Patent Scope' (1990) 90 *Columbia Law Review* 839.

Mossoff, A, 'The Rise and Fall of the First American Patent Thicket: The Sewing Machine War of the 1850s' (2011) 53 *Arizona Law Review* 165.

Nieder, M, 'Eingeschränkter Unterlassungsanspruch im europäischen Patentrecht: Folgen auf der Abnehmerseite' [2023] *Gewerblicher Rechtsschutz und Urheberrecht* 995.

Nikolic, I, 'Are Patent Assertion Entities a Threat to Europe?' (2019) 14 *Journal of Intellectual Property Law & Practice* 477.

Nikolic, I, *Licensing Standard Essential Patents: FRAND and the Internet of Things* (Hart Publishing, 2021).

Norrgård, M, 'The Role Conferred on the National Judge by Directive 2004148/EC on the Enforcement of Intellectual Property Rights' (2005) 6 *ERA Forum* 503.

Nuninga, T, 'Recht, Plicht, Bevel, Verbod' (2018) *Nederlands Tijdschrift voor Burgerlijk Recht* 152.

Nuninga, T, *Recht, Plicht, Remedie* (Wolters Kluwer, 2022).

Ohly, A, '"Patenttrolle" oder: Der patentrechtliche Unterlassungsanspruch unter Verhältnismäßigkeitsvorbehalt? Aktuelle Entwicklungen im US-Patentrecht und ihre Bedeutung für das deutsche und europäische Patentsystem' (2008) 57 *Gewerblicher Rechtsschutz und Urheberrecht International* 787.

Ohly, A, 'Three Principles of European IP Enforcement Law: Effectiveness, Proportionality, Dissuasiveness' in J Drexl et al (eds), *Technology and Competition: Contributions in Honour of Hanns Ullrich* (Larcier, 2009).

Ohly, A, 'Der Ausgleichsanspruch gemäß § 139 I 4 PatG als Rechtsfortwirkungsanspruch' [2022] *Gewerblicher Rechtsschutz und Urheberrecht* 303.

Ohly, A, 'Injunctions in the UPC and the Principle of Proportionality' (2022) 5 *Stockholm IP Law Review* 58.

Ohly, A and Stierle, M, 'Unverhältnismäßigkeit, Injunction Gap und Geheimnisschutz im Prozess' [2021] *Gewerblicher Rechtsschutz und Urheberrecht* 1229.

O'Malley, K and Lynn, B, 'Decision-Making in the Unified Patent Court: Ensuring a Balanced Approach' in C Geiger, CA Nard and X Seuba (eds), *Intellectual Property and the Judiciary* (Edward Elgar, 2018).

Osterrieth, C, 'Kriterien der Angemessenheit des Ausgleichs nach § 139 I 4 PatG' [2022] *Gewerblicher Rechtsschutz und Urheberrecht* 299.

Parcu, P-L, Innocenti, N and Carrozza, C, 'Ubiquitous Technologies and 5G Development: Who Is Leading the Race?' (2022) 46 *Telecommunications Policy* 102277.

Peukert, A, 'Intellectual Property as an End in Itself?' (2011) 33 *European Intellectual Property Review* 67.

Picht, P and Contreras, J, 'Proportionality Defenses in FRAND Cases – A Comparative Assessment of the Revised German Patent Injunction Rules and US Case Law' (2023) 72 *Gewerblicher Rechtsschutz und Urheberrecht International* 435.

Pila, J, 'The European Patent: An Old and Vexing Problem' (2013) 62 *International & Comparative Law Quarterly* 917.

Pila, J, 'Pluralism, Principles and Proportionality in Intellectual Property' (2014) 34 *OJLS* 181.

Reilly, G, 'Patent Litigation Reform in the United States' in T Takenaka, *Research Handbook on Patent Law and Theory* (Edward Elgar, 2019).

Rognstad, O-A, *Property Aspects of Intellectual Property* (Cambridge University Press, 2018).

Sarnoff, J, 'Lessons from the United States in Regard to the Recent, More Flexible Approach to Injunctive Relief' in CM Correa (ed), *Research Handbook on the Interpretation and Enforcement of Intellectual Property under WTO Rules* (Edward Elgar, 2010).

Scharen, U, 'The Practice of Claiming Injunctive Relief for Patent Infringement in Germany' (2019) 14 *Journal of Intellectual Property Law & Practice* 112.

Schauer, F, 'Giving Reasons' (1995) 47 *Stanford Law Review* 633.

Schauer, F, 'Do Cases Make Bad Law?' (2006) 73 *University of Chicago Law Review* 883.

Schellhorn, M, *Der Patentrechtliche Unterlassungsanspruch im Lichte des Verhältnismäßigkeitsgrundsatzes* (Carl Heymanns Verlag, 2020).

Seaman, C, 'Permanent Injunctions in Patent Litigation after eBay: An Empirical Study' (2016) 101 *Iowa Law Review* 1949.

Shapiro, C, 'Navigating the Patent Thicket: Cross Licenses, Patent Pools, and Standard-Setting' in A Jaffe, J Lerner and S Stern (eds), *Innovation Policy and the Economy*, vol 1 (MIT Press, 2001).

Sichelman, T, 'Purging Patent Law of Private Law Remedies' (2014) 92 *Texas Law Review* 517.

Siebrasse, N et al, 'Injunctive Relief' in CB Biddle et al (eds), *Patent Remedies and Complex Products: Toward a Global Consensus* (Cambridge University Press, 2019).
Sikorski, R, 'Permanent Injunctions in Patent Law – in Search of Flexibility' in S Frankel (ed), *Is Intellectual Property Pluralism Functional?* (Edward Elgar, 2019).
Sikorski, R, 'Towards a More Orderly Application of Proportionality to Patent Injunctions in the European Union' (2022) 53 *International Review of Intellectual Property and Competition Law* 31.
Smith, S, *Rights, Wrongs, and Injustices* (Oxford University Press, 2020).
Stierle, M, *Das Nicht-Praktizierte Patent* (Mohr Siebeck, 2018).
Stierle, M, 'Patent Injunctions – Identifying Common Elements' (2019) 11 *Zeitschrift für geistiges Eigentum* 334.
Stierle, M, 'Zum Verhältnismässigkeitsvorbehalt Im Patentrechtlichen Unterlassungsrecht' (2020) *Mitteilungen der deutschen Patentanwälte*.
Stierle, M and Hofmann, F, 'The Latest Amendment to the German Law on Patent Injunctions: The New Statutory Disproportionality Exception and Third-Party Interests' (2022) 71 *Gewerblicher Rechtsschutz und Urheberrecht International* 1123.
Strowel, A and Léonard, A, 'Cutting Back Patent Over-enforcement' (2020) 11 *Journal of Intellectual Property, Information Technology and Electronic Commerce Law* 3.
Sunstein, C, 'Problems with Rules' (1995) 83 *California Law Review* 953.
Thumm, N, 'The Good, the Bad and the Ugly – the Future of Patent Assertion Entities in Europe' (2018) 30 *Technology Analysis & Strategic Management* 1046.
Tilmann, W, 'Article 63' in C Plassmann and W Tilmann (eds), *Unified Patent Protection in Europe: a Commentary* (Oxford University Press, 2018).
Van Overwalle, G, 'Policy Levers Tailoring Patent Law to Biotechnology: Comparing US and European Approaches' (2011) 1 *UC Irvine Law Review* 433.
van Zeebroeck, N et al, 'Patent Inflation in Europe' (2008) 30 *World Patent Information* 43.
Vesala, J, 'Misuse of Patent Application Procedures: A Case for Condemning Non-misleading Strategies?' in RM Ballardini, M Norrgård and N Bruun (eds), *Transitions in European Patent Law: Influences of the Unitary Patent Package* (Kluwer Law International, 2015).
Vivant, M, 'Intellectual Property Rights and Their Functions: Determining Their Legitimate "Enclosure"' in G Ghidini, H Ullrich and P Drahos (eds), *Kritika: Essays on Intellectual Property*, vol 2 (Edward Elgar, 2017).
Wagner, G, 'Die Aufopferung Des Patentrechtlichen Unterlassungsanspruchs' [2022] *Gewerblicher Rechtsschutz und Urheberrecht* 294.
Widdershoven, R, 'National Procedural Autonomy and General EU Law Limits' (2019) 12 *Review of European Administrative Law* 5.
Wu, P and Xiao-chuan Weng, C, 'Old Wine in a New Bottle? Assessing the Injunction Remedy for Intellectual Property Disputes in China' (2021) 11 *Queen Mary Intellectual Property Law Journal* 295.
Yu, L, 'Permanent Injunction on Intellectual Property Rights: Judicial Experiences in China' (2023) 45 *European Intellectual Property Review* 154.

Reports

Cowan R et al, 'Policy Options for the Improvement of the European Patent System' (IP/A/STOA/FWC/2005-28/SC16, European Parliament STOA 2007).
Darts-IP, 'NPE Litigation in the European Union: Facts and Figures' (February 2018) https://clarivate.com/lp/npe-litigation-in-the-european-union-facts-and-figures/.
European Patent Office, 'Top Technical Fields' (30 January 2023) www.epo.org/about-us/annual-reports-statistics/statistics/2022/statistics/patent-applications.html#tab3.
European Patent Office, 'Quality Report' (2020) www.epo.org/about-us/annual-reports-statistics/annual-report/2020.html.

European Patent Office, 'Report: Workshop on Patent Thickets' (2013) www.epo.org/mobile/news-events/news/2013/20130313.html.
Federal Trade Commission, 'To Promote Innovation: The Proper Balance of Competition and Patent Law Policy' (October 2003) www.ftc.gov/sites/default/files/documents/reports/promote-innovation-proper-balance-competition-and-patent-law-and-policy/innovationrpt.pdf.
Hall B et al, A Study of Patent Thickets (Intellectual Property Office 2013) 2013/26.
IPLytics, '5G Patent Study 2020' (24 February 2020) www.iplytics.com/report/5g-patent-study-2020/.

Executive and Legislative Materials

Assemblée Nationale, Rep min no 4621 JOAN 16 May 2023, p 4467 (Christophe Blanchet).
Commission, 'Antitrust: Commission Sends Statement of Objections to Teva over Misuse of the Patent System and Disparagement of Rival Multiple Sclerosis Medicine' IP/22/6062.
Commission, 'Combating Counterfeiting and Piracy in the Single Market' COM(98) 569 final.
Commission, 'Proposal for a regulation of the European Parliament and of the Council on compulsory licensing for crisis management and amending Regulation (EC) 816/2006' COM(2023) 224 final.
Commission, 'Proposal for a directive of the European Parliament and of the Council on measures and procedures to ensure the enforcement of intellectual property rights' COM(2003) 46 final.
EP Committee on Legal Affairs and the Internal Market, 'Report on the proposal for a directive on measures and procedures to ensure the enforcement of intellectual property (Janelly Fourtou)' A5-0468/2003.
Commission, 'Communication from the Commission to the European Parliament, the Council and the European Economic and Social Committee [providing] guidance on certain aspects of Directive 2004/48/EC of the European Parliament and of the Council on the enforcement of intellectual property rights' COM(2017) 708 final.
Commission, 'Communication from the Commission to the European Parliament, the Council and the European Economic and Social Committee setting out the EU approach to Standard Essential Patents' COM(2017) 712 final.
Commission, 'Proposal for a regulation of the European Parliament and of the Council on standard essential patents and amending Regulation (EU)2017/1001' COM(2023) 232 final.
Dutch Minister of Economic Affairs, Letter of 14 September 2010, Kamerstukken II 29 544, Nr 261.
Dutch Minister of Economic Affairs and Climate, Letter of 20 June 2022, DGBI-I&K / 22257631.
European Patent Office, 'Decision of the Administrative Council of 16 October 2013 amending Rules 36, 38, and 135 of the Implementing Regulations of the European Patent Office' [2013] OJ EPO 501.
Executive Office of the President of the US, 'Economic and Trade Agreement between the United States and The People's Republic of China Fact Sheet: Intellectual Property' (January 2020) https://ustr.gov/sites/default/files/files/agreements/phase%20one%20agreement/Phase_One_Agreement-IP_Fact_Sheet.pdf.
German Federal Council, Recommendations of the Committee (*Empfehlungen der Ausschüsse*) of 7 December 2020, Drs 683/1/20.
German Federal Ministry of Justice, Discussion proposal (*Diskussionsentwurf: Entwurf eines Zweiten Gesetzes zur Vereinfachung und Modernisierung des Patentrechts*) of 14 January 2020.
German Federal Ministry of Justice, Draft bill (*Referentenentwurf: Entwurf eines Zweiten Gesetzes zur Vereinfachung und Modernisierung des Patentrechts*) of 1 September 2020.
German Federal Parliament, Proposed bill (*Gesetzentwurf: Entwurf eines Zweiten Gesetzes zur Vereinfachung und Modernisierung des Patentrechts*) of 31 January 2021, BT-Drs 19/25821.
German Federal Parliament, Transcript (*Wortprotokoll der 132. Sitzung*) of 24 February 2021, BT-Drs 19/2581.
German Federal Parliament, Final recommendation and notice (*Beschlussempfehlung und Bericht*) of 9 June 2021, BT-Drucksache 19/30498.

Jinping X, 'Order of the President of the People's Republic of China No 55' of 17 October 2020 www.npc.gov.cn/englishnpc/c23934/202109/63b3c7cb2db342fdadacdc4a09ac8364.shtml.

Legal Group of the UPC Preparatory Committee, 'Responses to the Public Consultation of the Rules of Procedure of the UPC' (31 January 2014) www.veron.com/upc/various-documents/?lang=en.

Legal Group of the UPC Preparatory Committee, 'Table with Explanatory Notes to the Changes Made by the Legal Group of the Preparatory Committee in the 17th Draft of the Rules of Procedure' (31 October 2014) www.veron.com/upc/various-documents/?lang=en.

Legal Group of the UPC Preparatory Committee, 'Oral Hearing on the Rules of Procedure' (Trier, 26 November 2014) www.veron.com/upc/various-documents/?lang=en.

Office of the US Trade Representative, 'Findings of the Investigation into China's Acts, Policies and Practices Related to Technology Transfer, Intellectual Property, and Innovation Under Section 301 of the Trade Act of 1974' (22 March 2018) https://ustr.gov/sites/default/files/Section%20301%20 FINAL.PDF?mod=article_inline.

Miscellaneous

Chairman of the EPO Central Staff Committee, 'Petition from EPO Examiners' (9 March 2018 (https://regmedia.co.uk/2018/03/15/epo-examiners-letters.pdf.

Daimler, 'Annual Report 2016' https://group.mercedes-benz.com/documents/investors/reports/annual-report/daimler/daimler-ir-annualreport-2016.pdf.

Dijkman L, 'Guest Book Review: IP Accidents' (*IPKat*, 14 September 2022) https://ipkitten.blogspot.com/2022/09/guest-book-review-ip-accidents.html.

Dorn S, 'Those New European Patent Litigation Rules: A Report on the Oral Hearing on the 17th Draft' (*IPKat*, 1 December 2014) https://ipkitten.blogspot.com/2014/12/those-new-european-patent-litigation.html.

Editorial, 'Meer ontslagen bij Cordis in Roden' (*NRC Handelsblad*, 21 October 2005) www.nrc.nl/nieuws/2005/10/21/meer-ontslagen-bij-cordis-in-roden-11032009-a768204.

Editorial, 'Doek valt voor Cordis Roden' (*Groninger Internet Courant*, 17 October 2007) www.gic.nl/nieuws/doek-valt-voor-cordis-roden-700-medewerkers-staan-op-straat.

Editorial, 'IPCom Lands Cash Bonanza from D.Telekom Settlement-Sources' (*Reuters*, 3 July 2013) www.reuters.com/article/deutschetelekom-patent-idUSL5N0F72GN20130703.

Gellene D, 'Ruling Forces Kodak to Quit Instant Camera Field' (*LA Times*, 9 January 1986) www.latimes.com/archives/la-xpm-1986-01-09-fi-14373-story.html.

Glass I, 'When Patents Attack!' (*This American Life*, 22 July 2011) www.thisamericanlife.org/441/when-patents-attack.

Klos M, 'Europe's Industrial Companies Mobilise against Weaker Automatic Injunction' (*JUVE Patent*, 4 February 2021) www.juve-patent.com/news-and-stories/legal-commentary/europes-industrial-companies-mobilise-against-weaker-automatic-injunction/.

Knott B, 'A New Emoji for the IP World – the Emoji Troll is Born' (*IPKat*, 20 May 2022) https://ipkitten.blogspot.com/2022/05/a-new-emoji-for-ip-worldthe-emoji-troll.html.

Meyer A (dir), *The Patent Scam* (Genesis Studios 2017).

Brief of Nokia Corporation as Amicus Curiae, *eBay Inc v MercExchange LLC* 547 US 388 (2006).

Palmer M, 'Microsoft to Move Out of Germany' (*Financial Times*, 2 April 2012) www.ft.com/content/08b5913c-7ce2-11e1-a676-00144feab49a.

RPX Corp, 'Form S-1 Registration Statement under the Securities Act of 1933' filed 2 September 2011, www.sec.gov/Archives/edgar/data/1509432/000119312511240287/ds1.htm.

INDEX

www.ingramcontent.com/pod-product-compliance
Ingram Content Group UK Ltd.
Pitfield, Milton Keynes, MK11 3LW, UK
UKHW021909150926
475560UK00003B/273

9 781509 973620